I0327146

George Adlard

Amye Robsart and the Earl of Leycester

A Critical Inquiry into the Authenticity of the Various Statements in...

George Adlard

Amye Robsart and the Earl of Leycester
A Critical Inquiry into the Authenticity of the Various Statements in...

ISBN/EAN: 9783337185831

Printed in Europe, USA, Canada, Australia, Japan

Cover: Foto ©ninafisch / pixelio.de

More available books at **www.hansebooks.com**

AMYE ROBSART;

AND

THE EARL OF LEYCESTER;

A CRITICAL INQUIRY INTO THE AUTHENTICITY OF THE VARIOUS STATEMENTS IN RELATION TO THE DEATH OF AMYE ROBSART, AND OF THE LIBELS ON THE EARL OF LEYCESTER, WITH A VINDICATION OF THE EARL BY HIS NEPHEW SIR PHILIP SYDNEY.

AND A

History of Kenilworth Castle,

INCLUDING

AN ACCOUNT OF THE SPLENDID ENTERTAINMENT GIVEN TO QUEEN ELIZABETH BY THE EARL OF LEYCESTER, IN 1575, FROM THE WORKS OF ROBERT LANEHAM AND GEORGE GASCOIGNE;

TOGETHER WITH

Memoirs and Correspondence of Sir Robert Dudley, Son of the Earl of Leycester.

BY

GEORGE ADLARD,

AUTHOR OF 'THE SUTTON-DUDLEYS OF ENGLAND,' ETC.

LONDON:
JOHN RUSSELL SMITH,
36, SOHO SQUARE.
MDCCCLXX.

TO THE

HON^{BLE} FREDERICK WALPOLE, M.P.,

OF

RAINTHORPE HALL, NORFOLK,

A DESCENDANT OF THE ROBSART FAMILY AND POSSESSOR OF

AMYE ROBSART'S BIRTH-PLACE,

THIS VOLUME IS INSCRIBED

BY

THE AUTHOR.

に.

TABLE OF CONTENTS.

AMYE ROBSART.

PAGE

INTRODUCTORY CHAPTER.—Mr. Pettigrew's quotation from DRYDEN.—False estimate of the Character of Dudley, Varney, and others.—Sir Walter Scott's departure from historical truth in his Romance of "Kenilworth;"—some particulars in relation to same.—Mrs. Muhlbach on Historical Romance Writing.—Mystery connected with the Death of Amye Robsart.—Statements in "Leycester's Commonwealth" copied by subsequent writers.—Coroner's Inquest, and discovery of the Correspondence in reference thereto.—Queen Elizabeth's Proclamation and Sir Philip Sydney's Defence of the Earl of Leycester.—Character of Sir Richard Varney.—Original Letters in reference to Kenilworth and Sir Robert Dudley.—Von Raumer's Sketch of the Life of the Earl of Leycester . . . . . i to xi

ROBSART FAMILY, some Account of 1

SEDISTERN.—Sir John Robsart, Lord of the Manor.—Elizabeth his Wife, Daughter of John Scott, of Camberwell; Amye, their Daughter.—Elizabeth Scott, previously married to Roger Appleyard, of Stanfield Hall, Norfolk.—Sedistern descended to the Walpoles Earls of Orford 5

SCOTT OF CAMBERWELL, Pedigree of.—Some Account of the Family 8

APPLEYARD OF BRAKENASHE, some Account of.—Pedigree showing the connection of the Appleyard Family with Amye Robsart 10

TABLE OF CONTENTS.

	PAGE
STANFIELD HALL, Birthplace of Amye Robsart; on her Death in possession of her Half-brother, John Appleyard, afterwards sold to James Altham, Baron of the Exchequer, and then to Edward Flowerdew	12
RAINTHORPE HALL, formerly in possession of the Appleyards, now of Hon. Frederick Walpole, M.P. for Norfolk, brother of the Earl of Orford	15
MARRIAGE of AMYE ROBSART with Lord Robert Dudley, at Sheen, now Richmond, in the presence of Edward VI	16
LETTER of Lord ROBERT DUDLEY to John Flowerdew	ib.
FLITCHAM, in the Hollis Family, afterwards in that of Flowerdew	18
FLOWERDEW, Pedigree of	19
HAYS, in possession of the Scotts of Halden; purchased by the Right Hon. William Pitt, afterwards created Earl of Chatham	20
SCOTTS OF HALDEN	21
LETTER of AMYE DUDLEY to John Flowerdew	ib.
HYDES OF DENCHWORTH, short Account of	22
CUMNOR PLACE, Description of	24
———— Ballad, by Mickle	26
AMYE DUDLEY'S Death at Cumnor	30
———— CORRESPONDENCE between Lord Robert Dudley and his Cousin Blount on the Death of Amye Dudley, and Commentary on same by Mr. Bartlett	ib.
———— Examination of the various Statements made by Historians on the Death of Amye Dudley	43
———— 'Leycester's Commonwealth' and Ashmole's Statement compared	47
———— Funeral of, from the Dugdale MSS. in the Ashmolean Collection	52
LORD ROBERT DUDLEY, Vindication of, by the Queen, in answer to Throckmorton	55
———— ———— Vindication by the Privy Council	56
'LEYCESTER'S COMMONWEALTH' and Ashmole's County History,—False Statements in	58

TABLE OF CONTENTS.

	PAGE
LEYCESTER's 'Commonwealth,' Answer to, and Vindication of the Earl, by Sir PHILIP SYDNEY	65
PARSONS or PERSONS, reputed Author of the 'Commonwealth'	77
——— Proceedings against, by the Privy Council	78
BURGHLEY (Lord), Slanderous Reports against him	82
BLISS (Dr.), MS. Copy of the 'Ghost,' and Supplement to same, having reference to the Death of the Earl	84
Sir RICHARD VARNEY or VERNEY,—Particulars in reference to	85
——— Grandson of the Kenilworth Varney, married to the Sister and sole Heir of the first Lord Broke	88
——— Short Pedigree of the Family of Verney or Varney	89
Baron WILLOUGHBY DE BROKE, Short Pedigree showing the Connexion of the Verney Family therewith	90
LEYCESTER's LETTERS to Lord Burghley in reference to the Guardianship of "Young Varney"	92
ANTHONY FORSTER, of Cumnor Place, reference to	96

HISTORY OF KENILWORTH CASTLE . 97

Sir WILLIAM DUGDALE's Account from the Earliest Period, 101.—Round Table, 103.—In possession of John de Somery, Baron of Dudley, 103.—In that of Sir John Dudley (Duke of Northumberland), 104.—Granted to Robert Dudley, Fifth Son of the Duke, 106.—Descended by Will to Sir Robert Dudley, Son of the Earl, 107.—Frustrated in obtaining his Father's Possessions, left England for Italy, 107.—Kenilworth sold to Prince Henry, 107.—Afterwards descended to Prince Charles (Charles I), 108.—On the Death of the latter Oliver Cromwell took possession, 108.—At the Restoration it reverted to the Monmouth Family, afterwards to Laurence Lord Hyde, created Baron Kenilworth and Earl of Rochester, 108.—In possession of the Clarendon Family, 108.—Description of the Buildings and Grounds, by Camden and by Dugdale, 109.—Description by Leland the Antiquary, 111.—Remarks on the Survey made by the Officers under James I, by Dugdale, 111.—Description by Bishop Hurd, 113; by Sir Walter Scott, 115.

LIST OF ILLUSTRATIONS.

Old STANFIELD HALL (*front and back view*), the birthplace of AMYE ROBSART. From a drawing contributed by the Hon. Mrs. Walpole, of Rainthorpe Hall, Norfolk . . [*Face p.* 1

KENILWORTH CASTLE, in Ruins [*Face p.* 101

Portrait of ROBERT DUDLEY, EARL OF LEYCESTER .
Ground Plan of KENILWORTH CASTLE in 1575, at the time of the Kenilworth Festivities . } [*Face p.* 106

KENILWORTH CASTLE, Ruins of the GREAT HALL, PRESENCE CHAMBER, and ORIEL WINDOW . . . . [*Face p.* 111

The Porch or Entrance to the GATE-HOUSE . .
The LEYCESTER CHIMNEY-PIECE, removed from the Great Hall to the Gate-House . . . } [*Face p.* 112

Portrait of Sir ROBERT DUDLEY, Son of the Earl of Leycester. From a Miniature by *Nicholas Hilliard*, in the possession of Lord De L'Isle and Dudley, at Penshurst, in Kent. Engraved by J. Brown, from a drawing the exact size of the original by G. P. Harding . [*Face p.* 276

INTRODUCTORY CHAPTER.

"He who unfolds to his fellow-men one single truth that has heretofore laid hidden, has not lived in vain."—TOULMIN SMITH.

MR. PETTIGREW, in his inquiry into the particulars connected with the death of Amye Robsart,[1] thus aptly quotes from *Dryden*: —"We find but few historians, of all ages, who have been diligent enough in their search for truth; it is their common method to take on trust what they distribute to the public, by which means a falsehood once received from a famed writer becomes traditional to posterity."

It is the false estimate of the character of Lord Robert Dudley, of Sir Richard Varney, and others, and the doubtful statements as to the cause of the death of Amye Robsart, that have led to the present investigation.

Unfortunately for the admirers of Sir Walter Scott's romance of 'Kenilworth,' the historical interest in that work is entirely marred by the fact that the leading incidents, in that otherwise interesting novel, are at variance with historical truth.

Amye Robsart never was Countess of Leycester, inasmuch as her husband was not created an Earl till three years after her

---

[1] 'Inquiry read at the Congress of the British Archæological Association, held at Newbury in 1859, being a refutation of the calumnies charged against Sir Robert Dudley, K.G., Anthony Forster, and others.' 8vo. London, J. Russell Smith, 1859.

death, nor did she appear at the Kenilworth revels, for the reason that that splendid castle was not possessed by her husband till he became an earl, and the Kenilworth revels did not take place till fifteen years after her death. Nor was her marriage with Lord Robert Dudley kept secret, as related by Scott; on the contrary, her marriage was publicly solemnized in the presence of the youthful king Edward VI, and the incidents connected with the event were noted down by him in his diary, the original of which, among other numerous relics of the past, is to be found stored in the manuscript department of the British Museum.

It is much to be regretted that Sir Walter Scott should, in professing to write a *historical* romance, have so seriously perverted historical facts. If, as probably was the case, he conceived the idea that a *secret* marriage would add to the interest of his work, he might have chosen an *actual*, instead of a *supposed*, secret marriage, as the former did exist at the period of Elizabeth's visit to Kenilworth.

In 1573, thirteen years after the death of Lady Amye Dudley, and two years previous to the Kenilworth revels, Leycester had privately married Douglas Howard, Lady Sheffield, which marriage was kept a profound secret. In 1574 a son was born as the fruit of that marriage, and in the year following (1575) Elizabeth made her celebrated visit to Kenilworth. This, therefore, might have formed a real and legitimate plea for Sir Walter to have worked up his secret marriage, without sacrificing to the object he had in view the memory of poor Amye, who had been in her grave for fifteen years.

A celebrated German authoress of the present day thus writes as to the importance of adhering to historical *truth* in compiling historical romances:—"It is of very little consequence whether the personages of the historical romance actually spoke the words, or performed the acts, attributed to them, it is only necessary that those words and deeds should be in accordance with the spirit and character of such historical personages, and that the writer should not attribute to them what they could not have spoken or done. In historical romance, when circumstances or events are presented in accordance with historical tradition; when the characters are naturally described, they bear with them their own justification, and historical romance has need of no further defence.

"Historical romance should be nothing but an *illustration of history*. If the drawing, grouping, colouring, and style of such an illustration of any given historical epoch is admitted to be true, then the illustration rises to the elevation of works of art, worthy of a place beside the historical picture, and as equally useful."[1]

While adopting the above critical remarks, the writer would not be supposed to be insensible to the great charm evinced in Scott's delightful romance of 'Kenilworth'—the effect of which cannot be better portrayed than in the words of Dr. Beattie:

"The romance of 'Kenilworth,' it is probable, has brought within the last [forty] years more pilgrims to this town and neighbourhood—pilgrims of the highest rank—than ever resorted to its ancient shrine of the virgin, more knights and dames than ever figured in its tilts and tournaments."[2]

It is, perhaps, not too much to say that the mystery connected with the death of Amye Robsart will probably never be cleared up. Conjectures only may be started. The coroner's inquest, that was assembled immediately after her decease, failed to elicit more than that she met with an untimely death, by some "mischaunce;" further, that inquest did not succeed in unravelling the mystery, though every effort appears to have been then made. There was no undue haste, nor does there appear to have been any undue influence exercised to bias or to thwart the investigation.

---

[1] Mrs. Muhlbach in her Introduction to "Henry VIII, and Catherine Parr."
[2] Dr. Beattie's 'Castles of England.' Imperial 8vo, Lond., 1842.

Till within a few years past we have been left in entire ignorance on the subject, nothing but the scurrilous reports promulgated by the most "virulent and pestilent book" ever written, under the title of 'Leycester's Commonwealth,' supplying all the information, in the shape of atrocious falsehoods, that authors and writers have subsequently availed themselves of so freely in their attacks on the character of Leycester. Written by the noted jesuit Parsons, who, in connection with the still more notorious Edward Campion, was constantly prowling about in search of means to subvert the Protestant faith, and to create all the mischief he could in the endeavour to restore the powers that had been driven out. Parsons's book was not published till twenty-four years after the occurrences took place, which it so minutely describes, fresh as if they had occurred within the day or year of its publication.

The writers who have since taken up the subject have all followed in the same path, reiterating, under different phases, the same scurrilous untruths, only varying them under different disguises—first, "it is stated," "it is related;" then as "secret memoirs," all derived from the same source; and in their zeal to establish the *apparent* truth of their falsehoods, multiplying the number of authorities in justification of their statements, quoting, for instance, *John Aubrey*, as one of their authorities, who, it would be difficult for them to find, had ever written a line on the subject; the principal works by which that author is known, being the 'History of Wiltshire,' and the 'Natural History of the County of Surrey.'

Much stress has been laid by previous writers on the narrative given in ASHMOLE's 'History of Berkshire' as an authority worthy of belief. Now when we consider that that statement was not made till a century after the occurrences took place, and that no *authority* whatever is given by Ashmole, we should at least pause before we give credence to his detail. In the present work will be found (see pages 47 to 51) a comparative detail of the statements given by Ashmole, and those given in Leycester's Commonwealth; the candid reader cannot fail to discover that the former is taken (in many instances verbatim) from the libellous publication of Parsons.

Writers who have preceded us attach an importance to Ashmole's narrative which we think, on very little reflection, is without justification. The fact that no authority whatever is given by him, ought naturally to create a doubt; that doubt is further increased by the plagiarism already referred to.

Mr. PETTIGREW, in his 'Inquiry,' says: "Every production issuing from the pen of Elias Ashmole and Walter Scott must be deemed entitled to our best consideration, and any attempt to invalidate what has been recorded on their authority, must be regarded worthy of the most intimate scrutiny."

With regard to Sir WALTER SCOTT, his total perversion of historical facts must certainly condemn his authority for the statements given. We question whether Ashmole would himself have ventured to compromise his reputation by inserting such a statement in his *County* history, a work in which, of all others, we expect to find nothing but what can be substantiated from known or reputable authority. Ashmole's history was not published during his lifetime. That scurrilous statement in reference to the death of Amye Robsart we may well conceive may have been found among his "*Collections*" for the County history, and published by those who undertook the work after his death.

The finding of such a statement among Ashmole's papers, we conceive was the *sole* authority for its publication.

To show the mischief arising from the promulgation of such false statements, Mr. Pettigrew alludes to a recent writer in the 'Quarterly Review' (vol. 106, p. 211), in an article expressly on Berkshire, in which the writer says:—"The story of the murder of the poor young Countess, as told in *Kenilworth*, is, for the most part, faithful;" (!) and this in the face of Amye

Robsart having been in her grave fifteen years previous to the occurrences so graphically described by Scott. Poor Amye, who probably had never even been at Kenilworth Castle during her life.

The writer of that article also alludes to the statement of the Countess's (!) father having caused the body of his daughter to be taken up, and the coroner to sit upon it. Sir John Robsart, her father, died several years *previous* to the death of his daughter (!).

We had written thus far when, having occasion to refer to Lysons's History of Berkshire, in the Magna Britannia, we found the following, in corroboration of what we had premised:—

"Elias Ashmole, the Herald and Antiquary, whose Collections for this county have been published since his decease.

"*The work called* 'Ashmole's Antiquities of Berkshire' *is improperly so termed. It was published after his death, and has no other pretension to being called by his name than that it consists chiefly of church notes copied from such as were collected by that industrious herald and antiquary, and by him deposited in the Heralds' College. The scanty information which it contains of other matters was collected by the Editor.*" [1]

Now, after this, who will venture to quote either Ashmole or Scott as authority for the statements set forth and copied by writer after writer? What remains then to guide us in our investigations after the truth? Certainly not the scurrilous publication of Parsons.

The only evidence that has been handed down to us, upon which any reliance can be placed, is the correspondence that took

[1] 'Magna Britannia, Berkshire,' p. 216.

INTRODUCTORY CHAPTER. vii

place immediately after the death of Amye Dudley, between Lord Robert Dudley and his cousin Blount, in reference to the coroner's inquest that was summoned to inquire into the cause of her death. For this correspondence we are indebted to George Lillie Craik, who, in his 'Romance of the Peerage,' has given us these letters, which he discovered in the Pepysian Library at Oxford, where a contemporary copy of the correspondence has been preserved. Lord Braybrooke, also, about the same time, made the discovery of these letters, and he has printed them in the Appendix to his edition of 'Pepys's Diary and Correspondence.' They may also be found in 'Bartlett's History of Cumnor Place.' These letters are inserted in the present work, and, though they open to us no light as to the immediate cause of Amye's death, they give us all the information we are likely to obtain. They serve to evince, however, on the part of Leycester, but little regret at the loss he had sustained, and tend to show that he was only tenacious how far the occurrence might lead to suspicion, and throw obloquy on himself by implication. Instead of going immediately to Cumnor to inquire into the circumstances connected with her death, he coolly writes to his Cousin Blount, and requests him to make the investigation. Instead of paying the least regard to her remains by attending the funeral, he deputes that duty to others, and contents himself at the Court in attendance upon the queen. First he writes from Windsor, the day following the death of his wife; three days afterwards from Kew, where he had a mansion, given to him by the queen, and which was probably his domicile, while his wife was staying at Cumnor under the charge or care of Sir Anthony Foster. That she had been living in great distress of mind may be inferred from the tenor of her letter to Mr. Flowerdew, the only letter of hers known to have been preserved.

It is a somewhat singular coincidence that the opinion formed by the writer (as expressed on page 63 of this work), as to the immediate *cause* of the death of Amye Robsart, will be found to coincide with that given by Mr. Pettigrew in his 'Inquiry.' It may be as well here to state that the writer had committed that opinion to paper several years before Mr. Pettigrew's publication; the investigation made by the writer having occurred at least ten years previous thereto. It is gratifying, however, to find, after the able and thorough research on the subject made by Mr. Pettigrew, that the views entertained by the writer were not at all singular in this respect.

With this inquiry into the evidences before us, is given Queen Elizabeth's proclamation, vindicating Leycester from the aspersions cast upon him by Parsons' slanderous publication; and also Sir Philip Sydney's defence of his uncle—the latter, it is believed, having never been printed, except in the 'Sydney Papers,' edited by Collins, the author of the 'Peerage.' These documents cannot fail to be of interest.

The reader will also find some interesting facts connected with Amye Robsart's family—apparently overlooked by previous writers on this subject, and certainly not hitherto published—which have been discovered by the writer in a Pedigree in one of the Heralds' Visitations at the College of Arms, London.

Another topic, immediately connected with the main subject, and respecting which no little misapprehension has long prevailed, namely, the character of SIR RICHARD VARNEY, or, more correctly, VERNEY, will likewise appear (it is thought) in a new and very different aspect, as illustrated in the following pages.

Moreover, not a few striking incidents and illustrations in regard to the history of Kenilworth Castle, subsequent to the Earl of Leycester's death, together with original letters never before given to the public, connected with Leycester's son, Sir Robert Dudley, have also been embodied in the present work, together with a biographical sketch of Sir Robert Dudley and of his second wife, Alice Leigh, who was created *Duchess* Dudley by Charles I.

A very interesting volume in royal quarto entitled 'KENIL-WORTH ILLUSTRATED; or, the History of the Castle, Priory, and Church of Kenilworth,' appeared in 1821, from the press of Charles Whittingham, of Chiswick, in which were included "Laneham's Letter," and "Gascoigne's Princely Pleasures." Numerous engravings embellished the volume in the first style of art of that period.

In the same year a republication of LANEHAM and GASCOIGNE appeared, in post octavo, published by J. H. Burn, of London.

In 1825 appeared 'KENILWORTH FESTIVITIES,' comprising "Laneham's Description of the Pageantry," and "Gascoigne's Princely Pleasures," post octavo, published by Merridew, Coventry, with a frontispiece representing Elizabeth's entry into the castle. This volume is composed of the two tracts reprinted by Burn in 1821, bound together, with new title-page and frontispiece.

In 1859 appeared an 8vo pamphlet, 'THE MILITARY ARCHITECTURE OF THE MIDDLE AGES, AS ILLUSTRATED BY KENILWORTH, WARWICK, AND MAXTOKE CASTLES. By Geo. T. Robinson, Architect.'

'KENILWORTH BUFFET,' a pamphlet in extra super-royal quarto, appeared in 1851, descriptive of elaborately carved relievos of a *Buffet*, in Oak, manufactured by Cookes and Sons, of Warwick, from an ancient oak, which formerly stood on the grounds of Kenilworth. On the centre panel is represented Queen Elizabeth's entry into Kenilworth Castle; the discovery by the queen of Amye Robsart taking shelter in an alcove on the grounds of Kenilworth; and the queen reproaching Leycester for his duplicity towards her in keeping secret his marriage with Amye on the panel of the door on either side—the subjects taken from Scott's romance of 'Kenilworth,' forming a striking illustration of the ill effects produced by the perversion of historical truth—perpetuating the historical untruths contained in that work—and misleading the public mind in what might otherwise have proved a highly interesting illustration of history. Four richly carved statuettes, representing Sir Philip Sydney, Sir Walter Raleigh, Shakspeare, and Sir Francis Drake, also embellished the work. As a work of art great credit is due to the artists employed, as well as to Messrs. Cookes and Sons, of Warwick, from whom the work originated. It was exhibited in the Great Exhibition of 1851 in London, and is now preserved in Warwick Castle, it having been purchased by the inhabitants of the Town and County of Warwick, and presented to the Lord Brooke (now Earl of Warwick) on his marriage.

A short sketch of Robert Dudley, Earl of Leycester, from the pen of a foreign writer, may form a not inappropriate conclusion of these preliminary remarks.

"ROBERT DUDLEY, born in 1533, the fifth son of the Duke of Northumberland, who was executed, and grandson of Dudley, who, at the accession of Henry VIII, was accused and put to death as an unfaithful minister of finance, had rendered Elizabeth much service during the reign of Mary, and thereby, perhaps, laid the foundation for his future elevation. At this time, when Elizabeth created him Earl of Leicester, he was in the prime of life, was very handsome, danced admirably, and was considered as a model of a perfect courtier. Even his adversaries also confess that he was courageous in danger, condescending to inferiors, courteous to his rivals, a patron of learning, generous on all occasions, and very skilful in perceiving and taking advantage of favorable opportunities. But if this is the case, opportunities of obtaining the hand of Elizabeth cannot have been offered him; and indeed, notwithstanding he was so high in her favour, she always kept him at a due distance, and repeatedly said in private to her most confidential minister, Cecil, "That she would never give her hand to a subject." But as Leicester was in many respects inferior to other men whom Elizabeth had elevated, many persons believed (when meaner motives, and thoughts of marriage were rejected) in the influence of the stars, and others, in their anger at the favour shown to Leicester, accused him of being a hypocrite, arrogant, selfish, immoral, indifferent to the choice of means to attain his ends, nay, they affirmed, that in the hope to obtain the hand of Elizabeth he had caused the death of his own wife, and perhaps of many other persons. This censure of the envied favourite (like praise in similar cases) is doubtless exaggerated, and it is difficult to find the just medium. Leicester certainly never understood how to gain public opinion; though he had much penetration and ability in some points, he wanted the simple dignity of his opponent Sussex; and still more the superior understanding of Cecil; his way of life did not entirely coincide with the strict puritanical principles which he professed. But shall Elizabeth be so severely blamed for desiring, besides the great statesman whom she honoured, to have an amiable and ccomplished courtier about her? The opinion which she expressed to the French Ambassador Castelnau, "That Leicester was the most virtuous and perfect man that she knew," may be founded in error, but she added, in the consciousness of her dignity, "Yet she would never marry him." [1]

[1] *Von Raumer.* 'Political History of England during the 16th and 17th Centuries,' translated by Lloyd. 8vo, Lond., 1837, vol. i, pp. 194–6.

OLD STANFIELD HALL, NORFOLK, BACK VIEW.

SOME ACCOUNT

OF THE

ROBSART FAMILY.

"The father of Sir JOHN ROBSART, or ROBSERT, Knight Baronet and K.G. (who was famed for his valour and conduct in several actions in France in the reigns of Hen. IV. V. VI., and who was great-grandfather to Amie Robsart), was Robert, Baron of Cannon, in Heinalt, on which account he is mentioned in our historians by the name of Cannon Robsart, and was the son of John Robsart, who, in 14 Edw. III., was one of those expert captains that (with Richard Verchin, Lord High Seneschal of Heinalt) surprised John, Duke of Normandy, eldest son of King Philip of France, in his quarters at Montais, on the river Selle. The Lord Robert Robsart was likewise very serviceable to the English nation; and when King Edward lay at the siege of Rheims, A.D. 1359, signalised himself in taking the castle of Commercy, and the defeat of the Lord Gomeignes, being then governor of the young Earl of Coucy, and manager of his lands. He also behaved himself with great bravery and conduct in several other actions in that reign; and, accompanying the Duke of Lancaster and divers of the English nobility into France, in 47 Edw. III., landed with them at Calais; and, continuing in our service, took divers castles in Spain, in 5 Rich. II.

"He left issue three sons—John, Lewis,[1] and Theodorick (or Terrey as we write the name)—who all engaged in the English service, and were commanders of the greatest note

[1] Lodowicus, in the 'Inquisitiones post mortem.'

in their time; but I shall confine myself to the actions of John, the eldest son.[1]

"The said Sir John Robsart distinguished himself in the wars with the Saracens in the reign of Richard II., and was knighted before the reign of Hen. IV., which king, out of his especial grace, and for the good services of his beloved and faithful knight, Sir John Robsart, grants to him, for term of his life, £100 per annum out of his exchequer, by letters patent dated 17th November, 1399; and Hen. V., in consideration of his good services, confirms to him the said annuity, by letters patent dated at Westminster, 12th June, 1413. He attended on Hen. V. at his first landing in France, and after being at the siege of Caen, in Normandy (as was also his brother Sir Lewis Robsart), he became one of the principal commanders under the Duke of Gloucester, the king's brother, who in 5 Hen. V. especially appointed him to treat with the governors of the castles of Vire, Hambye, St. Lo., and Clarenton, for the surrender thereof, which in that year were at several times delivered to him. In 6 Hen. V. he was also specially appointed by the said duke to treat with the governor of Pont Down, as also with the governor, knights, esquires, burgesses, and inhabitants of Chierburgh, and with Mons. Robert de Frevile, Knight, governor of the castle of St. Saviour le Visconte; all which places being surrendered by agreement made with him, he was constituted governor of the castle of St. Saviour le Visconte, and on the decease of the Duke of Holland was elected a Knight Companion of the most noble Order of the Garter, but, continuing abroad, was installed at Windsor by his proxy, Sir Thomas Bar, 17 February, 1418-19. At the siege of Rohan he was one of the commissioners assigned by the king to confer with the French commissioners about the surrender of that city; and when eight days had been spent without concluding on one article, which induced the English commissioners to break off the treaty, and thereupon the townsmen, mutinying, had forced the magistrates to alter their opinions, they came to

[1] For the authorities whence these statements are taken, the reader is referred to Collins's 'Peerage,' by Sir Egerton Brydges, vol. v, pp. 644, &c.

the tent of Sir John Robsart, desiring him to move the king that the truce might be prolonged for four days, which being assented to, they surrendered that city on articles agreed on by the said Sir John Robsart, the Earls of Warwick, Salisbury, and others. In 7 Hen. V. he had, in recompense of his services, a grant of the castle and lordships of St. Saviour le Visconte, Neahou and Danvers. In 8 Hen. V. he was appointed, with the Duke of Exeter and others of the greatest note, to confer with the French king at 'Troys concerning the title of King Henry to the crown of France, and his marriage with the Lady Catharine, daughter of the said king. And when it was concluded on that King Henry should come to Troys and marry the said Lady Catharine, and the French king should make him heir of his realm, crown, and dignity, after his decease, Sir John Robsart was left to give his attendance on the said princess till the King of England should come to Troys to celebrate his nuptials. In 9 Hen. V. he returned with the king and his queen to England, and was present with his majesty in a chapter of the Garter held at Windsor on May 23rd, but being absent in a chapter held in the next ensuing year, his excuse was allowed by being abroad in the wars. On the death of his royal master he attended on his corpse into England, and, being Keeper of the Seal of the Order of the Garter, was present at the feast of St. George, held at Windsor in 1 Hen. VI., but returned to France the same year, and, being a knight banneret as well as a Knight of the Garter, was retained, with his brother, Sir Terrey Robsart, Captain of Hamby, to serve the regent, John, Duke of Bedford, in that kingdom, who made him Captain of Candebeck, and (after the death of his brother, Sir Terrey) of St. Saviour de Ive, in Normandy. In 7 Hen. VI. he was with the king in Normandy. In the eighth year of that king the Duke of Bedford sent the Earl of Huntingdon and this Sir John Robsart to the assistance of the Duke of Burgundy, then besieging Compeigne, who (as my author observes) were two *as expert in all warlike affairs as valiant in all bold attempts;* and they were so active in carrying on the siege that the gaining of the town in a short time was not doubted of; but the death of Philip, Duke of Brabant, happening in the interval, occasioned the Duke of Burgundy to leave the siege and the command to Lord John of Luxemburgh, who marched off when the town was reduced to despair, without the consent of the English commanders.

"This Sir John Robsart, being born in Heinalt, was naturalised in the second year of King Henry VI.; and in the preamble to the patent it is recited, 'That the King, in consideration of the long and faithful services of his beloved and faithful Sir John Robbessart, Knt., to his dear father and grandfather, and also because he did homage to his said father, with the advice and assent of the Lords Spiritual and Temporal and the Commons of England in Parliament, grants to the said that he should be made a native of this kingdom,' &c. On the death of Sir Lewis [or Lodowicus], Robsart, Knight of the Garter, and Lord Bourchier, who departed this life on Monday before the feast of St. Andrew, in 9 Hen. VI., he was found his brother and heir, and of the age of forty-one years; but Sir Lewis enjoying that barony only in right of his wife, Elizabeth, daughter and heir to Bartholomew, Lord Bourchier, this Sir John Robsart had not summons to Parliament among the barons, as his brother had; but, in 7 Hen. V. he had the baronies of St. Saviour le Visconte and Neahou, in Normandy. In 17 Hen. VI. he had a renewal of the grant of £100 per ann. made to him by Hen. IV., as also of £50 per ann. out of the castle, forest, and lordship of Rockingham, granted him by Hen. V., with remainder to John, his son, for life; and deceasing in 29 Hen. VI., was buried in St. Francis's Chapel, in the Grey-Fryers, London, now called Christ-Church, where a raised tomb was erected to his memory, with his effigies in the livery of the Garter, and this inscription:

"Hic jacet Strenuus Vir. Dom. Johannes Robsard, Valens Miles in Armis, qui obii 24 die Decembris, A.D. 1450."

SEDISTERN, SIDERSTERN, OR SYDERSTERN.

"SIR JOHN ROBSERT, second son of Sir Terry, was lord of the manor of Sedistern, Sheriff of Norfolk and Suffolk, in the 1st of Edward VI. I find that this John Robsert, called late of Windham, in Norfolk, Esq., alias of Stanfield, in the parish of Wymondham, to have a pardon from the said king, by the advice of Edward, Duke of Somerset, the Protector, and the Council, for all treasons, insurrections, rebellions, murders, felonies, before the 20th of January in the first year of that king. Witness the King at Westminster, the fifth day of May, in his first year.

"Soon after this he died, leaving by Elizabeth his wife, daughter of John Scot, of Camberwell, in Surrey, a daughter and heir, Anne.[1]

"Anne, his daughter, married Sir Robert Dudley, afterwards Earl of Leicester, who had a grant of this manor, with that of Hemesby, and advowson of the vicarage, lately belonging to the Cathedral Church of Norwich, the manor of Newton-by-Bircham, and the advowson, late John Robsert's, also the manor of Great Bircham; to hold Hemesby with Anne, his wife, and the heirs of their bodies *in capite*; and to hold Seidestern, Newton, and Great Bircham, to Anne and Robert, during the life of the said Robert, by a grant dated January 30, in the 3rd and 4th Philip and Mary.[2]

"The earl held this manor for life, dying lord of it in 1588, when it came to John Walpole, Esq., son and heir of Edward Walpole, Esq., of Houghton, and Lucy his wife, daughter of Sir Terry Robsert, and in this family it remains, the Earl of Orford being lord.[3]

"The office of steward of the manor of Rising, in the county of Norfolk, and the constableship of the castle there, was granted by Edw. VI. to Sir John Robsert and Sir

---

[1] Bloomfield, as well as several other writers, in error, say Anne, instead of Amie or Amye.
[2] Bloomfield's 'Norfolk,' vol. iii, pp. 181-2.
[3] Dugdale's 'Baronage,' vol. ii, p. 222.

Robert Dudley [a son of the Earl of Warwick, and that married the daughter and heir of the said Sir John] for life, and to the longer liver of them, with a fee of 40*s.* by the year for the office of stewardship, and for the constableship £13 8*d.* per ann., and for the office of master of the game £4 13*s.* 3*d.* per ann., and 53*s.* 4*d.* for the wages of two forests, to be paid by the receivers of the premises. Dated in December."[1]

In 1551 Sir John Robsert was appointed one of the Lord Justices and Lord Lieutenants, with the Earl of Sussex, Sir Roger Townsend, and Sir William Fermor, for the county of Norfolk.[2]

In May, 1552, he was reappointed, with the Earl of Sussex, Lord Robert Dudley, and Sir William Fermor.[3]

In May, 1553, the same appointments were made.[4]

AMYE[5] ROBSART was the daughter of Sir John Robsart, of Siderstern, in the county of Norfolk, the manor of which came into possession of his family by the marriage of his father, Sir Theodorick Robsart, with the daughter and heiress of Sir Thomas Kerdeston, of Sydersterm, in Norfolk.[6] Amye is mentioned by all writers as being the heiress of her father, and no mention made of any other children. She had, however, a brother, who was illegitimate, named Arthur Robsart, and two half-brothers, John and Philip Appleyard, as well as two half-sisters, Anne and Frances Appleyard, all of whom, it is presumed, were living in 1560, two of them in that year attending the coroner's inquest on the death of Amye.

Lord Robert Dudley, in his letter to Blount,[7] says, "I have sent for my brother Appleyard, because he is her brother."

[1] Strype's 'Memorials,' vol. ii, pt. 2, p. 215.
[2] Ib., vol. ii, pt. 1, p. 464.
[3] Ib., vol. ii, pt. 2, p. 162.
[4] 'Privy Council Register,' vol. iii, p. 554.
[5] Dugdale as well as other writers, in error, call her Anne, probably written Amie.
[6] 'Biographia Britannica,' article "Robert Dudley."
[7] From contemporary copies in the Pepysian Library at Cambridge.

Her mother was Elizabeth, daughter of John Scott, Esq., of Camberwell, in the county of Surrey; and though the fact is not mentioned by any writer that I have met with, she had previously been married to Roger Appleyard, Esq., lord of the manor of Stanfield or Stanfield Hall, in the county of Norfolk, who in 1528 left the manor to "Elizabeth" his wife, for life, and then to John Appleyard, his son and heir, who held it in 1549.[1]

[1] Bloomfield's 'Norfolk,' fol., vol. iii, p. 851.

PEDIGREE OF SCOTT, OF CAMBERWELL.

(*From the 'Visitation of Surrey,' Harl. MSS., 1561.*)

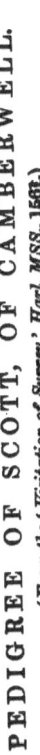

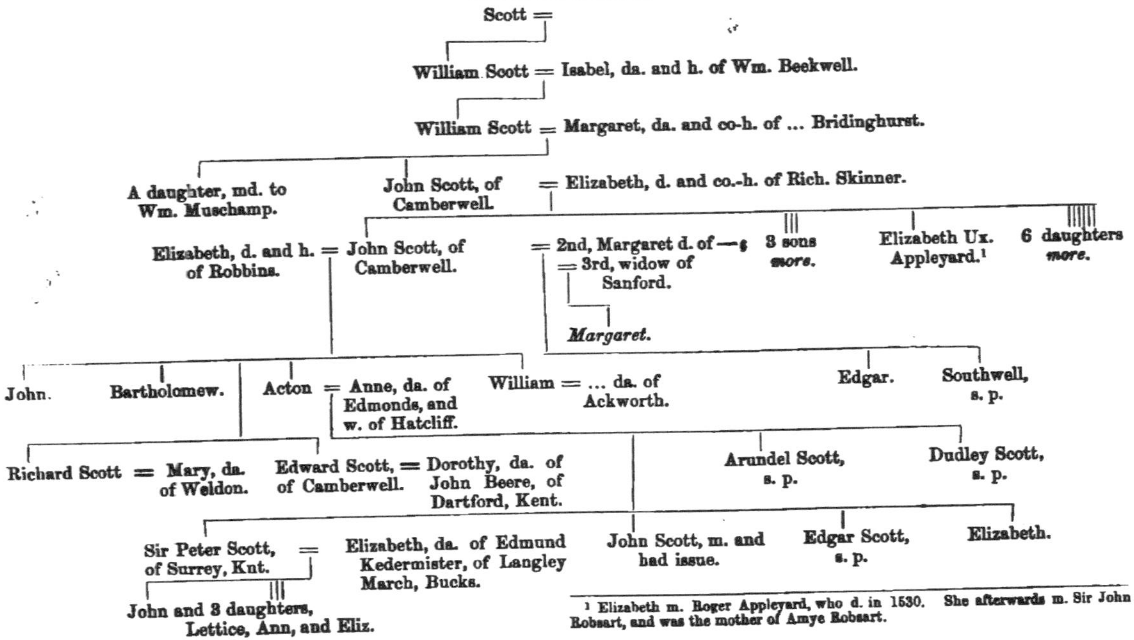

[Pedigree chart:]

Scott =

— William Scott = Isabel, da. and h. of Wm. Beckwell.
— William Scott = Margaret, da. and co-h. of ... Bridinghurst.
    — John Scott, of Camberwell = Elizabeth, d. and co.-h. of Rich. Skinner.
        — A daughter, md. to Wm. Muschamp.
        — Elizabeth, d. and h. of Robbins. = John Scott, of Camberwell = 2nd, Margaret d. of —; 3 sons *more*.
            = 3rd, widow of Sanford.
            — Margaret.
            — Anne, da. of Edmondes, and w. of Hatcliff. = William = ... da. of Ackworth.
                — John.
                — Bartholomew.
                — Acton.
                — Edgar.
                — Southwell, s. p.
            — Edward Scott, of Camberwell. = Dorothy, da. of John Beere, of Dartford, Kent.
                — Richard Scott = Mary, da. of Weldon.
                    — John and 3 daughters, Lettice, Ann, and Eliz.
                — Sir Peter Scott, of Surrey, Knt.
                — Elizabeth, da. of Edmund Kedermister, of Langley March, Bucks.
                    — Arundel Scott, s. p.
                    — John Scott, m. and had issue.
                    — Edgar Scott, s. p.
                    — Dudley Scott, s. p.
                    — Elizabeth.
        — Elizabeth Ux. Appleyard.[1]
        — 6 daughters *more*.

[1] Elizabeth m. Roger Appleyard, who d. in 1530. She afterwards m. Sir John Robsart, and was the mother of Amye Robsart.

SCOTT, OF CAMBERWELL.

"The manor of Camberwell-Buckingham, so called from having been in the possession of Edward Stafford, Duke of Buckingham, on whose attainder, in 1521 (13 Hen. VIII.), it was granted to John Scot, who had previously rented the estate under the duke, at £7 a year, as appears by an account of all the bailiffs of the castle, &c., of this duke, rendered to his auditors from Michaelmas to Michaelmas (3rd and 4th Hen. VIII.), 1511-12.[1]

"John Scot, the grantee, was made third Baron of the Exchequer in 1529, and died in 1553, leaving a son of his own name, mentioned by Hollinshed as having been concerned in some riots and misdemeanors with Lord Howard and Lord Ogle, for which they were all brought before the Court of Star Chamber.

"This last-named John Scot died 15 Aug., 1558, and lies buried in the Chapel of our Lady in the Church of Camberwell. In an inquisition taken on his death it was found that he died seized of the manor of Camberwell, late the Duke of Buckingham's, who was attainted.

"Richard Scot was his son and heir, then aged 32; and it is supposed that the manor of Camberwell, sometimes called the manor of Peckham, had been settled on him by his father during his lifetime, as the manor of Camberwell-Buckingham was bequeathed to his five other sons. Richard died 16 Dec., 1560, leaving Thomas, his son and heir, then only seven years of age, and he died 19 Jan. following. Edward Scot, brother to Richard, then succeeded as heir."[2]

[1] From a long roll in the British Museum.
[2] From Manning and Bray's 'Surrey,' fol., vol. iii.

APPLEYARD, OF BRAKENASHE, BRAKENE, OR BROKEN, CO. NORFOLK.

Sir JOHN ROBSART is described to be "late of Wyndham, alias Stanfeld," in Norfolk;[1] and it is most probable that on marrying the widow Appleyard he took up his residence at Stanfield Hall.

It is singular that no mention has been made of the previous marriage by any historian. Bloomfield, in his 'History of Norfolk,' says that Sir John Robsart is described as "late of Wyndham, alias Stanfeld," and in another place that "Sir John Robsart and Dame Elizabeth his wife resided at Stanfield Hall." Had he examined the 'Visitation of Norfolk,' in the Heralds' College (the only pedigree of the Robsart family that I have met with), he would there have discovered, not only the birth of the illegitimate son of Sir John Robsart, but also, in the same 'Visitation' the pedigree of the Appleyards, which would have furnished him with the fact of the previous marriage and the issue of that marriage.

Lord Braybrooke, in 'The Diary and Correspondence of Samuel Pepys,' has given a short table, showing "the connexion of the Robsarts and Appleyards," in which he states Sir John Robsart to be the first husband of Elizabeth Scott instead of the second, and that Arthur was the son of the latter, whereas Amye was the only child of that marriage, Arthur being illegitimate. He also states John Appleyard to be the only child of Roger Appleyard and Elizabeth Scott, whereas there were three other children.

It would appear from the records of the Privy Council that John Appleyard was mixed up with Lord Robert Dudley in the "Lady Jane" émeute, in the first year of Qu. Mary.[2]

In 1588 John Appleyard was High Sheriff of the counties of Norfolk and Suffolk.

[1] Bloomfield's 'Hist. of Norfolk.'
[2] See 'Extracts from Privy Council Registers,' in APPENDIX.

AMYE ROBSART.

The following PEDIGREE *will show the connexion of* AMYE ROBSART *with the Family of* APPLEYARD, *as well as with that of* FLOWERDEW.

(From 'Visitation of Norfolk,' by William Harvy, 1563, in the Heralds' College.)

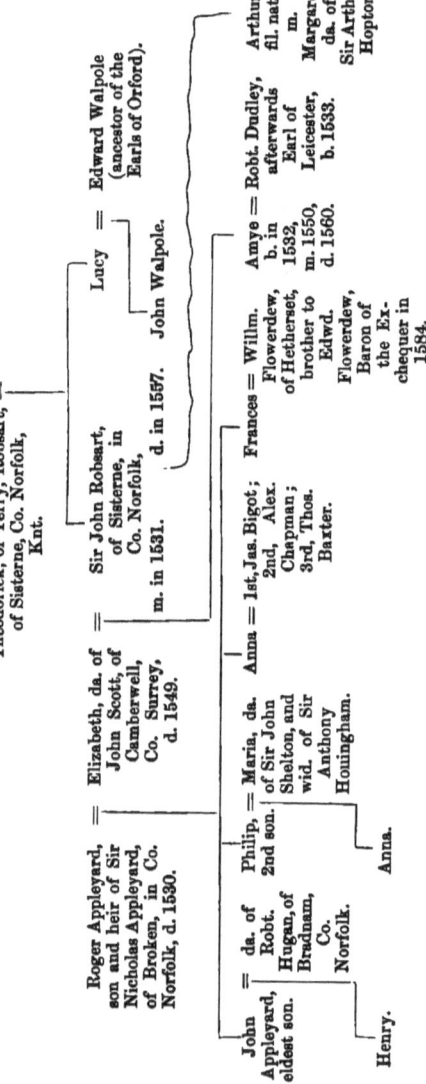

The marriage of the widow Appleyard to Sir John Robsart probably took place in 1531, her former husband having died in 1530. Amye was doubtless born at Stanfield Hall, in all probability in 1532. The death of Lady Elizabeth Robsart occurred (it is presumed) about twelve months before Amye's marriage, viz. in 1549, as Bloomfield states that the Manor of Stanfield Hall was held by John Appleyard, her son and heir, in that year. Of the death of Sir John Robsart I do not find any record, but as Lord Robert Dudley came into possession of the Robsart estates in January, 1557, we may conclude that Sir John died at that time.[1]

STANFIELD HALL, where it is probable Amye Robsart was born, after being in the possession of her half-brother, John Appleyard, to whom it had been bequeathed after the death of Amye's mother, was sold to James Altham, Esq. (Baron of the Exchequer), who in 1564 sold it to Edward Flowerdew, Esq. (afterwards Baron of the Exchequer), son of John Flowerdew, to whom Amye addressed a letter in 1559, and brother to William Flowerdew, who married Amye's half-sister, Frances Appleyard. Edward Flowerdew settled at Stanfield Hall, and purchased all the furniture from " John Appleyard, of Stanfield Hall." The estate afterwards came into the possession of William Jermy, Esq., by his marriage with the heiress of the then owner, and he was living there in 1735.[2] It had been in the family of the Appleyards for upwards of a century, and in that of the Jermys for a still longer period, when it became so fatally memorable by the murder committed there some few years since, on the person of Isaac Jermy, Esq., and his son.

Bloomfield, in his ' History of Norfolk,' says—

" Stanfield, or Stanfield Hall Manor, belonged to the Earl Warren in the Conqueror's time, and after to the Bigots, of whom it was held by Katherine, wife of Roger Fitz-Osbert, in 1306; and in 1346 Maud, widow of Oliver de Mouton, conveyed part of it to Bartholomew de Salle and Richard de

[1] For Copy of his Will see Appendix.
[2] Bloomfield's ' Norfolk,' fol., vol. i, pp. 721-2.

Bittering, who joined it to that part that Rob. de La Salle, of Norwich, had in 1280. Another part remained in John, son of Thomas de Mouton and Ivetta his wife, to the value of 100s. per annum. In 1348 the said Bartholomew held it at the 4th part of a fee. In 1394 William Appleyard paid his relief for it to Margaret, Duchess of Norfolk, it being then held of the honour of Forncet; and in 1448 Edmund Appleyard, of Windham, son of William, gave it to Anne his wife for life; remainder to William, Geoffrey, and Edmund, his sons. Another part of this manor belonged to the Rokeles, and after to the Cursons, and was held by Richard de Curson in 1256, who was then summoned to be made a knight, as holding a whole fee here and in Ketringham. In 1307 Sir William Curson held his part of Richard de la Rokele, by the 8th part of a fee, and had a capital messuage, in which he dwelt, 144 acres in domain, besides many lands, rents, and services, here and in Ketringham. In 1317, Katherine Kurson, widow of Sir William, is called Lady of Stanfield; she held it for life, and was succeeded by Sir John Curson, her son and heir, who in 1339 had Sir William Curson by Margaret his wife. In 1333 Oliver de Mouton and Maud his wife settled their part in this Sir John Curson, who had now married Ivetta, widow of Thomas de Mouton. In 1349 John de Berford; Roger Muirdegome, rector of Brakene; Ivan, widow of John de Bumpstead; Peter de Bumpstead; Emma, wife of Bartholomew, son of Nicholas de Appleyard; and Richard, son of Bartholomew de Salle, held jointly the manor of Stanfield, which they all settled on Emma for life, and afterwards released for ever to William Appleyard, who had possession in 1463. In 1514 Sir Nicholas Appleyard, Knt., granted an annuity of £6, issuing out of the manor, to John Griffith and Margaret his wife. In 1528 Roger Appleyard, Esq., of Brakene, gave it to Elizabeth his wife for life,[1] and then to John, his son and heir, who held it in 1549. It looks as if Philip Appleyard, Esq., sold it, for in 1563 James Altham, Esq., kept his first court, who in 1564 sold it with Hethill in common to Edward

[1] Elizabeth, widow of Roger Appleyard, who married Sir John Robsart.

Flowerdew, of Hetherset, Esq., and Henry, a younger son of Sir Robert Townsend, Knt., deceased; and the same year Flowerdew conveyed his half to Thomas Townsend, of Brakene-Ash, Esq.; Roger Townsend, of Raynham; Henry Heveningham, of Ketringham; William Curson, of Belagh; and Francis Windham, of Lincoln's Inn, Esqs., who in 1569 reconveyed their right to the said Edward Flowerdew and his heirs. This Edward settled at Stanfield Hall about 1566, for in that year, by the name of Edward Flowerdew, of the Inner Temple, gent., he purchased all the furniture of John Appleyard, of Stanfield Hall, in order to come and dwell there. In 1573 he was become an eminent barrister, for then Thomas Grimesdiche, of the Inner Temple, settled an annuity of 40s., issuing out of his manor called Joyces, in Little Hadham, in Hertfordshire, on him, in consideration of the good and faithful counsel he had given him. In 1575 he had such another grant of five marks a year for life, made him by Simon Harcourt, of Stanton Harcourt, in Oxfordshire, and Walter, his son and heir, issuing out of their manor of Stanton Harcourt. In Michaelmas term, 1580, he was called to the degree of serjeant-at-law; and in 1584, 23rd Oct., was made Baron of the Exchequer. By the inquisition taken after his death, in 1599, it was found that the manor was in feofee's hands, to the use of Elizabeth his wife, as her jointure, and that he was seized of a moiety of Hetherset Manor, in Hetherset, and of the site of the Abbey, and that Anthony Flowerdew, gent., was his cousin and heir, being son of William, his brother, and that he was 29 years old. In 1631 Sir Robert Gawdy had his share of Sir Nathaniel Bacon's lands in Stukey, in right of Winnefred, his wife, one of his daughters and co-heirs, and had this manor settled on him for life only—remainder to Dorothy, his daughter and sole heir, then married to Sir Philip Parker, of Arwarton, in Suffolk, Knt., and her heirs. In 1642 it was purchased by Sir Thomas Richardson, Knt., in which family it hath continued ever since, William Jermy, Esq., and Elizabeth his wife being the present owners (1739). The fine is at the lord's will.

"This Elizabeth was the only sister and heir of William, Lord Richardson, who died 28th July, 1735. She was married in August, 1735, to William Jermy, only son of John Jermy, of Bayfield, in Norfolk.

"Sir John Robsert, Knt., and Dame Elizabeth his wife, dwelt in Stanfield Hall in 1546."[1]

RAINTHORP HALL, Malherbis, otherwise called Myles or Mills Manor.[2]

"In 1444 a portion of the manor was conveyed to Nicholas Appleyard and Margaret his wife. In 1466 Margaret, relict of Nicholas Appleyard, Esq., conveyed Miles's Manor to John Appleyard, Esq., in tail; remainder to William, his brother; remainder to Henry, another brother; remainder to Bartholomew, another brother; with an over remainder to Elizabeth and Anne, their sisters, and their heirs. John Appleyard, Esq., inherited, and in 1498 settled it on trustees for the use of Nicholas, his son, who succeeded and left it to John, his son and heir. In 1515 Thomas Blowevyle was possessed of three parts of the manor. The fourth part passed as a single manor in the Appleyards, and in 1528 Roger Appleyard, Esq., died seized of it, and John, his son and heir, inherited after the death of Elizabeth,[3] his mother.

"In 1538 Robert Clere had it in trust, and afterwards Sir John Clere, Knt., for John Appleyard. In 1555 John Appleyard, of Brakenash, Esq., and Thomas Chapman, gent., son and heir of Alexander Chapman, Esq., deceased, sold to William Bigot, of Stratton, in Norfolk, gent., and John Strote, Esq., and their heirs in fee simple, the manor of Myles or Mills. In 1609 Thomas Baxter, gent., in right of his wife, who was late the wife of Alex. Chapman, and before that of James Bigot, gent."[4]

The marriage of Amye Robsart with Sir Robert Dudley

[1] Bloomfield's 'Norfolk,' fol., vol. i.   [2] Ibid., vol. iii, 44.
[3] Mother of Amye Robsart. The second marriage of Elizabeth Scott, omitted throughout by Bloomfield.
[4] James Bigot, gent., married Anne, sister to John Appleyard, and she was

took place at Sheen (now Richmond), on the 4th of June, 1550,[1] with great splendour, in the presence of Edward VI., who has recorded the fact in his journal, in his own handwriting, still preserved in the British Museum,[2] to the following effect:

"1550. June 4.—Sir Robert Dudley, third [surviving] son to the Earl of Warwick, married Sir John Robsart's daughter, after which marriage there were certain gentlemen that did strive who should first take away a goose's head, which was hanged alive on two cross posts."

Robert Dudley was born on the 24th June, 1532 or 1533. The date of his birth is not given by any historian; I discovered it in one of his letters to Queen Elizabeth, in which he says, "This is my birth-day." Amye Robsart, it is presumed, was born in 1532, so that they were nearly of the same age. We have no account as to where they took up their residence on their marriage, but it was probably at Siderstern.

In 1558 we have the following letter from Lord Robert Dudley, addressed to John Flowerdew,[3] who it is presumed was his steward or agent.

"GOOD MR. FLOWERDEW,—I do most heartily thank you for your pains and travail you have taken for me, as well touching the matter of Flitcham, as other mine affairs at Sidesterne. For the first, I would very gladly proceed therein, having it so as to be no loser by such rates as might be too over high set. For that, as I said before, I shall refer unto you, in thinking the prices too unreasonable, I must, if to dwell in that country, take some house other than mine own, for it were wanteth all such chief commodities as a house requireth, which is, pasture, wood, water, &c. To this I understand there is most of that the other wants, and besides it standeth somewhat nigh that little I have

secondly married to Alex. Chapman, and thirdly she married Thomas Baxter, as above.

[1] The day after the marriage of Dudley's elder brother John, then Lord Lisle, to the daughter of Protector Somerset.
[2] Cottonian MSS., Nero CX. British Museum.
[3] Harleian MSS., British Museum, 4712.

there. And where your care is so great for me in looking for my commodity herein, that you would have more advice than your own, for your contentation (though both your skill will suffice for a much greater matter than this, and my trust would not refuse that you should do in a greater matter also), I have required my brother Bige [Bigot][1] to take pains with you, and what order you take as well for the rent and prices, as for the year, I will accept and agree unto. Praying you that if you conclude that I may have a full certificate that the ground is—what the stock is upon it already—and what number of cattle you judge it may keep. And hearing hereof from you both, God willing, I will immediately come down to see it myself, and to take further order by your advices for my coming thither.

"I understand also that there is stuff or furniture in the house, which the executors will depart with all; I pray you I may have some little inventory what it is, and how they will leave it, and I will send word again what I will do. If it be good and worth the prices, I would not refuse it.

"For Sidestern, first for the fold-course [sheep-pens] at Boxford, I do mind to store and lay it myself, praying you to give your order for it; and for all things else that is out of order, I pray you to redress it at your discretion, as well [as] for placing or displacing such servants or shepherds as be unmeet to have charge there, even in such sort as any way I would or should do myself. And think myself much beholding and greatly in your debt, for the friendship you have divers ways showed me.

"And so with my hearty commendations, and ready to do you all the pleasure I may, I bid you farewell. From Hays, this Friday morning.

"Yours assured,
"R. DUDDELEY.

"*Sainte Magdylin's daye.*"[2]

Addressed—
"To my very friend,
"JOHN FLOWERDEW, Esq., with speed."

---

[1] James Bigot, the first husband of Anna Appleyard, half-sister to Amye Robsart.

[2] Saint Magdalen's day, Friday, 22nd July, 1558.

FLITCHAM, in the county of Norfolk, was formerly the property of Sir Thomas Hollis, whose son, William, married Elizabeth, daughter of this John Flowerdew, who was of Hetherset, in Co. Norfolk, and it is not improbable that this treaty of Lord Robert Dudley's for that estate was on the occasion of the death of William Hollis. It was not far from Newton and Great Bircham, which, with Sidestern, had been granted (30 Jan., 3 and 4 Philip and Mary) to Lord Robert for life.[1]

The Flowerdews were connected with Amye Robsart by the marriage of William Flowerdew, eldest son of the above John Flowerdew, of Hetherset, Co. Norfolk (to whom Dudley's letter is addressed), to Frances, daughter of Roger Appleyard and Elizabeth Scott, and half-sister of Amye Robsart.[2] Edward Flowerdew, Baron of the Exchequer,[3] and Lord of Stanfield Hall, was another son of this John Flowerdew.

[1] Bloomfield's 'Norfolk,' vol. iii, 851.
[2] Amye had two half-sisters—Frances Appleyard, married to William Flowerdew, and Anna, who married three times. She had also two half-brothers, John and Philip Appleyard, as will be seen by reference to the Pedigree at page 19.
[3] Edward Flowerdew was appointed Baron of the Exchequer 23rd Oct., 1584, 27 Eliz.

AMYE ROBSART. 19

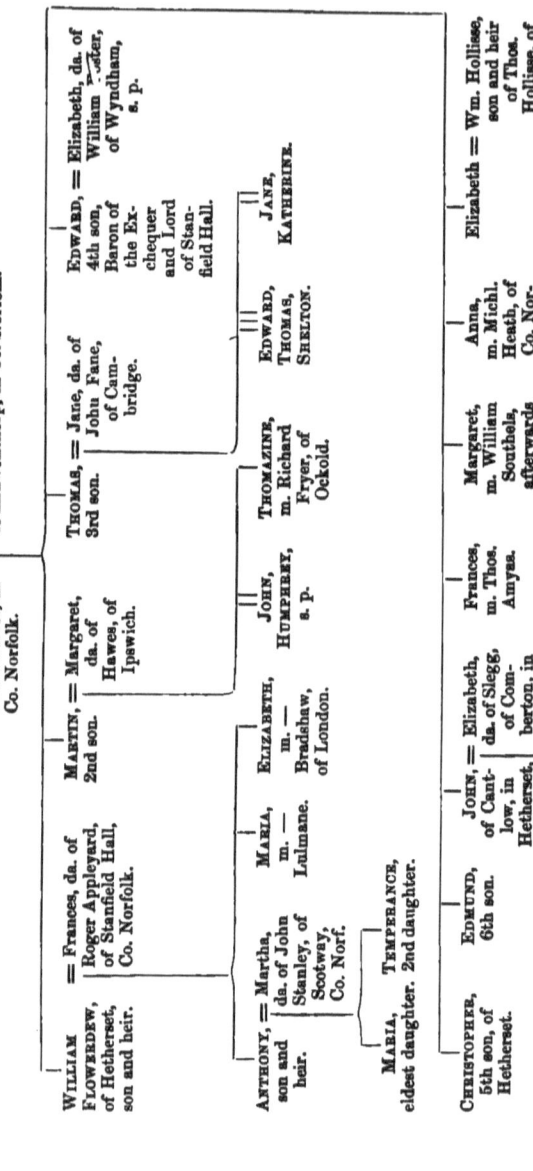

PEDIGREE OF THE FLOWERDEWS.

(From 'Visitation of Norfolk,' by W. Harvy, 1653, in College of Arms.)

JOHN FLOWERDEW, of Hetherset, in Co. Norfolk. = Katherine, da. of William Sheree, of Ashwellthorp, in Co. Norfolk.

- WILLIAM FLOWERDEW, of Hetherset, son and heir. = Frances, da. of Roger Appleyard, of Stanfield Hall, Co. Norfolk.
- MARTIN, 2nd son. = Margaret, da. of Hawes, of Ipswich.
- THOMAS, 3rd son. = Jane, da. of John Fane, of Cambridge.
- EDWARD, 4th son, Baron of the Exchequer and Lord of Stanfield Hall. = Elizabeth, da. of William —ter, of Wyndham, s. p.
- JANE. KATHERINE.
- Elizabeth = Wm. Hollisee, son and heir of Thos. Hollisee, of Flycham, Co. Norfolk, Knt.

Children of William Flowerdew:
- ANTHONY, son and heir. = Martha, da. of John Stanley, of Scotway, Co. Norf.
- MARIA, m. — Lulmane.
- ELIZABETH, m. — Bradshaw, of London.
- EDMUND, 6th son.
- JOHN, of Cantlow, in Hetherset, 7th son. = Elizabeth, da. of Slegg, of Comberton, in Co. Camb.
- Frances, m. Thos. Amyas.
- Margaret, m. William Southels, afterwards m. — Harman.
- Anna, m. Michl. Heath, of Co. Norfolk.

Children of Thomas:
- JOHN, HUMPHREY, s. p.
- THOMAZINE, m. Richard Fryer, of Ockold.
- EDWARD, THOMAS, SHELTON.

MARIA, eldest daughter. TEMPERANCE, 2nd daughter.

CHRISTOPHER, 5th son, of Hetherset.

EDWARD. WILLIAM. EDMUND. THOMAZINE.

HAYS, or HAYES, from which place Lord Robert writes his letter, was formerly in the possession of the Scotts of Halden, ancestors of the Scotts of Camberwell; it is situated south-west from Chislehurst, in the county of Kent.

"Hayes Place is a seat in this parish, situated about one hundred yards from the church, westward, which was once the ancient residence of a branch of the family of the Scotts of Halden, in this county. Sir Stephen Scott, Knt., one of the sons of John Scott, Esq., of Halden, who bore for his arms, *argent, a cross croslet, sable,* kept his shrievalty for this county at this seat in 1648, being then one of the gentlemen pensioners to Chas. I. He afterwards removed his residence to Cheshunt, in Hertfordshire, where he died in 1658, and was buried in this church.

"John Scott, his eldest son, became his heir in this seat, and was a gentleman of the King's Privy Chamber. In 1757 the estate was sold to the Right Honorable Wm. Pitt, second son of Robt. Pitt, of Boconnock, in Cornwall, Esq., descended from Thomas Pitt, Esq., sometime Governor of Fort St. George, in 1766 created Earl of Chatham. Soon after purchasing this seat he entirely rebuilt it, nearly on the old site, and added several parcels of land to it by purchase. In 1766 Pitt sold the estate to the Hon. Thomas Walpole, second son of Horatio, Lord Walpole, younger brother of Sir Robert Walpole, the first Earl of Orford of this family. Two years after it was resold to the Earl of Chatham, at his earnest request, and he then resided much here. 'The great Earl of Chatham' died here, 11th May, 1778, in consequence of the violent exertions he had made during a speech in the House of Lords, when, fainting away, he was carried home to his house in London, and from thence hither, where he languished but a short time till his death, and was afterwards buried in Westminster Abbey at the public expense.

"It afterwards came into the possession of the Earl of Dartmouth, who was possessor of it in 1797.

"The Right Honorable Wm. Pitt, second son of the great Earl of Chatham, was born at Hayes Place, 28th May, 1759, during his father's residence here."[1]

[1] From Hasted's 'Kent,' 8vo, vol. ii, 1797.

SCOTTS OF HALDEN.—John Scott died possessed of Halden House 21 Hen. VI.; his grandson, Henry Scott, of Halden, died, and was buried here in 1512, bearing for his arms, *argent, a cross-plate, fitchee, sable*. He left two sons, of whom Henry, the eldest, succeeded him at Halden, and Thomas, the second son, marrying the daughter and heir of Conghurst, of Hawkhurst, inherited that seat.

"From Henry, the eldest son, descended those of Hayes and Beckenham.

"Thomas Scott, the second son, mentioned just before, who married the co-heir of Conghurst, had two sons. From the eldest, George, descended the Scotts of Conghurst; and from Thomas, the youngest, those of Sutton-at-Hone, and of London. They bore for their arms, *argent, a cross-croslet, fitchee, sable*.[1]

We do not find any other letter from Lord Robert Dudley having reference to the Robsart estates, or in any way connected with Amye Robsart, but we have a letter from the latter, and the only letter of hers that has been discovered. It is preserved among the Harleian MSS. in the British Museum,[2] written "from Mr. Hyde's," and presumed to have been in 1559. It is addressed to Mr. Flowerdew the elder, the same person to whom Lord Robert Dudley's letter is addressed, in reference to the estate at Flitcham:

"MR. FLOWERDEW,—I understand by Gryse that you put him in remembrance of that you spake to me of, concerning the going of certain sheep at Siderstern; and although I forgot to move my lord thereof before his departing, he being sore troubled with weighty affairs, and I not being altogether in quiet for his sudden departing, yet, notwithstanding, knowing your accustomed friendship towards my lord and me, I neither may nor can deny you that request, in my lord's absence, of mine own authority, yea and [if] it were a greater matter, as if any good occasion may serve you to try me; desiring you further that you will make sale of the wool so soon as is possible, although you sell it for

[1] From Hasted's 'Kent,' vol. vii, 1797.
[2] Harleian MSS., British Museum, No. 4712.

vi! the stone, or as you would sell for yourself; for my lord so justly required me, at his departing, to see those poor men satisfied, as though it had been a matter depending upon life; wherefore I 'force not to sustain a little loss thereby to satisfy my lord's desire, and so to send that money to Gryse's house to London, by Bridewell, to whom my lord hath given order for the payment thereof. And thus I end, always troubling you, wishing that occasion may serve me to requite you, until that time I must pay you with thanks; and so to God I leave you.

"From Mr. Hyde's, this vii of August,
Your assured, during life,
"AMYE DUDDLEY."

(Superscription.)
"To my very friend, Mr. FLOWERDEW the elder,
give this. Norfolk."

This letter is spoken of by various writers as being in Amye's own handwriting, and comments have been made as to the boldness of her writing. I see nothing to justify such an inference. It should be borne in mind that at that period good writing was an accomplishment that every lady was not possessed of. It is the original letter, doubtless, but written, I conceive, by a clerk or secretary, and it would appear upon a careful examination that even the signature is not her own writing, but was either by the same clerk or one writing a similar hand. Neither is the name spelt as her husband and all others of that branch of the family wrote it, the *e* in Duddeley being omitted. It has the appearance as if she had commenced the signature, and after the first letter (A) that it had been finished by the clerk. We may presume from this circumstance that she was not skilled in writing, which may probably account for no other letter of hers having been discovered. The letter has no date to it, but from its contents it was probably written in 1559.

"Mr. Hyde's," at whose house Amye appears to have been staying when her letter was written, was in all probability William Hyde, son of William Hyde and Margery, daughter of John Cater, Esq., of Denchworth, in the hundred of Wanting and deanery of Abingdon, which lies about three miles north of Wantage, and nearly nine miles to the south-west of Abingdon. The manor of South Denchworth belonged to David Martun, Bishop of St. David's, who died in 1328. It was afterwards in the Corbets'; Sir Roger Corbet died seized of it in 1417. His daughter and sole heir, Sybella, married John Grevell. The manor afterwards became the property of the Hydes, who by some fabulous tradition in the family were said to have possessed it from the time of King Canute. A pedigree of the Hydes in the British Museum [1] states Sir George Hyde, K.B., who died in 1625, and sold the manor of South Denchworth to Sir William Cockayne, to have been the sixth in descent from the first of that family who settled at Denchworth, which will not be found inconsistent with the records, which prove the manor to have been in the Corbets' so late as the commencement of the fifteenth century. Lord Viscount Cullen, son of Sir William Cockayne, sold South Denchworth to the Geerings, of whom it was purchased, in 1758, by the provost and scholars of Worcester College, in Oxford.

"In the parish church are several monuments of the Hydes and Geerings.

"Wm. Hyde, Esq., as appears by his Will bearing date 1557, was seized of the manor of Hydes and Lovedays, in South and North Denchworth."[2]

Oliver Hyde, who died in 1570, was Member of Parliament for Abingdon, and was succeeded by Anthony Foster, of Cumnor. He was brother to the William Hyde, at whose house Amye's letter is supposed to have been written, and brother to Elizabeth, widow of John Odingsells, who is mentioned in Blount's letter to Lord Robert Dudley as residing with Anthony Foster, at Cumnor, at the time of Amye Dudley's death.

It was said that Lady Amye Dudley lived unhappily with her husband, but we have no clue to her private history beyond what is contained in her letter. From the expression

---

[1] Harleian MSS., 1535.   [2] Lysons's 'Berkshire.'

in the early portion of that letter, in speaking of her husband, we may be led to suppose that the reports in circulation were true. Queen Elizabeth ascended the throne on the 17th November, 1558, and Lord Robert was sworn of the Privy Council on the 4th June, 1559, two months previous to the date of Amye's letter. "He being sore troubled with weighty affairs," in all probability refers to his constant attendance on the queen, and consequent absence from her. Again, "I not being altogether in quiet for his sudden departing," evidently showing a mind ill at ease.

We hear nothing further of her till we find her residing at Cumnor, at the house of Anthony Forster, who was at that time tenant, but afterwards lord of the manor, and who was considered "a very amiable man, very learned, a great musician, builder, and planter."[1]

We now proceed to give a short account of Cumnor Place, where Amye had been living, we presume for a short time only, as her letter from Mr. Hyde's was written in 1559, and her death occurred in 1560. Cumnor was in the occupation of Anthony Forster at the time of her death.

CUMNOR PLACE.

CUMNOR PLACE was one of the country seats of the abbots of Abingdon, and, on the dissolution of the monasteries George Owen, Physician to Henry VIII., became the first lay proprietor, the king having granted it to him by Letters Patent, dated 5th October, 1546, in exchange for lands in Oxfordshire, which were surrendered to the crown. William Owen, son of the above, on the death of his father in 1561, sold the Cumnor property to Anthony Forster, who had occupied the mansion, as tenant, for some years previous. It was in September of the year previous that Amye Dudley died at Cumnor.

Forster died in 1572, and in his Will left the Cumnor pro-

[1] From his epitaph in Cumnor Church. See Lysons's 'Magna Brit.,' i, 270

perty to the Earl of Leicester, conditioned on the payment of twelve hundred pounds, which, however, does not appear to have been accepted by the earl.

Cumnor, after the death of Forster's widow, passed into the family of the Earl of Abingdon, where it still remains. It was for a long period deserted; the recollection of Amye Dudley's melancholy end was revived amongst the ignorant villagers, whose imaginations conjured up forms and horrors before unheard of, and hence arose the legendary tales that have descended to the present day. Decay followed fast on desertion, and with the aid of the wanton and mischievous, before a century had rolled away, it had become almost a ruin.

"When Cumnor Place was in the zenith of its splendour the great attraction must have been the park; the terrace walks which encircled it, the stately trees and capacious fish-ponds with which it was ornamented, and the church elevated conspicuously in the immediate rear of the mansion, all added their charms to the natural beauty of the spot, a pleasing contrast to the distant uncultivated downs which form the southern boundary of the vale. A complete change, however, has now swept over the former interesting aspect of the scene. The church, indeed, is an abiding representative of former ages, and the resting-place of some of those whose lives were spent at this monastic abode, while round the sacred edifice rest the remains of many who felt the bounty of its owners. The gardens and grounds, wherein the unfortunate Amye passed so many cheerless hours, have disappeared; their site is now in the occupation of the agriculturist, and for his convenience the present partition of them has been made. A few fine elms scattered here and there are all that is left to aid in realising the former picturesque appearance of this retreat, where we are privileged to sympathise with suffering innocence and blighted affection, although truth dispels from the story the exaggerated horrors with which those sufferings have been portrayed."[1]

[1] Bartlett's 'Cumnor Place,' Oxford, 1850.

"Part of the old mansion, which was formerly the abbot's place, is fitted up as a farmhouse. The shell of the remainder, though in a state of dilapidation, is nearly entire; some part of it appears to have been rebuilt after the Reformation, by Mr. Forster."[1]

This short description of Cumnor would be incomplete were we to withhold that delightful ballad of Mickle's, which cannot fail to be of interest.

The 'Ballad of Cumnor Hall,' which, it is said, first suggested to Sir Walter Scott to write the romance of "Kenilworth," was the work of William Julius Mickle, who died in 1788. It was first printed in Evans's 'Collection of Old Ballads,' in 1784, with the antique spelling of Queen Elizabeth's period. In a subsequent edition of this interesting work, in 1810, the poem was modernised, and from that the present excerpt has been made, which is now presented to the reader:[2]

"CUMNOR HALL.

THE dews of summer night did fall,
  The moon (sweet regent of the sky)
Silver'd the walls of Cumnor Hall,
  And many an oak that grew thereby.

Now nought was heard beneath the skies
  (The sounds of busy life were still),
Save an unhappy lady's sighs,
  That issued from that lonely pile.

"Leicester," she cried, "is this thy love
  That thou so oft hast sworn to me,
To leave me in this lonely grove,
  Immur'd in shameful privity?

"No more thou comest with lover's speed
  Thy once beloved bride to see;
But be she alive, or be she dead,
  I fear, stern Earl, 's the same to thee.

[1] Lysons's 'Magna Britannia,' vol. i, p. 454.
[2] Introductory Preface to Laneham's 'Letter,' 12mo, 1821.

"Not so the usage I received
    When happy in my father's hall;
No faithless husband then me grieved,
    No chilling fears did me appal.

"I rose up with the cheerful morn,
    No lark more blithe, no flower more gay;
And, like the bird that haunts the thorn,
    So merrily sung the livelong day.

"If that my beauty is but small,
    Among court ladies all despis'd,
Why didst thou rend it from that hall,
    Where, scornful Earl, it well was prized?

"And when you first to me made suit,
    How fair I was you oft would say!
And, proud of conquest—pluck'd the fruit,
    Then left the blossom to decay.

"Yes, now neglected and despis'd,
    The rose is pale—the lily's dead—
But he that once their charms so priz'd
    Is sure the cause those charms are fled.

"For know, when sick'ning grief doth prey,
    And tender love 's repaid with scorn,
The sweetest beauty will decay—
    What flow'ret can endure the storm?

"At court, I'm told, is beauty's throne,
    Where every lady 's passing rare;
That eastern flowers, that shame the sun,
    Are not so glowing, not so fair.

"Then, Earl, why didst thou leave the beds
    Where roses and where lilies vie,
To seek a primrose, whose pale shades
    Must sicken—when those gaudes are by?

"'Mong rural beauties I was one;
    Among the fields wild flow'rs are fair;
Some country swain might me have won,
    And thought my beauty passing rare.

"But, Leicester (or I much am wrong),
    Or 'tis not beauty lures thy vows,
Rather ambition's gilded crown
    Makes thee forget thy humble spouse.

"Then, Leicester, why, again I plead
    (The injur'd surely may repine),
Why didst thou wed a country maid,
    When some fair princess might be thine?

"Why didst thou praise my humble charms,
    And oh! then leave them to decay?
Why didst thou win me to thy arms,
    Then leave me to mourn the live-long day?

"The village maidens of the plain
    Salute me lowly as they go;
Envious they mark my silken train,
    Nor think a Countess can have woe.

"The simple nymphs—they little know
    How far more happy's their estate—
To smile for joy, than sigh for woe;
    To be content, than to be great.

"How far less blest am I than them?
    Daily to pine and waste with care!
Like the poor plant that, from its stem
    Divided, feels the chilling air.

"Nor, cruel Earl, can I enjoy
    The humble charms of solitude;
Your minions proud my peace destroy,
    By sullen frowns or pratings rude.

"Last night, as sad I chanced to stray,
    The village death-bell smote my ear;
They wink'd aside, and seemed to say,
    'Countess, prepare—thy end is near!'

"And now, while happy peasants sleep,
    Here I sit lonely and forlorn;
No one to soothe me as I weep,
    Save Philomel on yonder thorn.

"My spirits flag—my hopes decay—
  Still that dread death-bell smites my ear,
And many a boding seems to say,
  'Countess, prepare, thy end is near.'"

Thus sore and sad that lady grieved,
  In Cumnor Hall so lone and drear;
And many a heartfelt sigh she heaved
  And let fall many a bitter tear.

And e'er the dawn of day appeared
  In Cumnor Hall, so lone and drear,
Full many a piercing scream was heard,
  And many a cry of mortal fear.

The death-bell thrice was heard to ring,
  An aërial voice was heard to call;
And thrice the raven flapp'd its wings
  Around the tow'rs of Cumnor Hall.

The mastiff howl'd at village door,
  The oaks were shatter'd on the green;
Woe was the hour—for never more
  That hapless Countess e'er was seen.

And in that manor now no more
  Is cheerful feast and sprightly ball;
For ever since that dreary hour
  Have spirits haunted Cumnor Hall.

The village maids, with fearful glance,
  Avoid the ancient moss-grown wall,
Nor ever lead the merry dance
  Among the groves of Cumnor Hall.

Full many a traveller oft hath sigh'd,
  And pensive wept the Countess' fall,
As wandering onwards they've espied
  The haunted tow'rs of Cumnor Hall."[1]

---

[1] It will be perceived that Mickle erred in speaking of Leicester as the "Earl," and Amye as the "Countess," the former not having been created an Earl till some few years after Amye's death.

The death of Amye Dudley occurred on Sunday, the 8th of September, 1560, at Cumnor, under circumstances certainly of some suspicion. Without, however, giving credence to the various libels that appeared against Lord Robert Dudley, his own letters, which we now give, written upon that occasion to his cousin Blount (contemporary copies of which are still preserved in the Pepysian Library at Cambridge), serve very strongly to show that he at least manifested but very little feeling at the loss of his wife. The first letter, it will be seen, is from Windsor, the day after her death.

Bartlett, in his history of Cumnor Place, has given these letters, which were first printed by Craik, in his 'Romance of the Peerage,' and as well, about the same period, by Lord Braybrooke, in his edition of the 'Diary and Correspondence of Samuel Pepys.'[1]

The excellent observations or commentary on these letters by Mr. Bartlett serve so well to illustrate the subject, that I take the liberty to transfer them to these pages.

"On the 9th of September, when Dudley was in attendance on the queen at Windsor, a messenger arrived from Cumnor with a letter containing the intelligence of the death of his wife on the previous day by a fall down some stairs; and although it may be gleaned from the ensuing correspondence that Bowes, the messenger, was attached to the household at the mansion of Cumnor Place, where the disastrous occurrence had taken place, he was unable to give very little, if any, account of how it happened, being in all probability absent with the rest of the servants at the fair at Abingdon.

"Dudley's first impression on receipt of the news appears to have been most remarkable and mysterious; he at once expressed an opinion that her death had not been the result of an accident, but of violence, and that he should be accused of being implicated in her destruction. The most reasonable explanation of these expressions that can be suggested, consistent with a perfectly guiltless conscience, seems to be that he must have at once perceived that so unlooked for an event,

[1] See 'Romance of the Peerage,' 1848, vol. i, Appendix; and 'Pepys' Diary,' vol. iv, Appendix.

occurring in so extraordinary a manner, would give his enemies the opportunity of asserting that his wife had been murdered, and that, notwithstanding his absence from the scene, they would charge him with being the originator of the plot; and he could not but have felt that his past estrangement from her would be held up as a ground of suspicion, and would be generally interpreted as a strong presumption of guilt.

"His conduct also, as well as his expressions, exposes him to invidious remarks, and may be by the prejudiced regarded as additional evidence in proof of the grave charge that has been so strongly urged against him. One would have thought that he would at once have started for the scene of his bereavement, and have satisfied himself whether there were any grounds to support his suspicions; but, apprehensive of crimination from his wife's relations, he immediately despatches the news to them in Norfolk, that they might be present at the coroner's inquiry, which he knew to be inevitable, to satisfy themselves as to the true cause and manner of her death; and he then sits down and writes a letter of instructions on the subject to a gentleman in his confidence named Blount.

"Such a course of proceeding on the part of Dudley, coupled with his expressions, do not at first sight seem altogether consistent with a complete state of innocence; but his subsequent conduct, in promoting the inquiry before the coroner, tends greatly to relieve the distrust that otherwise would be felt, and must be properly weighed in arriving at an impartial conclusion of his guilt or innocence; indeed, it would be the extreme of prejudice to insinuate that there is anything in the ensuing correspondence that betrays an attempt on his part to conceal a crime or to baffle investigation.

"The following letter is the first that passed between Dudley and Blount, pending the coroner's inquest at Cumnor:

"*Lord Robert Dudley to T. Blount.*[1]

"COUSIN BLOUNT,—Immediately upon your departing from me there came to me Bowes, by whom I do understand that my wife is dead, and, as he saith, by a fall from a pair of stairs. Little other understanding can I have of him. The greatness and the suddenness of the misfortune doth so perplex me, until I do hear from you how the matter standeth, or how this evil should light upon me, considering what the malicious world will bruit, as I can take no rest. And, because I have no way to purge myself of the malicious talk that I know the wicked world will use, but one which is the very plain truth to be knowen, I do pray you, as you have loved me, and do tender me and my quietness, and as now my special trust is in you, that [you] will use all the devises and means you can possible for the learning of the troth; wherein have no respect to any living person. And, as by your own travail and diligence, so likewise by order of law, I mean by calling of the Coroner, and charging him to the uttermost from me to have good regard to make choice of no light or slight persons, but the discreetest and [most] substantial men, for the juries, such as for their knowledge may be able to search throughly and duly, by all manner of examinations, the bottom of the matter, and for their uprightness will earnestly and sincerely deal therein without respect; and that the body be viewed and searched accordingly by them; and in every respect to proceed by order and law. In the mean time, Cousin Blount, let me be advertised from you by this bearer with all speed how the matter doth stand. For, as the cause and the manner thereof doth marvellously trouble me, considering my case, many ways, so shall I not be at rest till I may be ascertained thereof; praying you, even as my trust is in you, and as I have ever loved you, do not dissemble with me, neither let anything be hid from me, but send me your

---

[1] "*Cousin Blount.*" Dudley's brother, Ambrose, Earl of Warwick, married for his second wife, Elizabeth daughter of Gilbert, Lord Talboys (and widow of Thomas Wimbishe). She was great granddaughter of Sir John Blount, of Kynlett, Co. Salop. I presume Thomas Blount to be of this family. The father of Sir John Blount married Anne, daughter of Sir Richard Croftes. A descendant of the latter (I presume), Sir James Croftes, who was comptroller of the household to Queen Elizabeth, Leicester called "Cousin Croftes."

true conceit and opinion of the matter, whether it happened by evil chance or by villany. And fail not to let me hear continually from you. And thus fa[re] you well in much haste; from Windsor, this ixth of September i[n] the evening [1560]. Your loving friend and kinsman, much perplexed. "R. D."

"I have sent for my brother Appleyard, because he is her brother, and other of her friends also to be there, that they may be privy and see how all things do proceed."

"From this letter, and the reply of Blount, it may be inferred that the latter had left Dudley at Windsor on the 9th Sept. for the purpose of proceeding to Cumnor, but that previously to his arriving at Abingdon, which lay in his route, he met with Bowes on his way to Windsor with the above news, and from him learnt what had happened to Lady Dudley. Bowes, it would seem, informed Blount all that he knew of the circumstances, and also that when it occurred all the domestics belonging to the establishment were absent at Abingdon Fair.

"It is somewhat strange that Blount, on being apprised of Lady Dudley's death, should, like Dudley, have felt distrust of fair means having been used towards her; and his manner is in some degree open to suspicion; inasmuch as he did not, upon hearing the disastrous intelligence, hasten on to Cumnor, or immediately return to Windsor, to consult or take fresh instructions from Dudley. He however continued on his journey as far as Abingdon, where he stayed the night at an inn, for the avowed but somewhat singular purpose of ascertaining the particulars relating to the catastrophe and the public feeling in the neighbourhood touching the cause. The better to accomplish this end he dissembles with the landlord, with whom he manifestly assumes to be unconscious of what had taken place, and leads him to believe that he is merely passing the night at his house, on his road into Gloucestershire, and while at supper sends for him to learn if there was any news stirring. As a matter of course, the all-engrossing topic of conversation, the death of Lady Dudley, is communicated, and he then proceeds to inquire how she had come by the fall; to which the landlord replied, he knew not. Dissatisfied with this answer, Blount asked what was his judgment and the judgment of his people; when the landlord, attempting an evasion of the question, replied, that some were disposed to say well, and some evil. This, however, was by no means satisfactory to Blount, who was bent upon extracting from his host more than he appeared willing to disclose, and whom he supposed, like the rest of his fraternity, to be more conversant with the tales and rumours of the locality than the generality of the public, a country inn in those days being the place where all the news that was abroad was sure to be discussed and propagated; he therefore presses the landlord more closely for his opinion. 'By my troth,' said he, 'I judge it a very misfortune, because it chanced at that honest gentleman's [Forster's] house, his great honesty doth much cut the evil thoughts of the people.' This remark in a measure appeased Blount, who, still pretending entire ignorance of everything connected with the sad affair, proceeded to interrogate his companion as to what explanation the domestics of the mansion gave of the matter, and was told that they were not at home at the time, but at Abingdon Fair. Upon this Blount proceeded to catechise the landlord as to how that chanced, and elicits in answer that, 'it is said how that she rose very early, and commanded all her sort to go to the fair, and would suffer none to tarry at home, and thereof much is judged.'

"It may here be remarked, that, previously to this conversation, Blount could not have received the above letter from Dudley, which was dispatched to him by a person of the name of Bristo, who, in all probability, delivered it to Blount on the next day, viz., the 10th, after he had arrived at Cumnor, and it is therefore beyond a doubt that the suspicions that presented themselves in the minds both of Dudley and Blount on hearing her ladyship was dead, were also rife in the vicinity of Cumnor before either the one or the other were made acquainted with the fact of her decease.

"The proceedings of Blount on reaching the scene of the calamity do not appear to have been characterised by any remarkable incident. He finds some of the jury already assembled at the house, and to them he communicates Dudley's wishes, and the directions he had received from him with reference to the inquiry about to be entered on, and he then sets about investigating the matter. He at once discovers that it is surrounded with such suspicious circumstances, and is so enveloped in mystery, that, to use his own language, 'it passeth the judgment of any man to say how it is.' But the details of Blount's proceedings are more fully disclosed in his own letter to Dudley, which was written from Cumnor on the day after his arrival there, and is as follows :

II.—" *T. Blount to Lord Robert Dudley.*

"May it please your Lordship to understand that I have received your letter by Bristo, the contents whereof I do well perceive ; and that your Lordship was advertised by Bowes upon my departing that my Lady was dead; and also your strait charge given unto me that I should use all the devises and policies that I can for the true understanding of the matter, as well by mine own travail as by the order of law, as in calling the Coroner, giving him charge that he choose a discreet and substantial jury for the view of the body and that no corruption should be used or person respected. Your Lordship's great reasons, that maketh you so earnestly search to learn the troth, the same, with your earnest commandment, doth make me to do my best therein. The present advertisement I can give to your Lordship at this time is, too true it is that my Lady is dead, and, as it seemeth, with a fall; but yet how or which way I cannot learn. Your Lordship shall hear the manner of my proceeding since I cam from you. The same night I cam from Windsor I lay at Abingdon all that night ; and, because I was desirous to hear what news went abroad in the country, at my supper I called for mine host, and asked him what news was thereabout, taking upon me I was going into Gloucestershire. He said, there was fallen a great misfortune within three or four miles of the town; he said, my Lord Robert Dudley's wife was dead; and I axed how; and he said, by a misfortune, as he heard, by a fall from a pair of stairs ; I asked him by what chance ; he said, he knew not: I axed him what was his judgment, and the judgment of the people ; he said, some were disposed to say well, and some evil. What is your judgment? said I. By my troth, said he, I judge it a misfortune because it chanced in that honest gentleman's house; his great honesty, said he, doth much curb the evil thoughts of the people. Mythinks, said I, that some of her people that waited upon her should somewhat say to this. No sir, said he, but little; for it was said that they were all here at the fair, and none left with her. How might that chance? said I. Then said he, It is said how that she rose that day very early, and commanded all her sort to go [to] the fair, and would suffer none to tarry at home; and thereof is much judged.

"And truly, my lord, I did first learn of Bowes, as I met with him coming towards your lordship, of his own being that day and of all the rest of their being, who affirmed that she would not that day suffer one of her own sort to tarry at home, and was so earnest to have them gone to the fair, that with any of her own sort that made reason of tarrying at home she was very angry, and cam to Mrs. Odingsells (?),[1] the widow that liveth with Anthony Forster, who refused that day to go to the fair, and was very angry with her also, because she said it was no day for gentlewomen to go in, but said the morrow was much better, and then she would go. Whereunto my lady answered and said that she might choose and go at her pleasure, but all hers should go; and was very angry. They asked who should keep her company if all they went. She said Mrs. Owen[2] should keep her company at dinner. The same tale doth Pirto (?), who doth dearly love her, confirm. Certainly, my Lord, as little while as I have been here, I have heard divers tales of her that maketh me to judge her to be a strange woman of mind. In asking of Pirto what she might think of this matter, either chance or villany, she said by her faith she doth judge very chance, and neither done by man nor by herself. For herself, she said, she was a good virtuous gentlewoman, and daily would pray upon her knees; and divers times she saith that she hath heard her pray to God to deliver her from desperation. Then, said I, she might have an evil toy (?) in her mind. No, good Mr. Blount, said Pirto, do not judge so of my words; if you should so gather, I am sorry I said so much. My Lord, it is most strange that this chance should fall upon you. It passeth the judgment of any man to say how it is; but truly the tales I do hear of her maketh me to think she had a

[1] Sister of Oliver Hyde, M.P., and of William Hyde, at whose house Amye's letter was written.
[2] Wife of George Owen, Physician to Hen. VIII, and owner of Cumnor Place.

strange mind in her; as I will tell you at my coming. But to the inquest you would have so very circumspectly chosen by the Coroner for the understanding of the troth, your Lordship needeth not to doubt of their well choosing. Before my coming the most were chosen, and part of them at the house. If I be able to judge of men and of their ableness, I judge them, and specially some of them, to be as wise and as able men to be chosen upon such a matter as any men, being but countrymen, as ever I saw, and as well able to answer to their doing before whosoever they shall be called. And for their true search, without respect of person, I have done your message unto them. I have good hope they will conceal no fault, if any be; for, as they are wise, so are they, as I hear part of them, very enemies to Anthony Forster. God give them, with their wisdom, indifferency, and then be they well chosen men. More advertisement, at this time, I cannot give your Lordship; but as I can learn so will I advertise, wishing your Lordship to put away sorrow, and rejoice, whatsoever fall out, of your own innocency; by the which in time, doubt not but that malicious reports shall turn upon their backs that can be glad to wish or say against you. And thus I humbly take my leave; from Comner, the xith of September. Your Lordship's life and loving, "T. B."

"Your Lordship hath done very well in sending for Mr. Appleyard."

"By this letter it is certain, that the chief ground of suspicion rested upon the fact, that at the time of the fall, both Lady Dudley's and Forster's servants were away at the fair, which it so happened this year fell on a Sunday. The truth of the very remarkable assertion of Lady Dudley being angry with Mrs. Odingsells (who, it must be borne in mind, was a lady of family and station), because she declined to go to the fair, and of her not suffering one of her own attendants to remain at home, was most likely proved to the jury as an explanation of the cause of so few being at Cumnor Place when the fatal fall took place. Forster's absence is not alluded to, and therefore it may be supposed that he was at home at the time, and probably the only male person in the house, and that from these untoward circumstances, and the very singular manner of her death, the suspicions against him arose.

"There is a passage in Blount's letter highly favorable to Forster, as it diminishes the probability of his having been accessory to the death of Lady Dudley. For in the conversation recounted to have passed between Lady Dudley and Mrs. Odingsells, the former states, that if Mrs. Odingsells should be absent, Mrs. Owen would be her companion at dinner. This lady may most reasonably be concluded to have been the wife of Mr. Owen, then proprietor of Cumnor. And so it would appear that both Mrs. Odingsells and Mrs. Owen were staying in the house, and that they were there when Lady Dudley met with her death. Under such circumstances, it is hardly possible to conceive, that Forster would have attempted so atrocious a crime under his own roof; and it would be most improbable to suppose that he could have secured the connivance of these two ladies, even if he had induced all the servants purposely to absent themselves. Moreover, it appears that it was Lady Dudley, and not Forster, that insisted on the visit of the servants to Abingdon Fair.

"Blount's letter reaches Dudley, who had in the mean time gone to Kew, and causes him very great uneasiness. His apprehension that his wife had been murdered, and that he should be considered privy to the act, appears, if anything, increased by this communication. Upon receipt of it he again writes to his friend and emissary, urging him to repeat to the jury his earnest desire that they should, without either fear or favour, proceed in the most rigid manner with the investigation. The following is the letter:

III.—"*Lord Robert Dudley to T. Blount.*

"COUSIN BLOUNT,—Until I hear from you again how the matter falleth out in very troth, I cannot be in quiet; and yet you do well to satisfy me with the discreet jury you say are chosen already: unto whom I pray you say from me, that I require them, as ever as I shall think good of them, that they will, according to their duties, earnestly, carefully, and truly deal in this matter, and find it as they shall see it fall out; and, if it fall out a chance or misfortune, then so to say; and, if it appear a villany

(as God forbid so mischievous or wicked a body should live), then to find it so. And, God willing, I have never fear [of] the due prosecution accordingly, what person soever it may appear any way to touch; as well for the just punishment of the act as for mine own true justification; for, as I would be sorry in my heart any such evil should be committed, so shall it well appear to the world my innocency by my dealing in the matter, if it shall so fall out. And therefore, Cousin Blount, I seek chiefly troth in this case, which I pray you still to have regard unto, without any favour to be showed either one way or other. When you have done my message to them, I require you not to stay to search throughly yourself all ways that I may be satisfied. And that with such convenient speed as you may. Thus fare you well, in haste; at Kew,[1] this xiith day of September. Yours assured,
"R. D."

"Again, Blount conveys to the jury Dudley's commands, and as the inquiry advanced it is unquestionable that there was a suspicion of Lady Dudley having been murdered, and of Forster being implicated in the crime. Blount appears faithfully to discharge his trust, and he resorts to every means he can conceive likely to ascertain the true facts; he endeavours secretly to discover the feeling of the jury, but is unsuccessful; and after remaining at Cumnor three days, he professes not to be able to regard her Ladyship's death otherwise than as an accident. He insinuates that some of the jury appeared to be quite desirous of criminating Forster if they could; and considers their not being able to prove anything against him, ought to produce a conviction that there were no grounds to consider it an act of violence. Blount's next communication is as under:

[1] Kew. In the year 1559 Lord Robert had a grant from the Queen of "a capital mansion, called the Dairy House," at Kew,[*] and was living there in 1560, whence this letter was written. This Dairy House had been held in time of Edw. VI., by Sir Henry Gate, but as he suffered with John Dudley, Duke of Northumberland, 1st Mary, it would then have been escheated to the crown.

---

[*] Manning and Bray's 'Surrey,' folio, vol. i, 446.

IV.—"*T. Blount to Lord Robert Dudley.*

"I have done your Lordship's message unto the jury. You need not to bid them to be careful: whether equity of the cause or malice to Forster do forbid (?) it, I know not, they take great pains to learn the troth. To-morrow I will wait upon your Lordship; and, as I come, I will break my fast at Abingdon; and there I shall meet with one or two of the jury; and what I can I will bring. They be very secret; and yet do I hear a whispering that they can find no presumptions of evil. And if I may say to your Lordship my conscience, I think some of them may be sorry for it, God forgive me. And, if I judge aright, mine own opinion is much quieted; the more I search of it, the more free it doth appear unto me. I have almost nothing that can make me so much to think that any man should be the doer thereof as, when I think your Lordship's wife before all other women should have such a chance, the circumstances and as many things as I can learn doth persuade me that only misfortune hath done it, and nothing else. Myself will wait upon your Lordship to-morrow, and say what I know. In the mean time I humbly take leave; from Comner, the xiii[th] of September. Your Lordship's life and loving [?], "T. B."

"It would seem before the receipt of the last letter, the foreman of the jury had written to Dudley, apprising him that his wife's death did appear plainly to have been caused by an accident, but it is evident that at the time the letter was penned, a verdict to that effect had not been returned. The receipt of such a communication under such circumstances will by some be suspiciously regarded; both on the part of Dudley and the foreman. This letter, however, seems in a great measure to have relieved his anxiety; nevertheless he does not abate in his expressions of eagerness to sift the transaction, and to push the inquiry to the utmost possible limit. He requests that another gentleman, Sir Richard Blount, and also Mr. Norris, will assist in furtherance of the investigation. His intimation to this effect is conveyed to his friend Thomas Blount at Cumnor, in the following letter:

V.—"*Lord Robert Dudley to T. Blount.*

"I have received a letter from one Smith, one that seemeth to be the foreman of the jury. I perceive by his letters that he and the rest have and do travail very diligently and circumspectly for the trial of the matter which they have charge of, and for anything that he or they by any search or examination can make in the world hitherto, it doth plainly appear, he saith, a very misfortune; which, for mine own part, Cousin Blount, doth much satisfy and quiet me. Nevertheless, because of my thorough quietness and all others' hereafter, my desire is that they may continue in their inquiry and examination to the uttermost, as long as they lawfully may; yea, and when these have given their verdict, though it be never so plainly found, assuredly I do wish that another substantial company of honest men might try again for the more knowledge of troth. I have also requested to Sir Richard Blount, who is a perfect honest gentleman, to help to the furtherance thereof. I trust he be with you, or thing long,[1] and Mr. Norris likewise. Appleyard, I hear, hath been there, as I appointed, and Arthur Robsert her brothers. If any more of her friends had been to be had, I would also have caused them to have seen and been privy to all the dealing there. Well, Cousin, God's will be done; and I wish he had made me the poorest that creepeth on the ground, so this mischance had not happened to me. But, good Cousin, according to my trust have care about all things, that there be plain, sincere, and direct dealing for the full trial of this matter. Touching Smith and the rest, I mean no more to deal with them, but let them proceed in the name of God accordingly: and I am right glad they be all strangers to me. Thus fare you well, in much haste; from Windsor. Your loving friend and kinsman, "R. D."

"What subsequently took place before the Coroner, or how long the inquest lasted after the 13th, or what became of Blount, are only subjects of conjecture, for there are no further documents extant; and here, so far as is known, ended the correspondence.

"There appears no ground for questioning the fairness of the inquiry, which, it must be borne in mind, was attended

---

[1] Here there appears to be some corruption of the text.

by Arthur Robsart, a relation[1] of Lady Dudley's, and by Mr. Appleyard, probably the owner of Stanfield Hall, an old friend of her family,[2] and ended, after a tedious and patient investigation, with a verdict of mischance, or what would now be termed accidental death, which was equivalent to an entire acquittal of Forster and all others of violence. It is, however, certain that there were circumstances of very grave suspicion, and that an unusual degree of public feeling was roused in all parts of the country."

"The only person known to have taken an active and conspicuous part in the public outcry was Thomas Lever, a distinguished preacher of the day, a prebendary of Durham, and Master of Sherborne Hospital, who appears to have been impressed with the general opinion that Lady Dudley had been murdered, in furtherance of her husband's ambitious designs, and that it was his intention to hush up the matter, and prevent an inquiry into the cause of her death; and possibly feeling that the sacred duties of his office demanded that he should step forward, and claim on behalf of the public a discovery of the truth or falsehood of the current rumours, he took upon himself to address the subjoined letter to two of the Queen's principal advisers, being, it may be gathered, at the time unaware that a coroner's jury had been impanelled for that purpose, and that Dudley himself was urging the unflinching discharge of their duty :[3]

"'The grace of God be unto your Honors, with my humble commendations and hearty thanks in Christ; for it hath pleased God to place you in authority with wisdom and wills to advance His glory, the Queen's Majesty's godly honor, and the peaceable wealth of this realm; and that also I am well assured of your favorable minds towards me, to take in writing according to my meaning, faithfully, reverently, and lovingly.

"'Therefore I am moved and boldened by writing to signify

[1] He was her illegitimate brother.
[2] Her half-brother John Appleyard. See Pedigree, page 11.
[3] Bartlett's 'Cumnor-place,' p. 58.

unto you, that here in these parts seemeth unto me to be a grievous and dangerous suspicion and muttering of the death of her which was the wife of my Lord Robert Dudley. And now my desire and trust is that the rather by your goodly discreet device and diligence, through the Queen's Majesty's authority, earnest searching and trying out of the truth with due punishment, if any be found guilty in this matter, may be openly known. For if no search nor inquiry be made and known, the displeasure of God, the dishonor of the Queen, and the danger of the whole realm is to be feared. And by due inquiry and justice openly known surely God shall be well pleased and served, the Queen's Majesty worthily commended, and her loving subjects comfortably quieted. The Lord God guide you by His grace in this and all other your goodly travels, as he knoweth to be most expedient in Christ.

"'Scribbled at Coventry, the 17th of September, by your faithfully in Christ,

"'THOMAS LEVER.

"'Unto the right honorable Sir Francis Knollys,
and Sir William Cecil, Knights, and to
either of them be these delivered.'[1]

"Whether Lever was satisfied with the verdict of the jury, there is nothing to show, but it may be presumed he was, as no more is afterwards heard of him on the subject."

Let us now proceed to examine the various statements made by historians as to the manner of her death, all of which (Dugdale's excepted) have their foundation in the most virulent libel that ever was published,[2] viz. 'Leycester's Commonwealth.'

Dugdale merely says,[3] "As to his wives, certain it is, that he first married Anne,[4] the daughter and heir to Sir John

[1] 'Burleigh State Papers,' 1560.
[2] See 'Collins's Memoirs,' attached to the 'Sydney Papers,' vol. i, p. 61; and 'Chalmers's Biographical Dictionary,' article "Dudley."
[3] 'Baronage,' vol. ii, p. 222.
[4] In which he is in error, as her own letter proves it to be "Amye:"

Robsart, Knight, which lady came to an unhappy death, at one Mr. Forster's house, in Cumnor, near Oxford (then his tenant [1]), by a fall from the stairs, *as 't was said,* and lyeth buried in St. Marie's Church, in that University."

Wood, in his 'Athenæ Oxoniensis,'[2] says, " The Lady Amey Robsert, the first wife of Robert Earl of Leicester, whose body having been at first buried in Comnore Church near Abendon (for there she died, or rather was murdered, in the manor house there belonging to Anth. Forster, gent., 8 September, 1560) was taken up, and reburied in the Church of St. Mary the Virgin, in Oxon." Afterwards in speaking of " Robert Persons or Parsons, a Jesuit,"[3] the reputed author of 'Leycester's Commonwealth,' "This book, tho' commonly reported to be Persons' (and that he had most of his materials for the composition thereof from Sir William Cecil, Lord Burleigh), which I presume did arise from Dr. Thomas James his affirmation, that he was the Author of it."[4]

Osborn, in his ' Historical and Traditional Memoirs of the Reign of Queen Elizabeth,'[5] says, " Amongst all her minions, none (according to report) bad fairer for the Queen's Bridbed than Lecester." . . . " Nor could Lecester render his bed vacant to a more thriving end (as he is rumor'd to have done) than to make roome for the greatest and most fortunate Princess the Sun ever looked upon, without blushing in relation to oppression or blood."

Dr. Campbell, in the ' Biographia Britannica,'[6] in reference to Amye Dudley's death, says, " And so it falls out, that the

---

Vincent, in the second edition of Brooke's 'Catalogue of Nobility,' 1622, makes the same error, correcting Brooke, who in the first edition was right.

[1] Forster was tenant to Mr. Owen. Cumnor was never owned by Dudley.
[2] Vol. i, fo., 1691, col. 166.   [3] Vol. i, col. 304.
[4] See James's 'Life of Parsons,' at the end of the 'Jesuits' Downfall,' 4to, 1612, pp. 55, 56.
[5] 12mo, 1658, pp. 69—71.   [6] Article " Robert Dudley," Note D.

industrious John Aubrey, Esq., speaking of Cumnor, in Berkshire, where this happened, inserts the following relation, which is very circumstantial, and carries in it strong pretences to absolute certainty. At all events it is very curious, and much clearer than anything else that is to be met with on this subject." Dr. Campbell then gives the statement as written by *Ashmole*, for it was Elias Ashmole who was the author of it,[1] and not "the industrious John Aubrey," a singular error that the Doctor here committed. Aubrey wrote nothing in relation to Amye Dudley. This error of Dr. Campbell's is the more remarkable, inasmuch as he, in speaking of Aubrey, quotes "his ' History of Berkshire,' pp. 149—154," which is the reference to Ashmole's history. Strange that his successor, Dr. Kippis, did not detect this.

Dr. Kippis, in the second edition of the ' Biographia Britannica,' condemns the reliance that his predecessor (Dr. Campbell) had placed on Aubrey's story (for he also has fallen into the same error, as to Aubrey instead of Ashmole), and points out that this narrative, quoted by Dr. Campbell, is merely a plagiarism from ' Leycester's Commonwealth.'

Dr. Samuel Jebb, in his ' Life of Robert, Earl of Leicester,'[2] gives an abbreviated account of Ashmole's relation.

In the ' Bibliotheca Topographia Britannica,' " Berkshire Collections,"[3] will be found the same account as in Dr. Jebb's Life, in which the writer (Mr. Mores, the Antiquary) quotes that work as his authority, as well as Wood's ' Athenæ Oxoniensis,' Osborne's ' Memoirs of Elizabeth,' and ' Secret Memoirs of Robert Earl of Leicester, with Preface by Dr. Drake.' The latter, however, is merely a reprint of ' Leycester's Commonwealth ' under another title.

Bloomfield, in his ' History of Norfolk,'[4] says, " This lady

---
[1] See Ashmole's " Antiquities of Berkshire,' vol. i, pp. 149—154.
[2] 8vo, 1727, pp. 7, 8.
[3] Vol. iv, No. 16, p. 34*.   [4] Folio, vol. iii, pp. 851-2.

came to an unhappy death at Mr. Forster's house at Cumnore, near Oxford, by a fall from the stairs, and was buried at St. Mary's, the University Church at Oxford. The Earl is said not to be overkind to her, and that she was either thrown, or tumbled down a pair of stairs, and broke her neck."

Lysons, in the 'Magna Britannia,'[1] thus speaks of Cumner-House, "the seat of Anthony Forster, Esq., who lies buried in Cumner Church. His epitaph represents him as a very amiable man, very learned, a great musician, builder, and planter; but his character stands by no means clear of the imputation of having been accessary to the murder of the *Countess of Leicester*,[2] at his own house at Cumner, whither she was sent for that purpose by her husband. Sir Richard Verney, one of the Earl's retainers, was the chief agent in this horrid business. A chamber is shewn in the ruined mansion, which adjoins the churchyard at Cumner, called the Dudley-Chamber, where the Countess is said to have been murdered, and afterwards thrown down stairs, to make it appear that her death was accidental."

The authorities quoted by Lysons are Ashmole's 'Berkshire' and Dugdale's 'Baronage.'

Chalmers, in his 'Biographical Dictionary,' has doubtless copied from the 'Biographia Britannica,' as he also has fallen into the same error as to "Aubrey." Chalmers nevertheless states, "This narrative [Ashmole's], however, appears doubtful, because it is, in fact, almost closely copied from 'Leicester's Commonwealth,' a work which, with some truth, contains also much misrepresentation."

Ashmole's relation, and the story in 'Leycester's Commonwealth,' would occupy too much space to be here given, but the following parallel passages will serve to show the plagiarism committed by Ashmole: —

[1] Vol. i, p. 270.
[2] Amye Dudley never was Countess of Leicester; her husband was not created an earl till September, 1564, four years after her death.

Commonwealth.

"As for example, when his Lordship was in full hope to marry her Majesty, and his own wife stood in his light, as he supposed; he did but send her aside to the house of his servant Forster of Cumner by Oxford, where shortly after she had the chance to fall from a pair of stairs, and so to break her neck, but yet without hurting of her hood that stood upon her head. But Sir Richard Varney, who by commandment remained with her that day alone, with one man only, and had sent away perforce all her servants from her, to a market two miles off, he (I say) with his man can tell how she died, which man being taken afterward for a felony in the marches of Wales, and offering to publish the manner of the said murder, was made away privily in the prison; and Sir Richard himself dying about the same time in London, cried piteously and blasphemed God, and said to a gentleman of worship of mine acquaintance, not long before his death, that all the devils in hell did tear him in pieces. The wife also of Bald Butler, kinsman to my Lord, gave out the whole fact a little before her death." [1]

"Secondly, it is not also unlike that he prescribed unto Sir Richard Varney at

Ashmole.

"It was thought, and commonly reported, that had he been a bachelor or widower, the Queen would have made him her husband; to this end, to free himself of all obstacles, he commands, or perhaps with fair flattering entreaties, desires his wife to repose herself here, at his servant Anthony Forster's house, who then lived in the aforesaid Manor-house; and also prescribed to Sir Richard Varney (a prompter to this design) at his coming thither, that he should first attempt to poison her, and if that did not take effect, then by any other way whatsoever to dispatch her. This, it seems, was proved by the report of Dr. Walter Bayly, sometime Fellow of New College, then living at Oxford, and Professor of Physic in that University; who, because he would not consent to take away her life by poison, the Earl endeavoured to displace him from the Court. This man, it seems, reported for most certain that there was a practice, in Cumnor among the conspirators, to have poisoned this poor innocent lady, a little before she was killed, which was attempted after this manner. They seeing the good lady sad and heavy (as one that well knew by her other handling, that her death

[1] Page 22. Edition of 1641.

Commonwealth.

his going thither, that he should first attempt to kill her by poison, and if that took not place, then by any other way to dispatch her howsoever. This I prove by the report of old Doctor Bayly, who then lived in Oxford (another manner of man than he who now liveth about my Lord of the same name), and was Professor of the Physic Lecture in the same University. This learned grave man reported for most certain, that there was a practice in Cumnor among the conspirators to have poisoned the poor lady a little before she was killed, which was attempted in this order:

"They seeing the good lady sad and heavy (as one that well knew by her other handling that her death was not far off), began to persuade her that her disease was abundance of melancholy and other humours, and therefore would needs counsel her to take some potion, which she absolutely refusing to do, as still suspecting the worst, they sent one day (unawares to her) for Doctor Bayly, and desired him to persuade her to take some little potion at his hands, and they would send to fetch the same at Oxford upon his prescription, meaning to have added also

Ashmole.

was not far off) began to persuade her, that her present disease was abundance of melancholy, and other humours, &c., and therefore would needs counsel her to take some potion, which she absolutely refusing to do, as still suspecting the worst; whereupon they sent a messenger on a day (unawares to her) for Dr. Bayly, and entreated him to persuade her to take some little potion by his direction, and they would fetch the same at Oxford, meaning to have added something of their own for her comfort, as the Doctor, upon just cause and consideration did suspect, seeing their great importunity, and the small need the lady had of physic, and therefore he peremptorily denied their request, misdoubting (as he afterwards reported) least if they had poisoned her under the name of his potion, he might have been hanged for a colour of their sin; and the Doctor remained still well assured, that this way taking no effect, she would not long escape their violence, which afterwards happened thus:

"For Sir Richard Varney aforesaid (the chief projector in this design) who by the Earl's order remained that day of her death alone with her,

Commonwealth.

somewhat of their own for her comfort, as the Doctor upon just causes suspected, seeing their great importunity, and the small need the good lady had of physic; and therefore he flatly denied their request, misdoubting (as he after reported) lest if they had poisoned her under the name of his potion, he might after have been hanged for a colour of their sin. Marry the said Doctor remained well assured that this way taking no place, she should not long escape violence, as after ensued. And the thing was so beaten into the heads of the principal men of the University of Oxford by these and other means; as for that she was found murdered (as all men said) by the Crowner's inquest, and for that she being hastily and obscurely buried at Cumnor (which was condemned above, as not advisedly done), my good Lord, to make plain to the world the great love he bare to her in her life, and what a grief the loss of so virtuous a lady was to his tender heart, would needs have her taken up again and reburied in the University Church at Oxford, with great pomp and solemnity; that Doctor Babington, my Lord's chaplain, making the public funeral sermon at her second burial, tript once or twice in

Ashmole.

with one man only and Forster, who had that day forcibly sent away all her servants from her to Abingdon market, about three miles distant from this place, they (I say, whether first stifling her, or else strangling her) afterwards flung her down a pair of stairs, and broke her neck, using much violence upon her; but, however, though it was vulgarly reported that she by chance fell down stairs (but yet without hurting her hood that was upon her head), yet the inhabitants will tell you there that she was conveyed from her usual chamber where she lay, to another where the bed's head of the chamber stood close to a privy postern door, when they in the night-time came and stifled her in her bed, bruised her head very much, broke her neck, and at length flung her down stairs, thereby believing the world would have thought it a mischance, and so have blinded their villany. But behold the mercy and justice of God, in revenging and discovering this lady's murder, for one of the persons, that was a coadjutor in this murder, was afterwards taken for a felony in the marches of Wales, and offering to publish the manner of the aforesaid murder, was made away in the prison by the Earl's appointment.

Commonwealth.

his speech by recommending to their memories that virtuous lady so pitifully murdered, instead of so pitifully slain."[1]

Ashmole.

"And Sir Richard Varney the other, dying about the same time in London, cried miserably, and blasphemed God, and said to a person of note (who hath related the same to others since) not long before his death, that all the devils in hell did tear him in pieces. Forster likewise after this fact, being a man formerly addicted to hospitality, company, mirth, and music, was afterwards observed to forsake all this with much melancholy and pensiveness (some say with madness) pined and drooped away. The wife also of Bald Butler, kinsman to the Earl, gave out the whole fact a little before her death. Neither are these following passages to be forgotten, — That as soon as ever she was murdered, they made great haste to bury her, before the Coroner had given in his inquest (which the Earl himself condemned as not done advisedly), which her father, or Sir John Robsart (as I suppose) hearing of, came with all speed hither, caused her corpse to be taken up, the Coroner to sit upon her, and further inquiry to be made concerning this business to the full, but it was generally thought that the Earl stopped his mouth, and made up the business betwixt them, and the good Earl,

[1] Pp. 35, 36. Edition of 1641, 4to.

Commonwealth.

Ashmole.
to make plain to the world the great love he bare her while alive, what a grief the loss of so virtuous a lady was to his tender heart, caused (though the thing by these and other means, was beaten into the heads of the principal men of the University of Oxford,) her body to be re-buried in St. Marie's Church in Oxford, with great pomp and solemnity.

"It is remarkable when Dr. Babington (the Earl's chaplain) did preach the funeral sermon, he tript once or twice in his speech, by recommending to their memories that virtuous lady so pitifully murdered, instead of saying pitifully slain."[1]

Dr. Kippis, who has compared the two statements, thus observes :

"Our predecessor [Dr. Campbell] has laid too much stress upon Aubrey's [Ashmole's] narrative, which he considers as carrying in it strong pretences to absolute certainty. But the fact is, that Aubrey's [Ashmole's] story is manifestly copied from 'Leycester's Commonwealth.' This will appear by the many correspondent passages. Aubrey [Ashmole] has managed the matter so clumsily, as to retain words which betray the plagiarism ; such as 'fetch the same at Oxford.' Nothing in the narrative seems to be Aubrey's [Ashmole's] own, excepting the sentence that begins 'Yet the inhabitants will tell you,' &c., which has much the air of a circumstantiated idle tale. Stories of a similar nature, with regard to other events, may be met with in every county in Britain."[2]

[1] '*Antiq. of Berkshire*,' 8vo., vol. i, pp. 140—154.)
[2] '*Biog. Brit.*,' second edition, article "Robert Dudley," note, p. 466.

The funeral of Amye Robsart took place at the Church of Our Lady at Oxford, on Sunday, the 22nd of September, 1560, of which the following account will be found among the Dugdale MSS. in the Ashmolean Collection.[1]

"*The funerall of the lady Amye Robsert, wife of the lord Robert Dudley, knight of the Garter, anno* 1560.

"Thenterment of the right noble lady Amey Robsert, late wyffe to the right noble the lord Robert Dudelley, knight and compaignion of the moste noble ordre of the Garter and master of the horsse to the queenes moste excellent majestie, whoo departed out of this world on Sounday, beinge Our Lady day the viij. day of September,[2] at a keepe of one Mr. Forster, iij. myle of Oxford, in the seconde yere of the reigne of our soveraigne lady queene Elizabeth, by the [3] [grace of God] queene of England, Fraunce, and Irelaund, defendour of the Faith, &c. Anno domini, 1560.

"Fyrste, after that the said lady was thus departed out of this transsetory world, she was saffely cered and coffened, and so remayned there tyll Fryday the [4] day of the said moneth of September, on the which day she was secreately brought to Glouster college a lytell without the towne of Oxford, the which plasse of Gloster couledge was hanged with blake cloth and garnesshed with skocheons of his armes and heres in palle,[5] that is to say, a great chamber where the morners did dyne, and at there chamber where the gentillwomen did dyne, and beneth the steres a great hall, all which places as afforesaid were hanged with blake cloth and garnesshed with skochions; the howsse beinge thus furnesshed ther the corsse remayned till the buryall, and till suche tyme as all things were redy for the same.

"*The mannour of the garnessinge of the churche with the hersse.*

"Item, it was appoynted that the said corsse should be buryed in Our Lady churche in the said towne of Oxfourd, the which churche was hanged with blake cloth and garnesshed with skochions, and in the mydell eyle, in the upper ende, ther was maid a hersse iiij. square, conteynynge in leingth x. fote, and in

[1] Dugdale MSS., T. 2, fo. 77, Ashmolean Collection. Printed in the 'Gentleman's Magazine,' August, 1850.
[2] The day of the nativity of the Virgin Mary. [3] So in MS.
[4] Blank in the MS. [5] So, for *hers in pale.*

bredth vij. fote and a haulf, and in height x. fote on the sydes, and on the tope xiiij. fote, and from the tope came rochements to eche corner of the said square frame; in the which tope of the hersse was set ij. skochions of armes on paste paper in metall wrought with compartements of gold, and bereth ther penseles round aboute them; beneth that the said tope was kevered all over with fyne blake cloth, and in every square ther was set iij. skochions in metall, then on the rochements ther was set penseles of sarsenet in metall with bages;[1] then on the square beneth the saide rochements went a bredth of blake velvet, on the which ther was pyned skochions in metall, on eche syde iij. and on eche end ij., and at the upper ege of the velvet ther was set penseles rounde aboute, and at the neither ege ther was fastyned a vallence of blake sarsenet wrytten with lettres of gold and frynged with a fringe of blake sylke; ther was a flouer[2] of bords, and under that flouer ther was a vallence of bokeram with armes on the same; the iiij. postes were kovered with fyne blacke clothe, and on eche poste was fastened ij. skochions, and on the tope of every poste ther was a great skochion of armes on past paper with a compartement on the nether parte of the rayles of the saide hersse was hanged doubled with blake cloth and garnesshed with skochions. Then iiij. foote from the same hersse went a rayll of tymber, the which was covered with blake and garnesshed with skochions in lyke manner as aforsaid, and betwene the sad ralle and the hersse there was set vii. stoles, that is to say, at the hedd one and one eche side iij. the which were covered with blake cloth, and cussions at the same to knele on; the quere was also hounge and garnesshed in lyke maner, and at the upper end of the said quere was maid a vaute of bryke where the said crosse was buryed. Thus all things redy the day of the buryall was appoynted, the which was Sonday, the [3] [22nd] day of September, on the which day they proced to the churche in lyke manner.

"*The ordre of the procedinge to the churche with the said corsse from Gloster colledge to Our Lady Churche in Oxford.*

"Furste, the ij. conductors with blake staves in there hands to led the waye.

"Then the pore men and women in gownes to the nomber of iiij^{xx}.

[1] Badges.   [2] Floor.   [3] Blank in the MS.

"Then the universssities ij. and ij. together, accordinge to the degres of the colleges, and before every housse ther officers with ther staves.

"Then the quere in surpleses singenge, and after them the mynester.

"Then Rouge Crosse pursuvant in his mornynge gowne, his hod on his hed, and his cote of armes on his bake.

"Then gentillmen havinge blake gownes with there hoods on ther shoulders.

"Then Lancaster herauld in his longe gowne, his hod on his hed.

"Then the baner of armes borne by Mr. Appelyard in his longe gowne, his hod on his hed.

"Then Clarenceulx, king of armes, in his longe gowne, and his hood on his hed, and in his cote of armes.

"Then the corpes bore by viij. talle yeomen, for that they[1] wey was farre and iiij. assystants to them, and on eche syde of the corsse went ij. assystants touching the corse in long gownes, and ther hoods on ther hedds, and on eche corner a banerolle borne by a gentleman in a longe gowne, his hod on his hed.

"Then the cheiffe morner, Mrs. Norrys, daughter and heire of the lord Wylliams of Thame, her trayne borne by Mrs. Buteller the younger, she being assysted by Sir Richard Blunte, knight.

"Then Mrs. Wayneman and my lady Pollard.

"Then Mrs. Doylly and Mrs. Buteller thelder.

"Then Mrs. Blunte and Mrs. Mutlowe.

"Then iij. yeomen in blake cotes, to seperate the morners from the other gentlewomen.

"Then all other gentlewomen, haveing blake, ij. and ij.

"Then all yeomen, ij. and ij. in blake cotes.

"Then the majour of Oxford and his bretheren.

"Then after them all that would, and in this ordre they proced to the churche in at the weste dore, and so to the hersse, wher the corsse was plased, and on eche syde of the hersse without the ralles stod ij. gentlemen holdinge the bannerroles, and at the fete stod he that held the great banner; then the morners were plased, the chieff at the hed, and on eche syde iij.; thus, every man plassed, the service began, firste sarteyne prayers, then the x. commandments, the quere answeringe in prykesong, then the pystel and the gospell began, and after the gospell the offering began in manner followinge:—

[1] Sic in MS. [Qy. the way was far.]

"*Firste,*

"*The order of the offeringe.*

"Fyrste the cheff morner came fourth havinge before her the officers of armes, her trayne beinge borne, the assystante ledyng her, and thother morners followinge her, went to the offeringe and offered and retorned agayne to the hersse.

"Then after she had maid her obeyssyaunce to the corsse she went upe agayne, havinge before her Garter, and offered for herself and retorned.

Then offered the assystante to the cheiffe morner, and thother iiij. assystants havinge Clarenceulx before them.

"Then offered thother vj. morners, ij. after ij. havinge before them Lancaster herauld.

"Then offered all gentillmen, ij. and ij. havinge the Rugecrosse pursivante before them.

"Then the mayor and his brethren offered, havinge an offycer of armes before them.

"Item, the offeringe thus don the sermon began, mad by Doctor Babyngton, Doctor of Devynytie, whose antheme was *Beati mortui qui in Domino moriuntur.*"

"In whatever manner the death of Lord Robert Dudley's lady took place, it is certain that, on his becoming a widower, his ambition raised him to the hopes of marrying the Queen; and that there was a general opinion, both at home and abroad, of her Majesty's inclination to the match. Indeed it was not disclaimed by Elizabeth herself."[1]

The Queen took much pains to vindicate Leicester from the aspersions that were cast upon him. An instance of that may be found in her answer to Mr. Jones, who had been sent with despatches from Sir Nicholas Throckmorton, then ambassador in France, who says[2] that, in reference to the report that Lord Robert had caused his wife to be privately

---

[1] Biog. Brit. Article, "Robert Dudley," note 446.
[2] See his letter, dated 30th November, 1560 (little more than two months after Amye's death), printed in Lord Hardwicke's 'State Papers,' vol. i, pp. 163-9.

murdered, *"She thereupon told me that the matter had been tried in the country,[1] and found to be contrary to that which was reported, saying that he was then in the Court, and none of his at the attempt at his wife's house, and that it fell out as should neither touch his honesty nor her honour."*

Some years afterwards (in 1585) letters signed by Burghley and the rest of the Council were sent to the justices of the peace for the suppression of the libels in circulation against Leicester, and a letter with the Queen's sign manual was sent to the Lord Mayor, Sheriffs, and Aldermen of London, to the same effect, as follows:

"After our very hearty commendations. Upon intelligence given to her Majesty in October last past, of certain seditious and traitorous books and libels couvertly spread and scattered abroad in sundry parts of her realms and dominions, it pleased her Majesty to publish proclamations throughout the realm for the suppressing of the same, and due punishment of the authors, spreaders abroad, and detainers of them, in such sort and form, as in the said proclamation is more at large contained. Sithence which time, notwithstanding her Highness hath certainly known, that the very same and divers other such like most slanderous, shameful, and devilish books and libels have been continually spread abroad and kept by disobedient persons, to the manifest contempt of her Majestie's regal and sovereign authority, and namely, among the rest, one most infamous containing slanderous and hateful matter against our very good Lord the Earl of Leycester, one of her principal noblemen and Chief Counsellor of State, of which most malicious and wicked imputations, her Majesty in her own clear knowledge doth declare and testify his innocence to all the world, and to that effect hath written her gracious letters signed with her own hand, to the Lord Mayor, Sheriffs, and Aldermen of London, where it was likely these books would chiefly be cast abroad. We therefore, to follow the course taken by her Majesty, and knowing manifestly the wickedness and falsehood of these slanderous devices against the said Earl, have thought good to notify her further pleasure and our own consciences to you in this case.

[1] Meaning the coroner's inquest.

"First, that as in truth her Majesty hath noted great negligence and remissness in the former execution of her commandment, forasmuch as the said seditious libels have been suffered, since that time, to be dispersed and spread abroad, and kept by contemptuous persons, without severe and due punishment inflicted for the same; so now upon the *second* charge and admonition given unto you, she verily looketh for the most strict and precise observation thereof, in the sharpest manner that may be devised. Testifying in her conscience, before God, unto you, that her Highness not only knoweth in assured certainty, the libels and books against the said Earl, to be most malicious, false and slanderous, and such as none but the devil himself could deem to be true; but also thinketh the same to have proceeded of the fullness of malice, subtilly contrived to the note and discredit of her princely government over this realm, as though her Majesty should have failed in good judgment and discretion in the choice of so principal a Counsellor about her, or be without taste or care of all Justice and conscience in suffering such heinous and monstrous crimes (as by the said libels and books be infamously imputed) to have passed unpunished. Or finally, at the least, to want either goodwill, ability, or courage (if she knew these enormities were true) to call any subject of hers whatsoever, to render sharp account for them, according to the force and effect of her laws. All which defects (God be thanked), we and all good subjects, to our unspeakable comforts do know and have found to be far from the nature and virtue of her most excellent Majesty.

"And of the other side, both her Highness of her certain knowledge, and we, to do his Lordship but right, of our sincere consciences must needs affirm these strange and abominable crimes to be raised of a wicked and venomous malice against the said Earl, of whose good service, sincerity of religion, and all other faithful dealings towards her Majesty, and the realm, we have had long and true experience. Which things considered and withall knowing it an usual trade of traiterous minds, when they would render the prince's government odious, to detract and bring out of credit the principal persons about them.

"Her Highness taking the abuse to be offered to her own self, hath commanded us to notify the same unto you, to the end that knowing her good pleasure, you may proceed therein, as in a matter highly touching her own estate and honor. And therefore we wish and require you to have regard thereof accordingly, that the former negligence and remissness showed in the execution of her Majestie's commandment may be amended by the diligence and severity that shall be hereafter used. Which amendment and carefullness in this cause chiefly, her Highness assuredly looketh for, and will call for account at your hands.

"And so we bid you heartily farewell. From the Court at Greenwich, the 26th day of June, 1585.

(Signed by) "Your very loving friends,

"T. BROMLEY, Canc., F. BEDFORD,   H. SYDNEY,
W. BURGHLEY,   C. HOWARD,   CHR. HATTON,
GEO. SHREWSBURY,   J. HUNDSDEN,   FR. WALSINGHAM,
H. DERBY,   F. KNOLLYS,   WAL. MYLDMAY."

(*Endorsed*) "*Slanderous Books.*"
(*And in Lord Burghley's writing*), "1585. *A Copy of a Letter writ by her Majestie's Commandment to the Mayor of London, in defence of the Earl of Leicester.*"

That 'Leycester's Commonwealth' was a most virulent libel, every one must admit. Yet Ashmole, whose statement has been quoted by most subsequent writers, not satisfied with adopting the 'Commonwealth' story as his own, has added some statements at direct variance with the truth, for instance,—"That as soon as ever she was murdered, they made great hast to bury her, before the Coroner had given in his Inquest (which the Earl himself condemned, as not done advisedly) which her father, or Sir John Robertsett (as I suppose) hearing of, came with all speed thither, caused her corps to be taken up, the Coroner to sit upon her, and further enquiry to be made concerning this business to the full, but it was generally thought that the Earl stopped his mouth, and made up the business betwixt them."

Now, it so happens that her father, Sir John Robsart, had then been dead above three years, for Dudley came into possession of the Robsart estates in January, 1557. Then, again,

"That as soon as ever she was murdered, they made great hast to bury her, before the Coroner," &c., and that her father "caused her corps to be taken up, the Coroner to sit upon her," &c. The 'Commonwealth' story says, "My good Lord would needs have her taken up again and reburied." All which is evidently false; there is nothing in Dudley's letters to Blount (before quoted) to warrant such an inference, and the following extract from a letter written immediately after the occurrence shows clearly that such was *not* the case; it is from W. Honyng to the Earl of Sussex, then Lieutenant of Ireland, and is dated from Hampton Court, 6th October, 1560, less than a month after her death.[1]

"This said bearer seeth the Court stuffed with mourners (yea many of the better sort in degree) for the Lord Robert's wife, who was upon the mischancing death, buried in the head church of the University of Oxford. The cost of the funeral esteemed at better than two thousand marks."

Dudley, on the 9th of September, the day after her death, desires the coroner may be summoned, "charging him to the uttermost from me to have good regard to make choice of no light or slight persons, but the discreetest and [most] substantial men, for the juries, such as for their knowledge may be able to search throughly and duly, by all manner of examinations, the bottom of the matter, and for their uprightness will earnestly and sincerely deal therein without respect; and that the body be viewed and searched accordingly by them; and in every respect to proceed by order and law."[2]

As we before stated, her illegitimate brother, Arthur Robsart, and her half-brother, John Appleyard, were present at the coroner's inquest.[3] We have been unable to find any report of the proceedings at the inquest, or of the finding of the jury, other than what may be gathered from the answer given by the Queen to Jones, the bearer of Sir Nicholas Throckmorton's despatches.[4]

[1] Cottonian MSS., in the British Museum, Vespacian, F. xii, 151.
[2] Letter to Blount. See p. 32. [3] Ibid., p. 41. [4] See p. 55.

In the Harleian Collection,[1] in the British Museum, there is preserved a manuscript entitled 'English Pedigrees,' which, in speaking of Leicester, says—

"In hatred of him chiefly it is thought that Parsons, the Jesuit, wrote that pestilent book called 'Leycester's Commonwealth,' which, though it be stuffed with innumerable falsehoods, was secretly put into the hands of many men that would seem to know somewhat, but never sought into the depth of the Jesuit's contrivances, and so did as much mischief in that age and the following as any book that hath been printed."

It is not necessary here to enter on the inquiry as to who was the author of 'Leycester's Commonwealth.' Writers differ in opinion as to whether it was Parsons, *alias* Persons. Dr. James, in his 'Life of Parsons,' asserts that it was written by him, and calls it "an inormous libell written against one of the Peeres of this land."

Dr. Campbell, in the 'Biographia Britannica,' remarks that "Dr. Thomas James, who was a very learned and knowing man, ascribed it to Robert Parsons, the Jesuit. Anthony Wood[2] says that it was commonly supposed to be written by him, and adds, in a parenthesis, that he had most of his materials for the composition thereof from Sir William Cecil, Lord Burghley. Upon what foundation this report stands, it is not easy to say; but this is certain, that Parsons himself denied that he was the author of it, neither is it reckoned amongst his works either by Pits or Rybadeneira. Yet whoever considers and compares the 'Conference about the Succession,' which Parsons published under the name of Dolman, will not easily believe that he was not the author of this book also, though perhaps he might not call it 'Leicester's Commonwealth,' and therefore might think himself at liberty to deny his writing a book under that title.[3]

---

[1] No. 6071. [2] 'Athenæ Oxoniensis,' fo., vol. i, col. 360.
[3] The original title under which the book was first published is 'The copy of a letter written by a Master of Arts in Cambridge to his friend in London,

As to Lord Burghley's furnishing the materials, when we consider the paper signed by him,[1] it must appear very improbable. It may not, however, be amiss to observe that it is on all hands agreed that our famous historian, Mr. Camden, had his materials for the first part of the 'Annals of Queen Elizabeth' from that noble person, and many are of opinion that he actually wrote them. Now, upon examination it will be found that a great many of the facts in 'Leycester's Commonwealth' are likewise related, though in a softer and less peremptory style, in those 'Annals.'"

Dr. Campbell was not the advocate of Leicester, for Dr. Kippis, his successor, charges him with having "departed from his usual biographical character, and to have been as ready to believe things to the prejudice of the Earl of Leicester, as he was, in the preceding lives, to palliate the conduct of the Dudleys."

It will be seen by the foregoing that all the writers on this subject more or less quote from each other, and in some cases give their authority for the several statements made.

Not so, however, with Ashmole; in his statement we have no authorities cited. The details given by him are in that conversational style as though derived from sources of undoubted authority, and it has therefore been found necessary to supply his omissions by giving the parallel passages from each writer, showing the plagiarism committed by Ashmole throughout his narrative, and to which not one word of truth can attach.

We will now sum up the various writers quoted, and the authorities cited by them.

Dugdale, who has but little to say, and no authority given.

concerning some talk passed of late between two worshipfull and grave men about the present estate and some proceedings of the Earl of Leicester and his friends in England. Conceived, spoken, and published with most earnest protestations of all dutiful goodwill and affection towards her most excellent Majesty and the Realm, for whose good it is made common to many.' First edition was 1584.

[1] Letters signed by Burghley and the rest of the Council, 26th June, 1585, before referred to, pp. 56-58.

Wood (Anthony), 'Athenæ Oxoniensis,' speaks from general report only.

Campbell (Dr.), in 'Biographia Britannica,' quotes from Ashmole (which by some unaccountable blunder he has stated as "the industrious John Aubrey").

Kippis (Dr.), in new edition of same work, has fallen into the same error as to Aubrey (named by his predecessor), and shows the statement to be derived from the 'Commonwealth.'

Jebb (Dr. Samuel), in his 'Life of Robert Earl of Leicester,' gives a short account from Ashmole, and which is word for word with the next work,—

'Bibliotheca Topographia Britannica,' quoting as their authority Wood's 'Athen. Oxon.,' 'Secret Memoirs of Earl of Leicester,' Osborne's 'Memoirs of Elizabeth,' Dr. Jebb's 'Life of Leicester.'

Bloomfield, in his 'History of Norfolk,' says but little, citing no authority.

Lysons, in 'Magna Britannia;' authorities given—"Ashmole and Dugdale."

Chalmers, in his 'Biographical Dictionary,' evidently copied from 'Biographia Britannica,' at the same time showing the plagiarism from the 'Commonwealth.'

'Secret Memoirs of the Earl of Leicester,' with Preface by Dr. Drake, is a mere reprint of the 'Commonwealth,' without, however, naming or referring to that work.

Bartlett, in his 'History of Cumnor,' quotes from Ashmole and from Dugdale.

Ashmole, in his 'History of Berkshire,' is now the only one that remains to be accounted for. Having given a fair illustration that his statement is taken wholly from the 'Commonwealth,' which was not published till twenty-four years after the death of Amye Robsart, and his own history not written till upwards of a century had elapsed from the time of the occurrences he so minutely describes, it will clearly be seen that no reliance whatever can be placed on any of the statements.

If, after the critical examination we have given the subject and the most searching inquiry into all the evidence before us, we have succeeded in showing that Amye Robsart was *not murdered*, it might be asked, How, then, account for her death? Our reply is—the verdict of the coroner's jury—that of "mischance," or in other words "accidental death." Whether it was a voluntary or involuntary act can only be known to the Searcher of all hearts. We have no evidence on record to determine that matter, though from the expression in her letter, in speaking of her husband, where she says, "he being sore troubled with weighty affairs, and I not being altogether in quiet for his sudden departing."[1] And again in Letter II., where Blount relates his conversation with Pirto (who was evidently her waiting-woman), in which Pirto says "she was a good virtuous gentlewoman, and daily would pray upon her knees; and divers times she saith that she hath heard her pray to God to *deliver her from desperation*."[2] From these facts we may infer that, goaded to despair by the neglect of her husband, there might exist an aberration of mind which would be likely to lead to an involuntary act of self-destruction.

We should bear in mind that she had no settled home, no establishment of her own; she was living, or rather visiting, from place to place; at one time at Mr. Hyde's, a distant connection of her family by marriage, where she wrote, or rather indited, that letter, only twelve months before her death; then we find her at Cumnor, at the residence of one of the retainers of her husband. Evidently neglected by her husband, who was living at an establishment of his own at Kew, which had been given to him by the Queen, we have no evidence to show that he had ever visited her after his "sudden departing" from her. These facts would tend to infer a state of mind possibly driven to desperation.

If we have succeeded in removing one stain from the character of Leicester, one reproach from the character of Elizabeth, who held him in so high estimation, and if we shall succeed in removing any suspicion against Sir Richard

[1] See p. 21. [2] See p. 36.

Varney, as being concerned in this "horrid business," and if also it can be shown that Sir Anthony Forster was not in the least implicated in Amye's death, our labour will not have been in vain.

Bartlett, in his account of "Cumnor Place," speaking of the various statements in circulation, says, "It is somewhat to be regretted that those authors who have promulgated the reports should have received as authentic such scandals, without endeavouring to ascertain what proof there was for their foundation." And in reference more particularly to Anthony Forster, he observes, "The insinuations of a rival political party and the tattle of the village were magnified upon every repetition of the story, and, as is invariably the case, time and tradition added to the horrors of the tale."[1]

And in reference to Scott's statements in his interesting historical novel, 'Kenilworth,' he remarks, "The reader will be surprised to find the extent to which his account varies from sober history." In speaking of Dudley, he says, "It is not to be conceived that Lord [Robert] Dudley would have been raised to an earldom, had the imputation of guilt really attached to him after the coroner's inquest; and much less that the Queen would entertain affection for a nobleman whose fame was so dishonoured."[2]

Not the least reliance can be placed on any of the statements or charges contained in 'Leycester's Commonwealth.' It should be borne in mind that that work was not written till twenty-four years after the death of Amye Dudley; and how the author should be in possession of the circumstantial details which he there gives it would be difficult to conjecture, unless from the mere vague reports and surmises, which are most frequently at variance with historical truth. A very able answer to the 'Commonwealth,' and refutation of the statements made therein, was written by Sir Philip Sydney[3] immediately after its first appearance in 1584, but which, however, does not appear to have been printed at the time, owing probably to Sydney's death occurring so soon

[1] 'Historical Account of Cumnor Place,' 8vo, Oxford, 1850. [2] Ibid.
[3] Nephew of the Earl of Leicester.

after. It was not till many years after that it was brought to light by the publication of the 'Sydney Papers,' by Arthur Collins.[1]

SIR PHILIP SYDNEY'S DEFENCE OF THE EARL OF LEICESTER,

Being a Reply or Answer to 'Leycester's Commonwealth,' written, it is presumed, in 1584 or 1585. In his own handwriting, preserved at Penshurst.

"Of late there hath been printed a book, in form of dialogue, to the defaming of the Earl of Leicester, full of the most vile reproaches, which a wit, used to wicked and filthy thoughts, can imagine. In such manner truly, that if the author had as well feigned new names, as he doth new matters, a man might well have thought his only meaning had been, to have given a lively picture of the uttermost degree of railing. A thing contemptible in the doer, as proceeding from a base and wretched tongue, and such a tongue, as, in the speaking, dares not speak his own name. Odious to all estates, since no man bears a name, of which name, how unfitly soever to the person, by an impudent liar, anything may not be spoken; by all good laws sharply punished, and by all civil companies, like a poisonous serpent, avoided. But to the Earl himself, in the eyes of any men, who, with clear judgments, can value things, a true and sound honour grows out of these dishonorable falsehoods. Since he may justly say, as a worthy senator of Rome once in like case did,—That no man, these twenty years, hath borne a hateful heart to this estate, but that, at the same time, he hath shewn his enmity to this Earl; testifying it hereby, that his faith is so linked to her Majesty's service, that who goes about to undermine the one, resolves withal to overthrow the other. For it is not now, first that evil-contented and evil-

[1] 'Sydney Papers,' "Lives of the Dudleys," vol. i.

minded persons, before the occasion be ripe for them, to shew their hate against the Prince, do first vomit it out against his Councillors; nay, certainly, so stale a service it is, as it is to be marvelled, that so fine wits, whose inventions a fugitive fortune hath sharpened, and the air of Italy perchance purified, can light upon no gallanter way than the ordinary pretext of the very clownish rebellions. And yet that this is their plot, of late, by name, first to publish something against the Earl of Leicester, and after, when time served, against the Queen's Majesty, by some of their own intercepted discourses, is made too manifest. He himself, in some places, brings in the examples of Gaveston, Earl of Cornwall, Robert Vere, Duke of Ireland, and Delapole, Duke of Suffolk. It is not my purpose to defend them, but I would fain know, whether they that persecuted those Councillors, when they had had their will in ruining them, whether their rage ceased, before they had as well destroyed the Kings themselves,—Edward, and Richard the Second, and Henry the Sixth? The old tale testifieth that the wolves, that mean to destroy the flock, hate most the truest and valiantest dogs. Therefore the more the filthy empostume of their wolfish malice breaks forth, the more undoubtedly doth it raise this well-deserved glory to the Earl, that [he] who hates England and the Queen, must also withal hate the Earl of Leicester.

"And as for the libel itself, such is it, as neither in respect of the writer, nor matter written, can move, I think, the lightest wits to give thereto credit, to the discredit of so worthy a person. For the writer (whom in truth I know not, and, loth to fail, am not willing to guess at,) shews yet well enough of what kennel he is, that dares not testify his own writings with his own name. And which is more base (if anything can be more base than a defamatory libeller), he counterfeits himself in all the Treatise, a Protestant, when any man, with half an eye, may easily see he is of the other party; which filthy dissimulation, if few honest men of that religion will use, to the helping of themselves, of how many carats of honesty is this man, that useth it (as much as his poor power can) to the harm of another? And lastly, evident enough it is, to any man that reads it, what poison he means to her Majesty, in how golden a cup soever he dress it.

"For the matter written, so full of horrible villanies, as no good heart will think possible to enter into any creature, much less to be likely in so noble and well-known a man as he is, only thus accused to be by the railing oratory of a shameless libeller. Perchance he had read the rule of that sycophant, that one should backbite boldly; for, though the bite were healed, yet the scar would remain. But sure that schoolmaster of his would more cunningly have carried it, leaving some shadows of good, or, at least, leaving out some evil, that his Treatise might have carried some portable show of it: for as reasonable commendation wins belief, and excessive gets only the praiser the title of a flatterer, so much more in this far worse degree of lying, it may well rebound upon himself, the vile reproach of a railer, but never can sink into any good mind. The suspicion of any such unspeakable mischiefs, especially it being every man's case, even from the meanest to the highest, whereof we daily see odious examples, that even of the great Princes, the dear riches of a good name are sought in such sort to be picked away by such night thieves. For through the whole book, what is it else, but such a bundle of railings, as if it came from the mouth of some half-drunken scold in a tavern, not regarding while evil were spoken, what was fit for the person of whom the railing was, so the words were fit for the person of an outrageous railer. Dissimulation, hypocrisy, adultery, falsehood, treachery, poison, rebellion, treason, cowardice, atheism, and what not, and all still so upon the superlative, that it was no marvel, though the good lawyer he speaks of made many a cross to keep him from such a father of lies, and in many excellent gifts passing all shameless scolds, in one he passeth himself with an unheard-of impudence, bringing persons, yet alive, to speak things which they are ready to depose, upon their salvation, never came in their thoughts. Such a gentlewoman spake of a matter no less than treason, belike she whispered, yet he heard her; such two Knights spake together of things not fit to call witnesses to, yet this ass's ears were so long that he heard them. And yet see his good nature all this while would never reveal them till now, for secresy sake, he puts them forth in print; certainly such a quality in a railer, as I think never was heard of, to name persons alive, as not only can, but do disprove his falsehoods, and yet with such familiarity to name them. Without he learnt it of Pace, the Duke of Norfolk's fool, for he, when he had used his tongue, as this heir of his hath done his pen, of the noblest persons, sometimes of the Duke himself, the next that came fitly in his way, he would say he had told it him of abundance of charity, not only to slander, but to make bait. What therefore can be said to such a man? or who lives there . . . . but that so stinking a breath may blow infamy upon? Who hath a father, by whose death the son inherits, but such a nameless historian may say his son poisoned him? Where may two talk together, but such a spirit of revelation may surmise they spake of treason? What need more, or why so much? As though I doubted that any would build belief upon such a dirty seat, only when he, to borrow a little of his ink-horn when he plays the statist, wringing very unluckily some of Machiavel's axioms to serve his purpose then, indeed, then he triumphs. Why, then, the Earl of Leicester means and plots to be king himself, but first to rebel from the Prince to whom he is most bound, and of whom he only dependeth, and then to make the Earl of Huntingdon king, and then to put him down, and then to make himself. Certainly, sir, you shoot fair, I think no man, who hath wit and power to pronounce this word, *England*, but will pity a sycophant so weak in his own faculty. But of the Earl of Huntingdon, as I think all indifferent men will clear him from any such foolish and wicked intent of rebellion, so I protest before the Majesty of God, who will confound all liars; and before the world, to whom effects and innocency will witness my truth; that I could never find, in the Earl of Leicester, any one motion of inclination toward any such pretended conceit in the Earl of Huntingdon. I say no future wit, for as for the present, or for drawing it to himself, I think no devil so wicked, nor no idiot so simple, as to conjecture; and yet, being to him as I am, I think I should have some air of that, which this gentle libel-maker doth so particularly and piece-meal understand, and I do know the Earls of Warwick, of Pembroke, my father, and all the rest he names there, will answer the like. And yet such matters cannot be undertaken without good friends, nor good friends be kept without knowing something; but the Earl's mind hath ever been to serve only and truly, setting aside all hopes, all fears, his Mistress, by undoubted right, Queen of England, and most worthy to be the Queen for her Royal Excellencies, and most worthy to be his Queen, having restored his overthrown house, and brought him to this case; that curs for only envy bark at. And this his mind is not only (though chiefly) for faith knit in conscience and honour, nor only (though greatly) for gratefulness, where all men know how much he is bound, but even partly for wisdom's sake, knowing by all old lessons and examples, that, how welcome soever treasons be, traitors to all wise Princes are odious, and that as Mutius answered Tully, who wrote to him how he was blamed for shewing himself so constant a friend to Cæsar, that he doubted not, even they that blamed him would rather choose such friends as he was, than such as they were. For wise Princes well know, that these violent discontentments arise out of the parties' wicked humours, as in sick folks, that think, with change of places, to ease their evil, which indeed is inward, and whom, nor this Prince, nor that Prince, can satisfy, but such as are led by their fancies, that is to say, who leave to be Princes. But this gentle libel-maker, because he would make an evident proof of an unquenchable malice, desperate impudency and falsehood, which never knew blushing, is not content with a whole dictionary of slanders upon these persons living, but, as if he would rake up the bones of the dead, with so apparent falsehoods toucheth their houses, as if he had been afraid, else he should not have been straight found in that wherein he so greatly labours to excel. First, for Hastings, he saith, the Lord Hastings conspired the death of his master King Edward's sons; let any man but read the excellent treatise of Sir Thomas More, compare but his words with his libel-makers, and then judge him, if he who in a thing so long since printed, and, as any man may see by other of his allegations of him diligently read, hath the face to write so directly contrary; not caring, as it seems, though a hundred thousand find his falsehood, so some dozen, that never read Sir Thomas More's words, may be carried to believe his horrible slanders of a nobleman so long ago dead. I set down the words of both, because, by this only lively comparison, the face of his falsehood may be the better set forth. And who then can doubt, but he that lies in a thing, which, with one look, is found a lie, what he will do, where yet there is though as much falsehood, yet not so easy disproof.

"Now to the Dudleys, such is his bounty, that when he hath poured out all his flood of scolding eloquence, he saith they are no gentlemen, affirming that the then Duke of Northumberland was not born so; in truth, if I should have studied with myself of all points of false invectives which a poisonous tongue could have spit out against that Duke, yet would it never have come into my head, of all other things, that any man would have objected want of gentry unto him; but this fellow doth like him, who, when he had shot off all his railing quiver, called one cuckold that was never married, because he would not be in debt to any one evil word. I am a *Dudley* in blood, that Duke's daughter's son, and do acknowledge, though, in all truth, I may justly affirm that I am, by my father's side, of ancient, and well-esteemed and well-matched gentry, yet I do acknowledge, I say, that my chiefest honour is to be a *Dudley*, and truly am glad to have cause to set forth the nobility of that blood whereof I am descended, which, but upon so just cause, without vainglory, could not have been uttered; since no man, but this fellow of invincible shamelessness would ever have called so palpable a matter in question. In one place of his book he greatly extolleth the great nobility of the house of *Talbot*, and truly with good cause, there being, as I think, not in Europe a subject house which hath joined longer continuance of nobility, with men of greater service and loyalty. And yet this Duke's own grandmother, whose blood he makes so base, was a *Talbot*, daughter and sole heir to the Viscount of Lisle; even he, the same man, who, when he might have saved himself, chose rather manifest death, than to abandon his father, that most noble *Talbot*, Earl of Shrewsbury, of whom the histories of that time make so honorable mention.

"The house of Grey is well known; to no house in England in great continuance of honour, and for number of great houses sprung from it, to be matched by none; but, by the noble house of Nevill, his mother was a right Grey, and a sole inheritrix of that Grey of the house of Warwick which ever strove with the great house of Arundel, which should be the first Earl of England; he was likewise so descended, as that justly the honour of the house remained chiefly upon him, being the only heir to the eldest daughter, and one of the heirs of that famous Beauchamp, Earl of Warwick, that was Regent of France; and although Richard Nevill, who married the youngest sister, because she was of the whole blood to him that was called Duke of Warwick, by a point in our law carried away the inheritance; and so also I know not by what right the title, yet in law of Heraldry and Descents, which doth not consider those quiddities of our law, it is most certain that the honour of the blood remained upon him chiefly who came of the eldest daughter. And more undoubtedly is it said of the house of *Berkeley*, which is affirmed to be descended lineally from a King of Denmark, but hath ever been one of the best houses in England, and this Duke was the only heir-general to that house, which the house of Berkeley doth not deny; however, as sometimes it falls out between brothers, there be question of land between them. Many other houses might herein be mentioned, but I name these because England can boast of no nobler, and because all these bloods so remained in him, that he as heir might (if he had listed) have used their arms and name, as in old time they used in England, and do daily, both in

Spain, France, and Italy. So that I think it would seem as great news as if they came from the Indies, that he, who by right of blood, and so accepted, was the ancientest Viscount of England, heir in blood and arms to the first or second Earl of England; in blood of inheritance a Grey, a Talbot, a Beauchamp, a Berkeley, a Lisley, should be doubted to be a gentleman. But he will say, these great honours came to him by his mother, for these I do not deny they came so; but that the mother being an heir, hath been in all ages and countries, sufficient to nobilitate, is so manifest, that, even from the Roman time to modern times, in such case they might, if they listed, and so often did use the mother's name; and that Augustus Cæsar hath both name and empire of Cæsar, only by his mother's right, and so both moderns.[1] But I will claim no such privilege; let the singular nobility of his mother nothing avail him, if his father's blood were not, in all respects, worthy to match with hers. If ancient, undoubted, and untouched nobility be worthy to match with the most noble house that can be, this house, therefore, of Dudley, which in despite of all shamelessness he so doth deprave, is, at this day, a Peer, as we term it, of the Realm, a Baron, and, as all Englishmen know, a Lord of the Parliament, and so a companion, both in marriage, Parliament, and trial, to the greatest Duke that England can bear; so hath it been ever esteemed, and so, in the constitution of all our laws and ordinances, it is always reputed. Dudley house is so to this day, and thus it hath been time out of mind; in Harry the Fifth's time, the Lord Dudley was his Lord Steward, and did that pitiful office in bringing home, as chief mourner, his victorious master's dead body; as who goes but to Westminster, in the Church may see. I think, if we consider together the time which was of England the most flourishing, and the King he served, who, of all English Kings, was most puissant, and the office he bare, which was, in effect, as great as an English subject could have, it would seem very strange; so that Lord Dudley, if he could out of his grave hear this fellow make question, whether his lawful

[1] *i.e.* both name and arms.

posterity, from father to son, should be gentlemen or no? But though he only had been sufficient to erect nobility to his successors, bringing, as the Romans termed it, so noble an image into the house, yet did he but receive his nobility from his ancestors, who had been Lords of that very Seignory of Dudley Castle, many descents before, even from King Richard the First's time; at which time Sir Richard Sutton married the daughter and heir of the Lord Dudley; since which time all descended of him, as divers branches there be, left the name of Sutton, and have all been called Dudleys, which is now above four hundred years since; and both these houses of Sutton and Dudley having been before that time of great nobility; and that Sutton was a man of great honour and estimation, that very match witnesseth sufficiently, it being a dainty thing in that time, that one of Saxon blood, as Sutton's name testifieth he was, should match with such an inheritrix as Dudley was; the like example whereof I remember none but the great house of Raby, who matched with Nevill, who of that match, as the Suttons were called Dudleys, so did they ever since take the name of Nevill; so, as of a house, which, these four hundred years, have been still owners of one Seignory, the very place itself, to any that sees it, witnessing; such as, for any that I know, in England none, but the noble house of Stafford hath the like, considering the name of the house, the length of time it hath been possest, the goodliness of the seat, with pleasures and royalties about it; so, as I think, any that will not swear themselves brothers to a reproachful tongue, will judge of his other slanders by this most manifest; since all the world may see he speaks against his own knowledge; for if either the house of Dudley had been great anciently, and now extinguished, or now great, and had not continued from old time, or that they had been unentitled gentlemen, so as men must not needs have taken knowledge of them, yet there might have been cast some veil over this untruth; but in a house now noble, long since noble, with a nobility never interrupted, seated in a place which they have each father and each son continually owned, what should be said, but

that this fellow desires to be known; suitably, having an untrue heart, he will become it with an untrue tongue. But perchance he will seem to doubt, for what will he not doubt, who will affirm that which beyond all doubt is false, whether my great grandfather, Edmond Dudley, were of the Lord Dudley's house or no. Certainly, he might, in conscience and good manners, if so he did doubt, have made some distinction between the two houses, and not in all places have made so contemptible mention of that name of Dudley, which is borne by another Peer of the Realm; and even of charity sake he should have bestowed some father upon Edmond Dudley, and not leave him not only ungentled, but fatherless. A railing writer extant, against Octavius Augustus, saith his grandfather was a silversmith; another Italian, against Hugh Capet, though with most absurd falsehood, saith his father was a butcher. Of divers of the best houses of England, there have been such foolish dreams, that one was a Farrier's son, another a Shoemaker's, another a Miller's, another a Fiddler's; foolish lies, and by any that ever tasted any antiquities, known to be so. Yet those houses had luck to meet with honester railers, for they were not left fatherless clean, they descended from somebody; but we, as if we were of Deucalion's brood, were made out of stones, have left us no ancestors from whence we are come. But, alas, good railer, you saw the proofs were clear, and therefore for honesty sake, were contented to omit them; for, if either there had been difference of name, or difference of arms between them; or, if though in name and arms they agreed, yet, if there had been many descents fallen since, the separating of those branches (as we see in many ancient houses, it so falls out, as they are uncertain whether they came out of other), then, I say yet, a valiant railer may venture upon a thing, where, because there is not an absolute certainty, there may be some possibility to escape; but in this case, where not only name and arms, with only that difference, which acknowledgeth our house to be of the younger brother, but such nearness of blood, as that Edmond Dudley was no further off than son to the younger brother of the same Lord

Dudley, and so as he was to be Lord Dudley if the Lord Dudley had died without heirs: and by the German and Italian manner, himself was to have been also called Lord Dudley; that his father, being called John Dudley, married to the daughter and heir of Bramshot, in Sussex; 'twas the only descent between him and the Lord Dudley, who was his grandfather: his great grandfather being that noble Lord Dudley, whom before I mentioned, and no man need doubt that this writer doth not only know the truth hereof, but the proofs of this truth. This John, Edmond's father, being buried at Arundel Castle, who married Bramshot, and left that land to Edmond, and so to the Duke, in Sussex, which, after the Duke sold, by confiscation came to the Crown. This tomb any man at Arundel Castle may see. This Bramshot land I name, a thing not in the air, but which any man, by the ordinary course of those things, may soon know whether such land did not succeed unto Edmond from his father. So as were this inheritance of land, and monuments in churches, and the persons themselves little more than in man's memory; truly this libeller deserves many thanks, that, with his impudent falsehood, hath given occasion to set down so manifest a truth.

"As to the *Dudleys*, he deals much harder withal, but no wit truer; but therein I must confess I cannot allege his uncharitable triumphing upon the calamities fallen to that house, though they might well be challenged of a writer of whom any honesty were to be expected; but God forbid I should find fault with that, since, in all his book, there is scarce any one truth else. But our house received such an overthrow; and hath none else in England done so? I will not seek to wash away that dishonour with other honorable tears. I would this island were not so full of such examples; and I think, indeed, this writer, if he were known, might in conscience clear his ancestors of any such disgraces; they were too low in the mire to be so thunderstricken; but this I may justly and boldly affirm—let the last fault of the Duke be buried.

"And, in good faith, now I have so far touched there, as

any man that listeth to know a truth (if at least there be any that can doubt thereof), may straight be satisfied. I do not mean to give any man's eyes or ears such a surfeit, as by answering to repeat his filthy falsehoods, so contrary to themselves, as may well show how evil lies can be built with any uniformity. The same man, in the beginning of the book, was potent, to use his term, in that the Queen had cause to fear him; the same man, in the end thereof, so abject, as any man might tread on him; the same man, so unfriendly as no man could love him; the same man, so supported by friends that Court and country were full of them; the same man, extremely weak of body and infinitely luxurious; the same man, a dastard to fear anything; the same man, so venturesome as to undertake, having no more title, such a matter, that Hercules himself would be afraid to do, if he were here among us. In some, in one the same man, all the faults that in all the most contrary humoured men in the world can remain; that sure, I think, he hath read the devil's roll of complaints which he means to put up against mankind, or else he could never have been acquainted with so many wretched mischiefs. But hard it were if every goose-quill could any way blot the honour of an Earl of Leicester, written in the hearts of so many men throughout Europe. Neither for me shall ever so worthy a man's name be brought to be made a question, where there is only such a nameless and shameless opposer. But because that, though the writer hereof doth most falsely lay want of gentry to my dead ancestors, I have to the world thought good to say a little, which, I will assure any that list to seek, shall find confirmed with much more. But to thee I say, thou therein liest in thy throat, which I will be ready to justify upon thee, in any place of Europe, where thou wilt assign me a free place of coming, as within three months after the publishing hereof, I may understand thy mind. And as till thou hast proved this, in all construction of virtue and honour, all the shame thou hast spoken is thine own, the right reward of an eviltongued schelm,[1] as the German, especially, call such people.

[1] A knave, a villain.

So, again, in any place, whereto thou wilt call me, provided that the place be such as a servant of the Queen's majesty have free access unto; if I do not, having my life and liberty, prove this upon thee, I am content that this lie I have given thee, return to my perpetual infamy. And this which I write I would send to thine own hands, if I knew thee; but I trust it cannot be intended that he should be ignorant of this printed in London, which knows the very whisperings of the Privy Chamber. I will make dainty of no baseness in thee, that art, indeed, the writer of this book. And, from the date of this writing, imprinted and published, I will three months expect thine answer."

The following endorsements are on the original:

"A discourse in defence of the Earl of Leicester" . . { This is Sir P. Sidney's brother's hand-writing viz., Robert Sidney, the first Earl of Leicester of the name of Sidney.

"In my uncle's own hand, worthy to be better known to the world" . . . . { This is the handwriting of Robert, second Earl of Leicester, son and heir to the aforesaid Robert, and nephew to Sir P. Sidney.

Collins says, in relation to the above, "copied from his own handwriting, at Penshurst Place, and attested both by Robert Sydney, Earl of Leicester, his brother; and Robert, the 2d Earl of Leicester, his nephew."

"Seems to have been wrote immediately after the first publication, An. 1584; but I never heard of any one that has seen it in print."[1]

ROBERT PARSONS or PERSONS, the reputed author of 'Leycester's Commonwealth,' is thus spoken of by Camden, in his 'Annals of Queen Elizabeth:

" Robert Persons and Edmund Campian, English Jesuits, came into England at this time, 'to set Romish affairs forward.'

"This Robert Persons was a Somersetshire man, of a vehement and savage nature, of most uncivil manners and ill behaviour.

[1] Memoirs attached to the Sydney Papers.

"Edward Campian was a Londoner, of a contrary carriage; both were Oxford men, and I knew them while I was in the same University.

"Campian, being out of St. John's College, professed the place of Attorney in the said University in the year 1568, and being established Arch Deacon, made a show to affect the Protestant faith until that day he left England.

"Persons being out of Baliol College, in which he openly made profession of the Protestant religion, until his wicked life and base conversation purchasing him a shameful exile from thence, he retired himself to the Papists' side.

"Since both of them returning into England, were disguised, sometimes in the habits of soldiers, sometimes like gentlemen, and sometimes much like unto our ministers; they secretly travelled through England, from house to house, and places of popish nobility and gentry, valiantly executing by words and writings their commission.

"Persons, who was established chief and superior, being of a seditious nature and turbulent spirit, armed with audacity, spoke so boldly to the Papists to deprive Queen Elizabeth of her sceptre, that some of them were once determined to accuse and put him into the hands of justice. Campian though something more modest, presumed to challenge by a writing the ministers of the Church of England to dispute with him," &c. &c.

In the 'Privy Council Records' we find the following notices of proceedings against Campion and his associates:

"Greenwich, 26 July, 1581.

"Present—Lord Chancellor, Earl of Leycester, and five others.

"A warrant to Sir Thomas Heneage, Knight, Treasurer of Her Majesty's chamber, to pay unto the Sheriff of Berkshire for bringing up of one Edmund Campion, a Jesuit, three other Popish priests, and thirteen other persons, taken in that shire, and by their Lordships' order committed to the Tower, the sum of £33."[1]

[1] 'Privy Council Registers, Elizabeth,' vol. v.

"Greenwich, 30 July, 1581.

"Present—Lord Chamberlain, Earl of Leycester, and four others.

"A Letter to Mr. Lieutenant of the Tower, D. Hammond, Robert Beale, and Thomas Norton, advertising them how they are further to proceed with Campion, in manner as followeth :

"First, they shall demand of him whether he acknowledgeth himself to be Her Majesty's subject or no; which, if he shall confess, &c., then shall they minister unto him a corporal oath upon a Bible of St. Hierome's translation, for avoiding of loss of time, and also of further cavil to be by him made hereafter, to answer truly and directly to such things as by them shall be demanded of him, &c. And upon perusing of his former examinations and consideration of such points where he denies answer, and those which their Lordships are desirous to have added to his former interrogatories, contained in a paper herewith sent unto them. They are required to proceed to his further examination; and in case he continues wilfully [not] to tell the truth, then to deal with him by the rack.

"They are also required to take his answers to such articles as are herewith sent unto them touching one Rochfort, an Irishman. With the two other priests they are required likewise to proceed in propounding unto them the question of their allegiance to Her Majesty, and in ministering an oath to them to declare where they have lain, and whether there were a mass said in Mrs. Yates' house, or no, at their last being there. And if they shall find them to halt, then to put them in fear of the torture, &c. And after this Mr. Lieutenant is required to send to the Knight Marshal to remain under his charge, for which purpose he shall receive their Lordships' warrant unto him to receive them.

"Touching Weblin and Masfeld offering to conform themselves, after they shall have caused them both to be dealt with by some godly and learned preachers, who upon conference may persuade them voluntarily, in some open place, to acknowledge their former error and offence, and promise to come to the Church, and receive the sacraments by the laws appointed; they may upon bonds taken of either of them to be of good behaviour towards Her Majesty's laws set them at liberty.

"Postscript.—Whereas we are given to understand that you, Mr. D. Hammond, have, out of Sander's book, 'De Monarchia Eccliæ,' and 'Bristow's Motives,' drawn certain points touching the acknowledgment of their allegiance towards Her Majesty; we think it good that you propound the same to Campion and the priests, requiring their direct answer to the same.[1]

"At Greenwich, 2d August, 1581.

" Present—Earl of Leycester and four others.

" A letter to Sir John Byron, Sheriff of Lancaster, Sir Edmund Trafford, or any of them, requiring them forthwith, &c., to repair into the dwelling-houses of certain persons in their Lordship's letter mentioned, having been harbourers of Edmund Campion, lately sent from Rome, contrary to Her Majesty's proclamation, and to cause the said persons to be examined, whether the said Campion hath been there or no; whether he said mass there, together with such other particularities as they shall think meet to be inquired of. And further, to cause the said houses to be searched for books and other suspicious stuff; and especially the house of Richard Houghton, where, it is said, the said Campion left his books; and to inquire what is become of the said books; and also of Ralph Emerson, his man; and to understand from whence he came thither, how he was accompanied, and whither he went, and what things the said Campion or Emerson carried thence. Of all which they are required to advertise the Earl of Derby, to the intent his Lordship may assist them further, as need shall require, and hereof to advertise their Lordships.

[1] 'Privy Council Registers, Elizabeth,' vol. v.

"A letter to the Earl of Derby, advertising his Lordship of their Lordships' said letters written unto the aforesaid Sheriff of Lancaster, &c., for the apprehending, examining, and searching of the houses of the parties in the said letter specified. Requiring his Lordship to give them his assistance in the said service, as need shall require.[1]

"At Greenwich, 14th August, 1581,
"Present—Lord Treasurer, Lord Chamberlain, Leycester, and two others.

"A letter to Mr. Lieutenant of the Tower, Mr. D. Hammond, and Robert Beale, or to any three or two of them, thanking them for their pains taken in the examinations taken of Campion, and further requiring Mr. Lieutenant to remove Filby and Jacob unto the prison of the Marshalsea. They are required to examine Campion, Peters, and Ford, who refuse to confess whether they have said any masses or no; whom they have confessed, and where Parsons and the other priests be; touching those points, and to put them in fear of the torture, if they shall refuse to answer directly thereto.[2]

"Campion and other Romish Priests were this year [1581] executed for sedition, and attempting the ruin of the Queen and her kingdom."[3]

Hatton and Leicester lived on great terms of friendship with each other. Nicolas, in his life of Hatton, says that, in 1572, scandal (in reference to the Queen's regard for both of them) was equally rife to one as to the other. In August 1570, several persons were tried, and some executed at Norwich, for treasonable speeches and designs. "They had set out four proclamations; one was touching the wantonness of the Court," and one of the conspirators, called Marsham, having said that "my Lord of Leicester had two children by the Queen," was sentenced to lose both his ears or pay a fine of one hundred pounds.[4]

[1] P. C. R. Eliz., vol. v. [2] Ibid.
[3] Camden's 'Annals of Elizabeth,' 1625.
[4] Lodge's 'Illustrations Br. History,' 8vo, vol. i. See also Murdin's 'State

To show that Leicester was not alone in the slanderous reports made against him, Lord Burghley complains of the same thing, in a letter to his friend and steward, William Herle, under date 14th August, 1585.

"By your letter of the 11th, I perceive that you have heard the vile, false, and devilish exclamations and execrations [made] me by such as I know not, and therefore I can less judge what to think of them, in their degrees of the malice, and the causes thereof. . . .

"I am therefore determined to adhere to God, my only Patron, and shall be ready to answer all spirits, wheresoever I may find them blasting, and doubt not but if they would to myself but breathe any of these speeches, in presence of any honest company, I would with apparent truth confound their blasphemies. And therefore as you show yourself friendly in reporting these villanies to me, so you might show me friendship in effect, to my good, if you would advise them to charge me herewith, and if they do think me guilty hereof, they need not fear to accuse me, for I am not worthy to continue in this place, but I will yield myself worthy not only to be removed, but to be punished for an example to others, that should not abuse Her Majesty, and the office I hold. If they cannot prove all the lies they utter, let them make of any one point, wherewith to prove me guilty of falsehood, of injustice, of bribery, of dissimulation, of double-dealing in advice in Council, either with her Majesty or with the Counsellors; let them charge me in any point that I have not dealt as earnestly for the Queen's Majesty, to aid the afflicted in the Low Country, to withstand the increasing power of the King of Spain, the assurance of the King of Scots, to be tied to her Majesty with reward, yea, with the greatest pension than any other hath, if in any of these I may be proved to have been behind or slower than any, in a discreet manner, as becometh a servant and a counsellor. I will myself worthy of perpetual reproach, as

Papers' as to the traitorous speeches of Mather, and Berney's confession to Leicester.

though I were guilty of all that they use to bluster against me.

"They that say that in a rash and malicious mockery, that England has become 'Regnum Cecilianum,' may please their own cankered humour with such a device, but if my actions be considered, if there be any cause given by me of such a nickname, there may be found out in many others juster causes to attribute other names than mine."

He then goes on to speak of his houses, and the expenses he has been at in building, and in entertaining the Queen at Theobalds, and the lands he sold to enable him to build, lands that he had of " good King Edward 6th." " My house of Burghley is of my mother's inheritance, who liveth and is the owner of it, and I but a farmer." His charges at Court and in keeping house, " by report of suitors at more than any counsellor in England." His fees as Treasurer only the same as the last " four hundred years, whereas the Chancellor and others hath been doubly augmented within these few years, and these I do affirm that my fees of my treasurership doth not answer to my charge of my stable, I mean not my table; and in my household, I do seldom feed less than one hundred persons."

Addressed

"To my loving friend, Wm. Herle."

On a copy of another letter is endorsed,

"1585. Letters to Wm. Herle from the Lord Burghley, Lord Treasurer of England, found amongst his writings, and brought to the Earl of Leycester at the death of Herle," apparently in Burghley's writing.[1]

Dr. Bliss, in his notes to Wood's 'Athenæ Oxoniensis,' under the article of " Persons," vol. ii, 4to, p. 74, thus observes:

"It is rather singular that before I had resided in the University a fortnight, chance threw in my way a MS.

[1] 'Domestic Papers,' State Paper Office.

copy of the "Ghost," which contained a *supplement* of a very curious and interesting nature. This MS. was delivered to a person in Oxford, with orders to transcribe it, and from the marks on the volume, I conjecture it came from some college library. The transcriber could not read it, and brought it to me for assistance in deciphering the abbreviations. I immediately knew it to be a MS. copy of Leycester's "Ghost," and lent the writer my own printed copy, on condition of being allowed to transcribe the *supplement*. The person who paid for his transcript has probably been deceived by the substitution of a text already printed (for I do not accuse the transcriber of a collation of the text, although I recommended it to him), whilst I obtained the following contemporary statement.

"The author hath omitted the end of the Earl, the which may thus and truly be supplied : the Countess Lettice fell in love with Christopher Blunt, Gent., of the Earl's horse, and they had many secret meetings, and much wanton familiarity, the which being discovered by the Earl, to prevent the pursuit thereof, when General of the Low Countries, he took Blunt with him, and there purposed to have him made away, and for this plot there was a ruffian of Burgundy suborned, who, watching him one night going to his lodging at the Hague, followed him, and struck at his head with a halbert or battle-axe, intending to cleave his head. But the axe glanced, and withal pared off a great piece of Blunt's skull; which wound was very dangerous and long in healing, but he recovered, and afterwards married the Countess, who took this so ill, as that she, with Blunt, deliberated and resolved to dispatch the Earl. The Earl, not patient of the great wrong of his wife, purposed to carry her to Kenilworth, and to leave her there until her death by natural or by violent means, but rather by the last. The Countess, also, having suspicion or some secret intelligence of this treachery against her, provided artificial means to prevent the Earl, which was by a cordial, the which she had no fit opportunity to offer him till he came to Cornbury Hall, in Oxfordshire, where the Earl, after his gluttonous manner, surfeiting with excessive eating and drinking, fell so ill that he was forced to stay there. Then the deadly cordial was propounded unto him by the Countess. As Mr. William Haynes, sometime the Earl's page, and then a gentleman of his chamber, told me, who protested he saw her give that fatal cup to the Earl, which was his last draught, and an end of his plot against the Countess, and of his journey, and of himself; and so *Fraudis fraude sua prenditur artifex.*" Which may be thus Englished: '*The cunning deviser of deceit contracted for, is taken in his own snare.*'

SIR RICHARD VARNEY OR VERNEY,

OF WARWICKSHIRE.

But little information has been handed down to us in reference to Sir Richard Varney, who is so conspicuously mixed up with the death of Amye Robsart, according to the 'Commonwealth' story, transferred by Ashmole to his county history of Berkshire, and afterwards forming one of the principal characters in Sir Walter Scott's romance of 'Kenilworth.' It is gratifying to be able to trace out some portion of his lineage, to show who and what he was, and thereby somewhat to redeem his character from the obloquy which has been cast upon him by most writers who have preceded us. Not so, however, with Mr. BARTLETT, who, in his remarks on Scott's statements in 'Kenilworth,'[1] observes, "As regards Sir Richard Varney and the accomplice who, it is said, by Leicester's direction, *was privately made away with in prison*, their names must have originated with other groundless assertions of the period, as no allusion whatever is made to them in the correspondence respecting the death, or in any authenticated document."

Mr. PETTIGREW, in his 'Inquiry into the Particulars connected with the Death of Amye Robsart,' doubts the existence

[1] Bartlett's 'Historical and Descriptive Account of Cumnor Place.' 8vo, London, 1850.

even of such a person as Varney, so blackened had been his character by all who had referred to him, pointing him out as one of the greatest monsters in existence, capable of any crime; to such an extent was he vilified, that Mr. Pettigrew conceived that such a character was nothing more than a myth. He states—

"Of Sir RICHARD VARNEY I can ascertain no particulars. He is mentioned, in no measured terms, as an instigator to baseness, as the chief prompter to the murderous design, and as having been left with a man-servant, an underling, and Anthony Forster, to effect the diabolical business. We know nothing of Varney, save the mention of him in Ashmole's narrative, drawn by the Jesuit, as I have shown in *'Leycester's Commonwealth,'* and by the very important rôle he is made to play in the novel of *'Kenilworth.'* His name does not occur in any authentic documents connected with Sir Robert Dudley or Amy Robsart, nor indeed does he appear to have had any real existence."[1]

The statements made in 'Leycester's Commonwealth,' as to the participation of Sir Richard Varney in the death of Amye Robsart, so grossly scurrilous, are unsupported by any evidence whatever, and are entirely refuted by the correspondence in reference to the coroner's inquest, where no mention is made that Varney was present at Cumnor, either before the death or at the inquest; in fact, throughout that correspondence his name is not even mentioned.

Though we have been unable to find any particulars of the life of Sir Richard Varney, we fortunately are enabled to throw some light on his family connections by the following pedigrees, accompanied by two letters from Leycester to Burghley in 1574-75, having immediate reference to the grandson of Sir Richard Varney, who bore the same name— sufficient, we trust, to remove from the character of Sir

---

[1] 'Inquiry read at the Congress of the British Archæological Association, held at Newbury in 1859, being a refutation of the calumnies charged against Sir Robert Dudley, K.G., Anthony Forster, and others.' 8vo. London, 1859.

Richard the obloquy so infamously heaped upon him. Of the connexions by marriage of his immediate descendants some very interesting particulars have been collected, which are here presented to the reader, in connection with the pedigrees which follow.

In speaking of Varney, Scott says, "Varney, who sprung from an ancient but somewhat decayed family, was the Earl's page during his earlier and more obscure fortunes, and, faithful to him in adversity, had afterwards contrived to render himself no less useful to him in his rapid and splendid advance to fortune; thus establishing in him an interest, resting both on present and past services, which rendered him an almost indispensable sharer of his confidence."

Sir Richard Varney was Sheriff of Warwickshire in 1562 (4 Eliz.);[1] in what year he died we have no record, but presume before 1574, as in the month of July of that year we have a letter from Leycester in reference to the wardship of "young Varney," who was Sheriff of Warwickshire in 1591 (33 Eliz.),[2] afterwards knighted, and again Sheriff of that County in 1605 (3 Jas. I.).[3] It was the latter who married Margaret, daughter of Sir Fulke Greville (father of the first Lord Brooke), during the latter part of Elizabeth's reign, and who, by that marriage, became the ancestor of the present Lord Willoughby de Broke.

The family of *Verney* descended from William de Verney, who lived *temp.* Hen. I.

BARON WILLOUGHBY DE BROKE.

1503. Robert Willoughby, son and heir of Robert Willoughby, Baron Willoughby de Broke, summoned to Parliament fr. 3 Hen. VIII. (1511) to 7 Hen. VIII. (1515)—ob. 1522. s. p. m.

Edward, eldest son of the above, *d. vit. pat.* s. p. m. previous

[1,2,3] Dugdale's Warwickshire.

to 1522, left two daughters; Elizabeth, the eldest, m. Sir Fulke Greville. The barony being in abeyance, in 1696 it was claimed by, and allowed to,—

Richard Verney, second son and heir to Sir Greville Verney, who was son and heir of Sir Richard Verney, by Margaret, sister and sole heir of Fulke Greville, 1st Baron Broke. This Richard Verney d. in 1711.

Thus—

Sir Richard Verney[1] = Margaret, sister and sole heir of Fulke Greville, 1st Lord Broke, who was son and heir of Sir Fulke Greville, who m. Elizabeth Willoughby, as above.

Sir Greville Verney =

Richard Verney, second son, = summoned to parliament as Lord Willoughby de Broke, in 1691; died 1711. [2]

In the church at Norton, near Daventry, is a monument thus inscribed—
" Die Novem., Anno Dom. 1633.

"ELIZABETH, 3rd daughter of RICHARD VERNEY, de Compton Verney, in Com. Warw., Milit., by Margaret his wife, sister and heir of Fulco Grevill, late Baron Brooke de Beauchamps Court, in Com. Warw."

MARGARET, daughter of SIR RICHARD VARNEY, of Compton, in Com. Warw., Knt., married Robert Shurley, of Isfield, Esq., eldest son of Sir Geo. Shurley, Chief Justice in Ireland. She was living in 1633.[3]

---

[1] The " *Young Varney*" mentioned in Leycester's letter to Burghley.
[2] Nicholas' ' Synopsis of the Peerage,' vol. ii, p. 692.
[3] 'Visitation of Sussex, 1633-4.' Harleian MSS., 6164.

PEDIGREE OF VERNEY, OR VARNEY, OF WARWICKSHIRE.

(*From the 'Visitation of Warwickshire,' taken in 1619 by SAMSON LENNARD and AUGUSTIN VINCENT, Marshals and Deputies for WILLIAM CAMDEN, Clarencieux.—Harl. MSS., 1167, 1100, 1563.*)

```
Sir Thomas Verney, == ..., sister and co-heir of Sir Edward Thame, Knt.
of Compton, in Co. Warwick.
                │
    ┌───────────┴─────────────────────────┐
Sir Richard Verney,¹ == ..., da. of ... Rawley,²
of Compton.              of ......... Co. Warwick.
    │
    ┌──────────────────┬──────────────────────┐
George Verney,    Jane, da. of Wm. Lucy,³   Elizabeth, Ux.    Dorothy, Ux.
of Compton.       of Charlcot, Co. War.     ... Roydon.       ... Danvers.

Richard Verney, == Margarett,⁴ da. of Foulke Greville, Knt.
of Compton, Knt.
    │
    ┌──────────────────┬──────────────────┬──────────────────┐
Greville Verney,⁵ == Catherine,⁵ da. of   Mary, Ux.         Anne, Ux.      John,      Richard.   George.
æt. et her., æt. 32.  Robt. Southwell,    Richd. Damwell,   John Bretton,  æt. 30.
(b. 1587.)            of ... Co. Norfolk. of ... Co. Northmptn. of ... Co. Northmptn.
    │
    ┌──────────────┬──────────────┐
George Verney,   (Richard,)     A daughter,
or Greville, æt. 3. 2nd son.⁶    æt. 1.
(b. 1616.)
```

¹ The friend or retainer of the Earl of Leycester. ² *Query* a connexion of Sir Walter Raleigh.
³ Sister (?) of Sir Thomas Lucy (Justice Shallow), before whom Shakespeare was arraigned for deer-stealing.
⁴ Sister and sole heir of Fulke Greville, first Lord Brooke, who was son and heir of Sir Fulke Greville, who married Elizabeth Willoughby, one of the heiresses to the Barony of "Willoughby de Broke."
⁵ Sister of Elizabeth Southwell, who eloped with Sir Robert Dudley to Italy, habited as his page; their father, Sir Robert Southwell, was one of the naval commanders who most distinguished themselves in the year of the Armada.
⁶ Succeeded as Baron Willoughby de Broke in 1696.

BARON WILLOUGHBY DE BROKE.

(*From* BANKS's '*Dormant and Extinct Baronetage,*' *Vol. II, p.* 609.)

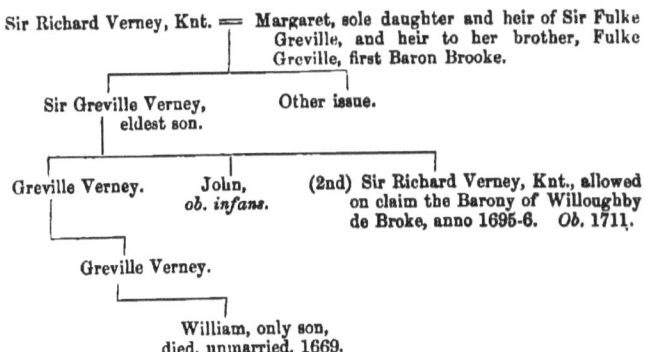

Present (1868) BARON WILLOUGHBY DE BROKE, Henry Verney, 10th Baron, who succeeded in 1862.

BARON AND EARL BROOKE AND EARL OF WARWICK.

Margaret, daughter of *Sir Fulke Greville* (father of the first Lord Brooke), *tempe* Elizabeth and James I., married *Sir Richard Verney*,[1] ancestor of the present Lord Willoughby of Broke.

It was Sir Fulke (the brother of this Margaret) who obtained, 2nd James I., " a grant of Warwick Castle, with the gardens and other dependencies about it. He then found it in a ruinous condition, the towers and other strong places of it being used for the common gaol of the county ; but at an expense of about £20,000 he repaired and adorned it for

[1] Sir Richard Verney was Sheriff of Warwickshire 33 Eliz., and again 3 James I.—Dugdale's ' Warwickshire.'

the seat of his family. Moreover, he made a purchase of the Temple grounds adjoining, and beautified them with large and stately plantations, with the intention, as it would seem, to put in execution the design which George, Duke of Clarence, formerly had of making a park of them under his windows; a design which Francis, the present Earl Brooke and Earl of Warwick, since he became lord of the manor, has been able to accomplish. Upon the whole, he so repaired this great and venerable but ruinous castle, as to render it (as Dugdale says) not only a place of great strength, but extraordinary delight, with most pleasant gardens, walks, and thickets, such as this part of England can hardly parallel; so that now it is the most princely seat that is within the midland parts of this realm."[1]

FRANCIS GREVILLE, son and heir of William, 7th Baron Brooke, who died in 1727, was created Earl Brooke of Warwick Castle in 1746, and Earl Warwick in 1759; he died in 1773, and was succeeded by his son—

GEORGE GREVILLE, 2nd Earl of Warwick, who died in 1816, and was succeeded by—

HENRY RICHARD GREVILLE, as 3rd Earl of Warwick; he died in 1853, and was succeeded by the present Earl, George Guy.[2]

Whether any or what relation Sir Richard Verney bore to the family of the Verneys of Fleetmarston, Co. Bucks, afterwards of Penley, Co. Herts, and ultimately of Middle Claydon, Co. Bucks, we have not been able to discover. A pedigree of this family, commencing in 1216, which is attached to the letters and papers of the Verney family published by the Camden Society,[3] does not give any reference to

[1] Collins's 'Peerage,' vol. iv, 347-8.
[2] Nicholas's 'Synopsis of the Peerage,' vol. i, p. 87; and 'Burke's Dictionary of Heraldry.'
[3] 'Letters and Papers of the Verney family down to the end of the year 1639, printed from the original MSS. in the possession of Sir Harry Verney, Bart.' Edited by John Bruce, Esq. 1853.

the Verneys of Warwickshire, from whom Sir Richard was descended.

The following are the letters from Leycester to Burghley in reference to " young VARNEY :"

Earl of Leycester to Lord Burghley, Lord Treasurer.

" *Woodstock ;* 30 *July,* 1574. (*Original.*)

" MY VERY GOOD LORD,—

" I have thought good to let you understand, that where of late I sent unto your Lordship, my solicitor, Nutthall, touching the lands of young Varney, by reason there is hitherto no order taken, nor any man appointed for the looking thereunto, both the lands and the house go to much rack, and if speedy remedy be not provided, it cannot but greatly turn to the loss and harm of the child. The meadows stand yet undealt withal, whereby the hay of the ground is like to be utterly spoiled, for want of some that should look to the inninge of it. And I, for my part, albeit divers have called upon me (for that your Lordship granted unto me the wardship of the child), to take some order in it, yet have forborne still to do anything, expecting some direction from your Lordship. And now very lately I understand by Sir Thomas Lucye,[1] there be divers that offer to make entries upon the land by virtue of statutes and other foolish bonds made by his father in his lifetime; wherein your Lordship is to take some speedy order, otherwise it cannot but turn to the child's undoing, or extreme prejudice, at the least. But not perceiving any man appointed, neither yet any of his friends very willing to meddle with the land, considering how foolishly the late father hath left the whole encumbered, I have thought good for the young child's sake to put your Lordship in remembrance, that the matter, in time for his more benefit hereafter, may be looked into presently, which if your Lordship cannot find any that will carefully deal for him, I will myself take what charge thereof you will require or

---

[1] The Justice Shallow of Shakespeare ; uncle to young Varney.

appoint, upon the survey of such as your Lordship shall assign for it, which for the poor child's sake, I pray your Lordship may be in as convenient time as the cause requireth, for all goeth almost to spoil. And so I wish your Lordship right heartily to farewell. From Woodstock this 30th of July, 1574.

"Your Lordship's most assured,

"R. LEYCESTER."

(Superscribed)
"To the Right Honorable, my very good Lord, the Lord Treasurer of England."[1]

Earl of Leycester to Lord Burghley, Lord Treasurer.

"*Tudington;* 16 *June,* 1575. (*Holograph.*)

"MY VERY GOOD LORD,—

"I have sent you the note the Queen's Majesty talked with you of at Hatfield, which I could not come by before I came hither to Tudington, for that my coffers were gone thither with some of my stuff. Your Lordship will better conceive of the matter than I can, and may have conference with such as are able to inform you the ways to further such a plot.[2]

"I have one other matter to request your Lordship's order for, before the term ends; it is for young Varney, whom your Lordship, I thank you, did grant unto me,[3] and I assure your Lordship I desired him only for the good of that house, knowing that he was likely to receive else much harm, and as I was desirous and willing to make offer of his marriage to your Lordship for one of Mr. Cave's daughters, your nieces, before any other, so am I still

[1] Lansdowne MSS. B. Museum, vol. 18.
[2] In reference to regulating the prices of some "wares," from which revenue was derived.
[3] "As guardian of one of the tenants of the Crown, who was a minor, this would give him the profits of the lands till the heir should reach the age of twenty-one. It was an arrangement which, at the same time, would be accounted a favor shown to the heir, as taking him out of the hands of the officers of the Crown and leaving him in the care of a friend of his late father."—*Craik.*

desirous that match should take place, as well for the good worship of the house as chiefly the alliance with your Lordship, by whose means he may receive his greatest benefit, and because your Lordship shall perceive my meaning was wholly for the young child's benefit to have him, even as I offered his match in marriage with your Lordship, hereafter if God give liking between the parties, so did I as freely offer all other things that were to be looked unto of his to Sir Thomas Lucy, his uncle, who I know hath loved the father and grandfather, and would willingly further this, yet upon perusing the state of things as they stand, would by no means deal with them, neither take the charge of them. I offered likewise to any other of his nearest kin the same with all commodities that they would make or that I could procure, at your Lordship's hands, for them, also that his house and other things might be well governed and preserved for the young man. There was none would meddle with them, and I protest to God (my Lord) they should have had all, and even as I had it from your Lordship, which indeed I thought could not be but some commodity to such as should have it at such reasonable rates as you use to let such things. Yet in the end all his own friends refusing, as I tell your Lordship, to deal with it, I was driven to desire and entreat Sir John Hibbotts to take it in hand, always foreseeing he should not hinder himself, or be a loser; whereupon, at my request, he hath so done, and we have had such a business with the mother[1] of the young boy as I assure your Lordship she wearied us all, and without your lordship sets your favorable help hereafter, as occasion shall serve justly, the boy shall scant, while he lives, be able to keep the countenance of a mere gentleman, and yet is his living worth together well a thousand marks a year. But his father,[2] the unthrift, that your Lordship and I had so much to do withal, hath made such bargains and leases, and in debt £2000 when he died, whereby except the young boy find good friends, when he comes to man's estate, he shall have all his lands subject to bonds and forfeitures, wherefore Sir John, being very careful to preserve all, as much as may be possible, I think will, at your coming to Kenilworth, confer with your Lordship how some order may be taken, whereby

[1] Catherine, daughter of Sir Robert Southwell, and sister of Elizabeth, who, disguised as a page, accompanied Sir Robert Dudley to Italy, and was afterwards, by a dispensation of the Pope, married to him.
[2] Son of the Sir Richard Varney mentioned by Sir Walter Scott.

some of his debts may in this time be paid, and so the child less burdened hereafter, and also Sir John hath great care in bringing him up, and so have I chiefly, till he be a little bigger to go to some other place to get more knowledge; and as hitherto he hath had no allowance for him, so my request to your Lordship is that you will appoint him some reasonable portion, which I dare undertake at the least shall be employed toward him every way. And, according to my promise to your Lordship, as soon as he cometh to years that you shall think good to have him dealt with for the matter of Mr. Cave's daughter, he shall be, God willing, only kept for it, and as you shall think of him then meet for such a one so shall find all his friends, at least the chief, to deal in it as I know already they are most willing and desirous should take place. And I wish he may prove one that your Lordship may like so to bestow him, and then your Lordship shall have him even as I had him of you. Thus desiring your Lordship that this bearer, Clark, Sir John Hibbott's solicitor, may attend you to receive your pleasure herein, I will for this time commit you to God, and bid your Lordship most heartily farewell. From Tudington, this 16th of June.

"Your Lordship's assured friend,
"R. LEYCESTER."

"I pray your Lordship send the book with your letter that Ellis hath, with as much speed as you may, and as your Lordship shall think best to write for the furtherance thereof."

"To the Right Honorable, my very good Lord,
the Lord Burghley, Treasurer of England
and Knight of the Order."[1]

[1] Lansdowne MSS., Brit. Museum.

ANTHONY FORSTER, OF CUMNOR PLACE.

BARTLETT, in his 'Historical Account of Cumnor Place,' has given a memoir of Anthony Forster as fully as could be collected "after the lapse of nearly three centuries." The reader is referred to that memoir, containing, as it does, a full and complete vindication of the character of Anthony Forster from the foul aspersions cast upon him; in fact, nothing further is required to show the utter falsity of the charges in the '*Commonwealth,*' in Ashmole's *statements*, and in Sir Walter Scott's '*Kenilworth*.' Bartlett very justly observes, " It is somewhat to be regretted that those authors who have promulgated the reports should have received as authentic such scandals without endeavouring to ascertain what proof there was for their foundation."

With this vindication we close our account of Amye Robsart and the inquiries as to the various statements in relation to her death.

Some very interesting observations in regard to Anthony Forster, his position, family connexions, his will, and distribution of his property, will be found in Mr. PETTIGREW's ' Inquiry concerning the Death of Amye Robsart.'

END OF AMYE ROBSART.

KENILWORTH.

HISTORY OF KENILWORTH CASTLE,

WITH AN

ACCOUNT OF THE SPLENDID ENTERTAINMENT

GIVEN TO QUEEN ELIZABETH,

BY THE EARL OF LEICESTER, IN 1575,

DESCRIBED BY ROBERT LANEHAM,

AN EYE-WITNESS.

KENILWORTH CASTLE.

"SIR WM. DUGDALE says that the land on which the Castle is situate was given by King Henry I. to a Norman named Geoffrey de Clinton, his Lord Chamberlain and Treasurer, by whom the building was first erected. By this proprietor also, he states, the Monastery of Black Canons of St. Augustine's Order to have been instituted at the same time, near the Fortress. In 1172 the Castle was garrisoned by King Henry II., to withstand the unnatural insurrection of his eldest son Henry, who was assisted by Louis VII., King of France, and several of the English barons. Although it is by no means certain that the building again reverted to the Clintons, yet, early in the reign of John, Henry Clinton, the grandson of the founder, released to that King all his interest in the Castle and lands. The son of the last possessor, who also bore his father's name, engaged himself in the wars of the tumultuous Barons during the reigns of John and Henry III.; but, in 1217, upon his submission to the latter monarch, he had livery of his father's land at Kenilworth. This appears to have been the last of the Clintons who held this estate. The castle had long been in the hands of the Crown, and was held for it by the successive Sheriffs for the Counties of Warwick and Leicester. In 1243 Henry III. constituted Simon Montfort, Earl of Leicester, Governor of Kenilworth Castle; and ten years afterwards granted it to him and his wife, Eleanora,[1] for their lives. This haughty and ambitious Baron was Commander-in-Chief of the insurrection against Henry III. concerning Magna Charta; and soon after his receiving the grant of this castle, himself and

[1] Eleanora his wife, sister of Hen. III.

his comrades met in arms at Oxford. The conclusion of this convocation was, that they marched against the Royal army, and Simon de Montfort was slain at the battle of Evesham, on 5th August, 1265. It is to the warlike disposition and death of this Baron that the Lady of the Lake alludes in her verses, where she says—

"The Earl, Sir Mountfort's force, gave me no heart."

"Kenilworth Castle, in the interim, was defended by Simon de Montfort the younger, son of the late Earl; and when the King's forces were besieging it, he, perceiving that it must shortly be surrendered, retired privately into France, to raise more soldiers in aid of the Baron's designs. In his absence Henry de Hastings was left Governor, whom he assured of a certain and early relief; but the King's reinforcements arriving first, after much doubt and delay the Castle was yielded to Henry III., on the feast of St. Thomas, December 21st, 1265. About the end of the siege, which lasted six months, and amounted to a very considerable sum, the King, by the advice of Ottobon, the Papal Legate, called a convention at Kenilworth, at which it was determined that persons who had forfeited their lands in the late rebellion might redeem them by a fine, to be paid to such as then possessed them. Some exceptions were, however, made, which were, the wife and children of the said Earl of Leicester; Robert Ferrers, Earl of Derby; Henry de Hastings, mentioned above; and those who wounded the King's messenger when he summoned Kenilworth Castle to surrender. On all these were imposed either heavier fines or imprisonment; and the Act by which the foregoing particulars were declared was called *Dictum de Kenilworth,* an entire copy of which may be found in some of the ancient statute books, or in the 'Statutes of the Realm,' printed by command, 1820.[1] Laneham also alludes to the statute of Kenilworth, in the following passage of his letter :—'A singular pattern of humanity may he be well unto us towards all degrees; of honour toward high estates, and chiefly whereby we may learn in what dignity,

[1] Vol. i, p. 12.

worship, and reverence, her Highness is to be esteemed, honoured, and received, that was never, indeed, more condignly done than here; so, as neither by the builders at first, nor by the *Edict of Pacification* after, was ever Kenilworth more ennobled than by this, his Lordship's receiving her Highness here now.' In the original edition of Lancham is the following marginal note to this passage :—' 1266, An. 50, Hen. III.' Immediately after the siege and surrender of the Castle, Philip Marmion, the first Lord of Scrivelsby and Tamworth, was made Constable by the King; but on the 16th of January, 1267, it was conferred, with many privileges, upon Edmund Crouchback, Earl of Lancaster, second son of the King, and to his lawful heirs. In 1296, Edmund died at Bayonne, and was succeeded by his eldest son Thomas, in whose time Roger Mortimer held at Kenilworth the feast of the Round Table. This festival, according to Dugdale, took place in 1378; and he thus describes it :—' The same year I find that there was a great and famous concourse of noble persons here at Kenilworth, called the Round Table, consisting of an hundred knights, and as many ladies; whereunto divers repaired from foreign parts for the exercise of arms, viz., tilting and martial tournaments; and the ladies dancing, who were clad in silken mantles, Roger Mortimer, Earl of March, being the chief, and the occasion thereof; which exercises began on the eve of St. Matthew the Apostle (21st September), and continued till the morrow after Michaelmas day ' (30th).[1] Roger Mortimer appears to have been one of the most fashionable gallants of his time, and his son Geoffrey named him 'The King of Folly.' But Thomas, Earl of Lancaster, joined the baronial party against the favorites of King Edward II., namely, Pierce Gaveston and the two Spencers; and although the King once pardoned him, and restored his forfeited lands, yet in 1322 he was taken in arms at the battle of Boroughbridge, and a few days after was beheaded.

" Kenilworth Castle was next delivered into the hands of John de Somery, Baron of Dudley; Ralph, Lord Basset of

[1] 'Antiq. of Warwicksh.,' edit. by Dr. Thomas, 1730, vol. i, 217.

Drayton; and Ranulph de Charun, for the King's use; but when the fortunes of King Edward were overthrown, his officers were expelled, and himself brought to the fortress as a prisoner in the power of Henry, brother of the late possessor, and others of his infamous fellow-subjects. After the cruel death of Edward II., at Berkeley Castle, whither he was conveyed from Kenilworth, the detestable Henry, Earl of Lancaster, was restored to his brother's possessions; and from him the castle descended, through his son and granddaughter, to John of Gaunt, Duke of Lancaster. At length the property of Kenilworth once more reverted to the Crown, by passing to the Duke's son, Henry of Bolingbroke, who afterwards became Henry IV.[1] This castle thus came a third time into the hands of the Crown.

Henry VII. united it to the Dukedom of Cornwall; and his son, Henry VIII., was at a considerable expense in repairing and ornamenting it. In 26th of Henry VIII., the monastery was valued at £643 14s. 9d. 29th Henry VIII. —On the 15th April, the Monastery of Kenilworth was surrendered by Simon Jekys, the last abbot, and sixteen monks, who had pensions allowed them by the King.

The Abbey lands were granted by Henry VIII. to Sir Andrew Flamoke, whose granddaughter and sole heiress carried them by marriage to John Colbourn, Esq., who afterwards buying some horses that had been stolen out of Lord Leicester's stables, was so much frightened by the threats of the Earl, that he was glad to make his peace by giving up the lands to him on easy terms, and they have ever since been annexed to the domain of the castle.

By the following letter, and the extract from the Privy Council Register, vol. 2, (Mary,) which immediately follows, it appears that Kenilworth was granted to Sir John Dudley, a fact which I have not seen mentioned by any writer.

---

[1] From 'Glossarial Notes to Gascoigne's Princely Pleasures of Kenilworth Castle,' 12mo, 1821.

Sir John Dudley (afterwards Duke of Northumberland) to Cromwell, Lord Keeper, 21st March, 153[ ].[1]

"Please it your Lordship; so it is that within two or three days after my coming home to Dudley, Andrew Flamoke[2] and his son came thither to me, and the same night sickened both in a bed in my house, and by the next day at night, the son was dead full of the marks, and the father hath a blain.[3] And no way with him but on as they that keepeth him can conjecture; they came both out of Gloucestershire from Mr. Poyntz, and whether they brought it from thence or by the way, God knoweth, for this country was as clear before their coming as any county in England. If it might please your good Lordship to be so good Lord unto me to be a meane for me to the King's highness for the office of Kenilworth, I were much bound to your Lordship, if not, your Lordship may do your pleasure for any other that you shall think meeter for it, for no man hath knowledge hereof by me but your Lordship. And sorry I am (as knoweth God) to send you word of such news, for the King's highness shall lose a tall man of him. His son died this last night, and he himself both raveth and hath the blain. No more to your Lordship at this time, but the merciful Lord have you in his merciful keeping, and all yours. Scribbled in haste, as appeareth, the 21st of March in the morning, with the rude hand of your most bounden through life.
"JOHN DUDLEY.

(Superscribed)
"To the Right Honorable and his singular good
Lord, my Lord Cromwell, Lord Keeper of the
Privy Seal, in haste."

"At Westminster, the 8th Oct., 1553.

"A letter to the Lord Rich and other the Commissioners for the attainted goods, to deliver unto the Duchess of Somerset, or to such as she shall send to receive the same, by bill indented, all such household stuff as remaineth in Kenilworth, lately belonging to the late Duke of Northumberland,

[1] State Paper Office, London.
[2] An officer in the navy acting under Sir John, when high admiral.
[3] Smallpox or plague.

and to send hither the said bill of the parcels that shall be delivered, to the end it may be considered whether the same be sufficient, or too much, for her furniture."[1]

Kenilworth, after the attainder of the Duke of Northumberland, descended to Queen Mary, and then to her sister Elizabeth, who, on the 9th June, 1563, granted it, with all the royalties belonging to it, to Robert Dudley, fifth son of the Duke of Northumberland, who on the 28th Sept., 1564, was created Baron of Denbigh, and, the day following, Earl of Leicester.

"It was under this haughty favorite that Kenilworth reached the summit of its grandeur. He, in 1571, erected the large pile of buildings on the south side of the inner court which bears his name, and the great gate-house on the north. This he made the principal entrance, and changed the front of the castle, which before was towards the lake. He likewise built a tower at each end of the tilt-yard, from whence the ladies had an opportunity to see the noble diversion of tilting and barriers; and greatly enlarged the lake, the chase, and the parks, which now extended over near twenty miles of country. He is said to have expended sixty thousand pounds (an immense sum in those days)[2] in these magnificent improvements. Here in July (Saturday, the 9th), 1575, having completed all things for her reception, Lord Leicester entertained Queen Elizabeth for the space of seventeen days, with excessive cost and a variety of delightful shows.[3]

"To honour this entertainment the more, there were then knighted here Sir Thomas Cecil (eldest son of the Lord Treasurer),[4] Sir Henry Cobham (brother of Lord Cobham), Sir Francis Stanhope, and Sir Thomas Tresham.

"The next year ensuing Lord Leicester obtained by grant of the Queen a weekly market here, upon the Wednesday, and a fair yearly on midsummer day.

[1] Privy Council Register, Mary, vol. ii.
[2] Probably equal to £600,000 in the present age.
[3] The expense of the entertainment was estimated at £1000 per diem.
[4] Some time afterwards created Earl of Exeter.

ROBERT DUDLEY, EARL OF LEYCESTER.

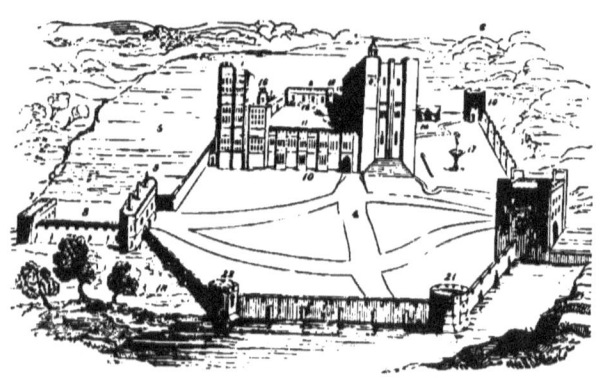

DESCRIPTION OF THE PLAN OF THE CASTLE AS IT APPEARED AT THE
QUEEN'S VISIT IN 1575.

1. Cæsar's Tower.
2. Lancaster Buildings.
3. Leycester Buildings.
4. Base Court or Outer Ballium.
5. Lake.
6. Chase.
7. Gallery Tower.
8. Tilt Yard.

9. Mortimer's Tower.
10. K. H. VIIIth's Lodgings.
11. Inner Court.
12. The Strong or Mervyn's Tower.
13. Kitchens.
14. Pleasance.
15. Great Hall.
16. Leycester's Chamber.

17. Gardens.
18. Orchard.
19. Swan Tower.
20. Great Gateway.
21. Lunn's Tower.
22. Water Tower.
23. St. Lowe Tower adjoins Mervyn's Tower S.W. and is not seen in this point.

(See *Appendix*, p. 342.)

"Lord Leicester (who died in 1588) left the castle and estate by his will to his brother Ambrose, Earl of Warwick, for his life, and after his death to Sir Robert Dudley, whom he styled his base son.

"The Earl of Warwick died in 1589, when Sir Robert came into possession, and determined to prove his legitimacy, and assert his claim to his father's titles. The case was thus— Lord Leicester privately married the widow of Lord Sheffield, by whom he had this son, but being apprehensive that the Queen would disapprove of his marriage, it was never made public; this the Earl took advantage of, and married Lady Essex (whom he fell violently in love with), though the Lady Sheffield was still living, and she (Lady Essex) had interest enough after his death to obtain a decree in the Star-Chamber, by which all Sir Robert Dudley's proceedings to prove his father's prior marriage with the Lady Sheffield (which he had nearly accomplished) were put a stop to. As a sentence in his favour would greatly have reflected on Lady Essex's character, she obtained from the Lords of the Council a command that all the depositions should be sealed and laid up with the records of the Star-Chamber. The hopes of Sir Robert Dudley for obtaining his father's possessions being thus frustrated, he left England for Italy, having received license to travel for three years. Some time after his departure a summons for his return was issued by a special writ of Privy Seal, which not being obeyed, the castle and lands of Kenilworth were seized on for the King's use, by virtue of the Statute of Fugitives, 31 Edwd. III., cap. 14. Although the castle and lands of Kenilworth were now vested in the Lord Privy Seal, through the contempt of Sir Robert Dudley, yet the amiable Henry Frederic, Prince of Wales, was unwilling to make them his dwelling without a compensation to the ejected owner. Through the medium of special agents, in 1811 he purchased of Sir Robert his interest for £14,500, to be paid within twelve months. At that time Kenilworth was considered one of the most magnificent places in the Kingdom. The Prince died on the 6th November, 1612, when not more than £3000 had been discharged, and even that amount never reached Sir Robert, as the merchant through whom it was paid had failed.

"Prince Charles, as his late brother's heir, took possession of Kenilworth, and procured an Act of Parliament (21 Jas. I., cap. 12), by which Lady Alice Dudley, the wife of Sir Robert, was enabled, on the 4th May, 1621, to alienate all her interest to him in right of her jointure, for the sum of £4000, which was paid to her from the Exchequer.

"1626, March 15.—Charles I. granted by patent to Robert Carey, Earl of Monmouth, and two of his family, the custody of the castle, park, and chase of Kenilworth for their joint and several lives; but after the king's death Oliver Cromwell divided the manor between his lawless followers, who wholly devastated the property. At the Restoration it again passed into the family of the Earl of Monmouth, and after their leases were expired, Charles II. granted the reversion of the whole manor to Lawrence, Lord Hyde (second son of Lord Chancellor Clarendon), afterwards created Baron of Kenilworth and Earl of Rochester. He died in 1711, and was succeeded in his titles and estate by Henry, his only son, who in 1723, by the death of Edward, third Earl of Clarendon, succeeded likewise to that earldom. He dying in 1753 without male issue, his grand-daughter, Lady Charlotte Capel (by William Capel, Earl of Essex, and the Lady Jane Hyde, his wife), became (her mother being before dead) the representative of the Hyde family, and pursuant to the will of the said Henry, Earl of Clarendon and Rochester, she took the name and arms of Hyde. In 1752 she married the Hon. Thomas Villiers, second son of the Earl of Jersey, who in 1756 was created by George II. Lord Hyde of Hindon, County Wilts, and in 1776 by George III. Earl of Clarendon. He died 11th December, 1786, and was succeeded by his eldest son, Thomas, second Earl, who died in 1824, unmarried, and was succeeded by his next brother, John Charles, the present peer. The family of the Clarendons have endeavoured to preserve the venerable ruins of the castle from farther dilapidations.[1]

[1] 'History of Kenilworth,' Coventry, 1781, 'Kenilworth Illustrated,' 4to, 1821. 'Gascoigne's Princely Pleasures of Kenilworth,' 12mo, 1821.

"It will be evident from the above slight history of Kenilworth that there exists a considerable difference between its real memoirs and those ascribed to it by Laneham. Camden, also, in the following passage condemns the inaccuracy of those legends which carry its foundation back to the Saxon period. 'More to the north-east,' says the learned antiquary, 'where a number of small streams, uniting among parks, form a lake, which, soon after being confined in banks, makes a canal, stands Kenilworth, anciently called Kenelworda, though now corruptly called Killingworth, which gives name to a large, beautiful, and strong castle, surrounded by parks, not built by Kenulphus, Kenelmus, or Kinegilsus, as some dream, but as can be made to appear from records by Galfridus Clinton, Chamberlain to King Henry I.[1]

"The Lord *Saintlowe*, who is mentioned as having once been possessor of Kenilworth, was most probably one of the family of Saintloe, or Saintloo, who, about the time of Elizabeth, were Lords of the manor of Tormarton, in the County of Gloucester. Sir William Saintloe was Captain of the Guard to the above Sovereign.

"Having thus given sufficient of a true history of Kenilworth Castle to be a perfect guide to the readers of the works of Gascoigne and Laneham, it remains to give some account of the buildings and grounds as given by those who saw them in all their original splendour. Dugdale commences with saying that the situation is of extraordinary strength and largeness, as may be seen by the circuit, breadth and depth of the outer moats, together with the parts called Cæsar's Tower, which, by the thickness of its walls and form of building, he considers to have been of the first foundation. In 1241, Henry III., to whom the Castle then belonged, made extensive improvements and repairs at Kenilworth; such as ceiling the chapel with wainscot, painting it, and making new seats for the King and Queen. The bell-tower also was repaired, and the south walls next the pool were newly erected. The Queen's chamber was likewise enlarged and painted. In 1391, Richard II. furnished John of Gaunt

[1] 'Camden's Britannia,' 1789, vol. ii, 329.

with materials for improving and building at this place; and he, according to Dugdale, 'began the structure of all the buildings here, except Cæsar's Tower, with the outer wall and turrets.' But little, however, appears to have been done towards making the Castle splendid as a nobleman's seat, or a palace fit for the visit of a Queen, until Elizabeth, on the 9th of June, 1562,[1] presented the building to the Earl of Leicester; who, Dugdale remarks, 'spared for no cost in enlarging, adorning, and beautifying thereof; witness that magnificent gate-house towards the north, where, formerly having been the back of the Castle, he made the front, filling up a great proportion of the wide and deep double ditch wherein the water of the pool came. And, besides that stately piece on the south-east part, still bearing the name of Leicester's Buildings, did he raise from the ground two goodly towers at the head of the pool, viz., the Floodgate or Gallery tower, standing at one end of the tilt-yard, in which was a spacious and noble room for ladies to see the exercises of tilting and barriers; and at the other Mortimer's Tower, whereupon the arms of Mortimer were cut in stone; which doubtless was so named by the Earl of Leicester, in memory of one more ancient, that stood there formerly; wherein, as I guess, either the Lord Mortimer, at the time of that great and solemn tilting formerly mentioned, did lodge; or else because Sir John Mortimer, Knight, prisoner here in Henry V.'s time, was detained therein. The Chase he likewise enlarged, impaling part of Blackwell within it; and also a large nook, extending from Rudfen-lane towards the pool, which, being then a waste, wherein the inhabitants of Kenilworth had common, in consideration thereof, he gave them all those fields called Prior's Fields, lying north of the Castle. I have heard some, who were his servants, say that the charge he bestowed on this Castle, with the parks and chase thereto belonging, was no less than sixty thousand pounds.'"

[1] Must be an error as to date. Dudley was not created Earl of Leicester till the 29th Sept., 1564. In the following month the Manor of Kenilworth was assigned to him, though lands in Kenilworth had been transferred to him by the Queen, in exchange for other lands, as early as May, 1563.

"Of the gardens made by Lord Leicester, Laneham gives a very particular account. Leland[1] makes but few observations on Kenilworth; so that it is evident that at his visit the castle had none of those marks of magnificence with which it was afterwards adorned. 'King Henry VIII.,' says he, 'did of late years great cost in repair of the Castle of Killingworth. Amongst these reparations the pretty banqueting-house of timber that stood thereby in the meere, and bore the name of Pleasant, was taken down, and part of it set up in the base-court of Killingworth Castle.'[2] The next notice which occurs in history concerning the appearance of Kenilworth is the survey taken by the officers of King James I. on the contempt of Sir Robert Dudley to the Royal Warrant of Privy Seal, sent after him to Italy, commanding his return. The following copy of remarks upon this survey will give a more perfect idea of the splendour of the castle than any other description can; since it was taken when the buildings were in their most perfect state, as well as being more numerous and magnificent than at any other period of their history.

"The Castle of Kenilworth, situate upon a rock.

1. The circuit thereof within the walls containeth seven acres, upon which the walks are so spacious and fair, that two or three persons together may walk upon most places thereof.

2. The Castle, with the four gate-houses, all built of free stone, hewen and cut; the walls, in many places, fifteen and ten foot thickness, some more, and some less; the least four foot in thickness square.

3. The Castle and four gate-houses, all covered with lead, whereby it is subject to no other decay than the glass, through the extremity of the weather.

4. The rooms of great state with the same; and such as are able to receive his Majesty, the Queen and Prince at one time, built with as much uniformity and conveniency as any

---

[1] 'It is worthy of remark that descendants of this celebrated antiquary are to be found, to this day, in Massachusetts, U.S. The writer is personally acquainted with the family of one of these descendants, located in the City of New York.

[2] Leland's 'Itinerary,' vol. iv, p. 191.

houses of later time; and with such stately cellars; all carried upon pillars, and architecture of freestone, carved and wrought as the like are not within this kingdom; and also all other houses for officers answerable.

5. There lieth about the same in Chases and Parks £1200 per annum, £900 whereof are grounds for pleasure; the rest in meadow and pasture thereto adjoining, tenants and freeholders.

6. There joineth upon this ground, a park-like ground, called the King's Wood, with fifteen several coppices lying all together, containing 789 acres, within the same; which in the Earl of Leicester's time, were stored with red deer. Since which the deer strayed, but the ground in no sort blemished, having great store of timber, and other trees of much value upon the same.

7. There runneth through the said grounds, by the walls of the Castle, a fair pool, containing 111 acres, well stored with fish and fowl; which at pleasure is to be let round about the Castle.

8. In timber and woods upon this ground, to the value (as hath been offered) of £20,000 (having a convenient time to remove them), which to his Majesty in the survey are to be valued at £11,722, which proportion, in a like measure, is held in all the rest upon the other values to his Majesty.

9. The circuit of the Castle, manors, parks, and chase lying round together, contain at least nineteen or twenty miles, in a pleasant country; the like, both for strength, state and pleasure, not being within the realm of England.

10. These lands have been surveyed by Commissioners from the King and the Lord Privy Seal, with directions from his Lordship to find all things under the true worth, and upon oath of jurors, as well as freeholders, as customary tenants; which course being held by them, are notwithstanding surveyed and returned at £38,554 15s. Out of which, for Sir Robert Dudley's contempt, there is to be deducted £10,000, and for the Lady Dudley's jointure, which is without impeachment of waste, whereby she may fell all the woods, which by the survey amount unto £11,722.

PORCH OR ENTRANCE TO THE GATE HOUSE.

CHIMNEY PIECE REMOVED TO THE GATE HOUSE.
(See *Appendix*, p. 343.)

The total of the survey ariseth as followeth.—In land		. £16,431	9	0
,, ,, ,, In woods		. 11,722	2	0
,, ,, ,, The castle		. 10,401	4	0

"His Majesty hath herein the mean profits of the Castle and premises, through Sir Robert Dudley's contempt during his life, or his Majesty's pardon; the reversion in fee being the Lord Privy Seal."[1] An original copy of the survey of Kenilworth Castle is preserved among the Cottonian MSS. in the British Museum.[2]

"Such was Kenilworth at its height of magnificence; the next notice is of its decline and overthrow, and almost ever since that time it has been," as Bishop Hurd remarks, "void and tenantless ruins; clasped with the ivy, open to wind and weather, and presenting nothing but the ribs and carcase, as it were, of their former state. When Oliver Cromwell portioned out this manor to his officers, it is related that they 'demolished the Castle, drained the great pool, cut down the King's woods, destroyed his parks and chase, and divided the lands into farms among themselves." This was the complete overthrow of that magnificent castle, and succeeding writers have had only to record how time and the storms of heaven have continued to cast down stone after stone of the interesting ruins. In 1716, the excellent Dr. Richard Hurd, afterwards Bishop of Worcester, visited Kenilworth Castle, and he has given a beautiful account of its state at that time, in the third of his 'Moral and Political Dialogues.' "When they alighted from the coach," says he, "the first object that presented itself was the principal gateway of the Castle. It had been converted into a farmhouse, and was indeed the only part of these ruins that was inhabited. On their entrance to the inner court they were struck with the sight of many mouldering towers, which preserved a sort of magnificence even in their ruins. They amused themselves with observing the vast compass of the whole, with marking the uses and tracing the dimensions of the several parts. All which it was easy for them to do by the very distinct traces that remained of them; and especially by means

---

[1] Dugdale's 'Warwickshire,' vol. i, p. 251.   [2] Vespas. F. ix, 302.

of Dugdale's plans and descriptions, which they had taken care to consult. After rambling about for some time they clambered up a heap of ruins which lay on the west side of the court; and thence came to a broken tower, which, when they had mounted some steps, led them to a pathway on the tops of the walls. From this eminence they had a very distinct view of the several parts they had before contemplated; of the gardens on the north side; of the winding meadow that encompassed the walls of the castle, on the west and south; and had, besides, the command of the country round about them for many miles. There was something so august in the mingled prospect of so many antique towers falling into rubbish, and in the various beauties of the landscape, that they were, all of them, as it were, suspended in admiration, and continued silent for some time.[1]

"Here then is the last state of that celebrated castle, in which the most splendid scenes of Elizabeth's most splendid reign were performed; like the great and magnificent cities of Babylon and Jerusalem, its goodliness is turned into ruins, and the beauty of it is exchanged for desolation. The flapping banners, rich with embroidered blazonings, and the gorgeous cloths of tissue and tapestry, which once covered the chambers, have all been rent from their places; and instead of them there is the ivy, and the long grass, the rush, the dock, and the 'hyssop that springeth out of the wall.' For the minstrel's music there are now the shrieks of the owl; and, for the court and presence of royalty, there are now silence and mournful solitude. One would have felt proud of the fall of Kenilworth had the walls been razed to the ground in battle; but to think that it was first dilapidated by the lawless bands of our own ancestors, and then left to the most cruel decay; it is like viewing a dear friend perishing, piecemeal, by consumption; and the feelings thus excited are the finest, though the most distressing which the heart can endure."[2]

[1] 'Moral and Political Dialogues,' 1759, 8vo.
[2] 'Glossarial Notes to Gascoigne's Princely Pleasures of Kenilworth,' 12mo, 1821.

KENILWORTH.

Sir Walter Scott, in his interesting historical romance of Kenilworth, says of this princely castle,—

"Upon improving which, and the domains around, the Earl of Leicester had, it is said, expended sixty thousand pounds sterling, a sum equal to half a million of our present money.

"The outer wall of this splendid and gigantic structure enclosed seven acres, a part of which was occupied by extensive stables, and by a pleasure garden with its trim arbours and parterres, and the rest formed the large base-court, or outer yard, of the noble castle. The lordly structure itself, which rose near the centre of this spacious enclosure, was composed of a huge pile of magnificent castellated buildings, apparently of different ages, surrounding an inner court, and bearing in the names attached to each portion of the magnificent mass, and in the armorial bearings which were there emblazoned, the emblems of mighty chiefs who had long passed away, and whose history, could ambition have lent an ear to it, might have read a lesson to the haughty favorite who had now acquired, and was augmenting the fair domain. A large and massive keep, which formed the citadel of the castle, was of uncertain though great antiquity. It bore the name of Cæsar, perhaps from its resemblance to that in the Tower of London so called. Some antiquaries ascribed its foundation to the time of Kenelph, from whom the castle had its name, a Saxon King of Mercia, and others to an early era after the Norman Conquest. On the exterior walls frowned the scutcheon of the Clintons, by whom they were founded in the reign of Henry I., and of the yet more redoubted Simon de Montfort, by whom, during the Baron's wars, Kenilworth was long held out against Henry III. Here, Mortimer, Earl of March, famous alike for his rise and his fall, had once gaily revelled, while his dethroned Sovereign, Edward II., languished in its dungeons. Old John of Gaunt, 'time-honoured Lancaster,' had widely extended the castle, erecting that 'noble and massive pile which yet bears the name of Lancaster's Buildings;' and Leicester himself had outdone the former possessors, princely and powerful as they were, by erecting another immense structure, which now lies crushed under its own ruins, the monument of its owner's ambition. The external wall of this royal castle was, on the south and west sides, adorned and defended by a lake partly artificial, across which Leicester had constructed a stately bridge, that Elizabeth might enter the castle by a path hitherto untrodden, instead of the usual entrance to the northward; over which he had erected a gate-house or barbican, which still exists, and is equal in extent, and superior in architecture, to the baronial castle of many a northern chief.

"Beyond the lake lay an extensive chase, full of red deer, fallow deer, roes, and every species of game, and abounding with lofty trees, from amongst which the extended front and massive towers of the castle were seen to rise in majesty and beauty. We cannot but add, that of this lordly palace, where princes feasted and heroes fought, now in the bloody earnest of storm and siege, and now in the games of chivalry, where beauty dealt the prize which valour won, all is now desolate. The bed of the lake is but a rushy swamp; and the massive ruins of the castle only serve to show what their splendour once was, and to impress on the musing visitor the transitory value of human possessions and the happiness of those who enjoy a humble lot in virtuous contentment."

"Laneham's account of the Queen's entertainment at Killingworth Castle, in 1575—a very diverting tract, written by as great a coxcomb as ever blotted paper. The original is extremely rare, but it has been twice reprinted; once in Mr. Nichols's very curious and interesting collection of the Progresses and Public Processions of Queen Elizabeth: and more lately in a work termed 'Kenilworth Illustrated,' beautifully printed at Chiswick." [1]

[1] It has since been published in a separate form in a small duodecimo volume, Lond., 1821, from a copy of which, formerly in the possession of Sir Harris Nicolas, is printed the full account in the present work.

ROBERT LANEHAM.

"Robert Laneham was born in the County of Nottingham, and was educated at St. Paul's School, and afterwards at that of St. Anthony, near the Royal Exchange, which, according to Stow, bore the highest "reputation in the City in former times." His father seems to have moved in a moderate, if not in a very inferior rank of life; for towards the conclusion of his letter he states that it was a great relief to his parent when the Earl of Leicester received him into favour and protection. Laneham appears to have held some situation in the Royal stables, where also his father was placed after his own advancement in the Court. In addition to this situation Laneham procured a patent, or license as it was then called, for serving the Royal Mews with beans, which, however, he neglected when promoted to the office of Clerk of the Council-Chamber door. It is to this office that he alludes in the commencement of his letter, when he says that he had the power, on such days as the Council did not sit, to visit whatever he thought proper to see, as well as the privilege of being present at any exhibition which should be prepared for the Queen. Hence it would appear that Laneham's duty was not confined to keeping the entrance of the Council-Room only, but that he also performed the office of a Gentleman-Usher, in preserving the Presence-Chamber, wherever that might be, free from the intrusion of strangers. It is evidently with this feeling that the author of 'Kenilworth' makes Laneham say to his patron Leicester, when requesting that he may visit the Castle in the Queen's suite, "Bethink you, my Lord, how necessary is this rod of mine to fright away all those listeners, who would else play at bo-peep with the honorable Council, and be searching for keyholes and crannies in the door of the Chamber, so as to render my staff as needful as a fly-trap in a butcher's shop."[1]
"It is not easy to imagine what the lordly and ambitious

[1] Kenilworth, by Sir Walter Scott.

Dudley could have discovered in the conceited and talkative Laneham to have induced him to become so excellent a patron; but the reasons might probably be the boldness of the latter, joined to his knowledge of several foreign languages, which rendered him peculiarly fitted for the duties of a Gentleman-Usher, who could, with official importance, keep order in the Court, and converse in their own tongues with any of the numerous foreigners who visited it. Nor is this supposition founded upon speculation only, for towards the conclusion of this letter Laneham expresses himself in terms like the following: "Now, Sir, when the Council sits, I am at hand, and attend them closely, I warrant you; if any should talk, then I say, 'Peace; know you where you are?' If I see one listening either at the aperture in the door, or between the spaces of it, then presently I am upon him for his rudeness."

"Such are some of the particulars extant concerning Laneham; and it is evident that these were in the mind of the author of 'Kenilworth,' when he wrote the admirable description of Laneham waiting in the ante-room at Greenwich Palace, where he even notices the convivial habits of that singular character, which gave a flushed and rosy tint to his face. This information was first given by Laneham himself in the ensuing letter, and in the following terms:—'But in faith it is not so; for sipped I no more sack and sugar than I do malmsey, I should not blush so much now-a-days as I do.' Having now so long dilated upon Laneham's life, and the duties of his station, it will not be uninteresting to extract his portrait from the romance of 'Kenilworth' itself; it may well be regarded as an authentic likeness, and nothing can more properly conclude these memoranda concerning him. 'Then the earl was approached with several fantastic *congées*, by a person quaintly dressed in a doublet of black velvet, curiously slashed and pinked with crimson satin. A long cock's feather in the velvet bonnet, which he held in his hand, and an enormous ruff, stiffened to the extremity of the absurd taste of the times, joined with a sharp, lively, conceited expression of countenance seemed to body forth a vain, hairbrained coxcomb, and small wit; while the rod he held, and an assumption of formal authority, appeared to express some sense of official consequence, which qualified the natural pertness of his manner. A perpetual blush which occupied rather the sharp nose than the thin cheek of the personage, seemed to speak more of ' good life,' as it was called, than of modesty."[1]

Queen Elizabeth visited Warwick, 12th August, 1572. On her way she dined at "Ichington, or Long Ichington," two miles from Warwick, which "belonged to Robert, Earl of Leicester, who on Saturday 9th July, 1575, gave Queen Elizabeth a glorious entertainment here, on her passage to Kenilworth Castle, erecting a tent of extraordinary largeness for that purpose ; the piers belonging whereto amounted to seven cart-loads, by which the magnificence thereof may be guessed at."[2]

"While on her visit here, she went to Kenilworth, and stayed from the Wednesday till Saturday; again on the Monday, and on the following Monday, staying till Saturday. While at Warwick, she stayed at the castle."[3]

The following is a particular account of the entertainment given to Queen Elizabeth at Kenilworth, in 1575, written by Robert Laneham, who was an eye-witness of the festivities.

[1] From Laneham's Kenilworth Castle in 1575. 12mo, 1821.
[2] Dugdale's ' Warwickshire,' p. 345.
[3] Black Book, printed in ' Nichols's Biblio. Topog. Brittanica.

A LETTER:

Whearin part of the Entertainment unto the Queen's Majesty at Killingworth[1] Castl in Warwiksheer in this Somers Progress—1575 is signified: from a freend officer attendant in the Court unto his freend a Citizen and Merchaunt of London.

DE REGINA NOSTRA ILLUSTRISSIMA.

Dum laniata ruāt vicina ob Regna tumultus,
Læta suos inter genialibus ILLA diebus
(Gratia Diis) fruitur: Rūpantur & ilia Codro.[2]

WITH EXPLANATORY NOTES.

---

[1] Killingworth, a corruption of Kenilworth, frequently so used and spelt at and after that period.
[2] Reprinted from the edition of 1821. 12mo, London.

LANEHAM'S LETTER.

"UNTO MY GOOD FRIEND,

"MASTER HUMPHREY MARTIN, MERCER,

"AFTER my hearty commendations, I commend me heartily to you. Understand ye, that since, through God and good friends, I am here placed at Court, as you know, in a worshipful room, whereby I am not only acquainted with the most, and well known to the best, and every officer glad of my company; but also at present have power, while the Council sits not, to go and to see things sight-worthy; and to be present at any show or spectacle, any where this progress represented unto her Highness: of part of which sports, having taken some notes and observations—for I cannot be idle at any rate in the world—as well to put from me suspicion of sluggishness, as to take from you any doubt of my forgetfulness of your friendship; I have thought it meet to impart them unto you, as frankly, as friendly, and as fully, as I can. You know well, the Black Prince was never stained with disloyalty of ingratitude towards any; I dare be his warrant he will not begin with you, that hath at his hand so deeply deserved. But herein, the better for conceiving of my mind, and instruction of your's, you must give me leave a little, as well to preface my matter, as to discourse somewhat of Killingworth Castle, a territory of the right honorable, my singular good Lord, my Lord the Earl of Leicester; of whose incomparable cheer and entertainment there unto her Majesty, I will show you a part, here, that could not see all; nor, had I seen all, could well report the half. Where things for the persons, place, time, cost, devices, strangeness and abundance, of all that ever I saw (and yet have I been, what under my *Master Bomsted*, and what on my own affairs, while I occupied merchandise, both in France and

Flanders long and many a day), I saw none any where so memorable, I tell you plain.

"The Castle hath the name of Killingworth, but of truth, grounded upon faithful story, Kenilworth. It stands in Warwickshire, seventy-four miles north-west from London, and as it were in the centre of England; four miles somewhat south from Coventry, a proper City; and a like distance from Warwick, a fair County-town on the north. Of air sweet and wholesome, raised on an easily mounted hill, it is set evenly coasted with the front strait to the east, and hath the tenants and town about it, that pleasantly shift from dale to hill sundry where, with sweet springs bursting forth; and is so plentifully well sorted on every side into arable, mead, pasture, wood, water, and good air, as it appears to have need of nothing that may pertain to living or pleasure. To advantage, it hath, hard on the west, still nourished with many lively springs, a goodly pool of rare beauty, breadth, length, depth, and store of all kinds of fresh-water fish, delicate, great, and fat; and also of wild fowl beside. By a rare situation and natural agreement, this pool seems conjoined to the Castle, that on the west lays the head, as it were, upon the Castle's bosom, embraceth it on either side, south and north, with both the arms, and settles itself as in a reach a flight-shoot broad, stretching forth body and legs a mile or two westward: between a fair park on the one side, which by the brays[1] is linked to the Castle on the south, sprinkled at the entrance with a few conies, that for colour and smallness of number seem to be suffered more for pleasure than commodity: And on the other side, north and west, a goodly chase; vast, wide, large, and full of red-deer and other stately game for hunting: Beautified with many delectable, fresh, and shaded bowers, arbours, seats, and walks, that with great art, cost, and diligence were very pleasantly appointed: Which also the natural grace, by the tall and fresh fragrant trees and soil, did so far forth commend, as *Diana* herself might have deigned there well enough to range for her pastime.

"The left arm of this pool, northward, hath my Lord adorned with a beautiful bracelet of a fair timbered bridge, that is of

[1] "The park at Kenilworth was separated from the Castle on the south side by a part of the pool, but was, as the text states, connected as it were with the building by the sloping banks next the water. The word Bra, Brae, or Bray, in the northern counties and Scotland is used for the acclivity of a hill, and the brink or bank of a river.—*Vide* Grose and Jamieson.

fourteen feet wide and six hundred feet long; railed on both sides, strongly planked for passage, reaching from the chase to the Castle. That thus in the midst it hath clear prospect over these pleasures on the back part; and forward over all the town, and much of the country beside.

"Here, too, is a special commodity at hand of sundry quarries of large building stone, the goodness whereof may the more easily be judged, in the building and ancient stateliness of the Castle, that (as by the name and histories well may be gathered) was first reared by *Kenulph*, and his young son *Kenelm*, born both indeed within the realm here, but yet of the race of Saxons; and reigned Kings of Marchland from the year of our Lord 798, for 23 years together, above 770 years ago; although the Castle hath one ancient, strong, and large keep, that is called Cæsar's Tower, rather, as I have good cause to think, for that it is square and high, formed after the manner of Cæsar's Forts, than that ever he built it. Nay, now that I am a little in, *Master Martin*, I will tell you all.

"This Marchland, that stories call *Mercia*, is numbered in their books the fourth of the seven kingdoms that the Saxons had whilom here divided among them in the realm. It began in Anno Dom. 616, one hundred and thirty-nine years after Horsa and Hengist; continued in the race of 17 kings, 249 years together, and ended in Anno 875, raised from the rest (says the book) at first by Penda's presumption,[1] overthrown at last by Buthred's hascardy,[2] and so fell to the kingdom of the West-Saxons. Marchland had in it London, Middlesex, herein a bishopric: had more of shires, Gloucester, Worcester, and Warwick, and herein a bishopric; Chester (that now we call Cheshire), Derby, and Stafford, whereunto one bishop that had also part of Warwick and Shrewsbury, and his See at Coventry that was then aforetime at Lichfield: Hereto Hereford, wherein a bishopric that had more to jurisdiction, half Shrewsbury, part of Warwick

[1] "In the year 642, Penda, king of Mercia, invaded the dominions of Oswald, king of Northumberland; who was slain after a fierce battle at Maserfield. Burthred or Buthred, who is mentioned in the context, was the last King of Mercia; whose kingdom was invaded in 874, by the West-Saxons, under Alfred. Thus overpowered, he fled to Rome, where he died.

[2] "The latter of these words signifies a dispersion or scattering, the cause of which has been related in the preceding note. Hascardy is derived from the Saxon Ἀρcaƀıan, which is of the same interpretation.—*Vide* Somner.

and also of *Gloucester*, and the See at Hereford: Also had Oxford, Buckingham, Hertford, Huntingdon, and half of Bedford; and to these Northampton, part of Leicester, and also Lincoln, whereunto a bishop; whose See at Lincoln City that sometime before was at Dorchester: hereto the rest of Leicester and in Nottingham, that of old had a special bishop, whose See was at Leicester, but afterwards put to the charge of the Archbishop of York.

"Now touching the name, that of old records I understand, and of ancient writers I find, is called Kenilworth; since most of the Worths in England stand nigh unto like lakes, and are either small islands, such one as the seat of this Castle hath been and easily may be, or is land-ground by pool or river, whereon willows, alders, or such like do grow: Which *Althamerus*[1] writes precisely that the Germans call 𝔚𝔢𝔯𝔡: joining these two together with the nighness also of the words and sybred[2] of the tongues. I am the bolder to pronounce, that as our English Worth, with the rest of our ancient language, was left us from the Germans, even so that their Werd and our Worth is all one thing in signification, common to us both even at this day. I take the case so clear, that I say not so much as I might. Thus proface ye with the preface ;[3] and now to the matter.

"On Saturday the ninth of July, at Long Ichington, a town and lordship of my Lord's, within seven miles of Killingworth, his Honour made her Majesty great cheer at dinner, and pleasant pastime in hunting by the way after, that it was eight o'clock in the evening ere her Highness came to Killingworth; where in the park, about a flight-shoot from the brays and first gate of the Castle, one of the ten Sibyls, that we read were all *Fatidicæ* and *Theobulæ*, as parties and privy to the Gods' gracious good wills, comely clad in a pall of white silk,[4] pronounced a proper poesy in

[1] "Andrew Althamer, a Lutheran minister of Nuremberg, who lived about 1560. The termination Worth, which is mentioned in the text to signify land situate by water, is more properly derived from the Saxon þorð, a court or farm; and hence the place was originally denominated Kenelm's Worth, or the Court of Kenelm.

[2] "A word signifying kindred, from the Saxon Sib-řeben—Consanguinity. —*Vide* Lye.

[3] Proface. An exclamation equivalent to "much good may it do you."— *Halliwell*.

[4] "A long and large upper mantle was denominated a pall, from the Latin *pallium*, or *palla*, a cloak. The great mantle worn by the Knights of the Garter, is by ancient writers called *pallium*.

English rhyme and metre: of effect, how great gladness her goodness' presence[1] brought into every stead[2] where it pleased her to come, and especially now into that place that had so long longed after the same; ending with prophecy certain of much and long prosperity, health, and felicity. This her Majesty benignly accepting, passed forth unto the next gate of the brays, which for the length, largeness and use, (as well it may so serve) they call now the tilt-yard, where a porter, tall of person, big of limb, and stern of countenance, wrapped also all in silk, with a club and keys of quantity according, had a rough speech full of passions, in metre aptly made to the purpose: Whereby (as her Highness was come within his ward,) he burst out in a great pang of impatience to see such uncouth trudging to and fro, such riding in and out, with such din and noise of talk within the charge of his office, whereof he never saw the like, nor had any warning afore, nor yet could make to himself any cause of the matter. At last, upon better view and avisement, as he pressed to come nearer, confessing anon that he found himself pierced at the presence of a personage so evidently expressing an heroical sovereignty over all the whole estates, and by degrees there beside, calmed his astonishment, proclaims open gates and free passage to all, yields up his club, his keys, his office and all, and on his knees humbly prays pardon of his ignorance and impatience; which her Highness graciously granting, he caused his trumpeters that stood upon the wall of the gate there, to sound up a tune of welcome; which, beside the noble noise, was so much the more pleasant to behold, because these trumpeters, being six in number, were every one eight feet high, in due proportion of person beside, all in long garments of silk suitable, each with his silvery trumpet of five feet long, formed taper-wise and straight from the upper part unto the lower end, where the diameter was 16 inches over; and yet so tempered by art, that being very easy to the blast, they cast forth no greater noise, nor a more unpleasant sound for time and tune, than any other common trumpet, be it never so artificially formed. These harmonious blasters, from the foreside of the gate, at her Highness' entrance, where they began: walking upon the walls unto the inner [court], had this music maintained from them very de-

---

[1] Another early copy reads "gracious presence."
[2] "That is to say, every where, or into every place; the word stead is from the Saxon Stede, a room or place.—*Vide* Somner.

lectably, while her Highness all along this tilt-yard rode unto the inner gate, next the base-court of the Castle, where the Lady of the Lake, (famous in King Arthur's book) with two nymphs waiting upon her, arrayed all in silks, awaited her Highness's coming: From the midst of the pool, where upon a movable island, bright blazing with torches, she floated to land, and met her Majesty with a well-penned metre and matter after this sort: [viz.] First, of the ancestry of the Castle, who had been owners of the same e'en till this day, most always in the hands of the Earls of Leicester; how she had kept this Lake since King Arthur's days; and now, understanding of her Highness's hither coming, thought it both her office and duty in humble wise to discover her and her estate: offering up the same, her lake, and power therein, with promise of repair unto the Court. It pleased her Highness to thank this lady, and to add withall: 'We had thought indeed the Lake had been ours, and do you call it yours now? Well, we will herein commune more with you hereafter.'

"This pageant was closed up with a delectable harmony of hautboys, shalms,[1] cornets, and such other loud music, that held on while her Majesty pleasantly so passed from thence toward the Castle-gate; whereunto, from the base-court, over a dry valley cast into a good form, there was framed a fair bridge of twenty feet wide, and seventy feet long, gravelled for treading, railed on either part with seven posts on a side, that stood twelve feet asunder, thickened between with well-proportioned turned pillars.

"Upon the first pair of posts were set two comely square wire cages, three feet long, and two feet wide; and high in them live bitterns, curlews, shovelers, hernshaws, godwits, and such like dainty birds, of the presents of *Sylvanus*, the God of fowl. On the second pair two great silvered bowls, featly apted to the purpose, filled with apples, pears, cherries, filberds, walnuts, fresh upon their branches, and with oranges, pomegranates, lemons, and pippins, all for the gifts of *Pomona*, Goddess of fruits. The third pair of posts, in two such silvered bowls, had (all in ears green and old) wheat, barley, oats, beans, and peas, as the gifts of *Ceres*. The fourth post, on the left hand, in a like silvered bowl, had grapes in clusters, white and red, gracified with their vine leaves: The match post against it had a pair of great white

[1] "The word shalm or shawm is derived from the German gehalme, a musical instrument; it however strictly signifies a psaltery or species of harp.

silver livery pots for wine: and before them two glasses of good capacity, filled full; the one with white wine, the other with claret, so fresh of colour, and of look so lovely, smiling to the eye of many, that by my faith methought, by their leering, they could have found in their hearts, (as the evening was hot,) to have kissed them sweetly and thought it no sin: And these were the potencial presents of *Bacchus*, the God of wine. The fifth pair had each a fair large tray, strewed with fresh grass;[1] and in them conger, burt, mullet, fresh herrings, oysters, salmon, crevis, and such like, from *Neptunus*, God of the sea. On the sixth pair of posts were set two ragged staves of silver, as my Lord gives them in his arms, beautifully glittering of armour, thereupon depending bows, arrows, spears, shield, head-piece, gorget, corslets, swords, targets, and such like, for *Mar's* gifts, the God of war. And the aptlier (methought) was it that those ragged staves supported these martial presents, as well because these staves by their tines seem naturally meet for the bearing of armour, as also that they chiefly in this place might take upon them the principal protection of her highness's person, that so benignly pleased her to take harbour. On the seventh posts, the last and next to the Castle, were there pight[2] two fair bay branches of four feet high, adorned on all sides with lutes, viols, shalms, cornets, flutes, recorders,[3] and harps, as the presents of *Phœbus*, the God of music, for rejoicing the mind, and also of physic, for health to the body.

"Over the Castle-gate was there fastened a table beautifully garnished above with her Highness's arms, and featly, with ivy wreaths bordered about, of ten feet square: the ground black, whereupon, in large white capital Roman fairly written, was a poem mentioning these Gods and their gifts, thus presented unto her Highness: which, because it remained unremoved, at leisure and pleasure I took it out, as followeth:—

[1] In another early copy " strewed a little with fresh grass."

[2] "This word is the ancient preterite and participle past of the verb *to pitch*. It signifies, generally, any thing placed, fixed, pitched, or determined. *Vide* Bailey.

[3] "These were wind-instruments somewhat resembling flutes, or rather clarionets.

"AD MAJESTATEM REGIAM.

"*Jupiter* hnc certos cernens te tendere gressus,
Cælicolas PRINCEPS actutum convocat Omnes:
Obsequium præstare jubet TIBI quenque benignum.
Unde suas Sylvanus Aves, Pomonaque fructus,
Alma Ceres fruges, hilarantia vina Liæus,
Neptunus pisces, tela et tutantia *Mavors*,
Suave Melos *Phœbus*, solidamq; longamq; salutem.
Dii TIBI REGINA hæc (cum sis DIGNISSIMA) præbent:
Hoc TIBI, cum Domino, dedit se et werda KENELMI.

"All the letters that mention her Majesty, which are here put in capitals, for reverence and honour, were there made in gold.

"But the night well spent, for that these verses by torch-light could easily be read; a poet, therefore, in a long ceruleous[1] garment, with side [i. e. long] and wide sleeves, Venetian-wise drawn up to his elbow, his doublet sleeves under that, of crimson, nothing but silk; a bay garland on his head, and a scroll in his hand, making first an humble obeisance at her Highness's coming, and pointing unto every present as he spake, the same were pronounced. Thus viewing the gifts, as she passed, and how the posts might agree with the speech of the poet: At the end of the bridge and entry of the gate, was her Highness received with a fresh delicate harmony of flutes, in performance of *Phœbus*' presents.

"So passing into the inner court, her Majesty (that never rides but alone) there, set down from her palfrey, was conveyed up to her chamber: When after did follow so great a peal of guns, and such lightening by fire-work a long space together, as though *Jupiter* would have shown himself to be no further behind with his welcome than the rest of his Gods: and that he would have all the country to know, for indeed the noise and flame were heard and seen twenty miles off. Thus much, *Master Martin*, (that I remember me) for the first day's *bien venu*. Be you not weary, for I am scant in the midst of my matter.

"On Sunday, the forenoon occupied as for the Sabbath-day, in quiet and vacation from work, and in divine service and preaching at the parish church: the afternoon in excellent music of sundry

---

[1] "Azure-blue, or sky-colour, from the Latin *ceruleus*. Anciently, blue dresses were worn by all servants. *Vide* Strutt.

sweet instruments, and in dancing of Lords and Ladies, and other worshipful degrees, uttered with such lively agility, and commendable grace, as whether it might be more strange to the eye, or pleasant to the mind, for my part indeed I could not discern; but it was exceedingly well, methought, in both.

"At night late, as though *Jupiter* the last night had forgot for business, or forborne for courtesy and quiet, part of his welcome unto her Highness appointed, now entering at the first into his purpose moderately (as mortals do) with a warning piece or two, proceeding on with increase, till at last the *Altitonant* [i. e. High Thunderer,] displays me his main power; with blaze of burning darts flying to and fro, leams of stars coruscant, streams and hail of fiery sparks, lightnings of wildfire on water and land, flight and shooting of thunderbolts, all with such continuance, terror, and vehemency, that the heavens thundered, the waters surged, the earth shook, and in such sort surely, as had we not been assured that the fulminant Diety was all hot in amity, and could not otherwise testify his welcome unto her Highness, it would have made me for my part, as hardy as I am, very vengeably afraid. This ado lasted until the midnight was passed, that it seemed well with me soon after, when I found me in my cabin. And this for the second day.

"*Monday* was hot, and therefore her Highness kept in till five o'clock in the evening; what time it pleased her to ride forth into the chase to hunt the hart of force: which found anon, and after sore chased, and chafed by the hot pursuit of the hounds, was fain of fine force, at last to take soil.[1] There to behold the swift fleeting of the deer afore with the stately carriage of his head in his swimming, spread (for the quantity) like the sail of a ship; the hounds harrowing after as they had been a number of skiffs to the spoil of a Carvell:[2] the one no less eager in the purchase of his prey, than was the other earnest in safeguard of his life: so as the yearning of the hounds[3] in continuance of their cry, the

---

[1] "A term used in hunting, when a deer runs into the water. *Vide* Phillips.

[2] "A Carvel, or Caravel, was a species of light round vessel, with a square stern, rigged and fitted out like a galley, and of about 140 tons burthen. Such ships were formerly much used by the Portuguese, and were esteemed the best sailers on the seas. *Vide* Phillips.

[3] "A hunting expression, used to signify the barking of beagles at their prey. *Vide* Bailey.

swiftness of the deer, the running of footmen, the galloping of horses, the blasting of horns, the hallooing and shouting of the huntsmen, with the excellent echoes between whiles from the woods and waters in valleys resounding; moved pastime delectable in so high a degree as for any person to take pleasure by most senses at once: in mine opinion, there can be none in any way comparable to this: and 'specially in this place, that of nature is formed so fit for the purpose; in faith, *Master Martin*, if ye could with a wish, I would you had been at it: Well, the hart was killed, a goodly deer, but so ceased not the game yet.

"For about nine o'clock, at the hither part of the chase, where torch light attended, out of the woods, in her Majesty's return, there came roughly forth *Hombre Salvagio* [i. e. a Savage Man,] with an oaken plant plucked up by the roots in his hand, himself foregrown all in moss and ivy; who, for personage, gesture, and utterance beside, countenanced the matter to very good liking; and had speech to this effect:—That continuing so long in these wild wastes, wherein oft had he fared both far and near, yet happed he never to see so glorious an assembly before: and now cast into great grief of mind, for that neither by himself could he guess, nor knew where else to be taught, what they should be, or who bare estate. Reports, some had he heard of many strange things, but broiled thereby so much the more in desire of knowledge. Thus, in great pangs, bethought he, and called he upon all his familiars and companions, the fawns, the satyrs, the nymphs, the dryades, and the hamadryades; but none making answer, whereby his care the more increasing, in utter grief and extreme refuge, called he aloud at last after his old friend *Echo*, that he wist would hide nothing from him, but tell him all, if she were here. ' Here ' (quoth *Echo*). ' Here, *Echo*, and art thou there ?' (says he) ' Ah ! how much hast thou relieved my careful spirits with thy courtesy onward. Ay me, good *Echo*, here is a marvellous presence of dignity ; what are they, I pray thee, who is Sovereign, tell me, I beseech thee, or else how might I know ?' ' I know,' (quoth she.) ' Knowest thou ?' says he ; ' marry, that is exceedingly well : Why, then, I desire thee, heartily show me what majesty, (for no mean degree is it) have we here : a King, or a Queen ?' ' A Queen !' (quoth *Echo*.) ' A Queen !' says he, pausing, and wisely viewing awhile, ' now full certainly seems thy tale to be true.' And proceeding by this manner of dialogue, with an earnest beholding her Highness awhile, recounts he, first, how justly that former reports agree with his present sight, touching the beautiful lineaments of countenance, the comely proportion of body, the princely grace of presence, the gracious gifts of nature, with the rare and singular qualities of both body and mind in her Majesty conjoined, and so apparent at eye. Then shortly rehearsing Saturday's acts, of *Sibyl's* salutation ; of the Porter's proposition ; of his Trumpeter's music ; of the Lake Lady's oration, and of the seven Gods' seven presents, he reported the incredible joy that all estates in the land have always of her Highness wheresoever she came ; ending with presage and prayer of perpetual felicity, and with humble subjection of him and his, and all that they may do. After this sort the matter went, with little difference, I guess, saving only in this point, that the thing which I here report in unpolished prose, was there pronounced in good metre and matter, very well endited in rhyme. *Echo* finely framed, most aptly, by answers thus to utter all. And I shall tell you, *Master Martin*, by the mass, of a mad adventure—As this Savage, for the more submission, broke his tree asunder, and cast the top from him, it had almost light upon her Highness's horse's head ; whereat he startled, and the gentleman much dismayed. See the benignity of the prince : as the footmen looked well to the horse, and he of generosity soon calmed of himself—— 'No hurt, No hurt,' quoth her Highness. Which words, I promise you, we were all glad to hear, and took them to be the best part of the play.

" *Tuesday*, pleasant passing of the time with music and dancing ; saving that toward night it liked her Majesty to walk afoot into the chase over the bridge, where it pleased her to stand : while upon the pool out of a barge, finely appointed for the purpose, to hear sundry kinds of very delectable music : thus recreated, and after some walk, her Highness returned.

" *Wednesday*, Her Majesty rode into the chase a hunting again of the hart of force. The deer, after his property, for refuge took the soil : but so mastered by hot pursuit on all parts, that he was taken quick in the pool : The watermen held him up hard by the head, while at her Highness's commandment, he lost his ears for a ransom, and so had pardon for life.

" *Thursday*, the fourteenth of this July, and the sixth day of her Majesty's coming, a great sort of Ban-dogs[1] were there tied in the

[1] "Bewick describes the Ban-dog as being a variety of the mastiff, but lighter, smaller, and more vigilant ; although at the same time not so power-

outer court, and thirteen bears in the inner. Whosoever made the pannel, there were enough for a quest, and one for challenge an need were. A wight of great wisdom and gravity seemed their foreman to be, had it come to a jury; but it fell out that they were caused to appear there upon no such matter, but only to answer to an ancient quarrel between them and the Ban-dogs, in a cause of controversy that had long depended, been obstinately full often debated, with sharp and biting arguments on both sides, and could never be decided: grown now to so marvellous a malice, that with spiteful upbraidings and uncharitable chaffings, always they fret, as any where the one can hear, see, or smell the other: and indeed at utter deadly feud. Many a maimed member, (God wot) bloody face, and a torn coat, hath the quarrel cost between them; so far likely the less yet now to be appeased, as there wants not partakers to back them on both sides.

"Well, Sir, the bears were brought forth into the court, the dogs set to them to argue the points even face to face; they had learned counsel also on both parts: what, may they be counted partial that are retainers but to a side? I ween no. Very fierce both the one and the other, and eager in argument: if the dog in pleading should pluck the bear by the throat, the bear with traverse would claw him again by the scalp: Confess an he list, but avoid he could not, that was bound to the bar; and his counsel told him that it could be to him no policy in pleading. Therefore thus with 'fending and proving, with plucking and tugging, scratching and biting, by plain tooth and nail on one side and the other, such expense of blood and leather was there between them, as a month's licking, I ween, will not recover; and yet remain as far out as ever they were.

"It was a sport very pleasant of these beasts; to see the bear with his pink eyes leering after his enemies approach, the nimbleness and wait of the dog, to take his advantage, and the force and experience of the bear again to avoid the assault: If he was bitten in one place, how he would pinch in another to get free; that if he was taken once, then what shift, with biting, with clawing, with roaring, tossing and tumbling, he would work to wind him-

ful. The nose is also less, and possesses somewhat of the hound's scent; the hair is rough, and of a yellowish grey colour, marked with shades of black. The bite of a Ban-dog is keen, and considered dangerous; and its attack is usually made upon the flank. Dogs of this kind are now rarely to be met with.

self from them; and when he was loose, to shake his ears twice or thrice with the blood and the slaver about his physiognomy, was a matter of a goodly relief.[1]

"As this sport was held at day-time, in the Castle, so was there abroad at night very strange and sundry kinds of fire-works, compelled by cunning to fly to and fro, and to mount very high into the air upward, and also to burn unquenchably beneath the water, contrary, ye wot, to fire's kind: This intermingled with a great peal of guns, which all gave both to the ear and to the eye the greater grace and delight, for that with such order and art they were tempered, touching time and continuance, that was about two hours space.

"Now, within also, in the mean time, was there showed before her Highness, by an Italian, such feats of agility, in goings, turnings, tumblings, castings, hops, jumps, leaps, skips, springs, gambols, summersets, caperings, and flights; forward, backward, sideways, downward, and upward, with sundry windings, gyrings[2] and circumflexions; all so lightly and with such easiness, as by me, in few words, it is not expressible by pen or speech, I tell you plainly. I blessed me, by my faith, to behold him; and began to doubt whether it was a man or a spirit; and I ween had doubted me till this day, had it not been that anon I bethought me of men that can reason and talk with two tongues, and with two persons at once, sing like birds, courteous of behaviour, of body strong, and in joints so nimble withal, that their bones seemed as lythie and pliant as sinews. They dwell in a happy island (as the book terms it,) four months sailing southward beyond Ethiopia. Nay, *Master Martin*, I tell you no jest; for both *Diodorus Siculus*, an ancient Greek historiographer, in his third book of the

---

[1] "There is a singular coincidence between Laneham's description of a bear-fight, and that given in the romance of 'Kenilworth,' where the Earl of Sussex presents a petition from Orson Pinnit, Keeper of the Royal Bears, against Shakspeare and the players. It is evident that the author of 'Kenilworth' had the passage in his mind; and as the reader may also like to compare the two passages, an extract from the romance is here inserted:—'There you may see the bear lying at guard with his red pinky eyes, watching the onset of the mastiff like a wily captain, who maintains his defence, that an assailant may be tempted to venture within his danger.' *Vide* 'Kenilworth.'

Kenilworth was visited by Queen Elizabeth in 1575. "Shakspeare and the players" did not begin to perform till (?) 1589.

[2] "An old English noun formed of the Latin *gyrus*, a circuit or compass; a career or circle.

acts of the old Egyptians ; and also from him *Conrad Gesnerus*,[1] (a great and learned man, and a very diligent writer in all good arguments of our time, but deceased ;) in the first chapter of his *Mithridates*, reporteth the same. As for this fellow, I cannot tell what to make of him, save that I may guess his back be metalled like a lamprey, that has no bone, but a line like a lute-string. Well, Sir, let him pass and his feats, and this day's pastime withal, for here is as much as I can remember me for Thursday's entertainment.

" *Friday* and *Saturday* there were no open shows abroad, because the weather inclined to some moisture and wind, that very seasonably tempered the drought and the heat, caused by the continuance of fair weather and sunshine all the while since her Majesty's thither coming.

" On *Sunday*, opportunely, the weather broke up again ; and after divine service in the parish church for the sabbath-day, and a fruitful sermon there in the forenoon: At afternoon, in worship of this Kenilworth Castle, and of God and Saint Kenelm, whose day, forsooth, by the Calendar this was, a solemn bridal of a proper couple was appointed : Set in order in the tilt-yard, to come and make their show before the Castle in the great court, where was pight a comely Quintain[2] for feats at arms, which when they had done, to march out at the north gate of the Castle homeward again into the town.

[1] "An eminent physician, naturalist, and scholar of the 16th century, who was born at Zurich in 1516. He was made Professor of Greek at Lausanne, and at Basil he took the degree of Doctor of Medicine. After having published many valuable works in Botany, Medicine, Natural History, and Philology, he died of the plague in 1565, aged forty-nine. His ' Mithridates,' mentioned in the text, is a work on the difference of tongues throughout the world.

[2] "In the Glossary to Bishop Kennet's Parochial Antiquities, it is stated that the Quintain was a customary sport at weddings. It consisted of an upright piece with a cross piece, one end of which is broad, and pierced full of holes, and to the other is appended a bag of sand, which swings round upon the slightest blow.—' The pastime was,' says Hasted, ' for the youth on horseback to run at it as fast as possible, and hit the broad part in his career with much force. He that by chance hit it not at all was treated with loud peals of derision ; and he who did hit it, made the best use of his swiftness, lest he should have a sound blow on his neck from the bag of sand, which instantly swang round from the other end of the quintain. The great design of this sport was to try the agility of the horse and man, and to break the board, which whoever did, he was accounted chief of the day's sport.'

"And thus were they marshalled. First, all the lusty lads and bold bachelors of the parish, suitably habited every wight, with his blue buckram bride-lace[1] upon a branch of green broom (because rosemary is scant there) tied on his left arm, for on that side lies the heart; and his alder pole for a spear in his right hand, in martial order ranged on afore, two and two in a rank: Some with a hat, some in a cap, some a coat, some a jerkin, some for lightness in doublet and hose, clean truss'd with points afore; Some boots and no spurs, this spurs and no boots, and he again neither one nor other: One had a saddle, another a pad or a pannel fastened with a cord, for girths were geazon:[2] And these to the number of sixteen wights, riding men and well beseen: But the bridegroom foremost in his father's tawny worsted jacket, (for his friends were fain that he should be a bride-groom before the Queen) a fair straw hat with a capital crown, steeple-wise on his head; a pair of harvest gloves on his hands, as a sign of good husbandry; a pen and ink-horn at his back, for he would be known to be bookish; lame of a leg that in his youth was broken at foot-ball; well beloved of his mother, who lent him a new muffler for a napkin, that was tied to his girdle for losing it. It was no small sport to mark this minion in his full appointment, that, through good tuition, became as formal in his action as had he been a bridegroom indeed; with this special grace by the way, that ever as he would have framed to himself the better countenance, with the worst face he looked.

"Well, Sir, after these horsemen, a lively morris-dance according to the ancient manner: six dancers, maid-marian, and the fool. Then three pretty pucelles,[3] as bright as a breast of bacon, of thirty years old a-piece; that carried three special spice-cakes of a bushel of wheat (they had by measure, out of my Lord's bakehouse) before the bride, Cicely, with set countenance and lips so demurely simpering, as it had been a mare cropping of a thistle. After these, a lovely loober-worts,[4] freckled-faced, red-headed, clean trussed in his doublet and his

[1] " Laces of this description were anciently presented to all the guests at weddings, and scarfs at funerals. *Vide* Ellis's edit. of Brand.
[2] " Or *Geason*, an ancient word, signifying rare or scarce. *Vide* Phillips.
[3] " A French word for maids or virgins.
[4] " A dull, heavy, and useless fellow. The word is probably derived from the Danish word *lubben*, gross or fat, and *vorte*, a wart or wen. *Vide* Wolff.—Shakspeare uses the latter word somewhat in this sense, when he makes Prince Henry say of Falstaff, 'I do allow this wen to be as familiar with me as my dog.'

hose, taken up now indeed by commission, for that he was loath to come forward, for reverence belike of his new cut canvas doublet; and would by his good will have been but a gazer, but found to be a meet actor for his office; that was to bear the bride-cup, formed of a sweet sucket-barrel,[1] a fair turn'd foot set to it, all seemly besilvered and parcell[2] gilt adorned with a beautiful branch of broom, gaily begilded for rosemary: from which two broad bride-laces of red and yellow buckram begilded, and gallantly streaming by such wind as there was, for he carried it aloft: this gentle cup-bearer had his freckled physiognomy somewhat unhappily infested, as he went, by the busy flies, that flocked about the bride-cup, for the sweetness of the sucket that it savoured of; but he, like a tall fellow, withstood their malice stoutly—see what manhood may do—beat them away, killed them by scores, stood to his charge, and marched on in good order.

"Then followed the worshipful bride, led, after the country manner, between two ancient parishioners, honest townsmen. But a stale stallion and a well spread (hot as the weather was,) God wot, and ill-smelling was she: thirty years old,[3] of colour brown-bay, not very beautiful indeed, but ugly, foul, and ill-favoured; yet marvelous fond of the office, because she heard say she should dance before the Queen, in which feat she thought she would foot it as finely as the best: Well, after this bride there came, by two and two, a dozen damsels for bride-maids, that for favour, attire, for fashion and cleanliness, were as meet for such a bride as a tureen ladle for a porridge-pot: More, but for fear of carrying all clean, had been appointed, but these few were enough.

"As the company in this order were come into the court, marvellous were the martial acts that were done there that day. The bride-groom, for pre-eminence, had the first course at the Quintain, and broke his spear with true hardiment; but his mare in her manege did a little so titubate, that much ado had his manhood to sit in his saddle, and escape the foil of a fall; With the help of his hand, yet he recovered himself, and lost not his stirrups (for he had none to his saddle,) had no hurt as it happened, but only that his girth burst, and lost his pen and ink-horn which he was ready to weep for: but his handkercher, as good hap was,

[1] "A vessel used for containing sweetmeats, for which sucket is the ancient word.
[2] "Partially, or partly.
[3] "Another early copy reads 'thirty-five years old.'

found he safe at his girdle: that cheered him somewhat, and had good regard it should not be soiled. For though heat and cold had upon sundry occasions made him some times to sweat, and sometimes rheumatic, yet durst he be bolder to blow his nose and wipe his face with the flappet of his father's jacket, than with his mother's muffler: 'tis a goodly matter, when youth are mannerly brought up, in fatherly love and motherly awe.

"Now, Sir, after the bride-groom had made his course, ran the rest of the band a while in some order; but soon after, tag and rag, cut and long tail: where the specialty of the sport was, to see how some for their slackness had a good bob with the bag; and some for their haste, too, would topple downright, and come down tumbling to the post: Some striving so much at the first setting out, that it seemed a question between the man and the beast, whether the course should be made on horseback or on foot: and put forth with the spurs, then would run his race by as among the thickest of the throng, that down came they together, hand over head: Another, while he directed his course to the quintain, his jument[1] would carry him to a mare among the people; so his horse was as amorous, as himself adventurous: Another, too, would run and miss the quintain with his staff, and hit the board with his head.

"Many such frolicsome games were there among these riders; who, by and by afterwards, upon a greater courage, left their quintaining, and ran at one another. There to see the stern countenances, the grim looks, the courageous attempts, the desperate adventures, the dangerous curvets, the fierce encounters, whereby the buff at the man, and the counterbuff at the horse, that both sometimes came topling to the ground: By my troth, *Master Martin*, 'twas a lively pastime; I believe it would have moved a man to a right merry mood, though it had been told him that his wife lay dying.

"And hereto followed as good a sport, methought, presented in an historical cue, by certain good-hearted men of Coventry,[2]

---

[1] "A French word for a mare.

[2] "Previous to the suppression of the English Monasteries, the City of Coventry was particularly famed for the Pageants which were performed in it on the 14th of June, or Corpus-Christi day. This appears to have been one of the ancient fairs; and the Gray Friars, or Friars Minors of the above City, had, as Dugdale relates, 'Theatres for the several scenes very large and high, placed upon wheels, and drawn to all the eminent parts of the City, for the

my Lord's neighbours there: who understanding among them the thing that could not be hidden from any: how careful and studious his Honour was, that by all pleasant recreations her Highness might best find herself welcome, and be made gladsome and merry, (the ground-work indeed and foundation of his Lordship's mirth, and gladness of us all,) made petition that they might renew now their old storial show: of argument how the Danes whilom here in a troublous season were for quietness borne withal and suffered in peace, that anon, by outrage and unsupportable insolency, abusing both Ethelred the King, then, and all estates every where beside; at the grievous complaint and counsel of Huna, the King's Chieftain in wars, on Saint Brice's night, Anno Dom. 1012, (as the book says, that falleth yearly on the thirteenth of November) were all dispatched and the Realm rid. And for because that the matter mentioneth how valiantly our English women, for love of their country, behaved themselves, expressed in action and rhymes after their manner, they thought it might move some mirth to her Majesty the rather. The thing, said they, is grounded in story, and for pastime wont to be played in our City yearly: without ill example of manners, papistry, or any superstition: and else did so occupy the heads of a number, that likely enough would have had worse meditations: had an ancient beginning and a long continuance till now of late laid down, they knew no cause why, unless it was by the zeal of certain of their preachers; men very commendable for their behaviour and learning, and sweet in their sermons, but somewhat too sour in preaching away their pastime: they wished therefore, that as they should continue their good doctrine in pulpit, so, for matters of policy and governance of the City, they would permit them to the Mayor and the Magistrates: and said, by my faith, *Master Martin*, they would make their humble petition unto her Highness, that they might have their plays up again.

"But aware, keep back, make room now, here they come—

"And first, Captain Cox, an odd man, I promise you: by profession a mason, and that right skilful; very cunning in fence, and hardy as Gawain; for his ton-sword hangs at his table's end; great oversight hath he in matters of story: For as for *King*

better advantage of the spectators: and contained the story of the Old and New Testament, composed in the old English rhyme.' Coventry appears to have derived great benefit from the numbers of persons who came to visit these pageants.

Arthur's Book; Huon of Bourdeaux; The Four Sons of Aymon; Bevis of Hampton; The Squire of Low Degree; The Knight of Courtesy, and the Lady Faguell; Frederick of Geneva; Sir Eglamour; Sir Tryamour; Sir Lamwell; Sir Isenbras; Sir Gawain; Oliver of the Castle; Lucrece and Euryalus; Virgil's Life; The Castle of Ladies; The Widow Edyth; The King and the Tanner; Friar Rush; Howleglas; Gargantua; Robin Hood; Adam Bell, Clym of the Clough, and William of Cloudesley; The Churl and the Bird; The Seven Wise Masters; The Wife lapt in a Morel's-skin; The Sack-full of News; The Serjeant that became a Friar; Scogan; Colin Clout; The Friar and the Boy; Elynour Rumming; and *The Nutbrown Maid;* with many more than I rehearse here—I believe he hath them all at his fingers' ends.

"Then in philosophy, both moral and natural, I think he be as naturally overseen; beside poetry and astronomy, and other hid sciences, as I may guess by the omberty of his books; whereof part, as I remember, *The Shepherds' Kalendar; The Ship of Fools; Daniel's Dreams; The Book of Fortune; Stans Puer ad Mensam; The Highway to the Spittle-house; Julian of Brentford's Testament; The Castle of Love; The Budget of Demands; The Hundred Merry Tales; The Book of Riddles; The Seven Sorrows of Women; The Proud Wives Pater-Noster; The Chapman of a Pennyworth of Wit.* Besides his ancient plays, *Youth and Charity; Hickskorner; Nugizee; Impatient Poverty;* and herewith Dr. Boord's *Breviary of Health.* What should I rehearse here; what a bunch of ballads and songs, all ancient: as *Broom broom on Hill; So woe is me begone, trolly lo; Over a Whinny Meg; Hey ding a ding; Bonny lass upon a green; My bonny one gave me a beck; By a bank as I lay:* and a hundred more he hath fair wrapt up in parchment, and bound with a whipcord. And as for Almanacs of antiquity, (a point for Ephemerides) I ween he can show from Jasper Laet of Antwerp unto Nostradamus of France, and thence unto our John Securiz of Salisbury. To stay ye no longer herein, I dare say he hath as fair a library of these sciences, and as many goodly monuments both in prose and poetry, and at afternoons can talk as much without book, as any inn-holder between Brentford and Bagshot, what degree soever he be.

"Besides this, in the field a good marshal at musters; of very great credit and trust in the town here; for he has been chosen ale-conner many a year, when his betters have stood by; and hath ever acquitted himself with such estimation, as to taste of a cup of *Nippitate*, his judgement will be taken above the best in the parish, be his nose ne'er so red.

"Captain Cox came marching on valiantly before, clean trussed and gartered above the knee, all fresh in a velvet cap (Master Golding lent it him,) flourishing with his ton-sword; and another fence-master with him: Thus in the forward making room for the rest. After them, proudly pricked on foremost, the Danish lance-knights on horseback, and then the English: Each with their alder pole martially in their hand. Even at the first entry, the meeting waxed somewhat warm; that by and by, kindled with courage on both sides, grew from a hot skirmish unto a blazing battle: first by spear and shield, outrageous in their races as rams at their rut; with furious encounters, that together they tumbled to the dust, sometimes horse and man, and after fall to it with sword and target, good bangs on both sides. The fight so ceasing, but the battle not so ended: then followed the footmen; both the hosts, one after the other:—first marching in ranks; then warlike turning; then from ranks into squadrons; then into triangles; from that into rings, and so winding out again. A valiant Captain of great prowess, as fierce as a fox assaulting a goose, was so hardy to give the first stroke: then got they so grisly together, that great was the activity that day to be seen there on both sides: the one very eager for purchase of prey, the other utterly stout for redemption of liberty: thus, quarrel enflamed the fury on both sides: twice the Danes had the better, but at the last conflict, beaten down, overcome, and many led captive for triumph by our English women.

"This was the effect of this show; that as it was handled, made much matter of good pastime, brought all, indeed, into the great court, even under her Highness's window, to have seen: but as unhappy it was for the bride, that came thither too soon, (and yet it was four o'clock,) for her Highness beholding in the chamber delectable dancing indeed, and therewith the great throng and unruliness of the people, was cause that this solemnity of bridal and dancing had not the full muster that was hoped for. Her Highness also saw but little of the Coventry play, and commanded it therefore on the Tuesday following to have it full out: as accordingly it was presented; whereat her Majesty laughed well: They were the merrier, and so much the more, because her Highness had given them two bucks and five marks in money, to make merry together: They prayed for her Majesty, long happily to reign, and oft to come thither, that oft they might see her: And what rejoicing upon their ample reward, and what triumphing upon the good acceptance, they vaunted their play was never so dignified, nor ever any players before so beatified.

"Thus, tho' the day took an end, yet slipped not the night all sleeping away: for as neither office nor obsequy ceased at any time to the full, to perform the plot his Honour had appointed, so after supper was there a play of a very good theme presented: but so set forth, by the actors well handling, that pleasure and mirth made it seem very short, tho' it lasted two good hours and more. But stay, *Master Martin*, all is not done yet.

"After the play, out of hand followed a most delicious and (if I may so term it) an ambrosial banquet: whereof, whether I might more muse at the daintiness, shapes, and the cost; or else, at the variety and number of the dishes (that were three hundred), for my part, I could little tell then; and now less, I assure you. Her Majesty eat smally or nothing; which understood, the courses were not so orderly served and sizely set down, but were, by and by, as disorderly wasted and coarsely consumed; more courtly, methought, than courteously: But that was no part of the matter: it might please and be liked, and do that it came for, then was all well enough.

"Unto this banquet there was appointed a masque: for riches of array of an incredible cost: but the time being so far spent, and very late in the night now, was cause that it came not forth to the show: And thus for *Sunday's* season, having staid you the longer, according to the matter, here make I an end: Ye may breathe ye awhile.

"*Monday* the eighteenth of this July, the weather being hot, her Highness kept the Castle for coolness, till about five o'clock, her Majesty in the chase hunted the hart (as afore) of force: that whether were it by the cunning of the huntsmen, or by the natural desire of the deer, or else by both; anon he got him to soil again, which raised the accustomed delight: a pastime indeed so entirely pleasant, as whereof at times who may have the full and free fruition, can find no more satiety (I ween) for the recreation, than of their good viands at times for their sustenance.

"Well, the game was gotten: and her Highness returning, came there upon a swimming mermaid, (that from top to tail was eighteen feet long,) *Triton*, Neptune's blaster: who with his

trumpet formed of a wrinkled welk, as her Majesty was in sight, gave sound very shrill and sonorous, in sign he had an embassy to pronounce. Anon her Highness was coming upon the bridge, whereupon he made his fish to swim the swifter: he then declared—' How the supreme salsipotent[1] monarch Neptune, the
' great God of the swelling seas, Prince of profundities, and
' Sovereign Signor of all lakes, fresh waters, rivers, creeks, and
' gulphs; understanding how a cruel Knight, one Sir Bruce sans
' pitié, a mortal enemy unto ladies of estate, had long lain about
' the banks of this pool, in wait with his bands here, to distress
' the Lady of the Lake, whereby she had been restrained not only
' from having any use of her ancient liberty and territories in
' these parts; but also of making repair and giving attendance
' unto you, Noble Queen, (quo' he) as she would; she promised,
' and also should; doth therefore signify, and hereto, of you, as
' of her good liege and dear friend, make this request, that you
' will deign but to shew your person toward this pool; whereby
' your only presence shall be matter sufficient of abandoning this
' uncourteous Knight, and putting all his bands to flight, and
' also deliver the Lady out of this thraldom.'

"Moving herewith from the bridge, and fleeting more into the pool, charged he in *Neptune's* name *Æolus* with all his winds, the waters with his springs, his fish and fowl, and all his clients in the same, that they ne be so hardy in any force to stir, but keep them calm and quiet while this Queen be present. At which petition her Highness staying, it appeared strait how *Sir Bruce* became unseen, his bands scaled,[2] and the Lady, by and by, with her two Nymphs floating upon her moveable Islands, *Triton*, on his mermaid skimming by, approached towards her Highness on the bridge,—as well to declare that her Majesty's presence had so graciously thus wrought her deliverance, as also to excuse her not coming to court as she promised, and chiefly to present her Majesty, as a token of her duty and good heart, for her Highness' recreation, with this gift: which was, *Arion*, that excellent and famous musician; in tire and appointment strange, well seeming to his person, riding aloft upon his old friend the dolphin, that from head to tail was four and twenty feet long, and swam hard

[1] "An epithet derived from the Latin *salsipotens*, which signifies one who has power over the salt seas; in which sense it is used by Plautus. *Ainsworth*.

[2] "Came away."

by these Islands. Herewith, *Arion*, for these great benefits, after a few well-couched words unto her Majesty of thanksgiving, in supplement of the same, began a delectable ditty of a song well apted to a melodious noise; compounded of six several instruments, all covert, casting sound from the dolphin's belly within: *Arion*, the seventh, sitting thus singing (as I say) without.

"Now, Sir, the ditty in metre so aptly endited to the matter, and after by voice deliciously delivered. .The song, by a skilful artist into his parts so sweetly sorted; each part in his instrument so clean and sharply touched; every instrument again in his kind so excellently tunable; and this in the evening of the day, resounding from the calm waters, where the presence of her Majesty, and longing to listen, had utterly damped all noise and din; the whole harmony conveyed in time, tune, and temper thus incomparably melodious; with what pleasure, (*Master Martin*,) with what sharpness of conceit, with what lively delight, this might pierce into the hearers' hearts, I pray ye imagine yourself, as ye may; for, so God judge me, by all the wit and cunning I have, I cannot express, I promise you. 'Mais j'ai ' bien vû cela, Monsieur, que fort grande est la pouvoir qu'avoit ' la très noble science de Musique sur l'esprit humain.' Perceive ye me? I have told you a great matter now: As for me, surely I was lulled in such liking, and so loath to leave off, that much ado a good while after had I, to find me where I was. And take ye this by the way, that for the small skill in music that God hath sent me (you know it is somewhat), I'll set the more by myself while my name is *Laneham*; and, grace of God, music is a noble art!

"But stay a while, see a short wit: by troth I had almost forgot. This day was a day of grace beside, wherein were advanced five gentlemen of worship unto the degree of Knighthood; *Sir Thomas Cecil*, son and heir unto the right honorable the Lord Treasurer; *Sir Henry Cobham*, brother unto the Lord Cobham; *Sir Thomas Stanhope; Sir Arthur Basset;* and *Sir Thomas Tresham*. And also by her Highness' accustomed mercy and charity, nine were cured of the painful and dangerous disease called the King's Evil; for that Kings and Queens of this Realm, without other medicine, save only by handling and prayers, do cure it: Bear with me, though perchance I place not those gentlemen in my recital here, after their estates; for I am neither a good herald of arms, nor yet know how they are set in the subsidy books: men of great worship I understand they are all.

"*Tuesday*, according to commandment, came our Coventry men. What their matter was, of her Highness' mirth and good acceptance, and reward unto them, and of their rejoicing thereat, I have informed you before, and so say the less now.

"*Wednesday*, in the forenoon, preparation was in hand for her Majesty to have supped in Wedgenall, three miles west from the Castle, a goodly Park of the Queen's Majesty.[1] For that cause a fair pavilion, and other provision was accordingly thither sent and prepared: but by means of the weather not so clearly disposed, the matter was countermanded again. Had her Highness happened this day to have come abroad, there was made ready a device of Goddesses and Nymphs, which, as well for the ingenious argument, as for the well handling of it in rhyme and enditing, would undoubtedly have gained great liking, and moved no less delight. Of the particularities whereof, however, I cease to entreat, lest like the bungling carpenter, by mis-sorting the pieces, I mar a good frame in the bad setting up; or by my bad tempering beforehand, blemish the beauty, when it should be reared up indeed. This day also was there such earnest talk and appointment of removing, that I gave over my noting, and hearkened after my horse.

"Marry, Sir, I must tell you: As all endeavour was to move mirth and pastime (as I told you), even so, a ridiculous device of an ancient minstrel and his song, was prepared to have been proffered, if meet time and place had been found for it. Once in a worshipful company, where I chanced to be, full appointed, he recounted his matter in sort as it should have been uttered. What I noted, here thus, I tell you.—

"A person very meet seemed he for the purpose, of forty-five years old, apparelled partly as he would himself. His cap of his head, seemly rounded tonsor-wise;[2] fair combed, that with a sponge daintily dipped in a little capon's grease was finely smoothed, to make it shine like a mallard's wing. His beard

[1] "The Duchess of Portland's copy reads 'a goodly park of the right honorable my very good Lord the Earl of Warwick.' It still belongs to that noble family, and is now called *Wedgnock Park.*—*Nichols's Progresses*, 1788, Vol. i.

[2] "More properly written tonsure-wise; that is to say, shaven in a circle after the manner of the monks. *Vide* Percy.

smugly shaven; and yet his shirt after the new trick, with ruffs fair starched, sleeked and glistering like a pair of new shoes; marshalled in good order with a setting-stick, and stout that every ruff stood up like a wafer. A side gown of Kendal green,[1] after the freshness of the year now; gathered at the neck with a narrow gorget, fastened afore with a white clasp, and a keeper, close up to the chin; but easily for heat to undo when he list, seemly begirt in a red Cadiz girdle; from that a pair of capped Sheffield knives hanging to a side: Out of his bosom drawn forth a lappet of his napkin, edged with blue lace, and marked with a truelove [knot], a heart, and a D. for *Damian*, for he was but a batchelor yet.

"His gown had side [i. e. long] sleeves down to mid-leg, slit from the shoulder to the hand, and lined with white cotton. His doublet-sleeves of black worsted; upon them a pair of poignets [i. e. wristbands] of tawny camblet, laced along the wrist with blue threaden points; a welt toward the hand of fustian-a-napes: a pair of red nether-stocks; a pair of pumps on his feet, with a cross cut at the toes for corns; not new indeed, yet cleanly blacked with soot, and shining as a shoe-ing horn. About his neck, a red riband suitable to his girdle. His harp in good grace dependent before him; his wrest tied to a green lace and hanging by. Under the gorget of his gown, a fair flaggon chain of pewter (for silver), as a *Squire Minstrel of Middlesex;* that travelled the country this summer season unto fairs, and worshipful men's houses. From his chain hung an escutcheon, with metal and colour, resplendent upon his breast, of the ancient arms of *Islington*: Upon a question whereof, he, as one that was well schooled, and conned his lesson perfect without book to answer at full, if question were asked him, declared: 'How the 'worshipful village of Islington in Middlesex, well known to be 'one of the most ancient and best towns in England next London 'at this day, for the faithful friendship of long time shown, as 'well at Cook's feast in Aldersgate-street yearly upon Holy-rood 'day, as also at all solemn bridals in the city of London all the 'year after; in well serving them of furmety for porridge, not

---

[1] "'*A side gown of Kendal green,*' was a long hanging robe of coarse green woollen cloth or baize, for the manufacture of which the town of Kendal in Westmoreland was very anciently celebrated.

'oversodden till it be too weak: of milk for their flawnes,[1] not
'pild nor chalked; of cream for their custards, not frothed nor
'thickened with flour; and of butter for their pasties and pie-
'paste, not made of well curds, nor gathered of whey in summer,
'nor mingled in winter with salt-butter watered or washed; did
'obtain long ago, these worshipful arms in colour and form as
'you see: which are—The arms: a field *Argent*, as the field and
'ground indeed wherein the milk-wives of this worthy town, and
'every man else in his faculty doth trade for his living. On a fess
'*tenné*, three plates between three milk-tankards *proper*. The
'three milk-tankards, as the proper vessels wherein the substance
'and matter of their trade is to and fro transported. The fess
'*tenné*, which is a colour betokening doubt and suspicion; so as
'suspicion and good heed-taking, as well to their markets and
'servants, as to their customers that they trust not too far, may
'bring unto them plates, that is coined silver; three, that is
'sufficient and plenty; for so that number in armory may well
'signify.

"'For crest, upon a wad of oat-straw for a wreath, a bowl of
'furmety. Wheat (as you know) is the most precious gift of
'*Ceres*; and in the midst of it, sticking, a dozen of horn-spoons
'in a bunch, as the instrument meetest to eat furmety porridge
'withal; a dozen, as a number complete for full cheer or a banquet;
'and of horn, as of a substance more estimable than is made for
'a great deal; being neither so churlish in weight, as metal; nor
'so froward and brittle to manure, as stone; nor yet so soily in
'use, nor rough to the lips, as wood; but light, pliant, and
'smooth: that with a little licking, will always be kept as clean
'as a die. With your patience, Gentlemen,' (quoth the Min-
'strel) 'be it said; were it not indeed that horns be so plenty,
'hornware, I believe, would be more set by than it is; and yet
'there are in our parts, those that will not stick to avow, that
'many an honest man, both in city and country, hath had his
'house by horning well upholden, and a daily friend also at need:
'And this with your favour may I further affirm; a very inge-
'nious person was he, that for dignity of the stuff, could thus by
'spooning devise to advance the horn so near to the head. With
'great congruity also were these horn-spoons put to the wheat;
'as a token and portion of *Cornucopiæ*, the horn of *Achelous*;

[1] "Phillips describes a flawn to be 'a kind of dainty made of fine flour,
eggs, and butter.'

' which the *Maiades* did fill with all good fruits, corn, and grain;
' and afterwards did consecrate unto abundance and plenty.

" ' This scutcheon with beasts, very aptly agreeing both to the
' arms and to the trade of the bearers; gloriously supported.
' Between a grey mare (a beast meetest for carrying of milk-
' tankards) her pannel on her back, as always ready for service at
' every feast and brid-ale at need; her tail displayed at most
' ease; and her filly foal, with a fallow and flaxen mane after the
' sire.

" ' In the scroll undergraven (quoth he) is there a proper word,
' an hemistich, well squaring with all the rest, taken out of
' Salerne's chapter of things that most nourish man's body: *Lac,
' Caseus infans*. That is: 'good milk, and young cheese.' And
' thus much, Gentlemen, an please you (quoth he) for the arms
' of our worshipful town:' " And therewithal made a mannerly
leg, and so held his peace.

"As the company paused, and the minstrel seemed to gape
after praise for his *beau parlé:* and because he had rendered his
lesson so well, says a good fellow of the company, 'I am sorry to
' see how much the poor Minstrel mistakes the matter; for
' indeed the arms are thus:—

" ' Three milk-tankards proper, in a field of clouted cream, three
' green cheeses upon a shelf of cake-bread. The furmety bowl and
' horn-spoons; cause their profit comes all by horned beasts.
' Supported by a mare with a galled back, and therefore still
' covered with a pannel, fisking with her tail for flies, and her filly
' foal neighing after the dam for suck. The words *Lac, Caseus
' infans*, that is, a fresh cheese and cream, the common cry that
' these milk-wives make in London streets yearly betwixt Easter
' and Whitsuntide: and this is the very matter, I know it well
' enough:' and so ended his tale and sat him down again.

"Hereat every man laughed much, save the Minstrel; that
though the fool was made privy all was but for sport, yet to see
himself thus crossed with a contrary cue that he looked not for,
would strait have given over all, and waxed very wayward, eager,
and sour: howbeit at last, by some entreaty and many fair words,
with sack and sugar, we sweetened him again; and afterward he
became as merry as a pye. Appearing then afresh, in his full
formality, with a lovely look; after three lowly courtesies, cleared
his voice with a hem and reach, and spat out withal; wiped his
lips with the hollow of his hand, for filling his napkin; tempered a

string or two with his wrest, and after a little warbling on his harp for a prelude, came forth with a solemn song, warranted for story out of King Arthur's acts, the 1st book and 26th chapter, whereof I got a copy; and that is this, viz.

"THE MINSTREL'S SONNET.

"So it befell upon a Pentecost day,
When King Arthur at Camelot[1] kept court royal,
With his comely Queen, dame Guenever the gay,
And many bold Barons sitting in hall;
Ladies apparelled in purple and pall,
When Heralds in hukes[2] herried full by,
Largess, Largess,[3] Chevaliers tres hardy!

"A doughty dwarf unto the uppermost deas[4]
Right pertly 'gan prick,[5] and kneeling on knee,
With steven[6] full stout amidst all the press,
Said, Hail, Sir King, God thee save, and see
King Ryence of North-Wales greeteth well thee,
And bids that thy beard anon thou him send,
Or else from thy jaws he will it off rend.

"For his robe of state, a rich scarlet mantle,
With eleven king's beards bordered about,
He hath made late, and yet in a cantle[7]
Is left a place the twelfth to make out,
Where thine must stand, be thou never so stout;

---

[1] "The city of Winchester.
[2] "The original word in this ballad is *hewkes*, which is derived from the French *huque*, a cloak. The tabards, or surcoats, of the ancient heralds, were often denominated houces, or housings; and this expression was applied, indiscriminately, to their coats of arms, as well as to a dark-coloured robe without sleeves, edged with fur, which they formerly wore.
[3] "A cry used by the heralds whenever they were rewarded by knights or sovereigns. It is still in use at a Coronation. It is a French expression, signifying a present or gift.
[4] "The highest or principal table in a hall, which usually stood upon a platform. The word comes from the French *dais*, a canopy, as such a covering was usually erected over the chief seats.
[5] "Pressed hastily forwards.
[6] "Voice, sounds.
[7] "A piece, or part. Shakspeare uses the word in King Henry IV. part I. act 3, scene 1.

"'And cuts me, from the best of all my land,
A huge half-moon, a monstrous *cantle* out.'

This must be done, I tell thee no fable,
Maugre the pow'r of all thy Round Table.

" When this mortal message from his mouth was past,
Great was the bruit in hall and in bow'r;
The King fumed, the Queen shrieked, Ladies were aghast,
Princes puff'd, Barons blustered, Lords began to lour,
Knights stamped, 'Squires startled as steeds in a stour,[1]
Yeomen and Pages yell'd out in the hall,
When herewith came in Sir Kay, Seneschal.

" ' Silence, my sufferaunce,' quoth the courteous Knight,
And in that stound the charm became still;
The Dwarf's dinner full dearly was dight,
For wine and wassail he had at his will;
And when he had eaten and fed his fill,
One hundred pieces of coined gold
Were given the Dwarf for his message bold.

" ' Say to Sir Ryence, thou Dwarf,' quoth the King,
' That for this proud message I him defy,
And shortly with basons and pans will him ring
Out of North Wales; whereas he and I
With swords and no razors, shall utterly try
Which of us both is the better barber:'
And therewith he shook his sword *Excaliber!*

" At this the Minstrel made a pause and a courtesy for *primus passus*. More of the song there is, but I got it not. As for the matter, had it come to the shew, I think the fellow would have handled it well enough.

" Her Highness tarried at Kenilworth till the Wednesday after, being the 27th of this July, and the nineteenth inclusive of her Majesty's coming thither; for which seven days, perceiving my notes so slenderly answering, I took it less blame to cease, and thereof to write you nothing at all, than in such matters to write nothing likely; and so much the rather, (as I have well bethought me) that if I did but ruminate the days I have spoken of, I shall bring out yet somewhat more meet for your appetite, (though a dainty tooth have ye) which I believe your tender stomach will brook well enough.

" Whereof part is, first, how according to her Highness' name *Elizabeth*, which I hear say, out of the Hebrew signifieth, among

[1] " A battle.

other, *the seventh of my God;* divers things here did so justly in number square with the same. As first, her Highness hither coming in this seventh month; then presented with the seven presents of the seven Gods; and after, with the melody of the seven sorted music in the dolphin, the Lake-Lady's gift. Then, too, consider how fully the Gods, as it seemed, had conspired most magnificently in abundance to bestow their influences and gifts upon her Court, there to make her Majesty merry.

"Sage *Saturn* himself in person (that because of his lame leg could not so well stir) in chair, therefore to take order with the grave officers of the household, holpen indeed with the good advice of his prudent niece *Pallas,* that no unruly body, or disquiet, disturb the noble assembly, or else be once so bold to enter within the Castle gates. Away with all rascals, captives, melancholic, wayward, froward conjurers and usurers, and to have labourers and under-workmen for the beautifying of any place, always at hand as they should be commanded.

"*Jupiter* sent personages of high honour and dignity; Barons, Lords, Ladies, Judges, Bishops, Lawyers, and Doctors; with them, Virtue, Nobleness, Equity, Liberality, and Compassion; due season, and fair weather; saving that, at the petition of his dear sister *Ceres,* he granted a day or two of some sweet showers for ripening of her corn that was so well set, and to get forward harvest. Herewith bestowed he such plenty of pleasant thunder, lightning, and thunderbolts, by his halting son and fire-master *Vulcan,* still fresh and fresh framed, always so frequent, so intellable, and of such continuance in the spending (as I partly told ye) consumed, that surely he seems to be as of power inestimable; so, in store of munition, unwasteable; for all *Ovid's* censure that says,

"Si quoties peccant homines sua fulmina mittat
Jupiter, exiguo tempore inermis erit.

If Jove should shoot his thunderbolts, as oft as men offend,
Assure you his artillery would soon be at an end !"

What a number of estates and of nobility had *Jupiter* assembled there, guess you by this, that of sort worshipful there were in the Court daily above forty, whereof the meanest of a thousand marks yearly revenue, and many of much more. This great gift beside did his Deity confer upon her Highness—to have fair and seasonable weather at her own appointment; according whereunto her Majesty so had. For her gracious presence, therefore, with this great gift endowed, Lichfield, Worcester, and Middleton, with many places more, made humble suit unto her Highness to come; to such whereof as her Majesty could, it came, and the season acceptable.

"*Phœbus*, beside his continual and most delicious music, (as I have told you) appointed he Princes to adorn her Highness' court, Counsellors, Heralds, and sanguine Youth, pleasant and merry, costly garments, learned physicians, and no need of them.

"*Juno*, Gold chains, ouches, jewels of great price and rich attire worn in much grace and good beseeming, without pride or emulation of any.

"*Mars*, Captains of good conduct, men skilful in feats of arms, politic in stratagems, of good courage in good quarrels, valiant and wise-hardy; abandoning pique-quarrels and ruffians: appointing also pursuivants, couriers, and posts, still feeding her Highness with news and intelligences from all parts.

"*Venus*, Unto the Ladies and Gentlewomen, beauty, good favour, comeliness, gallant attire, dancing with comely grace, sweet voice in song and pleasant talk, with express commandment and charge unto her son, on her blessing, that he shoot not a shaft in the Court all the while her Highness remained at Kenilworth.

"*Mercury*, Learned men in sciences; Poets, Merchants, Painters, Carvers, Players, Engineers, Devicers, and dexterity in handling of all pleasant attempts.

"*Luna*, Calm nights for quiet rest, and silver moonshine, that nightly indeed shone for most of her Majesty's being there.

"Blind *Plutus*, Bags of Money, Customers, Exchangers, and Bankers, with store of riches in plate and in coin.

"*Bacchus*, Full cups every where, every hour of all kinds of wine. There was no dainty that the sea could yield, but *Neptune* (though his reign at the nearest lay well nigh a hundred miles off) did daily send in great plenty, sweet and fresh. As for freshwater fish, the store of all sorts was abundant.

"And how bountiful *Ceres* in provision was, guess ye by this, that in little more than three days space, seventy-two tuns of ale and beer were piped up quite; what that might, whilst with it, of bread beside meat, I report me to you: and yet the Master

Comptroller, Master Cofferer, and divers Officers of the court, some honorable and sundry right worshipful were placed at Warwick, for more room in the Castle. But here was no ho! *Master Martin*, in devout drinking alway ; that brought lack unlooked for ; which being known to the worshipful my lord's good neighbours, came there in two days' space, from sundry friends, a relief of forty tuns, till a new supply was got again : and then to our drinking afresh as fast as ever we did.

"*Flora*, Abroad and within the house, ministered of flowers so great a quantity, of such sweet savour, so beautifully hued, so large and fair proportion, and of such strange kinds and shapes, that it was great pleasure to see : and so much the more, as there was great store of others that were counterfeit, and formed of feathers by art; alike glorious to the show, as were the natural.

"*Proteus*, His tumbler, that could by nimbleness cast himself into so many forms and fashions.

" *Pan*, His merry morrice-dance, with their pipe and tabor.

" *Bellona*, Her Quintain Knights, and proper bickerings of the Coventry men.

"*Polyphemus*, Neptune's son and heir, (let him I pray, an it be but for his father's sake and for his good will, be allowed for a God,) with his bears, his bear-whelps, and ban-dogs.

"*Æolus*, Holding up his winds, while her Highness at any time took pleasure on the water, and staying of tempests during her abode here.

"*Sylvanus*, Besides his plentiful provision of fowl for dainty viands, his pleasant and sweet singing birds : whereof I will show you more anon.

" *Echo*, Her well endited dialogue.

" *Faunus*, His jolly savage.

" *Genius loci*, His tempering of all things within and without with apt time and place to pleasure and delight.

" Then the three *Charities*: [or Graces] *Aglaia*, with her lightsome gladness ; *Thalia*, her flourishing freshness ; *Euphrosyne*, her cheerfulness of spirit : and with these three in one assent, *Concordia*, with her amity and good agreement. That to how great effect their powers were poured out here among us, let it be judged by this, that by a multitude thus met of three or four thousand every day ; and divers days more, of so sundry degrees, professions, ages, appetites, dispositions and affections; such a drift of time was there passed, with such amity, love, pastime, agreement, and obedience where it should; and without quarrel, jarring, grudging, or (that I could hear) of ill words between any. A thing, *Master Martin,* very rare and strange, and yet no more strange than true.

"The *Parcæ,* [or Fates] as erst I should have said, the first night of her Majesty's coming, they hearing and seeing so precious ado here at a place unlooked for, in an uplandish country so far within the realm: pressing into every stead where her Highness went, whereby so duddled with such variety of delights, did set aside their huswifery, and could not for their hearts tend their work a whit. But after they had seen her Majesty a-bed, got them a prying into every place: Old hags! as fond of novelties as young girls that had never seen court before: but neither full with gazing, nor weary with gadding; left off yet for that time, and at high midnight gat them giggling, (but not aloud) in the Presence Chamber: minding indeed, with their present diligence, to recompense their former slackness.

"So, setting themselves thus down to their work, 'Alas!' says *Atropos,* 'I have lost my sheers:' *Lachesis* laughed apace and would not draw a thread: 'And think ye, dames, that I'll hold the distaff, while both ye sit idle? Why, no, by my mother's soul,' quoth *Clotho.* Therewith, carefully lapped in fine lawn, the spindle and rock,[1] that was dizened with pure purple silk, laid they safely up together; that of her Majesty's distaff, for eighteen days, there was not a thread spun, I assure you. The two sisters after that (I heard say) began their work again, that long may they continue: but *Atropos* heard no tiding of her sheers, and not a man that moaned her loss. She is not beloved surely; for this can I tell you, that whether it be for hate to the hag, or love to her Highness, or else for both, every man prays God she may never find them for that work; and so pray I daily and duly with the devoutest.

"Thus partly you perceive now, how greatly the Gods can do for mortals, and how much always they love where they like: that what a gentle *Jove* was this, thus courteously to contrive here such

[1] "A distaff held in the hand, from which the wool was spun by a ball fixed below on a spindle, upon which every thread was wound up as it was done. It was the ancient way of spinning, and is still in use in many northern counties. *Vide* Bailey.

a train of Gods? Nay then rather, *Master Martin*, to come out of our poeticalities, and to talk on more serious terms, what a magnificent Lord may we justly account him, that could so highly cast order for such a *Jupiter* and all his Gods beside: that none with his influence, good property, or present, were wanting; but always ready at hand, in such order and abundance for the honouring and delight of so high a Prince, our most gracious Queen and Sovereign. A Prince (I say) so singular in pre-eminence, and worthiness above all other Princes and Dignities of our time: though I make no comparison to years past, to him that in this point, either of ignorance—(if any such can be), or else of malevolence, would make any doubt: *sit liber Judex* (as they say); let him look on the matter, and answer himself, he has not far to travel.

"As for the amplitude of his Lordship's mind, albeit that I, poor soul, can in conceit no more attain unto, than judge of a gem whereof I have no skill: yea, though daily worn and resplendent in mine eye; yet some of the virtues and properties thereof, in quantity, or quality, so apparent as cannot be hidden, but seen of all men, might I be the bolder to report here unto you; but as for the value, your jewellers by their carats let them cast, an they can.

"And first, who that considers unto the stately seat of Kenilworth Castle, the rare beauty of building that his Honour hath advanced, all of the hard quarry-stone: every room so spacious, so well belighted, and so high roofed within: so seemly to sight by due proportion without; In day-time on every side so glittering by glass; at nights, by continual brightness of candle, fire, and torch-light, transparent thro' the lightsome windows, as it were the Egyptian Pharos relucent unto all the Alexandrian coast: or else, (to talk merrily with my merry friend,) thus radiant, as though *Phœbus* for his ease would rest him in the Castle, and not every night so to travel down unto the Antipodes. Here, too, so fully furnished of rich apparel and utensils apted in all points to the best.

"Unto this, his Honour's exquisite appointment of a beautiful garden, an acre or more in quantity, that lieth on the north there: Wherein hard all along by the Castle wall, is reared a pleasant terrace, ten feet high, and twelve feet broad, even under foot, and fresh of fine grass; as is also the side thereof towards the garden: In which, by sundry equal distances, with obelisks, and spheres,

and white bears,[1] all of stone upon their curious bases, by goodly
shew were set; To these, two fine arbours redolent by sweet trees
and flowers, at each end one, the garden plot under that, with fair
alleys, green by grass, even voided from the borders on both sides,
and some (for change) with sand, not light, or too soft, or soily
by dust, but smooth and firm, pleasant to walk on, as a sea-shore
when the water is availed. Then, much gracified by due proportion of four even quarters: in the midst of each, upon a base of
two feet square, and high, seemly bordered of itself, a square
pilaster rising pyramidically fifteen feet high. Symmetrically
pierced through from a foot beneath to two feet of the top:
whereupon, for a capital, an orb of ten inches thick; every of
these, with its base, from the ground to the top, of one whole
piece; hewn out of hard porphyry, and with great art and heed
(think me) thither conveyed and there erected. Where, further
also, by great cast and cost, the sweetness of savour on all sides,
made so respirant from the redolent plants and fragrant herbs and
flowers, in form, colour, and quantity so deliciously variant; and
fruit-trees bedecked with apples, pears, and ripe cherries.

"And unto these, in the midst, against the terrace: a square
cage, sumptuous and beautiful, joined hard to the north wall,
(that on that side guards the garden, as the garden the Castle) of
a rare form and excellency was raised: in height twenty feet,
thirty long, and fourteen broad. From the ground strong and
close, reared breast-high, whereat a framing of a fair moulding
was couched all about: from that upward, four great windows,
in front, and two at each end, every one five feet wide, as many
more even above them, divided on all parts by a transom and
architrave,[2] so likewise ranging about the cage. Each window
arched at the top, and parted from the other at even distances by
flat fair bolteld columns[3] all in form and beauty alike, these supported a comely cornice couched all along upon the bold square.
Which with a wire net, finely knit, of meshes six square, an inch

[1] "These effigies were allusive to the ancient badge of the Earls of Warwick, which was, *a bear erect Argent, muzzled Gules, supporting a ragged
staff of the first.* In 1561, Ambrose Dudley, Robert's elder brother, was made
Earl of Warwick, and consequently the badge was thus introduced.

[2] "The word architrave signifies the lowest member of the cornice, and an
architrave window is one with an ogee, or wreathed moulding. A transom is
a beam or lintel crossing over a window.

[3] "Boltel is a term used in building, to signify any prominence or jutting-
out beyond the flat face of the wall.

wide (as it were for a flat roof) and likewise the space of every window with great cunning and comeliness, even and tight was all over-strained. Under the cornice again, every part beautified with great diamonds, emeralds, rubies, and saphires: pointed, tabled, rock and round, and garnish'd with gold;[1] by skilful head and hand, and by toil and pencil so lively expressed, as it might be great marvel and pleasure to consider how near excellency of Art could approach unto perfection of Nature.

"Bear with me, good countryman, though things be not showed here as well as I would, or as well as they should. For indeed I can better imagine and conceive that which I see, than well utter, or duly declare it. Holes were there also and caverns in orderly distances and fashion, voided into the wall, as well for heat, for coolness, for roost at nights and refuge in weather, as also for breeding when time is. More; fair, even, and fresh holly trees for perching and pruning, set within, toward each end one.

"Here, too, their diversity of meats, their fine several vessels for their water and sundry grains; and a man skilful and diligent to look to them and tend them.

"But, shall I tell you, of the silver sounded lute, without the sweet touch of hand; the glorious golden cup, without the fresh fragrant wine: or the rich ring with gem, without the fair featured finger: is nothing, indeed, in his proper grace and use: even so his Honor accounted of this mansion till he had placed there tenants according. Had it, therefore, replenished with lively Birds, English, French, Spanish, Canarian, and I am deceived if I saw not some African. Whereby, whether it became more delightsome in change of tunes, and harmony to the ear; or else in difference of colours, kinds, and properties to the eye, I'll tell you, if I can, when I have better bethought me.

"One day, *Master Martin*, as the garden door was open, and her Highness hunting, by licence of my good friend *Adrian*, I

[1] "It is evident that these precious stones were imitated in painting; and that they were meant to represent the gems in their various appearances. *Pointed*, or rose, as it is termed by the lapidaries, is when a stone is cut with many angles rising from an octagon, and terminating in a point. *Tabled* is when a diamond is formed with one flat upper surface; and the word table also signifies the principal face. *Rough* is understood to mean the gem in its primary state, when its radiance is seen to sparkle through the dross of the mine. *Round* denotes the jewel when it is cut and polished with a convex surface. The expression 'Garnished with their gold,' which follows in the text, signified ornamented with their settings.

came in at a beckon, but would scant out with a thrust: for sure I was loath so soon to depart. Well may this, *Master Martin*, be somewhat to magnitude of mind, but more thereof as ye shall know, more cause ye shall have so to think: hear out what I tell you, and tell me when we meet.

"In the centre, as it were, of this goodly garden, was there placed a very fair fountain, cast into an eight-square, reared four feet high; from the midst whereof, a column upright, in shape of two *Athlants,* joined together a back half: the one looking east, the other west, with their hands upholding a fair-formed bowl of three feet over; from whence sundry fine pipes did lively distil continual streams into the reservoir of the fountain, maintained still two feet deep by the same fresh falling water: wherein pleasantly playing to and fro, and round about, carp, tench, bream, and for variety, pearch and eel, fish fair-liking all, and large: In the top, the ragged staff; which, with the bowl, the pillar, and eight sides beneath, were all hewn out of rich and hard white marble. On one side, *Neptune* with his tridental fuskin[1] triumphing in his throne, trailed into the deep by his marine horses. On another, *Thetis* in her chariot drawn by her dolphins. Then *Triton* by his fishes. Here *Proteus* herding his sea-bulls. There *Doris* and her daughters solacing on sea and sands. The waves surging with froth and foam, intermingled in place, with whales, whirlpools, sturgeons, tunneys, conches, and whealks, all engraven by exquisite device and skill, so as I may think this not much inferior unto *Phœbus'* gates, which *Ovid* says, and peradventure a pattern to this, that *Vulcan* himself did cut: whereof such was the excellency of art, that the work in value surmounted the stuff, and yet were the gates all of clean massy silver.

"Here were things, ye see, might inflame any mind to long after looking: but whoso was found so hot in desire, with the wrest of a cock was sure of a cooler: water spirting upward with such vehemency, as they should, by and by, be moistened from top to toe; the he's to some laughing, but the she's to more sport: this sometime was occupied to very good pastime.

"A garden then so appointed, as wherein aloft upon sweet shadowed walk of terrace, in heat of summer, to feel the pleasant whisking wind above, or delectable coolness of the fountain-spring beneath; to taste of delicious strawberries, cherries, and

[1] "A term derived from the Latin *fuscina*, an eel-spear, trident, or three-forked mace.—*Vide* Ainsworth.

other fruits, even from their stalks; to smell such fragrancy of sweet odours, breathing from the plants, herbs, and flowers; to hear such natural melodious music and tunes of birds; to have in eye for mirth sometime these underspringing streams; then, the woods, the waters (for both pool and chase were hard at hand in sight), the deer, the people (that out of the east arbour in the base Court, also at hand in view), the fruit-trees, the plants, the herbs, the flowers, the change in colours, the birds flittering, the fountain streaming, the fish swimming, all in such delectable variety, order, and dignity; whereby, at one moment, in one place, at hand, without travel, to have so full fruition of so many God's blessings, by entire delight unto all senses (if all can take) at once: for etymon of the word worthy to be called Paradise:[1] and though not so goodly as Paradise, for want of the fair rivers, yet better a great deal by the lack of so unhappy a tree. Argument most certain of a right noble mind, that in this sort could have thus all contrived.

"But *Master Martin*, yet one windlass must I fetch, to make you one more fair course, an I can: and cause I speak of One, let me tell you a little of the dignity of One-hood; wherein always all high Deity, all Sovereignty, Pre-eminence, Principality, and Concord, without possibility of disagreement, is contained: As, One God, One Saviour, One Faith, One Prince, One Sun, One Phœnix; and as One of great wisdom saith, One heart, One way. Where One-hood reigns, there Quiet bears rule, and Discord flies apace. Three again may signify company, a meeting, a multitude, plurality; so as all tales and numberings from two unto three, and so upward, may well be counted numbers, till they mount unto infinity, or else to confusion, which thing the sum of two can never admit; nor itself can well be counted a number, but rather a friendly conjunction of two Ones; that, keeping in a sincerity of accord, may purport unto us charity to each other; mutual love, agreement and integrity of friendship without dissimulation. As is in these: The two Testaments; the Two Tables of the Law; the Two great Lights, *Duo luminaria magna*, the Sun and Moon. And, but mark a little, I pray, and see how of all things in the world, our tongues in talk do

[1] "Laneham, in making use of this expression, gave to Lord Leicester's gardens a name which it was customary to apply to pleasure-grounds and houses in the sixteenth and seventeenth centuries, as in the instances of Wressell and Lekinfield, in the East Riding of Yorkshire.

always so readily trip upon two's, pairs, and couples; sometimes as of things in equality, sometime of difference, sometime of contraries, or for comparison, but chiefly, for the most part, of things that between themselves do well agree, and are fast linked in amity: As, first, for pastimes, Hounds and Hawks; Deer red and fallow; Hare and Fox; Partridge and Pheasant; Fish and Fowl; Carp and Tench. For Wars, Spear and Shield; Horse and Harness; Sword and Buckler. For sustenance, Wheat and Barley; Pease and Beans; Meat and Drink; Bread and Meat; Beer and Ale; Apples and Pears.

"But lest by such dualities I draw you too far; let us here stay, and come nearer home. See what a sort of friendly binites[1] we ourselves do consist and stand upon: First, our Two feet, Two legs, Two knees, so upward; and above, Two shoulders, Two arms, and Two hands. But chiefly our principal Two; that is, body and soul: Then in the head, where all our senses meet, and almost all in Two's; Two Nostrils, Two ears, and Two eyes: So are we of friendly Two's from top to toe. Well, to this number of binites, take ye one more for an upshot, and here an end.

"Two dials nigh unto the battlements, are set aloft upon two of the sides of Cæsar's Tower; one east, the other south; for so stand they best to show the hours to the town and country: both fair, large, and rich, blue bice for ground, and gold for letters,[2] whereby they glitter conspicuous a great way off. The clockbell, that is good and shrill, was commanded to silence at first, and indeed, sung not a note all the while her Highness was there; the clock stood also still withal. But mark now, whether were it by chance, by constellation of stars, or by fatal appointment (if fates and stars do deal with dials) thus was it indeed. The hands of both the tables stood firm and fast, always pointing at two o'clock. Which thing beholding by hap at first, but after seriously marking in deed, enprinted into me a deep sign and

---

[1] "A word probably coined by Lancham to express duality, or the quality of being two. Its principal derivation is evidently from the Latin *binus*, two.

[2] "Bice is a pale blue colour prepared from the Armenian stone, formerly brought from Armenia, but now from the silver mines of Germany; in consequence of which smalt is sometimes finely levigated, and called bice. The dials alluded to in the text were enamelled, and with the sun's reflection on the gold figures, heightened by the azure ground, must have had a most splendid appearance.

argument certain: that this thing, among the rest, was for full significance of his Lordship's honourable, frank, friendly, and noble heart towards all estates: which, whether they come to stay and take cheer, or strait to return; to see, or to be seen; come they for duty to her Majesty, or love to his Lordship, or for both: come they early or late: for his Lordship's part, they come always all at two o'clock, e'en jump at two o'clock: that is to say, in good heart, good acceptance, in amity, and friendly welcome: who saw else that I saw, in right must say as I say. For so many things beside, *Master Humphrey*, were herein so consonant unto my construction, that this pointing of the clock (to myself) I took in amity, as an oracle certain. And here is my windlass like your course, as please you.

"But now, Sir, to come to an end. For receiving of her Highness, and entertainment of all the other estates. Since of delicates, that any way might serve or delight; as of wine, spice, dainty viands, plate, music, ornaments of house, rich arras and silk (to say nothing of the meaner things), the mass by provision was heaped so huge, which the bounty in spending did after bewray. The conceit so deep in casting the plat at first: such a wisdom and cunning in acquiring things so rich, so rare, and in such abundance: by so immense and profuse a charge of expense, which, by so honourable service, and exquisite order, courtesy of officers, and humanity of all, were after so bountifully bestowed and spent: what may this express, what may this set out unto us, but only a magnific mind, a singular wisdom, a princely purse, and an heroical heart? If it were my theme, *Master Martin*, to speak of his Lordship's great honour and magnificence, though it be not in me to say sufficiently, as bad a pen-clerk as I am, yet could I say a great deal more.

"But being here now in magnificence, and matters of greatness, it falls well to mind the greatness of his Honor's tent, that for her Majesty's dining was pight at Long Ichington, the day her Highness came to Kenilworth Castle. A tabernacle indeed for number and shift of large and goodly rooms, for fair and easy offices both inward and outward, all so likesome in order and eyesight: that justly for dignity may be comparable with a beautiful palace; and for greatness and quantity, with a proper town, or rather a citadel. But to be short, lest I keep you too long from the Royal Exchange now, and to cause you to conceive much matter in fewest words. The iron bedstead of Og,[1] the king of Basan (you know) was four yards and a half long, and two yards wide, whereby ye consider a giant of a great proportion was he: This tent had seven cart-load of pins pertaining to it: Now for the greatness, guess as you can.

"And great as it was (to marshal our matters of greatness together,) not forgetting a wether at Grafton, brought to the Court, that for body and wool was exceeding great; the measure I took not: let me show you with what great marvel a great child of Leicestershire, at this Long Ichington, by the parents was presented: great, I say, of limbs and proportion, of four feet and four inches high, and else lanuginous[2] as a lad of eighteen years; being indeed avowed to be but six years old, nothing more bewraying his age than his wit, that was, as for those years, simple and childish.

"As for unto his Lordship, having with such greatness of honourable modesty and benignity so passed forth, as *laudem sine invidia et amicos parit*. By greatness of well-doing, won with all sorts to be in such reverence as *de quo mentiri fama veretur*. In sincerity of friendship so great, as no man more devoutly worships *illud amicitiæ sanctum et venerabile nomen*. So great in liberality, as hath no way to heap up the mass of his treasure, but only by liberal giving and bounteous bestowing his treasure; following (as it seems) that saw of *Martial*, that saith,

"Extra fortunam est, quicquid donatur amicis:
Quas dederis, solas semper habebis opes.

"Out of all hazard dost thou set that to thy friends thou givest:
A surer treasure canst thou not have ever while thou livest.

What may these greatnesses bode, but only as great honour, fame, and renown for these parts here away, as ever was unto these two noble greats, the *Macedonian Alexander* in Emathia or Greece, or to *Roman Charles* in Germany or Italy.? Which, were it in me any way to set out, no man of all men by God, *Master Martin*, had ever more cause, and that hereby consider you.

"It pleased his Honor to bear me good will at first, and so to continue. To have given me apparel even from his back, to get me allowance in the stable, to advance me unto this worshipful

[1] "*Vide* Deuteronomy, chap. iii, verse 11.
[2] "An adjective derived from the Latin *lanuginosus*, downy, covered with soft hair.

office so near the most honourable Council, to help me in my licence of beans (though indeed I do not so much use it, for, I thank God, I need not) to permit my good father to serve the stable. Whereby I go now in my silks, that else might ruffle in my cut canvas: I ride now on horseback, that else many times might manege it on foot: am known to their Honors, and taken forth with the best, that else might be bidden to stand back myself. My good father a good relief, that he fares much the better by, and none of these for my desert, either at first or since, God knows. What say you, my good friend Humphrey, should I not for ever honour and extol him all the ways I can? Yes, by your leave, while God lends me power to utter my mind. And, having as good cause of his Honor, as *Virgil* had of *Augustus Cæsar*, will I poet it a little with *Virgil*, and say,

"Namque erit Ille mihi semper Deus, illius aram
Sæpe tener nostris ab ovilibus imbuet agnus.

"For he shall be a God to me, till death my life consumes,
His altars will I sacrifice with incense and perfumes.

"A singular patron of humanity may he be well unto us toward all degrees: of honour toward high estates, and chiefly whereby we may learn in what dignity, worship, and reverence her Highness is to be esteemed, honoured, and received, that was never indeed more condignly done than here; so as neither by the builders at first, nor by the edict of pacification after, was ever Kenilworth more ennobled, than by this his Lordship's receiving her Highness here now.

"But, Jesu, Jesu, whither am I drawn now? But talk I of my Lord once, even thus it fares with me: I forget all my friends, and myself too. And yet you, being a mercer, a merchant, as I am, my countryman born, and my good friend withal, whereby I know you are compassioned with me; methought it my part somewhat to impart unto you how it is here with me, and how I lead my life, which indeed is this:

"A mornings I rise ordinarily at seven o'clock: then ready, I go into the chapel; soon after eight, I get me commonly into my Lord's chamber, or into my Lord's presidents. There at the cupboard, after I have eaten the manchet served over night for livery, (for I dare be as bold, I promise you, as any of my friends the servants there; and indeed I could have fresh, if I would tarry; but I am of wont jolly and dry a mornings): I drink me up a good bowl of ale ; when in a sweet pot it is defecated[1] by all night's standing, the drink is the better, take that of me : and a morsel in a morning, with a sound draught, is very wholesome and good for the eyesight : Then I am as fresh all the forenoon after, as I had eaten a whole piece of beef. Now, Sir, if the Council sit, I am at hand; wait at an inch, I warrant you : If any make babbling, "Peace," say I, " wot ye where ye are ?" If I take a listener, or a pryer in at the chinks or at the lock-hole, I am by and by in the bones of him : but now they keep good order, they know me well enough : If he be a friend, or such a one as I like, I make him sit down by me on a form or a chest; let the rest walk, in God's name.

"And here doth my languages now and then stand me in good stead, my French, my Spanish, my Dutch, and my Latin : sometime among Ambassadors' men, if their masters be within the Council : sometime with the Ambassador himself, if he bid call his lacquey, or ask me what's o'clock; and I warrant you I answer him roundly, that they marvel to see such a fellow there : then laugh I, and say nothing. Dinner and supper I have twenty places to go to, and heartily prayed to : Sometimes I get to *Master Pinner;* by my faith a worshipful Gentleman, and as careful for his charge as any her Highness hath. There find I always good store of very good viands; we eat, and be merry, thank God and the Queen. Himself in feeding very temperate and moderate as you shall see any ; and yet, by your leave, of a dish, as a cold pigeon or so, that hath come to him at meat more than he looked for, I have seen him even so by and by surfeit, as he hath plucked off his napkin, wiped his knife, and eat not a morsel more; like enough to stick in his stomach two days after : (some hard message from the higher officers ; perceive ye me ?) Upon search, his faithful dealing and diligence had found him faultless.

"In afternoons and at nights, sometime am I with the right worshipful *Sir George Howard*, as good a Gentleman as any that lives. And sometime, at my good *Lady Sidney's* chamber, a Noble-woman that I am as much bound unto, as any poor man may be unto so gracious a Lady; and sometime in some other place. But always among the Gentlewomen by my good will ; (O, you know that comes always of a gentle spirit) : And

[1] "A participle formed of the Latin verb *defæco*, to purify liquors from their lees and foulness.

when I see company according, then can I be as lively too: Sometimes I foot it with dancing: now with my gittern, or else with my cittern, then at the virginals:[1] You know nothing comes amiss to me: Then carol I up a song withal; that by and by they come flocking about me like bees to honey; And ever they cry, "Another, good *Laneham*, another!" Shall I tell you? when I see *Mistress* —— (Ah! see a mad knave; I had almost told all!) that she gives once but an eye, or an ear; why then, man, am I blest; my grace, my courage, my cunning is doubled: She says, sometime, " She likes it ;" and then I like it much the better: it doth me good to hear how well I can do. And to say truth; what with mine eye, as I can amorously gloit it, with my Spanish sospires,[2] my French heighes, mine Italian dulcets, my Dutch hoves, my double releas, my high reaches, my fine foigning, my deep diapason, my wanton warbles, my running, my timing, my tuning, and my twinkling, I can gracify the matters as well as the proudest of them, and was yet never stained, I thank God: By my troth, countryman, it is sometimes high midnight, ere I can get from them. And thus have I told you most of my trade, all the live long day: what will you more, God save the Queen and my Lord. I am well, I thank you.

"Herewith meaned I fully to bid ye farewell, had not this doubt come to my mind, that here remains a doubt in you, which I ought (methought) in anywise to clear. Which is, ye marvel perchance to see me so bookish. Let me tell you in few words: I went to school, forsooth, both at Paul's and also at St. Anthony's; In the fifth form, passed Æsop's Fables, I wis, read Terence *vos istœc intro auferte*, and began with my Virgil *Tityre ta patulæ*. I conned my rules, could construe and parse with the best of them: since that, as partly you know, have I traded the

[1] The first two of these instruments, if not the same, were at least closely resembling each other. The words are a corruption from the Spanish *citara*, a guitar; or *Citron*, a guitar-maker. Citterns were a species of that extensive class of musical instruments of the guitar form, known in the best era of music in England, which went under the names of the Lute Ompharion, Bambora, &c. The *virginals* was a keyed instrument of one string to each note like a spinet, but in shape resembling a small piano-forte.

[2] Laneham gives in this passage a specimen of making love in the various languages in which he was skilled. *Suspiro*, in the Spanish tongue, signifies a very deep sigh: *Hé*, in the French, expresses the emotions of the soul in love; *Dolce*, in Italian, means dear or beloved; and in Dutch, *Hoofshied* is the word for courtship.

feat of merchandise in sundry countries, and so got me languages ; which do so little hinder my Latin, as I, thank God, have much encreased it. I have leisure sometimes, when I tend not upon the Council ; whereby, now look I on one book, now on another. Stories I delight in : the more ancient and rare, the more irksome to me. If I told you, I liked William of Malmesbury so well, because of his diligence and antiquity, perchance you would construe it because I love malmsey so well : But i' faith it is not so : for sipt I no more sack and sugar, (and yet never but with company,) than I do malmsey, I should not blush so much adays as I do : you know my mind.

"Well now, thus fare ye heartily well i' faith : If with wishing it could have been, ye had had a buck or two this summer : but we shall come nearer shortly, and then shall we merrily meet, an grace o' God. In the mean time commend me, I beseech you, unto my good friends, almost most of them your neighbours : *Master Alderman Pullison*,[1] a special friend of mine : And in any wise to my good old friend *Master Smith*, Customer, by that same token, —— " Set my horse up to the rack, and then let's have a cup of Sack." He knows the token well enough, and will laugh, I hold you a groat. To Master Thorogood : and to my merry companion (a Mercer, you know, as we be) *Master Denman, Mio fratello in Christo :* He is wont to summon me by the name of " *Ro. La.* of the County of Nosingham Gentleman :" A good companion, i' faith. Well, once again, fare ye heartily well. From the Court. At the City of Worcester, the twentieth of August, 1575.

" Your Countryman, companion, and friend assuredly : Mercer, Merchant-adventurer, and Clerk of the Council chamber-door, and also Keeper of the same :

El Prencipe Negro, Par me, R. L. Gent. Mercer

DE MAJESTATE REGIA

Benigno.

" Cedant arma togæ, concedat laurea linguæ,
Jactanter Cicero, at justius illud habe :
Cedant arma togæ, vigil et toga cedit honori,
Omnia concedant imperioque suo.

Deo Opt. Max. Gratiæ.

---

[1] " Afterwards Sir Thomas Pullison, and Lord Mayor in 1584.

END OF LANEHAM'S LETTER.

GASCOYNE'S
PRINCELY PLEASURES OF KENILWORTH.

INTRODUCTORY PREFACE.[1]

"THE festivities which took place at Kenilworth Castle being familiar to nearly all the reading public, as well by the reprint of Robert Laneham's letter, as by the admirable and interesting Romance of Kenilworth, it becomes a desirable appendage to both these works to have some specimens of the literary compositions which were prepared for the dramatic entertainments then displayed before Queen Elizabeth. Although Laneham's letter contains a perfect description of the arrangement and nature of the various pageants, yet he often professes himself unable to give more than a general abstract of the many laudatory orations, both in verse and prose, which were delivered in the course of the Queen's visit. For instance, such expressions as these convey only general information :—' A proper poesy in English rhyme and metre,'—' A rough speech full of passions,'—' A well-penned metre, and matter after this sort ;' and he also uses these apologetical terms, which may be considered as an excuse for all his omissions. ' Had her Highness happened this day to have come abroad, there was made ready a device of goddesses and nymphs, which, as well for the ingenious argument, as for the well-handling of it in rhyme and enditing, would undoubtedly have gained great liking, and moved no less delight. Of the particularities thereof, however, I cease to entreat, lest, like the bungling carpenter, by mis-sorting the pieces, I mar a good frame in the bad setting up ;

[1] Extracted from ' Gascoigne's Princely Pleasures,' 12mo. Lond., 1812.

or by my bad tempering before-hand, blemish the beauty when it should be reared up indeed.

"There are several sources whence these memoirs have been derived; firstly, the author's own works; secondly, the admirable life written by Mr. Chalmers, for his edition of the English Poets; and, lastly, from a curious biographical poem by Gascoigne's friend, George Whetstone.

"George Gascoigne, the son and heir of Sir John Gascoigne, was descended from an ancient and respectable family of Essex, and was first educated under a minister named Nevinson, who, as Mr. Chalmers observes, was probably 'Stephen Nevinson, LL.D., Prebendary and Commissary of the City and Diocese of Canterbury.' Gascoigne was next removed to the University; Wood supposes him to have studied both at Oxford and Cambridge, but from several passages in his works, it is most probable that he belonged only to the latter. From College, like many young gentlemen of his time, Gascoigne went to Gray's Inn, of which he became a member, and it is probable, that about this period, he entered upon that dissolute course of life, his repentance of which is so strongly marked in the greater part of his writings. With a mind certainly highly-gifted with poetic feeling, and a disposition amorous to a very great degree, it is not surprising, that the youthful poems of Gascoigne are all on the subject of love; Gabriel Harvey, in his *Gratulationes Valdinenses*, celebrates him, with Chaucer, and the Earl of Surrey, as a poetic champion of the female sex. It was most probably this dissipated course of life that caused Sir John Gascoigne to disinherit his son; although, from several passages in his poems, it would seem that his offences had been exaggerated by slanderous reports. Left entirely to himself, and cast into the world alone, he for some time endeavoured to brave it with independence; but, finding that the revellers with whom he had associated, and the mistresses on whom he had lavished his property, were alike insensible to his situation or unable to amend it, on March 19th, 1572, he sailed for Holland, and entered into the army of William, Prince of Orange. After a dangerous voyage, in which twenty of the crew were drowned through the pilot's intoxication, Gascoigne landed in Holland, and received a Captain's commission under the Prince. His poems entitled 'Gascoigne's Voyage into Holland,' 'The Fruites of Warre,' and 'The Fruite of Fetters, with the Complaint of the Greene Knight,' under which name it appears that Gascoigne was known in the army, contain much information respecting his life at this period. From these may be learned, that he was in a fair path to promotion, when an unfortunate dispute with his Colonel caused him to remove to Delf, in order to resign his commission to the Prince, who, however, exerted himself to bring about a reconciliation. During these events, while Gascoigne remained at Delf, a lady at the Hague, which was then occupied by the enemy's troops, sent a letter to him concerning his portrait which he had given her. This billet got into the possession of his Colonel and his enemies, who made such use of it as to excite considerable suspicion in the minds of many, especially the Dutch burghers, that Gascoigne was unfaithful to their cause. In consequence of this he underwent considerable privations, which lasted, as he remarks, 'a winter's tyde,' until the Prince coming into Zealand, Gascoigne laid the whole affair before him, and immediately received passports for visiting the lady, and an ample testimonial of his worth. Soon after, William of Nassau laid siege to Middleburg, and Gascoigne evinced such bravery in the capture of it, that the Prince, as he relates, presented him with,

> 'Three hundred guilders good above my pay,
> And bad me bide till his abilitie
> Might better guerdon my fidelitie.'

The credit which Gascoigne had thus attained, was certainly a principal cause of the misfortunes which succeeded it; since his enemies had then to add envy to their former hatred and suspicion. A reinforcement was at that period sent from England to the Spaniards, and Gascoigne was ordered, under the command of Captain Sheffield, to an unfinished fort at Valkenburg, which was immediately attacked. The Dutch forces there amounted only to five hundred men, while those of the Spanish were about three thousand; added to which, the fortification works were incomplete, and the garrison not supplied either with provision or ammunition. It was vain to contend when this miserable defence was assaulted, though Gascoigne and his companions held out until they were forced to retreat, which they at length did to Leyden, the gates of which were shut against them. The rest is easily imagined—they surrendered to the Spaniards, upon honourable terms, and after about four months' captivity, the officers were sent home to their own countries. After his return to England, Gascoigne resided at his chambers in Gray's Inn, and occasionally at Walthamstow, as he again began the study of the law, and also published such of his more serious poems as he expected would efface the memory of his amatory verses. In the summer of 1575, he attended Lord Leicester at Kenilworth, to assist Hunnis, Goldingham, Mulcaster, &c., in the production of masks and pageants for Queen Elizabeth's entertainment; and in the course of the following work, the reader will observe what share he took in their composition. When the Kenilworth festival was over, Gascoigne is supposed to have been employed at Walthamstow, in preparing his several works for the press; of which an accurate bibliographical account will be found at the end of this memoir. According to Whetstone, he wrote in this retirement, the satire of 'The Steele Glasse,' 'The Glass of Government,' 'The Delicate Diet,' 'a Book of Hunting,' and 'The Doom's Day Drum;' the latter of which was not published until after his death. Though Gascoigne was certainly admired and caressed in his own time, and enjoyed the friendship and patronage of many great and eminent men, 'yet,' says Mr. Chalmers, 'during this period he complains bitterly of what poets in all ages have felt, the envy of rivals and the malevolence of critics, and seems to intimate that, although he apparently bore this treatment with patience, yet it insensibly wore him out, and brought on a bodily distemper which his physicians could not cure. In all his publications, he takes every opportunity to introduce and bewail the errors of his youth, and to atone for any injury, real or supposed, which might have accrued to the public from a perusal of his early poems, in which, however, the proportion of indelicate thoughts is surely not very great.' In little more than two years after the Queen's visit to Kenilworth, on October the 7th, 1577, Gascoigne died, at Stamford, in Lincolnshire, according to Whetstone, in the presence of his wife and son, and with such calmness,

> 'as no man there perceiv'd
> By struggling sign or striving from his breath,
> That he abode the pains and pangs of death.'

It is supposed by his biographers, that his age did not exceed forty years.

"The above hasty sketch of Gascoigne's life cannot be better concluded, than by the following finely written poetic character, which Mr. Chalmers has given of him and of his works. 'If we consider the general merit of the poets in the early part of the Elizabethan period, it will probably appear that the extreme rarity of Gascoigne's works has been the chief cause of his being so much neglected by modern readers. In smoothness and harmony of versification, he yields to no poet of his own time, when these qualities were very common; but his higher merit is, that in every thing he discovers the powers and invention of a poet; a warmth of sentiment, tender and natural; and a fertility of fancy, although not always free from the conceits of the Italian school. As a satirist, if nothing remained but his Steele Glass, he may be reckoned one of the first. There is a vein of sly sarcasm in this piece, which appears to me to be original; and his intimate knowledge of mankind, acquired indeed at the expense probably of health, and certainly of comfort and independence, enabled him to give a more curious picture of the dress, manners, amusements, and follies of the times, than we meet with in almost any other author. To point out the individual beauties of his miscellaneous pieces, after the specimens exhibited by Mrs. Cooper, by Bp. Percy, Warton, Headley, and Ellis, would be unnecessary; but there are three respects in which his claims to originality require to be noticed, as æras in the history of poetry. His Steele Glass is among the first specimens of blank verse in our language; his Jocasta is the second theatrical piece written in that measure; and his Supposes is the first comedy written in prose.[1]

" ' *The Princely Pleasures at the Courte at Kenilwoorth*: That is to sayo, the copies of all such verses, Proeses, or Poeticall inuentions, and other deuices of pleasure, as were there deuised, and presented by Sundry Gentlemen, before the Quenes Maiesty: in the yeare 1575.

"Imprinted at London by Richard Jhones, 1576. 8vo.

"Of this edition, which is the first, only one copy is known. At the sale of Dr. Wright's library, in April, 1787, Dr. Farmer obtained it for the very trifling sum of ten shillings! On the demise of Dr. Farmer, in 1798, his library was also dispersed by the hammer, and this unique copy was purchased by Mr. Jeffery of Pall Mall, for the late George Ellis, Esq., for two pounds six shillings, which is somewhat surprising, as the rarity of the volume had then become more generally known; it subsequently

---

[1] A list of Gascoigne's Works, in verse and prose, will be found in the "Princely Pleasures," 12mo. Lond. 1821, from which the present work is extracted.

passed through the hands of Mr. Park to Messrs. Longman and Co., from whom it was transferred to its present possessor, William Staunton, Esq., of Longbridge. The existence of this edition was unknown to Mr. Nichols, while editing the Progresses of Queen Elizabeth; and the 'Princelye Pleasures,' of Gascoigne, are there given from a transcript from the subsequent edition of 1587; nor does it appear, that although Ritson had noticed this edition in his *Bibliographia Poetica*, that Mr. A. Chalmers knew anything more respecting it than Mr. Nichols, as in the preliminary notices prefixed to his republication of Gascoigne's poems, speaking of this work' he observes, 'This piece was first printed in the posthumous edition of his works.'"[1]

[1] 'Works of the English Poets,' 1810, vol. ii, p. 450.

THE PRINCELY PLEASURES
AT
KENILWORTH CASTLE.

A brief rehearsal, or rather a true copy of as much as was presented *before her Majesty at Kenilworth, during* her last abode there, as followeth.[1]

[1] Reprinted from the edition of 1821. 12mo, London.

THE PRINTER TO THE READER.

[From the first edition 'Imprinted at London by Richard Jhones, 1576.']

BEING advertised (gentle reader) that in this last Progress, her Majesty was (by the Right Noble Earl of Leicester) honourably and triumphantly received and entertained at his Castle of Kenilworth: and that sundry Pleasant and Poetical Inventions were there expressed, as well in verse as in prose. All which have been sundry times demanded for, as well at my hands, as also of other printers, for that indeed all studious and well-disposed young gentlemen and others, were desirous to be partakers of those pleasures by a profitable publication: I thought meet to try by all means possible if I might recover the true copies of the same, to gratify all such as had required them at my hands, or might hereafter be stirred with the like desire. And in fine, I have with much travail and pain obtained the very true and perfect copies of all that were there presented and executed; over and besides, one moral and gallant Device, which never came to execution, although it were often in readiness. And these (being thus collected,) I have (for thy commodity, gentle reader) now published: the rather because of a report thereof lately imprinted by the name of the Pastime of the Progress: which (indeed) doth nothing touch the particularity of every commendable action, but generally rehearseth her Majesty's cheerful entertainment in all places where she passed: together with the exceeding joy that her subjects had to see her: which report made very many the more desirous to have this perfect copy: for that it plainly doth set down every thing as it was indeed presented, at large: And further doth declare, who was Author and Deviser of every Poem and Invention. So that I doubt not but it shall please and satisfy thee both with reason and contentation: In full hope whereof, I leave thee to the reading of the same, and promise to be still occupied in publishing such works as may be both for thy pleasure and commodity.

This 26th of March, 1576.

KENILWORTH CASTLE.

" HER Majesty came thither (as I remember) on Saturday, being the ninth of July last past. On which day there met her on the way, somewhat near the Castle, *Sibylla*, who prophesied unto her Highness the prosperous reign that she should continue, according to the happy beginning of the same. The order thereof was this: *Sibylla* being placed in an arbour in the park near the highway, where the Queen's Majesty came, did step out and pronounced as followeth:

"ALL hail, all hail, thrice happy Prince,
    I am *Sibylla*, she
Of future chance, and after-haps,
    fore-shewing what shall be.
As now the dew of heavenly gifts
    full thick on you doth fall,
E'en so shall virtue more and more
    augment your years withal.
The rage of war bound fast in chains
    shall never stir nor move:
But peace shall govern all your days,
    encreasing subjects love.
You shall be called the Prince of Peace,
    and peace shall be your shield,
So that your eyes shall never see
    the broils of bloody field.
If perfect peace then glad your mind,
    he joys above the rest,
Which doth receive into his house
    so good and sweet a guest.
And one thing more I shall foretell,
    as by my skill I know:
Your coming is rejoiced at
    ten thousand times and mo.

And whiles your Highness here abides,
nothing shall rest unsought,
That may bring pleasure to your mind,
or quiet to your thought.
And so pass forth in peace (O Prince
of high and worthy praise):
The God that governs all in all,
encrease your happy days.

This device was invented, and the verses also written, by M. Hunnis, Master of her Majesty's Chapel.

"Her Majesty passing on to the first gate, there stood on the leads and battlements thereof six Trumpeters hugely advanced,[1] much exceeding the common stature of men in this age, who had likewise huge and monstrous trumpets counterfeited, wherein they seemed to sound: and behind them were placed certain trumpeters, who sounded indeed at her Majesty's entry. And by this dumb shew it was meant, that in the days and reign of King Arthur, men were of that stature. So that the Castle of Kenilworth should seem still to be kept by Arthur's heirs and their servants. And when her Majesty entered the gate, there stood *Hercules* for Porter, who seeming to be amazed at such a presence, upon such a sudden, proffered to stay them. But yet at last being overcome by view of the rare beauty and princely

---

[1] "This serves to explain a passage in Laneham's Letter which has excited considerable doubt; namely, that where he says, 'these trumpeters being six in number, were every one eight feet long,' see page 127 of the present work. It would appear that these were but figures constructed like all those used in ancient triumphs and pageants, of hoops, deal boards, pasteboard, paper, cloth, buckram, &c., which were gilded and coloured on the outside; and within this case the real trumpeter was placed. An exhibition similar to that mentioned in the text, is related by Holingshed, to have taken place when Queen Mary proceeded through London, before her Coronation, Sept. 30th, 1553. 'At the upper end of Grace's Street,' says that minute chronicler, 'there was another pageant, made by the Florentines, verie high, on the top whereof there stood four pictures, and in the middest of them and most highest, there stood an angell all in greene, with a trumpet in his hand: and when the trumpetter (who stood secretlie in the pageant) did sound his trumpet, the angell did put his trumpet to his mouth, as though it had been the same that had sounded, to the great marvelling of many ignorant persons.'—*Chronicles of Eng.* 1586, fol. vol. iii. p. 1091. Selden, in his 'Table Talk,' when speaking of Judges, alludes to such figures. 'We see,' says he, 'the pageants in Cheapside, the lions, and the elephants, but we do not see the men that carry them.'

countenance of her Majesty, yielded himself and his charge, presenting the keys unto her Highness, with these words :—

"What stir, what coil is here? come back, hold, whither now?
Not one so stout to stir, what harrying[1] have we here?
My friends a porter I, no poper here am plac'd:
By leave perhaps, else not while club and limbs do last.
A garboil[2] this indeed, what, yea, fair Dames? what yea,
What dainty darling's here? oh God, a peerless pearl;
No worldly wight no doubt, some sovereign Goddess sure:
Even face, even hand, even eye, even other features all,
Yea beauty, grace, and cheer, yea port and majesty,
Shew all some heavenly Peer, with virtues all beset.
Come, come, most perfect paragon, pass on with joy and bliss,
Most worthy welcome, Goddess guest, whose presence gladdeth all.
Have here, have here, both club and keys, myself, my ward, I yield,
E'en gates and all, yea Lord himself, submit and seek your shield.

"These verses were devised and pronounced by Master Badger of Oxford, Master of Arts, and Bedel in the same University.

"When her Majesty had entered the gate, and come into the base court, there came unto her a Lady attended with two nymphs, who came all over the pool, being so conveyed, that it seemed she had gone upon the water. This Lady named herself the Lady of the Lake,[3] who spake to her Highness as followeth:

"Though haste say on, let suit obtain some stay,
    (Most peerless Prince, the honour of your kind)
While that in short my state I do display,
    And yield you thanks for that which now I find,
Who erst have wish'd that death me hence had fet,[4]
If gods, not born to die, had ow'd death any debt.

"I am the Lady of this pleasant lake,
    Who since the time of great King Arthur's reign,

---

[1] "This word signifies an outry or chasing, and is derived from the Norman French *Haro* or *Harron*, which was a hue-and-cry after felons and malefactors —*vide* Phillips, and Jacob's 'Law Dictionary.'

[2] "Tumult or disorder—*vide* Phillips.

[3] See Laneham's description, page 128, of the present work.

[4] "The preterite and participle past of the ancient verb active to Fet, viz. to fetch, to go and bring. This word is evidently taken from the Saxon Feᴛᴛan, ᵹeᴛian, or ᵹeᴛiȝian, which are all of the same signification as the former—*vide* Bailey, Somner.

That here with royal court abode did make,
    Have led a low'ring life in restless pain.
Till now that this your third arrival here
    Doth cause me come abroad, and boldly thus appear.

" For after him, such storms this Castle shook,
    By swarming Saxons first who scourg'd this land,
As forth of this my pool I ne'er durst look,
    Though *Kenelm* King of *Merce* did take in hand
(As sorrowing to see it in deface)
    To rear these ruins up, and fortify this place.

" For straight by Danes and Normans all this isle
    Was sore distress'd, and conquered at last.
Whose force this Castle felt, and I therewhile
    Did hide my head, and though it straightway past
Unto Lord Saintlowe's hands, I stood at bay :
    And never shew'd myself, but still in keep I lay.

" The Earl Sir Mountford's force gave me no heart.
    Sir Edmund Crouchback's state, the prince's son,
Could not cause me out of my lake to part,
    Nor Roger Mortimer's ruff, who first begun
(As Arthur's heir) to keep the Table Round,
    Could not comfort my heart, or cause me come on ground.

" Nor any owner else, not he that's now,
    (Such fear I felt again, some force to feel)
Till now the Gods do seem themselves t' allow
    My coming forth, which at this time reveal
By number due, that your thrice coming here
    Doth bode thrice happy hope, and voids[1] the place from fear.

" Wherefore I will attend while you lodge here,
    (Most peerless Queen) to Court to make resort;
And, as my love to Arthur did appear,
    So shall 't to you in earnest and in sport.
Pass on, Madam, you need no longer stand,
    The Lake, the Lodge, the Lord, are yours now to command.

---

[1] "An old English verb active, originally derived from the French *Vider*, to empty or leave vacant. It was frequently used in the sixteenth and seventeenth centuries. Shakspeare in his Henry V. act v. scene vii. makes the King say,

    " ' Ride thou unto the horsemen on yon hill;
      If they will fight with us, bid them come down,
      Or *void* the field ; they do offend our sight.'

"These verses were devised and penned by M. Ferrers, sometime Lord of Misrule in the Court.[1]

"Her Majesty proceeding towards the inner court, passed on a bridge, the which was railed in on both sides. And on the tops of the posts thereof were set sundry presents, and gifts of provision: as wine, corn, fruits, fishes, fowls, instruments of music, and weapons for martial defence. All which were expounded by an actor clad like a Poet, who pronounced these verses in Latin:

"Jupiter è summi dum vertice cernit Olympi,
Huc, Princeps Regina, tuos te tendere gressus:
Scilicet eximiæ succensus imagine formæ,
Et memor antiqui qui semper ferverat ignis,
Siccine Cœlicolæ pacientur turpiter (inquit)
Muneris exortem Reginam hoc visere castrum,
Quod tam læta subit? Reliqui sensere tonantis
Imperium superi, pro se dat quisque libenter:
Musicolas Sylvanus aves; Pomonaque poma,
Fruges alma Ceres, rorantia vina Lyæus;
Neptunus pisces, tela et tutantia Mavors:
Hæc (Regina potens) superi dant munera divi:
Ipse loci dominus dat se Castrumque Kenelmi.

"These verses were devised by Master Muncaster,[2] and other verses to the very self-same effect were devised by M. Paton, and fixed over the gate in a frame. I am not very sure whether these

[1] For an interesting account of the Lord of Misrule, see note at end of the 'Princely Pleasures.'

[2] "From Fuller's *Worthies of England*, edit. 1662, part III, p. 139, Wood's *Athenæ Oxoniensis*, vol. I, p. 369, and Wilson's *Memorabilia Cantabrigiæ*, p. 112, a few particulars may be gained of the life of this eminent scholar, Dr. Richard Mulcaster. He was the son of William Mulcaster, was born at Carlisle, and was descended from an ancient family in Cumberland, which had been employed by King William I. to defend the border provinces of England from the depredations of the Scots. After having received his education on the foundation at Eton, in 1548, he was elected to King's College, Cambridge; but after taking one degree, he removed to Christ-Church, Oxford, to which he was elected in 1555. In December, 1556, he assumed his Bachelor's degree, and became so eminent for his Greek learning, that in 1561, he was made the first Master of the Merchant-Taylors' School, then recently founded. After passing upwards of twenty-five years in this situation, in 1596 he resigned it, and was made Head-master of St. Paul's, where he continued for twelve years more; and then, on the death of his wife, he retired to the Rectory of Stamford-Rivers, in Essex, which was given him by Queen Elizabeth. He

or Master Paten's were pronounced by the Author, but they were all to one effect. This speech being ended, she was received into the inner court with sweet music. And, so alighting from her horse, the drums, fifes and trumpets sounded: wherewith she mounted the stairs, and went to her lodging.

"On the next day (being Sunday) there was nothing done until the evening, at which time there were fireworks shewed upon the water, which were both strange and well executed; as sometimes passing under the water a long space, when all men had thought they had been quenched, they would rise and mount out of the water again, and burn very furiously until they were utterly consumed.

"Now to make some plainer declaration and rehearsal of all these things before her Majesty, on the tenth of July, there met her in the forest, as she came from hunting, one clad like a savage man, all in ivy, who, seeming to wonder at such a presence, fell to quarrelling with Jupiter as followeth:—

"O! thund'ring *Jupiter*,
  who swayest the heavenly sword;
At whose command all gods must crouch,
  and 'knowledge thee their Lord.
Since I (O wretch therewhiles)
  am here by thy decree,
Ordained thus in savage-wise
  for evermore to be.
Since for some cause unknown,
  but only to thy will;
I may not come in stately Court,
  but feed in forests still.
Vouchsafe yet, greatest god,
  that I the cause may know,
Why all these worthy Lords and Peers
  are here assembled so?
Thou knowest (O mighty god)
  no man can be so base,
But needs must mount, if once it see
  a spark of perfect grace.

---

was also, in 1594, made a Prebend of Salisbury, and was sometimes employed by the Queen in dramatic productions, since his name appears for two payments in the Council-Register. On April 15th, 1611, Mulcaster died at his rectory, and was buried, in his own church, by the side of his wife. The works of Dr. Mulcaster were, 'Positions;' a book on the training up of children, 1581, 4to.: 'Elementarie,' a volume on the English language, 1582, 4to.: and a Catechism for St. Paul's School, in Latin verse, 1599, 8vo.

And since I see such sights,
  I mean such glorious Dames,
As kindle might in frozen breasts
  a furnace full of flames,
I crave (great god) to know
  what all these Peers might be:
And what has moved these sundry shews,
  which I of late did see?
Inform me, some good man,
  speak, speak, some courteous knight:
They all cry mum; what shall I do,
  what sun shall lend me light?
Well, Echo, where art thou?
  could I but Echo find,
She would return me answer yet
  by blast of every wind.
Ho *Echo*—*Echo*, ho,
  where art thou, *Echo*, where?
Why, *Echo*, friend, where dwell'st thou now!
  thou wont'st to harbour here.

   (*Echo* answered.)
Echo.   Here.
  then tell thou me some news,
For else my heart would burst with grief,
  of truth it cannot chuse.
Echo.   Chuse.
Chuse? why? but thou me help:
  I say my heart will break:
And therefore even of courtesy,
  I pray thee *Echo* speak.
Echo.   Speak.
I speak? yes, that I will,
  unless thou be too coy,
Then tell me first what is the cause,
  that all the people joy?
Echo.   Joy.
Joy? surely that is so,
  as may full well be seen:
But wherefore do they so rejoice?
  is it for King or Queen?
Echo.   Queen.
Queen? what, the Queen of Heaven?
  they knew her long agone:
No sure some Queen on earth,
  whose like was never none.
Echo.   None.

O then it seems the Queen
    of England for to be,
Whose graces make the Gods to grudge:
    methinks it should be she.
Echo.   She.
And is it she indeed?
    then tell what was meant
By every shew that yet was seen,
    good *Echo* be content.
Echo.   Content.
What mean'd the woman first,
    which met her as she came?
Could she divine of things to come,
    as *Sibyls* use the same?
Echo.   The same.
The same? what *Sibyl?* she,
    which useth not to lie?
Alas! what did that beldame there?
    what did she prophesy?
Echo.   Prophesy.
O then by like she caus'd
    the worthy Queen to know:
What happy reign she still should hold,
    since heaven's ordained so.
Echo.   So.
And what mean'd those great men,
    which on the walls were seen?
They were some giants certainly,
    no men so big have been.
Echo.   Have been.
Have been? why then they served
    King Arthur man of might,
And ever since this castle kept,
    for Arthur's heirs by right.
Echo.   Right.
Well, *Hercules* stood by,
    why came he from his dorter?[1]
Or was it eke some monstrous man,
    appointed for a porter?
Echo.   A porter.
A porter? surely then,
    he either was acrazed,
Or else to see so many men,
    his spirits were amazed.
Echo.   Amazed.

---

[1] "A word derived from the French noun, *Dortoir*, a Dormitory. It originally signified, according to Phillips, 'the common room or place where all the Friars of one Convent sleep together and lie all night.'

Amazed? so methought,
    why did he let them pass:
And yield his keys? because he knew,
    his master's will so was.
Echo.   So was.
Well, then did he but well,
    yet saw I yet a Dame:
Much like the Lady of the Lake;
    perchance so was her name.
Echo.   Her name.
Alas, and what could she
    (poor dame distress'd) deserve?
I knew her well: percase she came
    this worthy Queen to serve.
Echo.   To serve.
So would I her advise:
    but what mean'd all those shifts,
Of sundry things upon a bridge?
    were those rewards of gifts?
Echo.   Gifts.
Gifts? what? sent from the god,
    as presents from above?
Or pleasures of provision,
    as tokens of true love?
Echo.   True love.
And who gave all these gifts?
    I pray thee (*Echo*) say.
Was it not he, who (but of late)
    this building here did lay?
Echo.   DUDLEY.
O DUDLEY, so methought:
    he gave himself and all,
A worthy gift to be receiv'd,
    and so I trust it shall.
Echo.   It shall.
What mean'd the fiery flames,
    which through the waves so flew?
Can no cold answers quench desire?
    is that experience true?
Echo.   True.
Well, *Echo*, tell me yet,
    how might I come to see
This comely Queen of whom we talk?
    oh were she now by thee!
Echo.   By thee.

By me? oh were that true,
  how might I see her face?
How might I know her from the rest,
  or judge her by her grace?
Echo.   Her grace.
Well then, if so mine eyes
  be such as they have been,
Methinks I see among them all,
  this same should be the Queen.
Echo.   The Queen.

"Herewith he fell on his knees and spake as followeth:—

"O Queen! I must confess,
  it is not without cause:
These civil people so rejoice,
  that you should give them laws.
Since I, which live at large,
  a wild and savage man,
And have run out a wilful race,
  since first my life began,
Do here submit myself,
  beseeching you to serve:
And that you take in worth my will,
  which can but well deserve.
Had I the learned skill,
  which in your head is found:
My tale had flow'd in eloquence,
  where now my words are drown'd.
Had I the beauteous blaze,
  which shines in you so bright:
Then might I seem a falcon fair,
  which now am but a kite.
Could I but touch the strings
  which you so heavenly handle;
I would confess, that fortune then,
  full friendly did me dandle.
O Queen (without compare)
  you must not think it strange,
That here amid this wilderness,
  your glory so doth range.
The winds resound your worth,
  the rocks record your name:
These hills, these dales, these woods, these waves,
  these fields pronounce your fame.
And we which dwell abroad
  can hear none other news,
But tidings of an English Queen,
  whom heaven hath deck'd with hues.

Yea, since I first was born,
    I never joy'd so much:
As when I might behold your face,
    because I see none such.
And death or dreary dole
    (I know) will end my days,
As soon as you shall once depart,
    or wish to go your ways.
But, comely peerless Prince,
    since my desires be great: -
Walk here sometimes in pleasant shade,
    to 'fend the parching heat.
On Thursday next (think I)
    here will be pleasant Dames:
Who bet than I[1] may make you glee,
    with sundry gladsome games.
Meanwhile (good Queen) farewell,
    the gods your life prolong:
And take in worth the Wild-Man's words,
    or else you do him wrong."

"Then he bad *Echo* farewell, thus:—

"*Echo* likewise farewell,
    let me go seek some death,
Since I may see this Queen no more,
    good grief now stop my breath."

"These verses were devised, penned, and pronounced by Master Gascoyne: and that (as I have heard credibly reported) upon a very great sudden.

"The next thing that was presented before her Majesty was the delivery of the Lady of the Lake: whereof the sum was this. *Triton* in likeness of a mermaid, came toward the Queen's Majesty as she passed over the bridge, returning from hunting. And to her declared that *Neptune* had sent him to her Highness, to declare the woeful distress wherein the poor Lady of the Lake did remain, the cause whereof was this. *Sir Bruce sans pitié*, in revenge of his cousin Merlin the Prophet,[2] (whom

---

[1] "An ancient poetical contraction, and also the original Saxon word Bet, used for better. During the repetition of the five lines preceding the above, a marginal note, in the first edition of the *Princely Pleasures*, states that 'the Queene saide the actor was blind,' in consequence of which, at p. 202, Audax, his Son, comes to entreat her Majesty to restore his father to sight.

[2] "The original of this story, as well as the history of the Lady of the Lake herself, is to be found in the well-known romance of *La Morte d'Arthur;* for

for his inordinate lust she had inclosed in a rock) did continually pursue the Lady of the Lake: and had (long since) surprised her, but that *Neptune* (pitying her distress) had environed her with waves. Whereupon she was enforced to live always in that Pool, and was thereby called the Lady of the Lake. Furthermore affirming that by Merlin's prophecy, it seemed she could never be delivered but by the presence of a better maid than herself. Wherefore *Neptune* had sent him right humbly to beseech her Majesty that she would no more but shew herself, and it should be sufficient to make *Sir Bruce* withdraw his forces. Furthermore, commanding both the waves to be calm, and the fishes to give their attendance: And this he expressed in verse as followeth:—

The Speech of *Triton* to the Queen's Majesty.

"Muse not at all, most mighty Prince,
  though on this lake you see
Me, *Triton*, float, that in salt seas
  among the gods should be.
For look what *Neptune* doth command,
  of *Triton* is obeyed:
And now in charge I am to guide
  your poor distressed maid;
Who, when your Highness hither came,
  did humbly yield her Lake;
And to attend upon your Court,
  did loyal promise make.
But parting hence that ireful knight,
  Sir *Bruce* had her in chace:
And sought by force, her virgin's state,
  full foully to deface.
Yes, yet at hand about these banks,
  his bands be often seen :
That neither can she come nor 'scape,
  but by your help, O Queen;
For though that *Neptune* has so fenc'd
  with floods her fortress long,
Yet *Mars* her foe must needs prevail,
  his batteries are so strong.

---

the first chapter of the fourth book is thus entitled: 'How Merlyn was assotted and dooted on one of the lades of the lake, and how he was shytte in a roche, vnder a stone, and there deyed.' The idea of Sir Bruce's revenge seems to be without foundation.

How then can *Dian, Juno's* force,
  and sharp assaults abide?
When all the crew of chiefest gods
  is bent on *Bruce's* side.
Yea, oracle and prophecy,
  say sure she cannot stand,
Except a worthier maid than she
  her cause do take in hand.
Lo, here therefore a worthy work,
  most fit for you alone;
Her to defend and set at large
  (but you, O Queen) can none:
And gods decree and *Neptune* sues,
  this grant, O peerless Prince:
Your presence only shall suffice
  her enemies to convince.

Herewith *Triton* sounded his trumpet and spoke to the winds, waters, and fishes, as followeth:—

"You winds return into your caves,
  and silent there remain:
You waters wild suppress your waves,
  and keep you calm and plain.
You fishes all, and each thing else,
  that here have any sway;
I charge you all in *Neptune's* name,
  you keep you at a stay.
Until such time this puissant Prince
  , Sir *Bruce* hath put to flight:
And that the maid released be,
  by sovereign maiden's might.

"This speech being ended, her Majesty proceeded further on the bridge, and the Lady of the Lake (attended with her two nymphs) came to her upon heaps of bulrushes, according to this former device: and spake as followeth:—

"What worthy thanks might I, poor maid, express,
  Or think in heart, that is not justly due
To thee (O Queen) which in my great distress
  Succours hast sent mine enemies to subdue?
Not mine alone, but foe to ladies all,
  That tyrant *Bruce sans pitié*, whom we call.

"Until this day, the lake was never free
  From his assaults, and other of his knights:
Until such time as he did plainly see
  Thy presence dread, and feared of all wights:
Which made him yield, and all his bragging bands,
  Resigning all into thy Princely hands.

"For which great grace of liberty obtain'd,
   Not only I, but nymphs, and sisters all,
Of this large lake, with humble heart unfeign'd
   Render thee thanks, and honour thee withal.
And for plain proof, how much we do rejoice,
   Express the same, with tongue, with sound, and voice.

"From thence her Majesty passing yet further on the bridge, *Proteus* appeared, sitting on a dolphin's back. The dolphin was conveyed upon a boat, so that the oars seemed to be his fins. Within which dolphin a concert of music was secretly placed, which sounded, and *Proteus* clearing his voice, sang this song of congratulation, as well in the behalf of the Lady distressed, as also in the behalf of all the nymphs and gods of the sea.

The Song of *Proteus*.

"O Noble Queen, give ear
   to this my floating muse:
And let the right of ready will
   my little skill excuse.
For herdmen of the seas
   sing not the sweetest notes:
The winds and waves do roar and cry
   where Phœbus seldom floats.
Yet since I do my best,
   in thankful wise to sing;
Vouchsafe (good Queen) that calm consent
   these words to you may bring:
We yield you humble thanks,
   in mighty *Neptune's* name,
Both for ourselves and therewithal
   for yonder seemly Dame.
A Dame, whom none but you
   deliver could from thrall:
No, none but you deliver us
   from loitering life withal.
She pined long in pain,
   as overworn with woes:
And we consum'd in endless care,
   to 'fend her from her foes.
Both which you set at large,
   most like a faithful friend:
Your noble name be prais'd therefore,
   and so my song I end.

"This song being ended, *Proteus* told the Queen's Majesty a pleasant tale of his delivery, and the fishes which he had in charge. The device of the Lady of the Lake was also by Master

Hunnis: and surely if it had been executed according to the first invention, it had been a gallant shew: for it was first devised, that (two days before the Lady of the Lake's delivery) a captain with twenty or thirty shot should have been sent from the heron house[1] (which represented the Lady of the Lake's Castle) upon heaps of bulrushes: and that *Sir Bruce*, shewing a great power upon the land, should have sent out as many or more shot to surprise the said Captain, and so they should have skirmished upon the waters in such sort, that no man could perceive but that they went upon the waves: at last (*Sir Bruce's* men being put to flight) the Captain should have come to her Majesty at the castle window, and have declared more plainly the distress of his mistress, and the cause that she came not to the court according to duty and promise, to give her attendance: and that thereupon he should have besought her Majesty to succour his mistress: the rather because *Merlin* had prophesied that she should never be delivered but by the presence of a better maid than herself. This had not only been a more apt introduction to her delivery, but also the skirmish by night would have been both very strange and gallant: and thereupon her Majesty might have taken good occasion to have gone in her barge upon the water, for the better execution of her delivery. The verses, as I think, were penned, some by Master Hunnis, some by Master Ferrers, and some by Master Goldingham.[2]

[1] "The marginal notes to the first edition of Gascoigne's Princely Pleasures, states that 'there was a Heron House in the Pool;' the original survey of the Manor preserved in the Cottonian Library, Tiberius, E. viii, 246, is, however, so damaged by fire, that this building is never mentioned.

[2] "Of Henry Goldingham only a very few memoranda are now extant: like many scholars of his time, he appears to have been employed, both as a writer and an actor of pageants, as in the present instance, when he performed Arion. A whole masque of his composing will be found in 'The receiving of the Queene's Majestie into her Citie of Norwich,' which was printed in Mr. Nichols's Progresses of Queen Elizabeth, vol. II, p. 26, of that particular tract. There is also in the Harleian Manuscripts, preserved in the British Museum, a poem by Goldingham, which is referred to in vol. III. of Queen Elizabeth's Progresses, p. x. In the Harleian Catalogue, edit. 1808, vol. III. p. 447, it is thus described: 'Numb. 6902. A Quarto containing a Poem inscribed to Queen Elizabeth by Henry Goldyngham, and entitled the Garden Plot. It is an allegorical poem, (118 verses) with a long introduction, (46 verses) in stanzas of six lines. This copy is prepared for introducing illuminations, but none are finished.' In another Harleian Manuscript, No. 3695, which is a collection of 'Merry Passages and Jeasts,' are two anecdotes con-

"And now you have as much as I could recover hitherto of the devices executed there; the Coventry shew excepted, and the merry marriage:[1] the which were so plain as needeth no further explication. To proceed then, there was prepared a shew to have been presented before her Majesty in the forest;

The argument whereof was this:

"*Diana* passing in chase with her nymphs, took knowledge of the country, and thereby called to mind how (near seventeen years past) she lost in those coasts one of her best beloved nymphs, called *Zabeta*.[2] She described the rare virtues of *Zabeta*. One of her nymphs confirmed the remembrance thereof, and seemed to doubt that *Dame Juno* had won *Zabeta* to be a follower of hers: *Diana* confirmed the suspicion; but yet affirming herself much in *Zabeta*'s constancy, gave charge to her

cerning Goldingham, one of which, as it relates to the Kenilworth Pageant, is here transcribed, but the other is wholly unworthy of being extracted.

"'221. There was a spectacle presented to Q: Elizabeth vpon the water, and amongst others, Har: Golding: was to represent Arion vpon the Dolphin's backe, but finding his voice to be very hoarse and vnpleasant when he came to performe it, he teares of his disguise, and sweares he was none of Arion, not he, but honest Har: Goldingham; which blunt discoverie pleasd the Queene better, then if it had gone thorough in the right way; yet he could order his voice to an instrument exceeding well.' In the romance of Kenilworth this incident is given to a fictitious but well-drawn character called Michael Lambourne, vide vol. III, p. 79. Before closing this note, it should be remarked, that in the text the name of Proteus is erroneously inserted for Arion.

1 "All the circumstances respecting the Coventry shew, and the merry marriage, here noticed, are particularly described in Laneham's Letter, see pages 136—143.

2 "A title formed from the last three syllables of the Queen's name, when translated into Latin, viz.: Elizabetha. She is, in page 214, called by several other appellations, as *Ahtebasile, Completa*, and *Complacida*. The first of these when divided thus, Ah te basile, signifies Ah thou Queen, taking the word basile, for Βασίλισσι; the second is the feminine gender in the nominative case, of the Latin adjective *Completus*, accomplished, complete; and the third is also a female name, expressive of pleasing or delighting. It is evident, that both the exhibitions in which these names were used, were composed to display to Elizabeth the national wish for her marriage with Lord Leicester; who is represented in the latter under the name of Deep-desire; while it is probable that Due-desire was meant for the Earl of Essex, and that all the other allegorical characters were but the types of real personages at the Court. Dudley in this manner showed his policy, by enforcing his own suit, and depreciating his rivals, even when the Queen had withdrawn from the intrigues of government, to pleasure and retirement.

nymphs, that they diligently hearken and espy in all places to find or hear news of *Zabeta:* and so passed on.

"To entertain *intervallum temporis,* a man clad all in moss came in lamenting, and declared that he was the wild man's son, which (not long before) had presented himself before her Majesty; and that his father (upon such words as her Highness did then use unto him) lay languishing like a blind man, until it might please her Highness to take the film from his eyes.

"The nymphs return one after another in quest of *Zabeta;* at last *Diana* herself returning, and hearing no news of her, invoked the help of her father *Jupiter. Mercury* cometh down in a cloud, sent by *Jupiter,* to recomfort *Diana,* and bringeth her unto *Zabeta. Diana* rejoiceth, and after much friendly discourse departeth: affying[1] herself in *Zabeta's* prudence and policy: She and *Mercury* being departed, *Iris* cometh down from the rainbow sent by *Juno:* persuading the Queen's Majesty that she be not carried away with *Mercury's* filed[2] speech, nor *Diana's* fair words; but that she consider all things by proof, and then she shall find much greater cause to follow *Juno* than *Diana.*

The Interlocutors were these:
Diana: Goddess of Chastity.
Castibula, Anamale, Nichalis: Diana's nymphs.
Mercury: Jove's messenger.
Iris: Juno's messenger.
Audax: the son of Silvester.

ACTUS 1. SCENA 1.
DIANA. CASTIBULA.

MINE own dear nymphs, which 'knowledge me your Queen,
And vow (like me) to live in chastity;
My lovely nymphs (which be as I have been)
Delightful Dames, and gems of jollity:
Rejoicing yet (much more) to drive your days
In life at large, that yieldeth calm content,
Than wilfully to tread the wayward ways
Of wedded state, which is to thraldom bent.
I need not now, with curious speech persuade
Your chaste consents, in constant vow to stand;
But yet beware lest Cupid's knights invade,
By slight, by force, by mouth, or mighty hand,

---

[1] "Assuring; the word is originally derived from the French verb active *Fier,* to trust or rely upon. Another edition reads affirming.
[2] "Smooth, polished.—Probably from Fÿlʋ, a folding or rolling.

The stately tower of your unspotted minds:
    Beware (I say) least while we walk these woods,
In pleasant chase of swiftest harts and hinds,
    Some harmful heart entrap your harmless moods:
You know these holts,[1] these hills, these covert places,
    May close convey some hidden force unseen;
You see likewise, the sundry gladsome graces,
    Which in this soil we joyfully have seen,
Are not unlike some court to keep at hand:
    Where guileful tongues, with sweet enticing tales,
Might (Circe like) set all your ships on sand:
    And turn your present bliss to after bales.
In sweetest flowers the subtle snakes may lurk:
    The sugar'd bait oft hides the harmful hooks;
The smoothest words draw wills to wicked work
    And deep deceits do follow fairest looks.

    Hereat pausing, and looking about her, she took
        knowledge of the coast, and proceeded:

But what? alas! oh whither wander we?
    What chase hath led us thus into this coast?
By sundry signs I now perceive we be
    In Brutus' land, whereof he made such boast,
Which Albion in olden days did hight,[2]
    And Britain next by Brute his noble name:
Then Hengist's land as chronicles do write:
    Now England short, a land of worthy fame.
Alas, behold how memory breeds moan:
    Behold and see, how sight brings sorrow in,
My restless thoughts have made me woe begone;
    My gazing eyes did all this grief begin.
Believe me (nymphs) I feel great grips of grief,
    Which bruise my breast, to think how here I lost
(Now long ago) a love to me most lefe.[3]
    Content you all: her whom I loved most:
You cannot choose but call unto your mind
    Zabeta's name, who twenty years or more
Did follow me, still scorning Cupid's kind,
    And vowing so to serve me evermore:
You cannot choose but bear in memory,
    Zabeta, her, whose excellence was such,
In all respect of every quality,
    As gods themselves those gifts in her did grudge.

---

[1] "Small woods, or groves,—derived from the Saxon Holte.
[2] "Named, called.
[3] "Dear-beloved.

My sister first, which *Pallas* hath to name,
    Envied *Zabeta* for her learned brain.
My sister *Venus* fear'd *Zabeta's* fame,
    Whose gleams of grace, her beauties blaze did stain;
Apollo dread to touch an instrument,
    Where my *Zabeta* chanc'd to come in place:
Yea *Mercury* was not so eloquent,
    Nor in his words had half so good a grace.
My step-dame, *Juno*, in her glittering guise,
    Was nothing like so heavenly to behold;
Short tale to make, *Zabeta* was the wight,[1]
    On whom to think my heart now waxeth cold.
' The fearful bird oft lets her food downfall,
    ' Which finds her nest despoiled of her young;'
Much like myself, whose mind such moans appal,
    To see this soil, and therewithal among,
To think how now near seventeen years ago,
    By great mishap I chanc'd to lose her here:
But, my dear nymphs, (on hunting as you go)
    Look narrowly: and hearken every where:
It cannot be, that such a star as she
    Can lose her light for any low'ring cloud:
It cannot be, that such a saint to see
    Can long inshrine her seemly self so shroud.
I promise here, that she which first can bring
    The joyful news of my *Zabeta's* life,
Shall never break her bow, nor fret her string.
I promise eke, that never storm of strife
Shall trouble her. Now nymphs look well about:
Some happy eye, spy my *Zabeta* out.

" CASTIBULA.

" O heavenly Dame, thy woeful words have pierc'd
    The very depth of my forgetful mind:
And by the tale which thou hast here rehears'd,
    I yet record those heavenly gifts which shined
Triumphantly in bright *Zabeta's* deeds:
    But therewithal, a spark of jealousy,
With nice conceit, my mind thus far-forth feeds;
    That she which always liked liberty,
And could not bow to bear the servile yoke,
    Of false suspect, which mars these lovers marts,
Was never one to like that smould'ring smoke,
    Without some feat, that passeth common arts.

---

[1] " A person.—Saxon Ƿihᚱ; a creature, an animal.

I dread *Dame Juno*, with some gorgeous gift,
Hath laid some snare her fancy to entrap,
And hopeth so her lofty mind to lift
On Hymen's bed, by height of worldly hap.

"DIANA.

"My loving nymph, even so fear I likewise,
And yet to speak as truth and cause requires,
I never saw *Zabeta* use the guise,
Which gave suspect of such unchaste desires.
Full twenty years I marked still her mind,
Nor could I see that any spark of lust
A loitering lodge within her breast could find.
How so it be (dear nymphs) in you I trust:
To hark, and mark, what might of her betide;
And what mishap withholds her thus from me.
High Jove himself my lucky steps so guide,
That I may once mine own *Zabeta* see.

Diana *with her nymphs proceed in chase: and, to entertain time, cometh in one clad in moss, saying as followeth:*

ACTUS 1. SCENA 2.
AUDAX solus.

"IF ever pity pierc'd
    a peerless Princess's breast;
Or ruthful moan mov'd noble mind
    to grant a just request;
Then, worthy Queen, give ear
    unto my woeful tale:
For needs that son must sob and sigh
    whose father bides in bale.
O Queen, O stately Queen,
    I am that wild man's son,
Which not long since before you here,
    presumed for to run.
Who told you what he thought
    of all your virtues rare:
And therefore ever since (and yet)
    he pines in woe and care.
Alas, alas, good Queen,
    it were a cruel deed
To punish him who speaks no more
    but what he thinks indeed.
Especially when as
    all men with him consent,
And seem with common voice to prove
    the pith of his intent.

You heard what Echo said
    to every word he spake;
You hear the speech of *Dian's* nymphs,
    and what reports they make.
And can your Highness then
    condemn him to be blind?
Or can you so with needless grief
    torment his harmless mind?
His eyes (good Queen) be great,
    so are they clear and grey:
He never yet had pin or web,
    his sight for to decay.
And sure the dames that dwell
    in woods abroad with us,
Have thought his eyes of skill enough,
    their beauties to discuss.
For proof your Majesty
    may now full plainly see:
He did not only see you then,
    but more he did foresee.
What after should betide,
    he told you that (ere long)
You should find here bright heavenly dames
    would sing the selfsame song.
And now you find it true,
    that he did then pronounce,
Your praises peyze[1] by them a pound,
    which he weigh'd but an ounce.
For sure he is nor blind,
    nor lame of any limb:
But yet because you told him so,
    he doubts his eyes are dim.
And I therefore (his son)
    your Highness here beseech,
To take in worth (as subjects due)
    my father's simple speech.
And if you find some film,
    that seems to hide his eyes:
Vouchsafe, good Queen, to take it off,
    in gracious wonted wise.
He sighing lies and says,
    god put mine eyes out clean,
Ere choice of change in England fall,
    to see another Queen.
        FINIS Actus 1.

---

1 Peyze—*weigh*. Fr. peser.

ACTUS 2. SCENA 1.
ANAMALE sola.

"WOULD god I either had some *Argus'* eyes,
    Or such an ear as every tiding hears;
Oh that I could some subtlety devise,
    To hear or see what mould *Zabeta* bears,
That so the mood of my *Diana's* mind
    Might rest (by me) contented or appeas'd
And I likewise might so her favour find,
    Whom, goddess like, I wish to have well pleas'd.
Some courteous wind come blow me happy news;
    Some sweet bird sing and shew me where she is;
Some forest god, or some of *Faunus'* crew,
    Direct my feet if so they tread amiss."

ACTUS 2. SCENA 2.
NICOLIS sola.

"If ever *Echo* sounded at request
    To satisfy an uncontented mind,
Then *Echo* now come help me in my quest;
    And tell me where I might *Zabeta* find.
Speak, *Echo*, speak, where dwells *Zabeta*, where?
    Alas, alas, or she, or I am deaf.
She answered not, ha! what is that I hear?
    Alas it was the shaking of some leaf.
Well, since I hear not tidings in this place,
    I will go seek her out in some place else:
And yet my mind divineth in this case,
    That she is here, or not far off she dwells."

ACTUS 2. SCENA 3.
DIANA *with her Train*.

"No news, my nymphs? well then I may well think,
    That carelessly you have of her enquired;
And since from me in this distress you shrink,
    While I (meanwhile) my weary limbs have tired;
My father, *Jove*, vouchsafe to rue my grief,
    Since here on earth I call for help in vain:
O, King of kings, send thou me some relief,
    That I may see *Zabeta* once again."

ACTUS 2. SCENA 4.

MERCURY, DIANA, *and the Nymphs.*

"O goddess, cease thy moan,
    thy plaints have pierc'd the skies,
And *Jove*, thy friendly father, hath
    vouchsaf'd to hear thy cries.
Yea more, he hath vouchsaf'd,
    in haste (post haste) to send
Me down from heaven to heal thy harm,
    and all thy miss to mend.
Zabeta, whom thou seek'st,
    (in heart) ev'n yet is thine,
And passingly in wonted wise
    her virtues still do shine.
But as thou dost suspect,
    Dame Juno train'd a trap,
And many a day to win her will,
    hath lull'd her in her lap.
For first these sixteen years
    she hath been daily seen,
In richest realm that Europe hath,
    a comely crowned Queen.
And *Juno* hath likewise
    suborned sundry kings,
The richest and the bravest both
    that this our age forth brings:
With other worthy wights,
    which sue to her for grace;
And cunningly, with quaint conceits,
    do plead the lover's case.
Dame Juno gives her wealth,
    dame Juno gives her ease,
Dame Juno gets her every good
    that woman's will may please.
And so in joy and peace
    she holdeth happy days:
Not as thou thought'st, nor done to death,
    or won to wicked ways.
For though she find the skill
    a kingdom for to wield,
Yet cannot *Juno* win her will,
    nor make her once to yield
Unto the wedded life,
    but still she lives at large,
And holds her neck from any yoke,
    without control of charge.

Thus much it pleased *Jove*
  that I to thee should say,
And furthermore, by words express,
  he bade I should not stay;
But bring thee to the place
  wherein *Zabeta* bides,
To prop up so thy staggering mind,
  Which in these sorrows slides.
O goddess, then be blithe,
  let comfort chase out grief,
Thy heavenly Father's will it is
  to lend thee such relief.

   " DIANA.

" O Noble *Mercury*,
  dost thou me then assure
That I shall see *Zabeta's* face,
  and that she doth endure
(Even yet) in constant vow
  of chaste unspotted life:
And that my step-dame cannot yet
  make her a wedded wife?
If that be so indeed,
  O Muses, help my voice,
Whom grief and groans have made so hoarse,
  I cannot well rejoice.
O Muses, sound the praise
  of *Jove*, his mighty name;
And you, dear nymphs, which me attend,
  by duty do the same.

Here *Diana*, with her nymphs, assisted by a concert of music unseen, should sing this song, or rondeau following:

" O Muses, now come help me to rejoice,
  Since *Jove* hath changed my grief to sudden joy;
And since the chance whereof I craved choice,
  Is granted me to comfort mine annoy:
   O praise the name of *Jove*, who promised plain
   That I shall see *Zabeta* once again.

" O gods of woods, and goddess *Flora* eke,
  Now clear your breasts and bear a part with me:
My jewel she, for whom I wont to seek,
  Is yet full safe, and soon I shall her see.
   O praise the name of *Jove*, who promised plain
   That I shall see *Zabeta* once again.

"And you, dear nymphs, who know what cruel care
   I bare in breast since she from me did part,
May well conceive what pleasures I prepare,
   And how great joys I harbour in my heart.
      Then praise the name of *Jove*, who promised plain
      That I shall see *Zabeta* once again.

             " MERCURY.

   Come, goddess, come with me,
         thy leisures last too long;
   For now thou shalt her here behold,
         for whom thou sing'st this song.
   Behold where here she sits,
         whom thou so long hast sought:
   Embrace her since she is to thee
         a jewel dearly bought.
   And I will now return
         to God in heaven on high:
   Who grant you both always to please
         his heavenly Majesty.
            Mercury departeth to heaven.

What do I dream? or doth my mind but muse?
   Is this my leefe, my love, and my delight?
Or did this god my longing mind abuse,
   To feed my fancy with a feigned sight?
Is this *Zabeta*, is it she indeed?
   It is she sure: *Zabeta* mine, all hail!
And though dame Fortune seemeth you to feed
   With princely port, which serves for your avail,
Yet give me leave to gaze you in the face,
   Since now (long since) myself, yourself did seek,
And be content, for all your stately grace,
   Still to remain a maiden always meek,
Zabeta mine (now Queen of high renown),
   You know how well I loved you always;
And long before you did achieve this crown,
   You know how well you seem'd to like my ways:
Since when, you (won by *Juno's* gorgeous gifts)
   Have left my lawns and closely kept in court;
Since when, delight and pleasure's gallant shifts
   Have fed your mind with many a princely sport.
But, peerless Queen, (sometime my peerless maid)
   And yet the same as *Mercury* doth tell,
Had you but known how much I was dismay'd
   When first you did forsake with me to dwell;

Had you but felt what privy pangs I had,
   Because I could not find you forth again,
I know full well yourself would have been sad,
   To put me so to proof of pinching pain.
Well, since *Dan Jove* (my father) me assures,
   That, notwithstanding all my step-dame's wiles,
Your maiden's mind yet constant still endures,
   Though well content a Queen to be therewhiles;
And since by prudence and by policy,
   You win from *Juno* so much worldly wealth,
And since the pillar of your chastity
   Still standeth fast, as *Mercury* me tell'th,
I joy with you, and leave it to your choice
   What kind of life you best shall like to hold;
And in meanwhile I cannot but rejoice
   To see you thus bedeck'd with glistering gold;
To see you have this train of stately dames,
   Of whom each one may seem some goddess peer,
And you yourself (by due desert of fame)
   A goddess full, and so I leave you here,
It shall suffice that on your faith I trust;
It shall suffice that once I have you seen;
Farewell; not as I would, but as I must,
Farewell, my nymph, farewell, my noble Queen.

            "*Diana with her Train departeth.*

ACTUS 2. SCENA ultima.

"IRIS sola.

"Oh lo, I come too late,
        oh, why had I no wings?
To help my willing feet, which fet
        these hasty frisking flings;
Alas, I come too late,
        that babbling god is gone:
And *Dame Diana* fled likewise,
        here stands the Queen alone.
Well, since a bootless plaint
        but little would prevail,
I will go tell the Queen my tale:
        O, peerless Prince, all hail,
The Queen of heaven herself
        did send me to control
That tattling traitor, *Mercury*,
        who hopes to get the goal,

By curious filed speech,
    abusing you by art:
But, Queen, had I come soon enough,
    he should have felt the smart.
And you, whose wit excels,
    whose judgment hath no peer,
Bear not in mind those flattering words
    which he expressed here.
You know that in his tongue
    consists his chiefest might;
You know his eloquence can serve
    to make the crow seem white.
But come to deeds indeed,
    and then you shall perceive
Which goddess means you greatest good,
    and which would you deceive.
Call you to mind the time
    in which you did insue[1]
Diana's chase, and were not yet
    a guest of *Juno's* crew.
Remember all your life
    before you were a Queen:
And then compare it with the days
    which you since then have seen.
Were you not captive caught?
    were you not kept in walls?
Were you not forc'd to lead a life
    like other wretched thralls?
Where was *Diana* then?
    why did she you not aid?
Why did she not defend your state
    which were and are her maid?
Who brought you out of briers?
    who gave you rule of realms?
Who crowned first your comely head
    with princely diadems?
Even *Juno*, she which mean'd,
    and yet doth mean likewise,
To give you more than will can wish,
    or wit can well devise.
Wherefore, good Queen, forget
    Diana's 'ticing tale:
Let never needless dread presume
    to bring your bliss to bale.

---

[1] Insue—*follow.*

How necessary were
    for worthy Queens to wed,
That know you well, whose life always
    in learning hath been led.
The country craves consent,
    your virtues vaunt each self,
And *Jove* in heaven would smile to see
    Diana set on shelf.
His Queen hath sworn (but you)
    there shall no more be such:
You know she lies with *Jove* a-nights,
    and night-ravens may do much.
Then give consent, O Queen,
    to *Juno's* just desire,
Who for your wealth would have you wed,
    and, for your farther hire,
Some Empress will you make,
    she bade me tell you thus:
Forgive me (Queen), the words are hers,
    I come not to discuss:
I am but messenger,
    but sure she bade me say,
That where you now in princely port
    have past one pleasant day:
A world of wealth at will
    you henceforth shall enjoy
In wedded state, and therewithal
    hold up from great annoy
The staff of your estate:
    O Queen, O worthy Queen,
Yet never wight felt perfect bliss,
    but such as wedded been.
            Tam Marti, quam Mercurio.

"This shew was devised and penned by Master Gascoigne, and being prepared and ready (every Actor in his garment) two or three days together, yet never came to execution. The cause whereof I cannot attribute to any other thing, then to lack of opportunity and seasonable weather.

"The Queen's Majesty hastening her departure from thence, the Earl commanded Master Gascoigne to devise some farewell worth the presenting; whereupon he himself clad like unto *Sylvanus*, god of the woods, and meeting her as she went on hunting, spake (*ex tempore*) as followeth:—

"'Right excellent, puissant, and most happy Princess, whiles

I walk in these woods and wilderness (whereof I have the charge) I have often mused with myself, that your Majesty being so highly esteemed, so entirely beloved, and so largely endued by the celestial powers: you can yet continually give ear to the counsel of these terrestrial companions; and so, consequently, pass your time wheresoever they devise or determine that it is meet for your Royal Person to be resident. Surely if your Highness did understand (as it is not to me unknown) what pleasures have been for you prepared, what great good will declared, what joy and comfort conceived in your presence, and what sorrow and grief sustained by likelihood of your absence, yea, (and that by the whole bench in heaven) since you first arrived in these coasts, I think it would be sufficient to draw your resolute determination for ever to abide in this country, and never to wander any further by the direction and advice of these Peers and Counsellors; since thereby the heavens might greatly be pleased, and most men thoroughly recomforted. But, because I rather wish the increase of your delights, than any way to diminish the heap of your contentment, I will not presume to stay your hunting for the hearing of my needless, thriftless, and bootless discourse; but I do humbly beseech that your excellency will give me leave to attend you as one of your footmen, wherein I undertake to do you double service; for I will not only conduct your Majesty in safety from the perilous passages which are in these woods and forests, but will also recount unto you (if your Majesty vouchsafe to hearken thereunto) certain adventures, neither unpleasant to hear, nor unprofitable to be marked.

Herewith her Majesty proceeded, and Sylvanus *continued as followeth :—*

"'There are not yet twenty days past (most noble Queen) since I have been, by the Procuror-General, twice severally summoned to appear before the great gods in their Council-chamber; and making mine appearance according to my duty, I have seen in heaven two such exceeding great contrarieties, or rather two such wonderful changes as draw me into deep admiration and sudden perplexity. At my first coming I found the whole company of heaven in such a jollity, as I rather want skill to express it lively, than will to declare it readily. There was nothing in any corner to be seen, but rejoicing and mirth, singing, dancing, melody and harmony, amiable regards, plentiful rewards, tokens of love, and great good will, trophies and triumphs, gifts and presents, (alas, my breath and memory fail me) leaping, frisking, and clapping of hands.

"'To conclude, there was the greatest feast and joy that ever eye saw, or ear heard tell of, since heaven was heaven, and the earth began to have his being. And enquiring the cause thereof, *Reason*, one of the heavenly Ushers, told me, that it was to congratulate the coming of your most excellent Majesty into this country. In very deed to confess a truth, I might have perceived no less by sundry manifest tokens here on earth; for even here in my charge, I might see the trees flourish in more then ordinary bravery, the grass grow greener than it was wont to do, and the deer went tripping (though against their death) in extreme delicacy and delight. Well, to speak of that I saw in heaven, every god and goddess made all preparations possible to present your Majesty with some acceptable gift, thereby to declare the exceeding joy which they conceived in your presence. And I, poor rural god, which am but seldom called amongst them, and then also but slenderly countenanced, yet for my great good will towards your Majesty no way inferior to the proudest god of them all, came down again with a flea in mine ear, and began to beat my brains for some device of some present, which might both bewray the depth of mine affections, and also be worthy for so excellent a Princess to receive. But whiles I went so amusing with myself, many, yea, too many days, I found by due experience that this proverb was all too true, *omnis mora trahit periculum*. For whiles I studied to achieve the height of my desires; behold, I was the second time summoned to appear in heaven. What said I? Heaven? no, no, most comely Queen, for when I came there, heaven was not heaven, it was rather a very hell. There was nothing but weeping and wailing, crying and howling, dole, desperation, mourning, and moan. All which I perceived also here on earth before I went up, for of a truth (most noble Princess) not only the skies scowled, the winds raged, the waves roared and tossed, but also the fishes in the waters turned up their bellies, the deer in the woods went drooping, the grass was weary of growing, the trees shook off their leaves, and all the beasts of the forest stood amazed.

"'The which sudden change I plainly perceived to be, for that they understood above, that your Majesty would shortly (and too speedily) depart out of this country, wherein the heavens have happily placed you, and the whole earth earnestly desireth to keep you. Surely (Gracious Queen) I suppose that this late alteration in the skies hath seemed unto your judgment drops of rain in accustomed manner. But, if your Highness will believe me, it was nothing else but the very flowing tears of the gods, who melted into moan for your hasty departure.

"' Well, because we rural gods are bound patiently to abide the censure of the celestial bench, I thought meet to hearken what they would determine, and for a final conclusion it was generally determined, that some convenient messenger should be dispatched with all expedition possible, as well to beseech your Majesty that you would here remain, as also further to present you with the proffer of any such commodities and delights, as might draw your full consent to continue here for their contentation, and the general comfort of men.'

"Here her Majesty stayed her horse to favour *Sylvanus*, fearing lest he should be driven out of breath by following her horse so fast. But *Sylvanus* humbly besought her Highness to go on, declaring that if his rude speech did not offend her, he could continue this tale to be twenty miles long. And therewithal protested that he had rather be her Majesty's footman on earth, than a god on horseback in heaven, proceeding as followeth:

"' Now to return to my purpose (most excellent Queen) when I had heard their deliberation, and called unto mind that sundry realms and provinces had come to utter subversion by over great trust given to Ambassadors, I (being thoroughly tickled with a restless desire) thought good to plead in person; for I will tell your Majesty one strange property that I have, there are few or none which know my mind so well as myself, neither are there many which can tell mine own tale better than I myself can do. And therefore I have continually awaited these three days, to espy when your Majesty would (in accustomed manner) come on hunting this way.

"' And being now arrived most happily into the port of my desires, I will presume to beseech most humbly, and to entreat most earnestly, that your Highness have good regard to the general desire of the gods, together with the humble petitions of your most loyal and deeply affectionate servants.

"' And for my poor part, in full token of my dutiful meaning, I here present you the store of my charge, undertaking that the deer shall be daily doubled for your delight in chase. Furthermore I will entreat *Dame Flora* to make it continually spring here with stores of redolent and fragrant flowers. *Ceres* shall be compelled to yield your majesty a competent provision, and *Bacchus* shall be sued unto for the first fruits of his vineyards. To be short, O peerless Princess, you shall have all things that may possibly be gotten for the furtherance of your delights. And I shall be most glad and triumphant, if I may place my godhead in your service perpetually. This tedious tale, O comely Queen, I began with a bashful boldness, I have continued in base eloquence, and I cannot better knit it up, than with homely humility, referring the consideration of these my simple words, unto the deep discretion of your Princely will. And now I will, by your Majesty's leave, turn my discourse into the rehearsal of strange and pitiful adventures.

"'So it is, good gracious Lady, that *Diana* passeth often-times through this forest with a stately train of gallant and beautiful nymphs.

"'Amongst whom there is one surpassing all the rest for singular gifts and graces: some call her *Zabeta*, some other have named her *Ahtebasile*, some *Completa*, and some *Complacida*: whatsoever her name be, I will stand upon it. But (as I have said) her rare gifts have drawn the most noble and worthy personages in the whole world to sue unto her for grace.

"'All which she hath so rigorously repulsed, or rather (to speak plain English) so obstinately and cruelly rejected, that I sigh to think of some of their mishaps. I allow and commend her justice towards some others, and yet the tears stand in mine eyes (yea and my tongue trembleth and faltereth in my mouth) when I begin to declare the distresses wherein some of them do presently remain. I could tell your Highness of sundry famous and worthy persons, whom she hath turned and converted into most monstrous shapes and proportions. As some into fishes, some others into fowls, and some into huge stony rocks and great mountains: but because divers of her most earnest and faithful followers (as also some sycophants) have been converted into sundry of these plants, whereof I have charge, I will shew unto your Majesty so many of them as are in sight in these places where you pass.

"'Behold, gracious Lady, this old oak, the same was many years a faithful follower and trusty servant of hers, named *Constancy*, whom, when she could by none other means overthrow, considering that no change could creep into his thoughts, nor any trouble of passions and perplexities could turn his resolute mind, at length she caused him, as I say, to be converted into this oak, a strange and cruel metamorphosis. But yet the heavens have thus far forth favoured and rewarded his long continued service, that as in life he was unmovable, even so now all the vehement blasts of the most raging winds cannot once move his rocky body from his rooted place and abiding. But to countervail this cruelty with a shew of justice, she converted his contrary, *Inconstancy*, into yonder poplar, whose leaves move and shake with the least breath or blast.

"'As also she dressed *Vain Glory* in his right colours, converting him into this ash-tree, which is the first of my plants that buddeth, and the first likewise that casteth leaf. For believe me, most excellent Princess, *Vain Glory* may well begin hastily, but seldom continueth long.

"'Again she hath well requited that busy elf, *Contention*, whom she turned into this bramble-brier, the which, as your Majesty may well see, doth even yet catch and snatch at your garments, and every other thing that passeth by it. And as for that wicked wretch *Ambition*, she did by good right condemn him into this branch of ivy, the which can never climb on high, nor flourish without the help of some other plant or tree, and yet commonly what tree soever it raiseth by, it never leaveth to wind about it, and straitly to enfold it, until it hath smouldered and killed it. And by your leave, good Queen, such is the unthankful nature of cankered ambitious minds, that commonly they malign them by whom they have risen, and never cease until they have brought them to confusion. Well, notwithstanding these examples of justice, I will now rehearse unto your Majesty such a strange and cruel metamorphosis as I think must needs move your noble mind unto compassion. There were two sworn brethren which long time served her, called *Deep-desire* and *Due-desert*, and although it be very hard to part these two in sunder, yet it is said that she did long since convert *Due-desert* into yonder same laurel-tree. The which may very well be so, considering the etymology of his name, for we see that the laurel-branch is a token of triumph in all trophies, and given as a reward to all victors, a dignity for all degrees, consecrated and dedicated to *Apollo* and the *Muses* as a worthy flower, leaf, or branch, for their due deserts. Of him I will hold no longer discourse, because he was metamorphosed before my time; for your Majesty must understand that I have not long held this charge, neither do I mean long to continue in it; but rather most gladly to follow your Highness wheresoever you shall become.

"'But to speak of *Deep-desire*, (that wretch of worthies, and yet the worthiest that ever was condemned to wretched estate,) he was such an one as neither any delay could daunt him; no disgrace could abate his passions; no time could tire him; no water quench his flames; nor death itself could amaze him with terror.

"'And yet this strange star, this courteous cruel, and yet the cruelest courteous that ever was, this *Ahtebasile, Zabeta*, or by what name soever it shall please your Majesty to remember her, did never cease to use imprecation, invocation, conjuration, and means possible, until she had caused him to be turned into this holly-bush, and as he was in this life and world continually full of compunctions, so is he now furnished on every side with sharp pricking leaves, to prove the restless pricks of his privy thoughts. Marry, there are two kinds of holly, that is to say, he holly, and she holly. Now some will say, that she holly hath no pricks, but thereof I intermeddle not.'

"At these words her Majesty came by a closer arbour, made all of holly; and while *Sylvanus* pointed to the same, the principal bush shaked. For therein were placed both strange music, and one who was there appointed to represent *Deep-desire*. *Sylvanus*, perceiving the bush to shake, continued thus :

"'Behold, most gracious Queen, this holly-bush doth tremble at your presence, and therefore I believe that *Deep-desire* hath gotten leave of the gods to speak unto your excellent Majesty in their behalf, for I myself was present in the council-chamber of heaven, when *Desire* was thought a meet messenger to be sent from that convocation unto your Majesty as ambassador; and give ear, good Queen, methinks I hear his voice.'

"Herewith *Deep-desire* spake out of the holly-bush as followeth :—

"STAY, stay your hasty steps,
O Queen without compare;
And hear him talk, whose trusty tongue
consumed is with care:
I am that wretch *Desire*,
whom neither death could daunt,
Nor dole decay, nor dread delay,
nor feigned cheer enchant.

Whom neither care could quench,
    nor fancy force to change;
And therefore turn'd into this tree,
    which sight, percase, seems strange.
But when the gods of heaven,
    and goddesses withall,
Both gods of fields and forest gods,
    yea, satyrs, nymphs, and all,
Determined a dole,
    by course of free consent:
With wailing words and mourning notes,
    your parting to lament.
Then thought they meet to choose
    me, silly wretch, *Desire*,
To tell a tale that might bewray
    as much as they require.
And hence proceeds, O Queen,
    that from this holly-tree
Your learned ears may hear him speak,
    whom yet you cannot see,
But, Queen, believe me now,
    although I do not swear;
Was never grief, as I could guess,
    which set their hearts so near,
As when they heard the news,
    that you, O royal Queen,
Would part from hence; and that to prove
    it may full well be seen.
For mark what tears they shed
    these five days past and gone:
It was no rain, of honesty,
    it was great floods of moan.
As first *Diana* wept
    such brinish bitter tears;
That all her nymphs did doubt her death,
    her face the sign yet bears.
Dame *Flora* fell on ground,
    and bruis'd her woeful breast:
Yea, *Pan* did break his oaten pipes;
    Silvanus and the rest,
Which walk amid these woods,
    for grief did roar and cry;
And *Jove*, to shew what moan he made
    with thund'ring crack'd the sky.
O Queen, O worthy Queen,
    within these holts and hills,
Were never heard such grievous groans,
    nor seen such woeful wills.

But since they have decreed,
    that I poor wretch, *Desire,*
In their behalf shall make their moan,
    and comfort thus require:
Vouchsafe, O comely Queen,
    yet longer to remain;
Or still to dwell amongst us here:
    O Queen, command again
This castle and the knight,
    which keeps the same for you;
These woods, these waves, these fowls, these fishes,
    these deer which are your due:
Live here, good Queen, live here,
    you are amongst your friends:
Their comfort comes when you approach,
    and when you part, it ends.
What fruits this soil may serve,
    thereof you may be sure:
Dame *Ceres* and Dame *Flora* both
    will with you still endure.
Diana would be glad
    to meet you in the chase:
Sylvanus and the forest-gods
    would follow you apace.
Yea, *Pan* would pipe his part,
    such dances as he can:
Or else *Apollo* music make,
    and *Mars* would be your man.
And to be short, as much
    as gods and men may do;
So much your Highness here may find,
    with faith and favour too.
But if your noble mind,
    resolved by decree,
Be not content, by me *Desire,*
    persuaded for to be,
Then bend your willing ears
    unto my willing note,
And hear what song the gods themselves
    have taught me now by rote.
Give ear, good gracious Queen,
    and so you shall perceive
That gods in heaven, and men on earth,
    are loth such Queens to leave.

" Herewith the concert of music sounded, and *Deep-desire* sang this song:

> "Come, Muses, come and help me to lament,
> Come, woods, come waves, come hills, come doleful dales,
> Since life and death are both against me bent,
> Come gods, come men, bear witness of my bales.
> O heavenly nymphs, come help my heavy heart,
> With sighs to see Dame *Pleasure* thus depart.
>
> "If death or dole could daunt a deep desire,
> If privy pangs could counterpoise my plaint:
> If tract of time, a true intent could tire,
> Or cramps of care, a constant mind could taint:
> Oh then might I at will here live and serve;
> Although my deeds did more delight deserve.
>
> "But out, alas, no gripes of grief suffice
> To break in twain this harmless heart of mine,
> For though delight be banish'd from mine eyes,
> Yet lives *Desire*, whom pains can never pine.
> Oh strange effects! I live which seem to die,
> Yet die to see my dear delight go by.
>
> "Then farewell, sweet, for whom I taste such sour,
> Farewell, delight, for whom I dwell in dole:
> Free will, farewell, farewell my fancy's flower,
> Farewell, content, whom cruel cares control.
> Oh farewell life, delightful death, farewell,
> I die in heaven, yet live in darksome hell.

"This song being ended, the music ceased, and *Sylvanus* concluded thus:

"'Most gracious Queen, as it should but evil have beseemed a god to be found fraudulent or deceitful in his speech: so have I neither recounted nor foretold any thing unto your Majesty, but that which you have now found true by experience, and because the case is very lamentable, in the conversion of *Deep-desire*, as also because they know that your Majesty is so highly favoured of the gods, that they will not deny you any reasonable request. Therefore I do humbly crave in his behalf, that you would either be a suitor for him unto the heavenly powers, or else but only to give your gracious consent that he may be restored to his pristinate estate. Whereat your Highness may be assured that heaven will smile, the earth will quake, men will clap their hands, and I will always continue an humble beseecher for the flourishing estate of your Royal Person.

Whom God now and ever preserve, to his good pleasure and
our great comfort. Amen.
Tam Marti, quam Mercurio.'"

LORD OF MISRULE.[1]

"WARTON, in his *History of English Poetry*, vol. II. sect. xxxiv. p. 293, states that this was George Ferrers, whom Holingshed mentions as Lord of Misrule in the time of King Edw. VI.; but Wood in his *Athenæ Oxoniensis*, when speaking of this eminent author, never mentions his having held such an office; probably supposing that it would be derogatory to his character, both as a scholar and a poet. Puttenham calls him by the name of 'Maister Edward Ferrys,' and this has created a supposition that these were two different persons, but the character which he has given of that author, has nearly identified him to be the same as the George Ferrers already mentioned. The latter writer, when speaking of him as a poet of Edward the Sixth's reign, says: 'But the principall man in this profession, at the same time was Maister Edward Ferrys, a man of no lessse mirth and felicitie that way, but of much more skil and magnificence in his meeter, and therefore wrate for the most part to the Stage in Tragedie, and sometimes in Comedie or Enterlude, wherein he gave the King so much good recreation, as he had thereby many good rewardes.'—Lib. I, ch. xxxi, p. 49, edit. 1589. Soon after, the same author again observes, 'for Tragedie the Lord Buckhurst and maister Edward Ferrys, for such doinges as I have sene of theirs, deserve the highest price.'—Ibid., p. 51. These passages are supposed by Warton sufficient to prove that Puttenham mistook the name of Edward for George, especially when joined to the fact, that 'no plays of an Edward Ferrers, or Ferrys, which is the same, are now known to exist, nor are mentioned by any writer of the times which are now concerned.' Notwithstanding this conclusion, Wood, in his *Athenæ*, mentions an Edward Ferrers, though his account of him is doubtful, short, and indefinite; as he professes himself unable to say where he was born, or to name the College in Oxford at which he was educated. The only particulars, therefore, which can be collected from Wood, are, that Edward Ferrers was of the family of Ferrers, of Baldesley Clinton, iu Warwickshire; that he continued at Oxford University several years, 'being then in much esteem for his poetry;' that about the time of his leaving College he wrote 'several Tragedies, Comedies, or Enterludes,' and that he 'was in great renown about 1564,' when he supposes him to have died, and to have been buried at Baldesley Clinton, leaving a son Henry. But although this dispute must perhaps long remain undecided, yet it is certain, that George Ferrers was the Lord of Mis-rule alluded to in the text; and of him, and his office, it will be interesting to give as full an account, as the materials now to be obtained will permit.

"George Ferrers, according to all his biographers, was born at St. Albans, in Hertfordshire, and received a part of his education at Oxford. After quitting College, he entered himself of Lincoln's Inn, where he became

---

[1] Referred to in note at page 181.

a Barrister; and as Wood remarks, was as 'eminent for the law, as before he was for his poetry, having been as much celebrated for it by the learned of his time, as any.' While studying the jurisprudence of England, Ferrers appears to have published his first work, entitled, 'The Great Charter, called in Latyn, Magna Carta, with diuers olde statutes :' no date. In the second edition of this work, the colophon declares the author's name in the following terms: 'Thus endeth the booke called Magna Carta, translated oute of Latyn and Frenshe into Englishe, by George Ferrerz. Imprynted at London, iu Paules church-yerde, at the signe of the Maydens head, by Thomas Petyt. M.D.XLII.' Mr. Haslewood, the unwearied and excellent illustrator of the Poetry and Biography of Queen Elizabeth's reign, has said in his introduction to the recent reprint of the 'Mirror for Magistrates,' that Ferrers 'was a polished courtier, and esteemed favourite with Henry the VIII. although that capricious monarch, for some offence, the nature of which has not yet been discovered, committed him to prison in 1542.' For the same King he also served in the army, and Wood states, was engaged in several battles; but in the year above mentioned he appears to have left the wars, as at that time he was returned Member of Parliament for Plymouth. Henry VIII. appears to have entertained a grateful sense of the services of Ferrers; since, in the will of that Sovereign, in 1546-7, his name appears as a Legatee, for one hundred marks, in a list with many others, who were to receive their bequests, as the instrument states, 'for the special love and favour that we bear to our trusty counsailours and others our said servaunts, hereafter following.' It is remarkable, that in this will there is not any christian name given to Ferrers. In the reign of Edward VI. Ferrers was employed in the suite of the Duke of Somerset, Protector to the King; and he was also one of the Commissioners in the Army, in the expedition to Scotland. In 1552, after the condemnation of the Duke of Somerset, the populace were greatly irritated against the Duke of Northumberland, whom they conceived to be the cause of it; and the young King himself was considerably grieved at the unfortunate fate of his uncle. On this account, as well to amuse the commonalty, as to give pleasure to the King, 'it was deuised,' says Holingshed, 'that the feast of Christs natiuitie, commonlie called Christmasse, then at hand, should be solemnlie kept at Greenwich, with open houshold, and franke resort to Court, (which is called keeping of the hall) what time of old ordinarie course there is alwaise one appointed to make sport in the court, called commonlie Lord of Mis-rule; whose office is not unknown to such as haue beene brought vp in noblemen's houses, and among great house-keepers, which vse liberall feasting in that season. There was therfore by order of the councell, a wise gentleman, and learned, named George Ferrers, appointed to that office for this yeare; who, being of better credit and estimation than comonlie his predecessors had beene before, receiued all his commissions and warrants by the name of the Maister of the King's pastimes. Which gentleman so well supplied his office, both in shew of sundrie sights and deuices of rare inventions, and in act of diuerse interludes, and matters of pastime plaied by persons, as not onlie satisfied the common sort, but also were verie well liked and allowed by the councell, and other of skill in the like pastimes;

but best of all by the young King himselfe, as appeered by his princelie liberalitie in rewarding that service.'—*Chronicle of Eng.*, vol. III, p. 1067. This office, which George Ferrers so ably filled, had too often been executed by those who possessed neither the wit nor the genius it required; but, as will be hereafter shewn in its history, persons of high talent were originally selected to perform the somewhat difficult duties of a Lord of Mis-rule. On the 30th of November, 1552, Ferrers received 100*l.* for the charges of his office; and afterwards the Lord Mayor, who probably had been at the royal festival, entertained him in London. Stowe, in his 'Annals,' thus relates the circumstances of his visit and rewards. 'The King kept his Christmasse with open houshold at Greenwich, George Ferrers, Gentleman of Lincolnes Inne, being Lord of the merry disports all the 12 dayes, who so pleasantly and wisely behaued himselfe, that the King had great delight in his pastimes. On Monday, the fourth of January, the said Lord of merry disports came by water to London, and landed at the Tower-wharfe, entered the Tower, and then rode through the Tower-streete, where he was receiued by Sergeant Vawce, Lord of Mis-rule to John Mainard, one of the Sheriffes of London, and so conducted through the Citie with a great company of young Lords and Gentlemen, to the house of Sir George Barne, Lord Maior; where he, with the chiefe off his company dined, and after had a great banquet; and, at his departure, the Lord Maior gave him a standing cup, with a couer of silver and guilt, of the value of ten pound, for a reward; and also set a hogshead of Wine, and a Barrell of Beere at his gate, for his traine that followed him; the residue of his Gentlemen and Seruants dined at other Aldermen's houses, and with the Sheriffes, and so departed to the Tower-wharfe againe, and to the Court by water, to the great commendation of the Maior and Aldermen, and highly accepted of the King and Councell.'—*Annals*, edit. 1631, fol., p. 608. In 1559, Ferrers again appeared as a poet in the celebrated 'Mirror for Magistrates,' in which he wrote, in conjunction with several of the best versifiers and most learned men of that period; and as the history of this book is a portion of his own life, it will not be irrelevant to give it so far as Ferrers was concerned.

"Richard Baldwyne, who may be considered as the first of that party which composed the Mirror for Magistrates, was a graduate of Oxford and an ecclesiastic; and he, in his Preface to the work, states, that Thomas Marshe, the printer, had invited him to take a share in the composition of a continuation of Lydgate's 'Fall of Princes;' in which the examples should be selected from English history. Baldwyne, however, was unwilling to engage in a work so laborious without assistance; but Marshe soon after provided 'divers learned men, whose manye giftes nede fewe praysee,—to take upon them parte of the travayle.' These met together to the number of seven, of whom George Ferrers was one, and who, after they had agreed upon the plan to be pursued, wrote the first tale, entitled, the Fall of Robert Tresillian, Chiefe Justice of England. Besides this, Ferrers wrote five other poems, which were, on the misfortunes of Thomas, of Woodstock; King Richard the Second; Eleanor Cobham; Humphrey, Duke of Gloucester; and Edmund, Duke of Somerset; and to the above, Wood adds other stories which he does not name. Most of these were scattered through the different editions of the Mirror for Magistrates, from 1559, till 1578. Of that published in the latter year, Mr. Haslewood is inclined to think Ferrers was the Editor, since it contains many exclusive alterations, and his two legends of the Duke and Duchess of Gloucester. In 1575, George Ferrers seems to have been employed by the Earl of Leicester, as one of the authors for the entertainment to be given to the Queen; at which time he appears still to have been in the Office of Lord of Mis-rule. In the elegant work, entitled, 'Kenilworth Illustrated,' William Hamper, Esq., of Birmingham, whose very extensive antiquarian learning and collections are so well known to the literary world, has printed an original MS. of Masques, which was long in the possession of Henry Ferrers, Esq., of Baddesley Clinton, in Warwickshire, who was, most probably, a very near relative of George. There is little doubt that they were the production of the courtly Master of Mis-rule; and that the first part, which is called 'A Cartell for a Challeng,' was exhibited in the Tilt-yard at Westminster, on November 17th, 1590; when Sir Henry Lee, the Queen's Champion, resigned the office to George Clifford, Earl of Cumberland. It is supposed that the remainder was presented on a progress, probably when the Queen visited Sir Henry Lee, at Quarendon, in Buckinghamshire. Only a small portion of this interesting composition has been printed before. Early in 1579, George Ferrers is supposed to have died at Flamstead in Hertfordshire; as, on the 18th of May in that year, administration was granted on his effects. Having thus recorded what is known of the life of Ferrers, the history and nature of his office are next to be considered.

"The title and the duties of a Lord of Mis-rule appear in England to have had a classical origin; since Warton, in his *Hist. of Engl. Poetry*, vol. II, sect. xvi, p. 378, mentions, that 'in an original draught of the Statutes of Trinity College, at Cambridge, founded in 1546, one of the Chapters is entitled, *De Præfecto Ludorum qui Imperator dicitur*, under whose direction and authority, Latin Comedies and Tragedies are to be exhibited in the hall at Christmas. With regard to the peculiar business and office of Imperator,' continues the same writer, 'it is ordered, that one of the Masters of Arts shall be placed over the juniors, every Christmas, for the regulation of their games and diversions at that season of festivity. At the same time, he is to govern the whole society in the hall and chapel, as a republic committed to his special charge, by a set of laws which he is to frame in Latin and Greek verse. His sovereignty is to last during the twelve days of Christmas; and he is to exercise the same power on Candlemas-day.' His fee amounts to forty shillings. Nor was this peculiar to the University of Cambridge; for Wood, in his *Athenæ Oxonienses*, speaks of a similar custom being used in several of the Colleges at Oxford, especially at St. John's and Merton. The Inns of Court also celebrated their Christmas sports under the direction of a Revel Master, who frequently received substantial honours and rewards. Warton mentions, that a Christmas Prince, elected by the society of the Middle Temple, in 1635, was attended by a Lord Keeper, Lord Treasurer, eight Officers with white staves, a band of Gentlemen Pensioners, and two Chaplains, who preached before him on the Sunday preceding Christmas-day. This holiday Sovereign also dined in the hall and chamber, under a cloth of estate; while his feasts were supplied with venison by Lord Holland, and by the Lord Mayor and Sheriffs of London with wine. After his reign was over, King James I.

knighted him at Whitehall.—The same system of appointing a Ruler of Pastimes seems to have been common through most ranks; for Stow observes, that 'the like had ye in the house of every Nobleman of honour or good worship, were he spiritual or temporal. The Mayor of London, and either of the Sheriffs, had their several Lords of Mis-rule, ever contending, without quarrel or offence, who should make the rarest pastime to delight the beholders. These Lords, beginning their rule at Allhallond-Eve, continued the same till the morrow after the Feast of Purification, commonly called Candlemas-day: in which space there were fine and subtle disguisings, masks, and mummeries, with playing at cards for counters, nayles, and points in every house, more for pastime than for gaine.'—*Strype's Edit. of Stowe*, Book I, p. 252. But the best account of the fees, duties, dress, and general use of the Lord of Misrule, is given by the most violent enemy of all sports that probably ever existed, namely, Philip Stubbs, the vehement author of the 'Anatomie of Abuses.' This singular writer, while he rails most immoderately at all the fashions and follies of his age, condemning them and their votaries to certain perdition, has nevertheless contrived most minutely to record them for the benefit of posterity; and frequently, where less scrupulous writers are deficient in their intelligence, their imperfections may be amply supplied by a reference to his pious invectives. Speaking of the Lord of Mis-rule, Stubbs writes thus: 'Firste all the wilde heades of the parishe, conventynge together, chuse them a grand Capitaine (of mischeef), whom they innoble with the title of my Lorde of Misserule, and hym they crown with great solemnitie, and adopt for their kyng. This kyng anoynted, chuseth forthe twentie, fourtie, threescore, or a hundred lustie guttes like to hymself, to waite uppon his lordely majestie, and to guarde his noble persone. Then every one of these his menne he investeth with his liveries, of greene, yellowe, or some other light wanton colour. And as though that were not (baudie) gaudy enough, I should saie, they bedecke themselves with scarffes, ribons, and laces, hanged all over with golde rynges, precious stones, and other jewelles: this doen, they tye about either legge, twentie or fourtie belles, with rich hande-kercheefes in their handes, and sometymes laied acrosse over their shoulders and neckes, borrowed for the moste parte of their pretie Mopsies and loovyng Bessies, for bussyng them in the darcke. Thus thinges sette in order, they have their hobby horses,[1] dragons, and other antiques, together with their baudie Pipers, and thunderyng Drommers, to strike up the Deville's dance[2] withall, then marche these heathen companies towardes the Churche and Churche-Yarde; their Pipers pipyng, Drommers thonderyng, their stumppes dauncyng, their belles jynglyng, their handkerchefes swyngyng about their heades like

---

[1] "These were formed with the resemblance of a horse's head and tail, having a light wooden frame to be attached to the body of the person who performed the hobby-horse. The trappings and footcloth, which were often very splendid, reached to the ground, and so concealed the actor's feet, while he pranced and curvetted like a real horse.
[2] "The Morris Dance.

madmen, their Hobbie horses and other monsters skyrmishyng amongst the throng: and in this sorte they goe to the Churche, (though the Minister bee at Praier or Preachyng) dauncyng and swingyng their handkercheefes over their heades in the churche, like Devilles incarnate, withe suche a confused noise, that no man can heare his owne voice. Then the foolishe people, they looke, they stare, they laugh, they fleere, and mount upon formes and pewes, to see these goodly pageauntes, solemnised in this sort. Then after this, aboute the Churche they goe againe and againe, and so forthe into the Churche-Yarde, where they have commonly their Sommer haules, their Bowers, Arbours, and Banquettyng houses set up, wherein they feaste, banquet, and daunce all that daie, and (peradventure) all night too. And thus these tertestriall furies spend their Sabbaoth daie. Then for the further innoblyng of this honourable Lurdane[1] (Lorde, I should saye), they have also certaine papers, wherein is paynted some bablerie or other, of Imagerie worke, and these they call my Lord of Misrule's badges; these thei giue to every one that will geve money for them, to maintaine them in this their heathenrie, devilrie, whoredome, drunkennesse, pride, and what not. And who will not shew himselfe buxome[2] to them, and give them money for these the Deville's Cognizaunces, they shall be mocked, and flouted at shamefully. And so assotted are some, that they not onely give them money, to maintaine their abhomination withall, but also weare their badges and cognizaunces in their hattes or cappes, openlye. Another sort of fantasticall fooles, bring to these Helhoundes (the Lorde of Mis-rule and his complices) some Bread, some goode Ale, some newe cheese, some olde cheese, some Custardes, some Cakes, some Flaunes,[3] some Tartes, some Creame, some Meate, some one thing, some another; but if they knewe that as often as they bring any to the maintenaunce of these execrable pastymes, they offer sacrifice to the Devill and Sathanas, they would repent, and withdrawe their haundes, which God graunt they maie.'—Edit. 1585, 8vo. fol. 92. b. Such was a Lord of Mis-rule, whose office, however, branched out into other circumstances than those now detailed, but his duties are all equally at an end, and the name only remembered. The puritans were the principal cause of this overthrow; as in the time of James I. the custom was preached against as a relic of the Saturnalian games, deduced from the pagan ritual."

---

[1] " A Blockhead.—Old French, *Lourdain*.
[2] " Compliant, lively, brisk.—Saxon, Bucrum.
[3] " According to Phillips, this was a species of cake, made with flour, eggs, butter, and sugar."

HAVING now completed the account of the splendid entertainment given by the Earl to Queen Elizabeth, as described in Laneham's Letter and in Gascoigne's Princely Pleasures, we will conclude the history of Kenilworth Castle by the insertion of the correspondence, hitherto (we believe) unpublished, which occurred after the death of the Earl of Leicester,[1] in reference to Kenilworth Castle, then in possession of Sir Robert Dudley, the Earl's son.

"16th April, 1590.

"*A letter to Sir Fulke Greville, Sir Thomas Lucye, Sir John Harrington, and Sir Henry Goodier, Knights, and Thomas Leigh, Esq., or to any two of them.*

"Whereas upon information given by you (Sir John Harrington) of a forcible entry made by certain the servants of Sir Christopher Blount, Knight, and others in the behalf of the Countess of Leicester, his lady, upon the Castle of Kenilworth, being then in the sole and quiet possession of Mr. Robert Dudley; We, the Lord Chancellor and the Lord Admiral and others, put in trust in the behalf of the young gentleman; doubting some further like disorderly proceedings, directed our letters unto you (Sir John) for the preservation of the gentleman's possession, and repressing of such like further attempts against him, if any should be offered, together with other directions by you to be given, as well to the tenants concerning the keeping of Courts, and payment of the rents, as also to the Ranger and Keeper of the Chase and Park there, for the preserving of their several charges, as by the same letters more at large may appear. Since which time, notwithstanding Sir Christopher Blount (as we are advertised by letters from our very good Lord, the Earl of Huntingdon, dated the 11th of this present), contrary to a former order and agreement made before you the Justices, that were there present for the peaceable keeping of a joint possession by an equal number on either part, hath with like force attempted to remove Captain Jeames and others, who held the possession for the late Earl of

[1] The Earl died on the 4th of September, 1588, at Cornbury, in Oxfordshire, under great suspicion that he was poisoned by, or at the instigation of, Lettice, Countess of Leicester. *See Statement at pp.* 84–5.

Warwick in his life time, and likewise for Mr. Dudley; by means whereof great mischief might and was likely to have grown, if the same had not been by the good advice and persuasion of the said Earl of Huntingdon wisely stayed and prevented. We, being thus informed of these disorders, and moved on the behalf of the said Mr. Dudley, for the redressing of this violent and unlawful course taken against him, as well to prevent the inconveniences which may therefore ensue, as also for the lawful preservation of his right, have thought good to address these our letters unto you in that behalf, praying and requiring you by authority hereof, as Justices of the Peace, not only to see that present force (if any be there still maintained), with the assistance of the Sheriff of that County, forthwith removed, and any like forcible or unlawful attempts that shall be hereafter moved against the gentleman, in like sort repressed according to law; but also that the gentleman's possession may be peaceably maintained by those which are or shall be authorised there for him, and the rents reserved, the Courts respited, and the game preserved, and all duly accomplished according to those former letters unto you (Sir John Harrington) directed; for which purpose you shall, in our names, also reiterate the warning given by the said letters, as well unto the tenants, as also to the Ranger and Keepers, so much as doth particularly concern them.

"Wherein praying you to use all care and endeavour for the preserving both of peace and quietness, and of the gentleman's right, we bid you heartily farewell.

"From," &c.[1]

"30*th April*, 1590.

"*A letter to Sir Fulke Greville, Sir Thomas Lucye, Knights, and Mr. Thomas Leigh, Esq.*

"We have received your letter written at Kenilworth, the 21st of this present, whereby you advertise us of your travel taken in removing of the forces assembled there together in the Castle, of which your proceedings as we deem well, so would we better have allowed the same, if you had communicated our last letter unto Sir John Harrington, unto whose further advice we referred you, having before directed our letters unto him, the cause whereof according to our appointment you should have

[1] Privy Council, Reg. Eliz., vol. viii.

followed. Since which time the parties, whom the possession of the said Castle concerneth, have agreed amongst themselves, that you, Sir Fulke Greville, shall for both parties, sequester the profits of the said Castle, reserve the rents, respite the Courts, and preserve the game, without any joint possession of the parties, until the matter in controversy be fully decided, and to require you to set the persons committed to the Gaol at Gloucester [at liberty], taking bonds to her Majesty's use, to answer the disorders by them committed, if hereafter it be called into question."[1]

"*At Farley, the 9th September*, 1591.

"*A letter to the Sheriff of the County of Warwick.*

"Whereas the late Earl of Leicester, in his lifetime, did compound with the tenants of Killingworth,[2] concerning the chase there, and for that purpose gave them satisfaction by payment of divers sums of money to their contentation at that time. Forasmuch as we are given to understand that notwithstanding the said composition, the tenants have lately threatened and have a disposition to enter again upon the same, for the which there hath been satisfaction given. These are to require you upon the receipt hereof (after you shall have conference with Sir Fulke Greville, having charge of the Castle, and of that which appertaineth thereunto), that you call all the tenants before you, and in her Majesty's name to charge and command them, that they forbear in any case to deal therein until the next term, that their pretences may be examined, and the cause heard and ordered according to justice, and hereof not to fail, as they will answer their doings to the contrary, at their perils."[3]

In 1605 (Jas. I.) Sir Robert Dudley had license to travel for three years. In 1607 a revocation of that license was sought for and sent to him, and he not complying therewith commissioners were appointed to take charge of his lands on behalf of the King. These commissioners were Sir Richard Verney,[4] Edward Boughton, and William Barnes,

[1] Privy Council, Reg. Eliz., vol. viii.
[2] A corruption of Kenilworth, frequently so written at that period.
[3] Privy Council, Reg. Eliz., vol. ix.
[4] The 'Young Varney,' ward of the Earl of Leycester, and brought up by him. (See 'Letters to Lord Burghley,' pp. 92, 93.)

reference to whom will be found in the following correspondence.

[*About March*], 1605.

"His Highness' directions about Kenilworth."

"A memorial of such things as are to be done at Kenilworth by Sir Thomas Challoner.

"In March next you shall go to Kenilworth and take with you the Officers of the works, who shall survey the castle, to inform themselves what reparation is needful, and what charges requisite.

"The garden shall be new planted with such herbs and trees as are green, winter and summer, and let the conduit and laver be repaired. Consider of the bridge that goes over the lake how it may be mended with saving most of the old timber.

"And if it may be, erect the heronry[1] again, and out of a nook of the lake to make an island for mews and other fowl to breed in.

"Cause the river to be stored with trout, and scours to be made for them, and from your own pond send three or four thousand carps to put into the lake.

"Also you shall make two large flat-bottomed boats, to fish the pool, and to help the hounds when the stag is at the soil.

"Take a particular view of the chase and old park, of such paling as is necessary to enclose them into one ground, and choose the driest soil to place stacks of hay for the deer, and make such divisions, with rails, as shall be most necessary.

"About Bestbige's Lodge in the old park, choose a dry plot to be railed in, to keep elk, roin-deer and bison deer, and other strange beasts.

"In convenient places, make fair and easy standings, and plant rows of trees and tufts such as are at 'Nonesuch,' and procure out of Italy and Germany, green oaks, pine trees, and fir trees.

"Let the smaller pools be scoured and stored for the provision of the house, and a large net to be made to fish the lake.

"Survey the woods and grounds which are to be compounded for with the Countess at Leicester, and consider whether they be worth the money demanded.

"Also, in convenient places, cause store of apple trees and

[1] Heronry, place for herons to breed.

pear tres to be planted, which may be had out of Worcestershire; and plenty of crab trees likewise.

"In conclusion, be careful to make a full relation of all things necessary to increase the game, and appoint such dotard trees to be felled for the paling, as may be least missed, and least disgrace the ground with their want; and this do with speed, that the King[1] may see it at his next progress to Rockingham.[2]

The Surveyors appointed to value Kenilworth, to the Lords of the Council.

Kenilworth, 10 Sept., 1609.

"May it please your good Lordships,

"After great labor and much time spent in surveying the castle and manor of Kenilworth, with Leeke, Wooton and Hill, members thereof, and also the manor and parks of Rudfen, finding ourselves enabled thereby to make some brief estimate thereof, albeit time will not afford us as yet to make up the same survey at large, to be returned with our commission, we hold it our duties in meantime to present unto your Lordships the same, our estimate, viz.:

"The castle and manor of Kenilworth.

"The site of the castle containeth within the walls 6 acres, 3 roods, 14 perches, wherein are many and goodly buildings, built all with very fair free-stone, hewn and all covered with lead.

	£ s. d.		£ s. d.
Rents of the freeholders heriotable,[3] the best beast	18 12 0½;	at 18 years' purchase	334 16 9
Rents of the copyholders for one, two, or three lives	10 14 5;	at 50 years' purchase	535 17 11
Rents of tenants by indenture, for one, two, or three lives improved	21 5 0;	at 16 years' purchase, deducting a third part of their estates	226 13 4
Rents of tenants by indenture, for years improved	20 0 8;	at 16 years' purchase, deducting a third part for the present estate	214 0 0

---

[1] King James was at Rockingham, 9 Aug., 1605; and again, 28 July, 1619.
[2] State Paper Office, London.
[3] HERIOTABLE. Heriot, the best beast (whether horse, ox, or cow) that the tenant dies possessed of, due and payable to the Lord of the Manor. A

Rents improved of tenants-at-will	327 13 8;			
The yearly value of the chase, as it may be improved with part of the old park, in the occupation of Francis Phipps, the deer to be taken away	264 16 2;	£612 9s. 10d. whereof deduct for rents resolute £13 0s. 19d.,[1] and so remaineth £599 8s. 3d., which, at 16 years' purchase, amounteth to	9590 12 0	
The rent of the fishing of the pond, containing 3 acres, improved	20 0 0;			

Perquisites of Courts, 40s.; at 12 years' purchase, £24.
Sum total of rents, £672 0s. 4½d.
Sum total perquisites thereof, as above, £10,926.

"The timber and woods in Kenilworth.

"Timber trees 14,138, amounting to 10,088 tons, valued at 8s. per ton, in toto £6744 sterling. Firewood trees 5041, with the underwood and tops of timber trees, amounting to 23,341¼ loads, valued at 3s. the load, in toto £3736 sterling.

Sum total of the timber and wood, £10,480.
Sum total of the purchase of the land, timber, and wood in Kenilworth } £21,406.[2]

Endorsed, "The Survey of Killingworth," being the report of the Surveyors John Hercy and Henry Adis, addressed to [the Lords of the Council] and dated Kenilworth 10th Sept., 1609, of the manor and castle of Kenilworth, and also the manor and park of Rudfen. Particulars of the valuation are given, and at the end is the following:

	£	s.	d.
Sum total of all the timber and wood in Kenilworth and Rudfen	14,625	6	0
Sum total of the purchase of the lands in Kenilworth and Rudfen	13,923	9	0
Sum total of the purchase of all the said lands, and price of all the timber and woods	£28,548	15	0
Sum total of the purchase of all the land, price of all the timber and woods, adding £20,364 8s. for the materials of the castle as it now standeth	48,913	3	0
Out of which, deducting the rate of workmanship, with spoil of the materials in taking it down, £10,000. And so remaineth for the whole purchase	38,913	3	0

custom first invented by the Danes. Some heriots are due by custom, some by tenure, and some by reservation on deeds.

HERIOTS. Not confined to beasts, sometimes a piece of plate or other personal property."—*Tomlins's Law Dict.*

[1] *Sic. Orig.*   [2] State Paper Office, London.

KENILWORTH CASTLE.

"It may also please your Lordships to be informed that we find here a manor of his Majesty's, called Kenilworth, sundry parcels whereof lie intermixed with the lands of this manor now by us surveyed, and some of them even in the midst of the chase and sundry houses thereof situate near the castle and some opposite against the castle gate, so that the sale of that manor may be very inconvenient if it be his Majesty's pleasure to have this. All which we thought in duty fit to signify unto your Lordships, humbly submitting ourselves and the same to your honorable considerations, whom we beseech Almighty God evermore to preserve and prosper.

"Your Lordships' most bounden,

"JOHN HERCY,
"HENRY ADIS."

"*At Kenilworth; 10th Sept.,* 1609.

(Endorsed)
"The Survey of Killingworth."[1]

1610. "Rudfen. The improved yearly value, at 16 years' purchase to be bought.

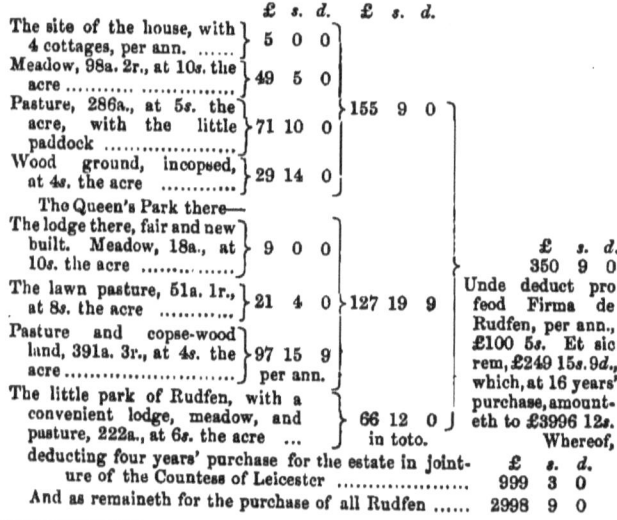

	£ s. d.	£ s. d.		£ s. d.
The site of the house, with 4 cottages, per ann.	5 0 0			
Meadow, 98a. 2r., at 10s. the acre	49 5 0			
Pasture, 286a., at 5s. the acre, with the little paddock	71 10 0	155 9 0		
Wood ground, incopsed, at 4s. the acre	29 14 0			
The Queen's Park there— The lodge there, fair and new built. Meadow, 18a., at 10s. the acre	9 0 0			350 9 0
The lawn pasture, 51a. 1r., at 8s. the acre	21 4 0	127 19 9	Unde deduct pro feod Firma de Rudfen, per ann., £100 5s. Et sic rem, £249 15s. 9d., which, at 16 years' purchase, amounteth to £3996 12s. Whereof,	
Pasture and copse-wood land, 391a. 3r., at 4s. the acre	97 15 9	per ann.		
The little park of Rudfen, with a convenient lodge, meadow, and pasture, 222a., at 6s. the acre		66 12 0 in toto.		
deducting four years' purchase for the estate in jointure of the Countess of Leicester				999 3 0
And as remaineth for the purchase of all Rudfen				2998 9 0

[1] State Paper Office, London.

Timber and woods in Rudfen—
Timber, 8807 trees, 7359½ tons, at 8s. the ton £2943 16 0
Firewood, 1580 trees, with the tops of the timber trees, 8010 loads, at 3s. the load 1201 10 0
} 4145 6 0
Sum total of the purchase of the land and price of the timber and woods in Rudfen .... 7142 15 0[1]

1610. Endorsed. "Reasons touching Killingworth on behalf of the Lord Lisle and the Lord of Kenclinan." [Clinclenyn]. (For raising of Rents, and removing some of the Officers.)

The value of Sir Robert Dudley's lands, forfeited to His Majesty, in Killingworth and Ladbrook, found by inquisition, and seized into his Majesty's hands, do amount to .... per ann. 717 9 0
The same remain uncertain in his Majesty's hands.
The Lady Dudley receiveth out of those lands, per ann. 300 0 0
One Fitch challengeth .... „ 100 0 0
A rent-charge granted by Sir Robert Dudley.
So *ultra repris.*, here will remain to the Lords but (pr. an.)[2] 300 9 0

1610. Endorsed. "The rents and values of divers places within the manor of Kenilworth."

"The increase of rents at Kenilworth will be made upon these places following :

	Per ann.	Per ann.
The chase, now let and 400 deer kept, is	£110 0 0	
The same number of deer kept will yield ...	...	· £160 0 0
The Abbey grounds, now let for	48 0 0	
The same will yield		58 0 0
The tithes of Kenilworth, now let for	20 0 0	
The same will yield	...	30 0 0
Whiting holdeth ground in the old park, for	68 0 0	
The same will yield	...	76 0 0
Wotton men hold ground in the old park, at	26 0 0	
The same will yield	...	30 0 0
Edward Mole holds ground in the old park, for	74 0 0	
The same will yield	...	80 0 0
John Benyon holdeth ground in the old park, for	50 0 0	
The same will yield	...	55 0 0
The pool and flood-gates will yield.............		13 6 8
The sum now answered cometh to	£396 0 0	
The increase will be made	per ann.	£502 13 4[3]

---

[1] State Paper Office, London.   [2] Ibid.   [3] Ibid.

1609-10, Feb. 8. "A Book of Entries of Privy Seals at large."
"James, by the grace of God, King of England, Scotland, France and Ireland, Defender of the Faith, &c. To the Treasurer and Undertreasurer of our Exchequer for the time being, greeting. We will and command you, out of our treasure in the receipt of our Exchequer, to pay or cause to be paid unto our right trusty and well beloved, the Lord Viscount Lisle,[1] or his assigns, the sum of Three score and fifteen pounds, nine shillings, ten pence, in full satisfaction of the like sum disbursed by him for the charges of our Commissioners, Counsellers and others, who were employed for the finding of Sir Robert Dudley's lands; the same to be taken to him without account, imprest, or other charge to be set upon him or them for the same; and these our letters shall be your sufficient warrant and discharge in that behalf. Given under our privy seal at our Palace of Westminster, the Eighth day of February in the sixth year of our reign of England, France and Ireland, and of Scotland the two and fortieth."[2]

Robert Sydney (Sir) succeeded as next heir male upon the death of his elder brother Sir Philip Sidney. This gallant person, like his predecessors, acquired renown in arms, first, under his uncle, Robert Dudley, Earl of Leicester, in the Netherlands, and afterwards with Sir Francis Verd, when he shared in the victory achieved at Turnholt in Brabant, anno 1597. For these, upon the accession of King Jas. I., Sir Robert was elevated to the Peerage as Baron Sydney of Penshurst in the County of Kent, by letters patent, dated 13th May, 1603, and upon the 24th July in the same year (it being the day of the King and Queen's coronation) he was appointed Lord Chamberlain to the Queen. The next year he was created Viscount Lisle. In 1616 he was installed a Knight of the Garter, and raised on 2nd August, 1618, to the Earldom of Leicester, the ceremony of creation being performed in the Hall of the Bishop's Palace at Salisbury."[3]

[1] Robert Sydney, created Viscount Lisle in 1604.
[2] 'Warrant Book,' p. 2, State Paper Office.
[3] Burke's 'Dictionary of the Peerages,' 1831.

1610. "Lessees to whom the estate escheated to his Majesty by the contempt of Sir Robert Dudley, Knight, is committed."

"Right honorable, our duties remembered,

"We have lately received the King's Majesty's letters patent under the Great Seal of England, whereby we are made lessees of all the lands late Sir Robert Dudley's, upon trust and confidence that we shall dispose of the profits thereof in such sort as by the said letters patent is appointed. Upon view of which letters patent we find some questions, how far we stand chargeable out of our own estates to perform the covenants contained in the said letters patent, and how we shall be answered of the charges to be by us disbursed, in execution of the trust reposed in us, from which there is no provision by the patent. Of which doubts, though we would willingly have been resolved upon the receipt of the said lease, and before we do enter into the business, yet assuring ourselves upon your honor's message delivered to us by Mr. William Emott, servant to the Lord Viscount Lisle, the bringer of the patent, that your honor will provide that we shall receive no prejudice thereby, we attending such further directions herein as your honor shall please hereafter to send us, we resolve, with as much speed as possibly we may, to enter into the business. And so most humbly do take our leaves, and rest,

"At your honor's command in all humble services,
"RICHARD VERNEY.
"EDWARD BOUGHTON.
"W. BARNES.

"*Warwick, this* 11*th of August*, 1610.
(Superscription.)
"To the right-honorable our very good Lord,
the Earl of Salisbury, Lord High Treasurer of England."[1]

1610–11, Jan. "To the right honorable the Earl of Salisbury, Lord high Treasurer of England.

"The humble petition of Francis Phipps, Keeper of the Chase of Kenilworth.

"Showing in all humbleness to your good Lordship that the petitioner, about ten years since, was by the means of Sir Thomas Leigh, Knight, at the earnest desire of Sir Robert Dudley, persuaded to leave a good farm wherein he was settled, at a place called Shustock, in the County of Warwick, and to serve the said

[1] State Paper Office, London.

Sir Robert in the place of Keeper of the Chase of Killingworth which he yielded unto, upon Sir Robert's promises of reward and good allowances, with a patent for the same during your petitioner's life, which are certified to your good Lordship in Sir Richard Verney's letter, both by Sir Thomas Leigh and the Lady Dudley, in which respect by Sir Robert's own direction a patent of the said Keepership was drawn up by Mr. Dyot, a Counsellor at Law, but not sealed by means of Sir Robert's sudden departure.

"May it please your Lordship, while Sir Robert Dudley continued there, the chase was fully furnished with deer, to the number of about 800, at which time it could yield no other benefit at all, but such as was allowed to your petitioner for his service and pains as aforesaid; but since his departure the deer were abated to 400; and the petitioner enjoined by Sir Thomas Leigh to pay £110 rent per annum, and for the herbage and pannage[1] of the chase, and to maintain those 400 deer.

"Forsomuch as since it hath been in the King's hands, the deer are increased to 500, so as your petitioner is not able to pay so great a rent, without either his undoing, or the spoil of the game.

"He doth, therefore, most humbly beseech your good Lordship that you will vouchsafe in this respect to have an honorable consideration of him, and that your Lordship will be pleased to establish him in his place, with an abatement from Michaelmas last of £30 per annum of the former rent, for the feeding of that 100 deer, increased by his diligence and care, which is but an ordinary rate for the keeping of 100 sheep in that country, although it is well known that a deer will take much more than a sheep. And that hereafter, as the game shall by view be found to be increased, a rateable abatement may be made of the rent accordingly. And he will daily pray for your Lordship's long life and happiness.[2]

1610-11, Feb. 5. "A letter or warrant from my Lord Treasurer to Sir Richard Varney and the other gentlemen, for the abatement of Francis Phippes his rent, for the chase and part of the park of Killingworth, now in the said chase, which the said Phippes holdeth upon the rent of £110 per annum, and is to maintain and keep there

[1] "Pannage,—the mast of the oak and beech, which swine feed on in the woods."—*Halliwell.*
[2] State Paper Office, London.

four hundred deer upon the same, for that there are five hundred deer, the said Phippes to have an abatement of £30, and to pay from Michaelmas last for this year £80, and so to have an annual abatement, after the rate of £6 for the increase of every twenty deer, made him accordingly as the deer shall be hereafter yearly found to be increased upon the view. And the view of the deer to be at all times taken some small time before the 25th day of March, by honest and sufficient men of knowledge and understanding in that science.

" A warrant for the allowance timber to build and repair barns and hovels in the chase and park of Killingworth, for paling, railing, and mending of bridges, in and about the said chase and park, with an allowance for the defraying the charge thereof as shall be needful.[1]

1610-11, Feb. 11. The Lessees applied to the Earl of Salisbury to be released from their charge of Killingworth, their lease containing a covenant to keep the Castle in repair, and they are informed that even a new lease, without that covenant, would still make them liable; they pray to be discharged from their trust altogether.[2]

Enclosed in the Letter of the 5th February from the Lessees or Commissioners.

1610-11, Jan. 2. " The allowance of Francis Phipps for the keeping of the chase and park of Killingworth, made unto him by Sir Robert Dudley, Knight, the which he hath continually had, is as followeth :

" First, the feeding and depasturing of twenty kine [cows], one bull, four geldings, and a convenient number of hogs for his provision.

" Secondly, the usual fees that belong to other keepers with convenient store of wood for his fire.

"And lastly, the hay and grass of the two meadows called Pleasant's Meadow and Constable's Meadow, for the deer and keeping of his own beasts and horses.

" THOMAS LEIGH.[3]
" A. DUDDELEY."

[1] State Paper Office, London.　　[2] Ibid.
[3] Sir Thomas Leigh was the father of Alice, Lady Dudley (whose signature is attached). He died in 1625.

Another enclosure in Letter of 5th February.

In a letter of Sir Thomas Leigh to the Commissioners or Lessees, dated from Stoneleigh, the 2nd of January, 1610-11, he concludes (after reiterating the terms as stated in the above certificate) thus,—

"And for the farming of the ground since Sir Robert's departure he hath had it upon a hundred and ten pounds rent per annum, keeping at his own charge four hundred deer, which is the number he is tied unto.[1]

Lessees or Commissioners of the Lands of Sir Robert Dudley, to Cecil, Earl of Salisbury.

"*Compton;* 5 *Feb.*, 1610-11.

"Right honorable and our especial good Lord,

"We have well conceived by your former letters, as by more later information we have received by Sir Richard Verney, how much you have desired to be freed of those unnecessary troubles which are brought unto you concerning the business of Killingworth. And all our hopes are, that your honor doth rightly judge that it is from our obedience to your commandments only, and out of the desire we have to perform all duties, that you shall be pleased to impose upon us, that we do willingly undergo so troublesome employments. Concerning the contents of your honor's letters, brought unto us by the Lord Lisle his solicitor, the 6th of January, we confidently answer (sparing your honor from the trouble of the repetition of the particulars), that, as well for the allowance of Francis Grammer, Bailiff and Woodward of Killingworth, as for all others that are employed in any necessary business there, we have ordered all things before the receipt of your honor's letters, with as small charge, and to as much advantage of the Lords, as our discretions could reach unto, guiding ourselves by the directions which we have received from your honor. Concerning Francis Phipps, Keeper of the chase at Killingworth, we have sent, here enclosed to your honor, the former note which we have received of the allowances intended to him from Sir Robert Dudley, and a later letter sent to us from Sir Thomas Leigh, justifying the same, with some other circumstances which we thought your honor would be willing to be informed of. The worth of these cattle keeping (considering the

[1] State Paper Office.

quality of the ground of the chase upon which they pasture) we value at forty pounds by the year. The deer we have caused to be viewed, and we are very well assured by the certificate that is returned us, that there are five hundred; whereof of deer of antler there are four score and six, and of rascal[1] deer four hundred and fourteen. We have likewise appointed Francis Phipps himself to be the messenger of these letters, for your honor's full satisfaction in all things. And herein we have endeavoured ourselves to fulfil your honor's intentions and commandments, with as little trouble to your honor as we could possibly devise. And now we most humbly take our leaves,

"Your honor's most humble at commandment,
in all dutiful services,
" RICHARD VERNEY.
" EDWARD BOUGHTON.
" W. BARNES.

" *From Compton, this 5th of Feby.*

(Superscribed.)
" To the right-honorable our especial good Lord,
the Earl of Salisbury, Lord High Treasurer of England."[2]

Robert [Sydney] Lord Lisle, to Robt. [Cecil] Earl of Salisbury.

"26 *Mar.* 1610–11. (*Holograph.*)

" My very good Lord,

" I understand by my Lord of Kinclenin that having attended upon your Lordship to acquaint you with the return of the commission for the seizing of Sir R. Dudley's land, your Lordship told him that the King had delivered his pleasure unto your Lordship, together with my Lord Privy Seal, and Mr. Chancellor of the Exchequer, touching the grant which his Majesty intends to my Lord of Kinclenin and me. The cause why I have not myself waited upon your Lordship is that I have been under the Philistines' hands these two or three days, and so shall continue for a day or two more, which done, I shall be ready to attend your Lordship, with my Lord of Kinclenin, when it shall please you to appoint us. I trust his Majesty doth remember as well what he hath heretofore promised me concerning this business, as also that

[1] " Rascal. A lean animal, neither fit to hunt or kill." — *Halliwell's Dictionary.*
[2] State Paper Office, London.

by his order I did follow it for him; and I dare confidently affirm that but for me there had not anything of Sir Robert Dudley's come to his Majesty's hands. I have likewise in this found your Lordship very favorable unto me, for which I yield you very humble thanks, and beseech you to continue it towards me, and to believe that I will ever be,

"Very affectionate to do your Lordship service,

"R. LISLE.

"*At Bainard's Castle; the 26th of March,* 1610.

(Superscription.)
"To the right honorable my very good Lord,
the Earl of Salisbury, Lord Treasurer of England, etc."[1]

1611. *The Lessees to the Earl of Salisbury, Lord High Treasurer, to be discharged from their trust.*

"Right honorable and our especial good Lord,

"According to your honor's commandment, we have entreated this gentleman, Mr. Mallett, to wait upon you, that by him your honor may understand in what great danger we be, by continuing tenants to his Majesty, for Sir Robert Dudley, his lands. Nothing doubting but by your wisdom, either by order of the Exchequer, or what other course shall seem fittest to your honor, upon whom we wholly rely and trust, we shall be cleared of such inconveniences as by these employments we are now subject unto. Whereof resting most confidently assured, with the remembrance of our most humble duties, we humbly take our leaves,

"Your Lordship's most humble at Commandment,
"In all dutiful services,
"RICHARD VERNEY,
"EDWARD BOUGHTON,
"W. BARNES.

"*Compton; this 19th of April.*

(Superscribed.)
"To the right hon^{ble} our special good Lord,
the Earl of Salisbury, Lord High Treasurer of England."[2]

[1] State Paper Office, London. [2] Ibid.

"LADY DUDLEY. Warrant for £300 yearly, during pleasure." With the sign manual of King James, and countersigned by Windebank.

"JAMES Rx.

"JAMES, by the grace of God, &c. To the Commissioners for the exercise of the office of our High Treasurer of England, greeting. Whereas of our Princely bounty, and in consideration of the distressed estate of the Lady Alice Dudley, wife of Sir Robert Dudley, Knight, we were pleased heretofore to grant unto the said Lady Dudley a yearly revenue and allowance of three hundred pounds, to be paid out of the rents and profits of the castle and manor of Killingworth, in our County of Warwick, which were seized into our hands for the contempt of the said Sir Robert Dudley in not repairing into our realm of England, from beyond the seas, according to our commandment, which heretofore she hath accordingly received from the Bailiffs and other officers there, half yearly by even portions, according to our direction, heretofore signified to our late Treasurer, deceased, until the feast of St. Michael the Archangel, last past, of which half year's annuity she is as yet unsatisfied. We, minding to continue the payment of the said yearly annuity of Three hundred pounds unto the said Lady Dudley, for maintenance of herself and children, do will and command you to cause payment to be made unto the said Lady Dudley, or her assignee, of the said sum of Three hundred pounds, out of such our Treasure, as from time to time shall be and remain in the receipt of our Exchequer, at the two usual feasts of the year, that is to say, at the feasts of St. Michael the Archangel, and the Annunciation of the Virgin Mary, by equal portions. The first payment thereof to begin at the feast of St. Michael the Archangel, last past, and so to continue half yearly during our pleasure. And these, &c. Given, &c.

"By order from Mr. Chancellor of the Exchequer,
"WINDEBANK.

(Endorsed.) "1612.
"Expedit apud Theobaldes, Vicesimo die
Novembri, anno R. Rx. Jacobi decimo,
per Windebank."[1]

---

[1] Docquets. State Paper Office, London.

"Warrant for payment of £500 to Thomas Stone, on account of Sir Robert Dudley, with the sign manual of King James, and countersigned by Windebank.

"JAMES Rx.

"JAMES, by the grace of God, &c. To the Commissioners for the exercise of the office of our High Treasurer of England, greeting. Whereas we were pleased of our princely bounty lately to bestow upon our late dearest son[1] Henry, Prince of Wales, the sum of seven thousand pounds towards the purchase of Killingworth and the Parks thereto belonging. And thereupon did direct to you, our said Commissioners, letters under our privy seal, bearing date the seven and twentieth day of July last, for the payment thereof unto our said son, the Prince, or to such as he by writing under his hand should authorise and appoint for the receipt thereof, part whereof hath already been received, and some part thereof as yet remaineth unsatisfied. And whereas we are informed that our said son, the Prince, in his lifetime, did, by letters under his privy seal, bearing date the seventh day of September last, directed unto you our said Commissioners, authorize and appoint Sir George More, Knight, Receiver-General of his possessions, to receive the sum of Three thousand and eight hundred and fifty pounds, being the remainder of the said sum of Seven thousand pounds, whereof One thousand pounds hath (as we are informed) been duly paid by you, our said Commissioners, unto him. And that by other letters under his privy seal, dated the tenth of September last, directed unto the said Sir George More, Knight, for payment of the sum of Five hundred pounds (out of the said sum of Three thousand eight hundred and fifty pounds, so by him to be received) unto Thomas Stone, Merchant, to be paid over unto Sir Robert Dudley, Knight, now remaining beyond the seas, according to the directions given to him in that behalf, which by reason of the decease of our said son, the Prince, neither the said Sir George More can receive the remainder of the said sum of Seven thousand pounds, being Two thousand eight hundred and fifty pounds, out of the receipt of our said Exchequer, nor can the said Stone receive the said sum of Five hundred pounds of the said Sir George More, for that those assignations,

[1] Henry, Prince of Wales, eldest son of James I, died at St. James's Palace, 6th Nov., 1612, and was buried in Westminster Abbey on the 7th Dec. following.

by the death of our said son, are now determined. We minding, nevertheless, but that the said Stone should receive the said sum of Five hundred pounds, which we are given to understand he hath already made payment of beyond the seas unto the said Sir Robert Dudley, do will and command you of such our Treasure as now is, or shall remain and be in the receipt of our said Exchequer, to cause payment to be made unto the said Thomas Stone, or his assignee, of the said sum of Five hundred pounds, so by him already disbursed, as aforesaid, without account, imprest,—or other charge to be set upon him, his executors, administrators, or assigns, for the same, or for any part thereof. And these, &c. Given, &c.

"By order from Mr. Chancellor of the Exchequer,
"WINDEBANK.

(Endorsed.) "1612.
"Expedit apud Theobaldes, Vicesimo die
Novembri, anno R. Reg. Jacobi decimo,
per Windebank."[1]

"Warrant under the sign manual of James 1st.
"JAMES Rx.
"JAMES, by the grace of God, &c. To the Treasurer, Chancellor, and Under Treasurer of our Exchequer, greeting. Whereas [   ] Wyatt hath been employed a Commissioner to Sir Robert Dudley, in Florence, to treat and compound with him for the Castle and Manors of Killingworth, which service he effected with all diligence and faithfulness, and disbursed therein divers sums of money, for which he hath not yet received any satisfaction. We will and command you, of such our Treasure as is now, or shall be remaining in the receipt of our Exchequer, forthwith to pay, or cause to be paid, to the said [   ] Wyatt, or his assigns, the sum of Fifty pounds by way of reward until farther consideration be had of his cause by those to whom the matter is referred; the said sum of Fifty pounds to be taken [paid] unto him without account, or other charge to be set upon him, the said Wyatt, for the same, or any part thereof. And these our letters, &c. Given, &c.

"By order of Mr. Secretary Lake,
"WINDEBANK.

(Endorsed.) "1616.
"Expedit apud Windsor, octavo die July,
anno R. Rx. Jacobi quarto decimo,
per Windebank."[1]

---

[1] Docquets. State Paper Office, London.

KENILWORTH CASTLE.

1617-18. "At Whitehall, on Friday afternoon, 20th of February, 1617.

"Whereas William Dyneley and John Wyatt have been long suitors to this Board, for satisfaction of charges and moneys disbursed in the execution of a commission under the great seal of England, concerning the concluding of a bargain, on his Majesty's behalf, with Sir Robert Dudley, Knight, for the castle and manors of Killingworth and Rudfen, in the County of Warwick, and for passing the fine and conveyances for the same. For the performance of which service they went twice to Leghorn, in Italy, where Sir Robert Dudley then was, and by their care and travaille[1] reduced the price from £38,000 (at which time it was surveyed by commission out of the Exchequer) unto £7000, which was paid for the lands. Forasmuch as it appeareth by a certificate under the hand of Francis Gofton, Esq., one of the Auditors of his Majesty's Imprests upon Depositions and Affidavits, taken before one of the Barons of His Majesty's Exchequer, by way of proof and voucher, that the petitioners have taken up at interest and disbursed the sum of £1332 19s. 5d. about the concluding of that purchase. And that their Lordships, in justice and conscience, think it meet that payment be made thereof; It is this day ordered, that his Majesty be moved, out of his gracious and princely favor, to grant a privy seal of £1500, in full satisfaction of the said petitioners, viz. £1332 19s. 5d. for moneys disbursed as aforesaid, and the overplus, by way of reward, which by the aforesaid certificate was left to the consideration of the Board, to be paid unto them, either out of such a suit, as they themselves shall find, and by this Board shall be thought fit to pass for their satisfaction in that behalf or otherwise, as shall be found meet."[2]

Besides the warrant of the 23rd Feb., 1621-2, as to Lady Alice Dudley, among the " Bills delivered into the upper house of Parliament," 19 Jas. I.—

"An act to enable Dame Alice Dudley, wife of Sir Robert Dudley, Knight, to assure the estate in the castle and manor of Killingworth, and other lands in the County of Warwick, for a valuable consideration, to the Prince his Highness and his heirs."[3]

[1] Travaille, Labor.—*Halliwell*.
[2] Pr. Council Regr., Jas. I., vol. iii.
[3] Journal, Ho. Lords, vol. iii.

1621. "7th December.

"Lord Chief Baron and Mr. Baron Bromley bring from the Lords a bill intituled, An Act to enable Dame Alice Dudley, wife of Sir Robert Dudley, Knight."[1]

"Docket of Warrants issued 23rd Feby., 1621-2.

"A grant (at the request of the Prince, his Highness) unto Sir Henry Compton, Knight, and others, to the use of the Lady Dudley, wife to Sir Robert Dudley, of the sum of £4000, paid to the said Lady by the Prince, upon relinquishing her estate of jointure, in the manor and park of Killingworth, with a declaration also that the Lady Dudley shall quietly enjoy the goods, chattels, and pensions, whereof she, or any other to her use, now are possessed, and all other goods and chattels which she shall hereafter obtain without any claim thereunto by his Majesty, by reason of any contempt or forfeiture of Sir Robert Dudley, and so that he shall not dispose thereof: Subscribed by Mr. Attorney General. By order under the sign manual."[1]

[1] 'Journal, Ho. Commons,' vol. i.

An Inventory

OF THE

Plate, Household Stuff, Pictures, &c.

In Kenelworth Castle,

Taken after the Death of Robert Earl of Leycester, 1588.[1]

An Inventorie of Plate, Glasses, Pewter Vessell, Kitchen Stuffe, and other Implements of Houshold, of the Right Honorable the Earle of Leycester, at Kenellworthe, in the charge of Thomas Cole, upon the view taken 1584, and perused since by W. George, Ed. Blounte, 1588.

Plate.

A rounde deepe bason and ewer of silver, pois lxiiij.*oz.*

Another greate plaine bason and ewer, with my lordes armes on the bottom and side of the ewer.

A nest of chalice bowles, with a cover, pois lxxvj.*oz.*

Fyve plaine silver juggs, with two eares a peice, pois cxlix.*oz.*

A salte, ship-fashion, of the mother-of-perle, garnished with silver and divers workes of warlike ensignes and ornaments, with xvj. peices of ordinance, whereof ij. on wheles, two anckers on the fore parte, and on the stearne the image of Dame Fortune, standing on a globe, with a flag in her hand, pois xxxij.*oz.*

---

[1] We are indebted to J. O. HALLIWELL, Esq. for this interesting Inventory of the property of the Earl of LEYCESTER at KENILWORTH CASTLE, at the time of his death in 1588. It was printed by him from a modern transcript of the Original MS. in *private hands*, which was exhibited at the Kensington Museum in 1863 or 1864.

Sir HARRIS NICOLAS states that "a list of the Furniture, Pictures, &c., at Kenilworth, whilst it belonged to Robert Dudley, Earl of Leicester, is in the possession of his representative, Sir John Sidney, at Penshurst. It is dated in June, 1583."

A gilte salte, like a swann, mother-of-perle, pois xxx.*oz.* iij. *quarters.*

Six rounde salts graven with armes, pois cxij.*oz.*

Two fayer plaine gilt saltes with covers, standing upon three bowles, pois liij.*oz.* iij. *quarters.*

One other, containing lvj.*oz.*

A dozen of silver spoons, xvj.*oz. quarter.*

Two stand juggs, with covers, brims, and feete of silver, and gilte chased.

Glasses.

Ffyve plaine bole glasses, without covers.

Ffyve indented bole glasses; two graven bole glasses; twelve beare glasses of severall fashions, iij. with covers; two plaine taper glasses with covers; two others ribbed taper glasses; an embossed glasse with a cover; two glass ewers.

Glass Dishes.

Tenne glasse dishes gilte, with the sinque foyle on the brims.

Eight graven dishes of glasse aboute the brims.

Twelve greate standing indented bole glasses for creame.

A deepe standing glasse, with a cover.

Ffyvteen glasses, brode brimed and narrowe bottoms.

Ffowertene greate deepe glasses, viij. of them plaine.

A dozen of dishe glasses of one sorte.

Two dozen and iiij. dishe glasses of another sorte.

Candlesticks.

Two greate candlesticks, gilte and graven, and coloured blew.

Two more, plaine white and graven.

Seaven without graving.

A George on horseback of wood, painted and gilt, with a case for knives in the tayle of the horse, and a case for oyster knives in the breast of the dragon.

Peawter.

Ffyve greate chargers, thyrteen great platters.

Six dozen and iij. platters of another sorte.

Twelve dozen and ffyve platters of a lesser sort then the last.

Tenn dozen dishes of a smaller sort.
Three dozen dishes more of severall sorts.
Six dozen of sallett dishes.
Three dozen sawcers of the ould sorte.
Three dozen and six of a latter supplie.
Ffowerteen pie plates of the greatest sorte.
Eight pie plates of the second sorte.
Ffyve pie plates of the third sorte.

Eleven pewter basons, eleven ewers, fowerteen pewter saltsellers, ffyve dozen and iiij. trencher plates, ffyve greate danske potts, ffowr lesser danske potts.

Ffyve great potts with greate bellies.
Ffyve close stooles of black velvet quilted, with panns.
Ffower of Flaunders worke, two of blacke velvet plaine.

A close stoole of black velvet, laced and fringed with black silck.

A lowe stoole of blacke vellet, quilted with black silck, with a panne.

Ffyve close stooles of black velvet.
Eight close stooles with locks to them.

A close stoole of black velvet, garnished with lace and fringe of silver, gould, and black silck.

Ffower close stooles, in fashion of chaiers of green clothe.

A close stoole of black vellet, garnished with black silck and silver.

Six other close stooles, two dozen of pewter chamber potts.
Ffyve basons, a greate pewter peice like a bason.

Aundyrons.

A greate pair of lattin andirons, with pillers graven antique.
Ffowre lesser paire of andirons, with pillers of lattin.

vij. pair of andirons, with rings and duble knopps of lattin, with vj. fyer-shovells and vj. pair of tongs.

Ffower pair of lowe andirons of lattin.

Ffower pair of andirons with single knobbs of lattin, and iiij. pair of tongs and shovells to them.

A little pair of a plaine andirons, with fyer shovells and tonges to them; paste service.

Three fyer shovells, and one pair of tongs with lattin knobbs.
Two greate fyer shovells with tynned handles.
Two pair of wallnut tree bellowes, carved.

A warming pann for a bed, scarce serviceable.
Fower perfuming panns of lattin; a greate candlestick of lattin, with xxiiij. socketts.
A hanging candlestick of lattin, with vij. socketts hanging aboute a staggs head.
A Greeke barge-clothe, embrothred with white lions and beares.
Wicker skreens, iiij.; a perfumine pann of silver, pois xix.*oz.*; two casting-bottles of silver and gilte, one flat, the other rounde.

Tables.

A long table to fould with leaves, standing upon a frame of wainscott.
A long table of deale borde, standing upon a frame of wainscott.
Three square tables of maple, inlaid and border'd with wallnutt tree, with frames to them.
Eighteen square tables of wainscott, with frames.
Ffyve foulding tables of wainscott.
Ffower long tables of firr, without frames.
Two square tables of ashe.
A foulding table of wallnuttree.
Thirty-nine formes of wainscott.
Fifty-fower stooles of wainscott.
Lyverie cupbords of wainscott.

In the Hall.

Tabells, long and short, vj.
Fformes, long and shorte, xiiij.ten.

This charge hath bin perused twice, once in my lord's lyfe tyme, the xxvj.th of June, 1583;[1] and since his deathe, xxvj.th of October, 1588, as appeareth by the originall, subscribed Thomas Underhill, testibus Edward Boughton, Alexander Neville, 1583; againe, 1588, Thomas Underhill, testibus Alex. Neville, Edw. Blount, William Gorges.

Bedsteds, with their Furniture.

1. A fayre, riche, new, standing square bedsted of wallnuttree, all painted over with crimson, and silvered with roses, iiij. beares and ragged staves, all silvered, standing upon the corners; the

[1] Referred to in Sir HARRIS NOCOLAS's note, see page 241.

teastar, cealar, dooble vallance, and bases of crimson velvet, richly embrothered with cinque-foiles of clothe of silver, with my lord's armes verie richly embrothered in the midst of the cealor and teastar, supported with the white lyon and the beare, silver; lyned throughe with red buckerom.—Three bases and duble vallance, fringed with deepe fringe of crimson silk and silver.

Fyne curteines of crimson sattin of xiiij. breaths, striped downe with a bone lace of silver, with xciiij. long buttons and loopes of silver, and a little small fringe of crimson silk and silver rounde aboute the curteins, lyned through with white taffata sarsenet.

2. A bedsted of wallnuttree toppe fashion, the pillers redd and varnished, the ceelor, tester, and single vallance of crimson sattin, paned with a broad border of bone lace of golde and silver; the tester richlie embrothered with my lords armes in a garland of hoppes, roses, and pomegranetts, and lyned with buckerom. Fyne curteins of crimson sattin to the same bedsted, striped downe with a bone lace of golde and silver, garnished with buttons and loopes of crimson silk, and golde, containing xiiij.ten bredths of sattin, and one yard iij. quarters deepe; the celor, vallance, and curteins lyned with crymson taffata sarsenet; a crymson sattin counterpointe, quilted and imbrodered with a golde twiste, and lyned with redd sarsenet, being in length iij. yards good, and in breadth iij. yards scant.

A chaire of crymson stattin suteable.

A fayre quilte of crymson sattin, vj. breadths iij. yards 3 quarters naile deepe, all lozenged over with silver twiste, in the midst a cinquefoile within a garland of ragged staves, fringed rounde aboute with a small fringe of crymson silke, lyned throughe with white fustian.

Ffyve plumes of coolored feathers, garnished with bone lace and spangells of goulde and silver, standing in cups knitt all over with goulde, silver, and crymson sattin, embrothered with a border of goulde twiste, aboute iij. parts of it fringed with silk and goulde, lyned with bridges sattin, length ij. yards and ij. bredths of satin.

3. A felde bedsted of wallnuttree toppe fashion, the pillors and bedshead carved and garnished, parcell-gilte, my lo. armes painted therein, and the beare and ragged staffe embossed at the topp. The celor and double vallance to the same bed being of

green velvet embro. with narrowe gards of green sattin and purfled goulde, the ragged staffe running along the midst of the same gardes; lyned througheout with yelloe and green braunched caffa, and the vallance fringed with a deepe call fringe of green silk and goulde. Ffyve curtaines of green velvet, and one little one for the tester, embr. and lyned like the rest, and fringed with a narrowe friuge of green silke and goulde. A counterpointe to the bed of green velvet, embrothered likewyse with my lo. armes in the garter, supported with the white lyon and the green; the beare and ragged staffe upon the creaste, lyned throughe with caffa, with buttons and loopes of green silke and goulde at the neather corner. A carpet for a cupboarde suteable, iiij. bredths of velvet ij. yards deepe, lykewise embrothered. Three bases of like velvet, in lyke manner embrothered and lyned, fringed with a narrowe fringe of green silke and goulde, with buttons and loopes, like the counterpointe. Ffyve cuppes for the top of the same bedd, carved with lybberds heads gilt, and fringed at the lower end with green silke and goulde.

4. A square bedsted of wallnuttree; the cielor, tester, and duble vallance of crymson sattin, embrothered richlie with cloth of goldo tissue, with my lo. armes, supported with the beare and white lyon embrothered within sundry parts of the vallance; fringed with a deepe fringe of goulde and crymson silke. A counterpoynte of crymson sattin, quilted and embrothered with crymson cloth of goulde, rounde aboute in a broade border and narrowe borders downright, and my lo. armes richlie embr. in the midst; six breadths of sattin and iij. yards iij. quarters long, lyned with buckerom. Ffyve curteines of crymson damaske to the same bed, of xiiij. bredths and ij. yards deepe, garnished downe the seames with a bone lace of golde, fringed about the sides with crymson silke and goulde; and iij. doz. and ij. buttons and loopes of goulde; iiij. beares of woode, silvered and parcell gilte, for the topp of the same bedd.

5. A great square bedsted of wallnuttree, carved, silver gilt, and painted very fayer; the tester, ceelor, and duble vallance and bases of clothe of silver and crymson sattin, embr. with goulde lace, my lo. fathers armes and my ladyes in sundry parts of it; the vallance fringed with a deepe fringe of goulde, silver, and crymson silke.

Ffyve curteins of crymson taffata, being vij. bredths, and in depth ij. yards quarter, and striped downe with goulde twiste, garnished with loope buttons and fringe of crymson silk and goulde.

A counterpointe of crymson taffita, embr. with goulde and silver twiste, having armes richlie embr. in the midst, suteable to the tester, and fringed with a narrowe fringe of goulde and silver, lacking at one end fringe a yard 3 quarters, being in length iij. yards 3 quarters, and in breadth iij. yards and quarter.

6. A field bedsted of wallnuttree topp fashion, varnished and gilte: the ceelor, tester, and vallance of crymson raised velvet, striped, with a bone lace of crimson silke and goulde, the tester and vallance lyned with crimson taffata. Ffyve curteins of crimson damaske, being in depth one yard 3 quarters, garnished with long buttons and fringe of crimson silke and goulde, and striped downe with open lace of goulde. Ffyve plumes of red and yello feathers, spangled with goulde, for the topp of the same bed. A counterpointe of crimson damaske of 5 bredths, striped downe with the like lace, fringed with a narrowe fringe of crimson silke and goulde, lyned with russet fustain being in depth iij. yards quarter.

7. A field bedsted of wallnuttree, painted red and gilt; the ceelor, tester, and single vallance of scarlet, embr. with goulde and red velvet, in fashion of broad gards; the vallance fringed with a deepe fringe of silke and goulde; the ceeler and tester embr. very thicke. Ffyve curteins of scarlet, likewise embr., garnished with loope buttons and fringe of red silke and goulde, and lyned with red sarsenet. A counterpointe for the same of crymson taffata, striped with a bone lace of goulde, and fringed rounde with a narrowe fringe of red silke, lyned with jean fustian.

8. A bedsted of wallnuttree; the ceilor, tester, and vallance of crymson damaske, embr. with flowers of goulde and silver, fringed with crimson silke, cauld with golde. Ffyve curteins of crimsou taffata, laied on with silver lace. Bases to the bed, fitt for the same, of crymson damaske. A counterpointe of crimson taffata, quilted and fringed with goulde and silver, and. embr. with a border of clothe of golde.

ix. A fielde bedsted of wallnuttree; the ceelor, tester and

vallance of crimson velvet, embr. with armes, beasts, &c., silver, lyned with crimson taffata.

Five curteins of crimson taffata, fringed with golde, &c., being in depth, xiij. bredths of the silk, in length 2 yards scant. A quilte crimson taffata sarsenett, lyned with chequier canvis, black and white, in length 3 yards quarter, in bredth 2 yards.

x. A square bedsted of wallnuttree; the ceelor, testor, and duble vallance of white tinsell sarsenett, embr. all over with purple velvet and copper goulde; the vallance fringed accordinglie. Fyve curteines to the same bed of purple and white taffata, paned, containing 22 panes, and 2 yards quarter deepe. A counterpointe to the same bed of purple sarsenett, quilted and fringed with a narrowe fringe of golde and silver rounde aboute, containing in bredth iiij. yards, in length iij. yards iij. quarters.

xi. A fielde bedsted, with ceelor, testor, and vallance of black velvet. Fyve curteines of black taff. sarsenett, containing 5 bredths, and in depth j. yard iij. quarters. A counterpointe of black taffata, containing in length iij. yards, in bredth 2 yards 3 quarters scant.

xii. A great square wainscot bedsted, gilte and carved; the ceelor, testor, and vallance of crimson velvet, clothe of tissue, and clothe of goulde, with the queens armes upon the celor and testor, paned; bought of the Lady Lenox; with bases, &c. Fyve curteines of crimson damaske, duble vallance, containing 15 panes, and 2 yards and quarter deepe. A quilte of carnacions and blew taffata, paned and chekered over with a twiste of goulde, and embr. with a border of clothe of golde, and fringed with goulde, lyned with Million [Milan] fustian, containing in length 4 yards quarter, in bredth iij. yards quarter.

xiii. A fielde bedsted of wallnuttree topp fashion; the ceelor, testor, and single vallance of clothe of Murrey and greene, garnished with lace of greene silke and copper goulde, with 3 curteines of the same clothe; the testor and vallance lyned with changeable sarsenett. A counterpointe to the same, of the same clothe, laide downe the seames and aboute with the like lace and fringed; lyned with fustian, containing in length 3 yards 3 quarters, and in bredth 3 yards scant. A cupboarde clothe suteable.

XIV. A fielde bed of wallnuttree; the ceelor, testor, and vallance of Murrey cloth, garnished with a lace of copper goulde and silke, with 3 curteines of iiij. bredths of clothe, fringed; the testor and vallance lyned with purple sarsenett. A counterpointe of the same clothe, lyned down the seames with the like lace, and fringed round with the like fringe, lyned with fustian. A cupboarde of clothe suteable.

XV. A fielde bedsted of wallnuttree; the ceelor, testor, and vallance of blew clothe, garnished with a chaine lace of goulde and silver copper. Three curteines of the same clothe, laced over with like lace, being iiij. bredths of the clothe fringed; the testor and vallance lyned with sarsenett. A counterpointe of the same clothe, in length iiij. yards 3 quarters, in bredth ij. yards, laid downe the seames with the like lace to the bed, fringed accordinglie; lyned with the same fustian; with a cupboard clothe suteable.

XVI. A fielde bedsted of wallnuttree; the ceelor, testor, and vallance of red clothe, garnisht with a flat lace, copper gilt. Three curteines of the same clothe, the ceelor and vallance lyned with red sarsenett. A counterpointe of the same clothe, contayning in length iij. yards iij. quarters naile, and in bredth iij. yards scant. A cupboarde clothe suteable.

XVII. A Venice bedstead, with iiij. teannes carved like men and women, varnished and gilded verie faire, with a sparver of crimson velvet and blacke clothe of goulde, paned. The ceelor and testor richlie embrothrd with my lo. armes in the garter, and all the rest sett out with beares, ragged staves and letters of clothe of goulde and silver, embrothrd; the sparver containing iiij. panes, whereof the two utter panes are in depthe iij. yards and quarter, the other 2 shorter by a yard. Fyve curteines to the said sparver of crimson taffata, containing eleven bredths; the seames laid downe with a bone lace of silver and goulde, garnished with long buttons and loopes of goulde and silver, fringed accordinglie; in depth iij. yards. A counterpointe of crimson sattin, embr. all over with twiste and spangells of golde and silver, embr. rounde

aboute with a border of the ragged staffe, roses and lillies, &c., verio richlie fringed with a narrowe fringe of golde and silver and silk; lyned with crimson taffata sarsenett; in length iij. yards iij. quarters and the 5 bredths of the sattin.

XVIII. A sparver bedsted of wallnuttree, with a sparver of crimson rased velvet and crymson tynsell sattin, striped, paned togeither, fringed with goulde and silke. Three curteines of taffata crimson. A counterpointe of crimson sattin, quilted and fringed rounde with goulde, containing 6 breaths of sattin, and iij. yards long.

XIX. A sparver bedsted of wallnuttree, with a sparver of yellow and blew caffa, with three curteines of yelloe and blewe sarsenett. A counterpointe of the same caffa, quilted and lyned with fustian, containing 5 bredths of the stuffe, in length iij. yards iij. quarters.

XX. A sparver bedsted of wallnuttree, with a sparver of red and greene caffa. Three curteines of red and green sarsenett, changeable, containing 7 bredths, and in depth iij. yards. A counterpointe of the same caffa, quilted and lyned with fustian.

XXI. A sparver bedsted of wallnuttree, with a sparver of yelloe and blew caffa, with three curteines of yellow and blewe sarsenett. A quilted counterpointe of the same.

XXII. A sparver bedsted of wallnuttree, with a sparver of red and yelloe caffa. Three curteines of red and yelloe sarsenett. A counterpointe of the same caffa, quilted and lyned with fustian.

XXIII. A sparver bedsted of wallnuttree, with turned and carved pillors, with a sparver of blewe and orange tawnie damaske, the vallance and curteines fringed with blewe and orange tawnie silke. A counterpointe of blew damaske, laced and fringed with tawnie and blew silke, and lyned with Jene fustian.

XXIV. A sparver bedsted of wallnuttree, with a greate sparver of redd damaske, and curteines of redd caffata sarsenett.

XXV. A slope bedsted, covered and furnished with broade clothe frost upon green, lined throughe with green sarsenett. A counterpointe to the same of green taffata sarsenett, not fringed :

the bed fringed, buttoned, and laced with greene silke and silver.

XXVI. A slope little bedsted for the field, of wallnuttree; the ceelon, testor, and curteines of green clothe, all trimed with lace and fringe of green and yelloe silke. A counterpointe of like green clothe, trimed with lace and fringe of greene and yelloe silke, lyned with fustian.

XXVII. A slope bedsted of wallnuttree; the testor and curteines of orange tawnie kersey, garnished with fringe lace, and buttons of blewe and orange tawnie silk.

XXVIII. A slope bedsted of wallnuttree, covered and furnished with peache-coller broade clothe. Counterpointe to the same, laced and fringed with ashe-coolor silke.

XXIX—XXX. Two ould joyned bedsted, the one with a wainscott testor.
Two bedsted cases of red leather.

XXXI. A canapie bedsted of wallnuttree, with a canapie of green and yelloe changeable taffata, garnished with lace of green silke and gould. Two curteines, containing 18 panes, and in depth ij. yards and quarter, with buttons, tassells, and fringe of green silke and goulde. A counterpointe of like taffata, lyned with Jene fustain, and fringed with goulde and silver fringe; in length iij. yards scant, bredth ij. yards 3 quarters.

XXXII. An other canepie of like taffata; curteines and counterpointe garnished with lace, buttons, tassells, and fringe of greene silke and silver.

XXXIII. A canapie of purple lawne, brainched with sundry colors, lyned with crimson tinsell sarsenett, and tasselld with silke and goulde. A counterpointe of changeable sarsenett, quilted, purpell and yelloe, in length iij. yards, in bredth ij. yards 3 quarters.

XXXIV. A canapie bedsted of wainscott, the canapie of green sarsenett, buttoned, tasselled, and fringed with green silke. A counterpointe of green sarsenett, quilted.

xxxv. A canapie of purple sarsenett, with buttons, tassells, and fringe of silk; the traine being of xiiij. panes, and in depth ij. yards, stained and neere woren. Counterpointe of like sarsenett, quilted and lyned with fustian, the coolor being vaded.

Killingworth Beddes, &c.

A principall bed of downe, the tyke of Millian fustian, in length ij. yards 3 quarters, in breadth iiij. breadths of the sayde fustian.
A bowlester to the same.
One other speciall bed of downe, the tyke being viij. quarters, and striped all over with blew; with a bowlester to the same.
Nine other beddes of downe, with their bowlesters.
Ninety fether beddes of different sizes, with their bowlesters.
Twenty-four lynnen quiltes.
Thirty-seven pair of fustian blancketts.
Twentie pair of playne white woollen blancketts.
Seventie pillowes of different lengths, from 3 quarters of a yard to one yard.
Eight white Spanish ruggs, xiv. and xvj. ells the peece.
Eighteen other white ruggs, tenn of them of a courser sorte.
One red rugg of xij. ells; one blew, of xij. ells; one green, of xij. ells; two white Irish ruggs of ij. breadths, iij. yards long.
Seven Spanish ruggs, white.
xiiij. course English bancketts.
Fower redd ruggs.
One green rugg.
Twentie-seaven other blancketts.
A counterpointe of watchett caffa quilted, in length iij. yards, in breadths iij. yards. A counterpointe of imagerie, being in length iij. ells and in breadth ij. ells.
Two counterpointes of tapestrie.
Fourteen other counterpointes of tapestrie.
Six counterpointes of imagerie tapestry, of different lengths and breadths.
Eighteen counterpointes of Vardures, lyned throughe with canvis.
Thirty-six counterpointes of course Vardures.
Thirty-seven mattresses of canvis, of different sizes.
Three pair of fine holland sheets, iij. breadths, in length iij. ells.

Twenty-four pair of course holland sheets.

Tenn pair of pallet sheets, ij. breadths, and ij. ells and quarter long.

Tenn pair of fine canvis sheets, of ij. ells broad, and ij. ells long.

Twelve pair of sheets, of iij. breadths, iij. ells and quarter long.

One pillowbere, wrought all over with hops, knotts, and roses of blew silke.

Two pillowberes, wrought with laide worke of red and yello silck, in length a yard, breadth a yard.

A pillobere, wrought with carnacions of golde, and carnacions of green silck; one square pillobere of open worke of goulde, silver, and sundry coloured silckes, lyned with cambricke.

Two pilloberes of cambrick, wrought with beares, &c., of goulde, silver, and silck of sundry colours.

Two pilloberes of Italian work, of sundrie coloured silck.

Two pilloberes, with pillows to them, wrought with gould, silver, and silcks of sundry colors.

Two pilloberes, with a border of lorne worck, black.

Two pilloberes of holland, with a border of open worcke of white thred.

Thirty-nine very fayre wrought pilloberes, sent to London, per Browne, for the Countisse, October 17, 1588.

Chayres, Stooles, and Cushens.

A chaier of crimson velvet, the seate and backe partlie embrothered with R. L. in clothe of goulde, the beare and ragged staffe in clothe of silver, garnished with lace and fringe of goulde, silver, and crimson silck; the frame covered with velvet, bounde abowte the edge with goulde lace, and studded with gilte nailes.

A square stoole and a foote stoole of crimson velvet, fringed and garnished suteable.

A long cushen of crimson velvet, embr. with the ragged staffe in a wreathe of goulde, with my lo. posie, "*Droyte et Loyale,*" written in the same, and the letters R. L. in clothe of goulde, being garnished with lace and fringe; buttons and tasseles of golde, silver, and crimson silck; lyned with crimson taff.; being in length 1 yard quarter.

A square cushen of the like velvet, embr. suteable to the long cushen.

A chaier of wallnuttree, carved with the cinque-foile and the ragged staffe, covered with crimson velvet, the back richlie embrothered with cinque-foiles of clothe of silver, with two beares and ragged staves standing on the topp; the seate all lozenged with silver twiste, trimed with fringe of crimson silck and silver; the back of the chaier lyned with crimson sattin. A case of buckerom to the same.

A square stoole and a foote stoole suteable to the same.

A long cushin of crimson velvet, embr. with cinquefoilles, with tassells of crimson silck and silver, lyned with crimson sattin suteable.

Two chaiers of crimson velvet, embr. with black clothe of goulde, lyned with purple taffata, and fringed with redd silck and goulde. Two square stooles suteable.

Two long cushins of the same sorte suteable, lyned with purple taffata, buttoned and tasselled with crimson silck and goulde, in length 1 yard, in breadth 1 yard.

Two chaiers of black velvet, embr. with clothe of gould, lyned on the backe with purple taffata; two square stooles suteable. Two long cushins of black velvet, embr. with clothe of goulde, suteable to the sayd chayers, with buttons and tassells at the corners of blacke silck and goulde; in length and breadth, 1 yard.

A chaier of purple velvet, embr. with my lo. armes in the quarter, and letters, &c., fringed with purple silck and silver; the back lyned with purple sattin, with ragged staves, and a white lyon on the backe.

A chaier of crimson velvet, embr. with a broade wreathe of goulde, lyned on the backe with purple taffata.

A square stoole suteable. A long cushin of the same suite, with iiij. buttons and tassells at the corners of crimson silck and goulde, length and breadth 1 yard.

A chaier of crimson velvet, the seate, back, and frame embr. all over with clothe of gould and silver; the beare and ragged staffe embr. in the back in clothe of goulde and silver, and garnished with lace and fringe of goulde and silver.

Two square stooles and a foote stoole suteable.

Two long cushins to the same, with buttons and tassells and fringe of goulde, and silver and crimson silck, lyned with crimson taffata; length, 1 yard and quarter.

Two square cushins suteable.

A foulding chayer of black velvet, embrothered with clothe of goulde fringe, with black silck and goulde. A square stoole suteable. A long cushin of the same suite, lyned with striped taffata, in length 1 yard and quarter.

Six highe stooles of wallnuttree, covered with black velvet quilted. A chayer, long cushins, and loe stoole of blacke clothe of golde, the frame of the chayer broken.

A lowe square stoole, covered with crimson velvet.

Two long cushins of crimson sattin, garded with velvet.

One long cushin of crimson velvet, lyned with red and green caffa.

Fower chayers (two highe and two lowe) of green velvet, embr. with green sattin, suteable to the green velvet bedd; the frames varnished and parcell gilte, with pomell and studds gilte.

Chayer Stooles and Cushins.

Fower square cushins, and one little one longwise, of greene velvet, both sides a like, embrothered with green sattin and goulde like the rest, with buttons and tasselles of green silck and goulde.

A chayer and lowe stoole of crymson raysed velvet, trimed with lace and goulde fringe.

A chayer of crimson clothe of goulde tinsell, lyned in the back with purple taffata; a square stoole suteable; a long cushin of the same suite, with iiij. buttons and tassells of redd silk and gould, in length 1 yard 1 quarter, in breadth one yard.

A chayer of purple clothe of silver, the back lyned with purple taffata, fringed with purple silck and goulde; a square stoole suteable; a long cushin of the same suite, with iiij. buttons and tassells of purple silck and goulde, in length 1 yard quarter, breadth the same.

A chayer, the frame wrought with bone, the back and seate of russett clothe of silver, embr., fringed, &c., paste service.

Two chayers of green rased velvet, the grownd tynsell, fringed with green silke and goulde; the back and sides leather.

A chayer of plaine clothe of silver, fringed with silver, the back and sides purple taffata; a square stoole suteable; a long cushin of the same suite, with two buttons and tassells of white silk and silver; in length 1 yard quarter, in breadth one yard good.

A chaier of brainched clothe of silver, the backside leather, and fringed with silver; a square stoole suteable; a long cushin of the same suite, with iiij. tassells of white silck and silver, lyned with white checked damask, in length 1 yard and quarter, in breadth 1 yard.

A chayer of purple clothe of golde, the backside leather, and fringed with silck and golde; a square stoole suteable; a long cushin suteable, lyned with crimson damask, with iiij. tassells.

A chaier of black velvet, the pomell and studds gilt, fringed with black silck and goulde, the back vellet, with two cheakes to the same.

Three foote stooles of purple clothe of silver, fringed with purple silck and goulde.

A chayer of silver tissue, fringed with white silck and silver, and lyned with purple taffata.

A chayer of crimson vellet, embr. with a lyon in a wreath, &c., silver, with ragged staves and roses.

A chaier of crimson silver tissue, fringed with crimson silck and silver, lyned with purple taffata.

A chaier of crimson sattin, embr. with a white beare and ragged staves, in a wreath of silver.

A lowe square stoole of crimson sattin, garnished with bone lace of gould, and fringed as the chaier.

A long cushin of crimson sattin, embr. and garnished as the rest, lyned with crimson caffa.

Two foote stooles of crimson vellet, fringed with crimson silck.

A long cushion of crimson vellet, embr. with gould and silver, fringed with gould and red silck, and lyned with crimson damask, with iiij. buttons at the corners.

A chayer, long cushin, and lowe stoole, embrothered with purple clothe of tynsell, fringed and tassell'd with black silck and silver.

A chayre of peache-color clothe of tyssue.

A chayer of crimson silver tyssue, fringed with crimson silck and silver, and lyned with purple taff.

Two long cushins of tawnie vellet, lyned with black satin, fringed with tawnie silck.

Two long cushins of redd vellett, lyned with damask, fringed with redd silck.

Two long cushins, redd vellet, lyned with crimson sattin and fringed with silck.

A long cushin of purple clothe of silver tissue, bordered with a contrarie kinde of stuffe, having seed perle in it, lyned with gould tinsell, with iiij. buttons and tassells of white silck and gould, in length 1 yard 3 nails, in breadth the same.

Six cushins of redd vellett, lyned with green sattin of Bridges [Bruges], fringed with silck.

A cushion, both sides redd vellet, fringed with redd silck, bordered rounde aboute with a bone lace of gould, with iiij. buttons and tassells of redd silcke and gould.

One long cushin of crimson clothe of golde, lyned with blewe clothe of goulde and rased vellett, and peeced at the one end crimson clothe of tissue, fringed with a narrowe uncutt fringe of goulde, with ij. buttons and tassells of purple silck and goulde, lyned with purple vellett, purled with gould.

Two long cushins of crimson sattin, seamed with one open lace of golde and silver, lyned with blewe Bridges sattin, with iiij. buttons and tassells a peece.

A cushin, both sides redd sattin, fringed with red silck, with iiij. buttons and tassells of red silck and goulde.

A long cushin of needle worke, the ground crimson silck, wrought with flowers, &c., of gould, silver, and greene silcke, fringed with gould and silcke, lyned with crimson sattin, iiij. buttons and tassells at the corners.

A long cushin of needle worke, wrought with knotts of sundry-colored silckes, fringed with yelloe and tawnie silcke, lyned with yelloe sattin, with iiij. buttons and tassells.

A highe square stoole of needle worke, the frame wallnutttree, wrought with blew and yelloe silke, and fringed accordinglie.

A cushin of silcke needle worke, with letters E. K. in goulde in the midst, fringed and tasselled with gold, silver, and silck of sundrie colors, lyned with crimson sattin, striped with goulde and silver.

Two square cushins of needle worke crewell, lyned with leather.

Two covers of chests of crimson rased vellet, layed on with a lace of crimson silcke and gould, fringed with a narrowe fringe of crimson silcke and golde.

A chayer and lowe stoole of murrey clothe, garnished with a lace of copper gould and silcke.

A chayer and lowe stoole of blewe clothe, garnished with a chaine lace, gold and silver copper.

A chaier and a square stoole of red clothe, garnished with copper gould lace.

A chayer and lowe stoole of murrey and greene clothe, garnished with lace, greene silcke, and copper goulde; twelve square cushins of blewe clothe, lyned with redd leather, and fringed with silck.

Twelve square cushins of greene clothe, lyned with leather and fringed with silck.

Twelve cushins of stamell; six leather chayers.

Twelve highe stooles of crimson vellet.

Eight long cushins of crimson vellet checkered.

Carpetts.

A carpett of crimson velvet, richlie embr. with my Lo. armes; posie, beares and ragged staves, &c., of clothe of gould and silver, garnished upon the seames and aboute with golde lace, fringed accordinglie; lyned with crimson taffata sarsenett; being iij. breadths of vellet, one yard 3 quarters long.

A carpett for a cupboarde, of green vellet, embr. with sattin and goulde, lyned and fringed, being iiij. breadths of vellet, ij. yards in length.

A carpett of crimson rased vellet, with a lace of crimson silcke and goulde rounde aboute it, fringed with a deepe fringe of crimson silcke and golde; in length 2 y. quarter, iij. breadths of the same vellet.

Two carpetts of crimson vellet, lyned with buckerome, fringed with red silck and gould.

One carpett of crimson vellet, lyned with buckerome, bound aboute with parchment lace of red silck.

A carpett of purple vellet, lyned with purple Bridges sattin.

A carpett for a windowe of crimson vellet, garnished on the one side and both ends with lace and narrowe fringe of gould, silver, and crimson silck, and lyned with red Bridges sattin.

A carpett of needle worko of sundrye coulored silcks, the grounde sad green, with a borders of roses, and sundrie posies aboute it, the ground of the borders orainge tawnie; in length vj. yards, in breadth j. yard 3 quarters; given by Mr. Griffin, of Warr, in Septr. 1581.

A silck carpett, straingelie wrought with naked images, garnished in sundry places with gold and perle, lyned with green taffata.

Hanginges.

Eight peeces of flowers, beasts, and pillors, arched, in depth 5 ells and quarter, and of different lengths, from 3 ells 3 quarters; lyned with canvas.

Eleaven peeces of fyne tapestrye of fforest worke, in depth 3 ells the p'ece, and of different lengths [as in the first article].

Eight peeces of deepe hanginges, bought of the Ladye Lennox, all quarter-lined with canvas.

Eight peeces of historie, quarter lyned with canvas, in depth 5 ells, lengths from 3 ells 3 quarters to 7 ells.

Twelve peeces of historie, 5 ells deepe, in length alltogether lxvj. ells.

Eight peeces of hangings, fforest worke, vj. ells deepe, of different lengths, from 3 ells 3 quarters to 7 ells.

Sixteene peeces of gilt leather hangings, having on the topp the picture of a man and a woman, being all in depth iiij. ells and quarter the peece, and in length ij. ells.

Three peeces of gilt leather hangings of the storie of Susanna, paned gilte and blew, in depth iiij. ells and quarter, in length iiij. ells iij. quarters the peece.

Three peeces of gilte leather hangings of the storie of the Prodigall Childe, paned gilte and blew, being in depth iiij. ells and quarter, and in length iiij. ells and 3 quarters the peece.

Two like peeces of the storie of Saule, paned gilte and blewe, the one in depth iiij. ells, the other ij. ells, and both in length iiij. ells 3 quarters.

Three peeces of gilt hangings of red leather, paned gilt and blew; the first 6 ells in length by iiij. ells and quarter in depth; the second, 5 ells 3 quarters by iiij. ells and quarter; the third, 7 ells by ij.

One pair of guilt leather hangings, gilt and greene, of the story of Tobie; in depth iij. ells and quarter, in length iiij. ells 3 quarters.

Fyve peeces of leather hangings, gilt and black; in depth iiij. ells quarter, in length 5 ells.

Ffower peeces of the historie of Sawle, lyned with canvas, all fyve ells in depth, in length vij., v., vij., and iiij. ells.

Six peeces of the historie of Hercules, being all in depth v.

Flemish ells 3 quarters, fower of them in length iv. ells, the other vj. ells and iv. ells.

Six peeces of Lady Ffame, &c., being all in depth vj. ells, lyned all through with canvis; lengths vij., vij. 3 quarters, vj. 3 quarters, viij., viij. quarter, viij. 3 quarters.

Six peeces of flowers and beasts, being all in depth 5 ells quarter, lyned with canvis; lengths, three of them 5 ells 3 quarters each, the others v., vj., and vij. ells each.

Ffower peeces of fflowers and beasts, being in depth iiij. ells and a peece, all quarter-lyned with canvis; their lengths, vij. ells and quarter, v. 3 quarters, vj. 3 quarters, iij. 3 quarters.

Nyne peeces of Hawking and Hunting, in depth 5 ells, all quarter-lyned with canvis; two in length iij. ells 3 quarters, the others vij. ells, iiij., v. quarter, iiij. 3 quarters, iiij. and quarter, v. 3 quarters, and vj. quarter.

Seaven peeces of the storie of Jezabell, in depth 5 ells quarter, lyned with canvis; length of the two first, vj. ells, two others iiij. ells 3 quarters, v. 3 quarters, vj. 3 quarters, vij. 3 quarters.

Eight peeces of the historie of Judith and Holofernes, six of them in depth 5 ells the peece; two of them iiij. ells 3 quarters; two of them in length iiij. ells 3 quarters; two others v., vj. 3 quarters, vij., iiij, ells scant, v. 3 quarters, iiij. ells scant.

Fyve peeces of the storie of David, in depth 5 ells, lyned with canvis; three of them in length v. ells, the fourth vj., and the fifthe iiij. ells.

Six peeces of the storie of Abraham; in depth 5 ells, all quarter lyned with canvis, their length vj., vij., iiij., iiij. ells and quarter.

Eight peeces of fflowers and beasts, all in depth 5 ells, lyned with canvis; their lengths, two of iij. ells 3 quarters, the others vij., iiij. 3 quarters, vj., vj. 3 quarters, iiij. 3 quarters, v. 3 quarters.

Fyve peeces of the storie of Sampson, of ould stuffe; being in depth iiij. ells; two of them in length iij. ells quarter; the others iij., iiij. quarter, vj. 2 quarters.

Six peeces of fflowers and beasts, in depth iiij. ells 3 quarters, lyned through with canvis.

Nyne fayre peeces of the storie of Hercules, antiques; in depth vij. ells; two are in length viij. ells, two others vij. ells and 3 quarters, the others ix. ells quarter, xj., ix., iiij., the nynth viij. ells scant.

Six peeces of the storie Hippolitus, 5 of them being in depth

5 ells the peece, the sixth iiij.; lyned with canvis; lengths vij. ells, v. 3 quarters, vj. and 3 quarters, iiij., iij., and iiij. ells and 3 quarters.

Eight peeces of the storie of Alexander the Great; in depth 3 ells the peece; in length, two of them v. ells and 3 quarters, two others iij. and 3 quarters, the rest iiij. ells, vij. and 3 quarters, vj., v. ells.

Six peeces of the storie of Naaman the Assyrian; in depth 5 ells and quarter; in length, two of them v. ells and 3 quarters; the others iiij., iij. and 3 quarters, v. scant, vj. ells and 3 quarters.

Eight peeces of the storie of Jacob; in depth 5 ells and 3 quarters; in length, the first two iiij. ells 3 quarters; two other iij. ells 3 quarters; the others vij. 3 quarters, vj. 3 quarters, vj. scant, v. 3 quarters; all quarter-lyned with canvis.

Eight peeces of fflowers and beasts pillard; in depth 5 ells; in length, two v. ells, two iiij. ells 3 quarters, two iij. 3 quarters, the seventh vij. ells, the eighth vj. ells 3 quarters.

Ffower peeces of leather hangings, gilte and blacke, being in depth iiij. ells scant, in length v. ells scant.

Six peeces of vardures, of very ould stuffe, in depth iiij. ells the peece.

A peece of hangings of red linsey wolsey, with borders and pillars painted, in depth ij. yards, in length xvj. yards.

Three peeces of stamell clothe, embrothered all over with armes, beasts, fflowers, &c., being in depth iiij. ells and quarter; the peece in length alltogether xvij. ells and quarter, all lyned through with canvis.

Turquoy Carpetts.

A greate Turquoy carpett, the grounde blewe, with a liste of yelloe at each end; being in length x. yards, in breadthe iiij. yards and quarter.

An other greate Turquoy carpett, of divers collours, with a frett of diverse collours in the midst; in length vij. yards 3 quarters, in breadth iij. yards quarter.

An other greate Turquoy carpett, wrought with roses and Stafford knots at the ends; in length v. yards 3 quarters, in breadth ij. yards and quarter.

An other greate Turquoy carpett, with greene wreths and flowers of white and black, the grounde tawnie; in length vj. yards, in breadth ij. yards naile.

A fine Turquoy carpett, wrought with orient colours; in length iiij. yards, breadth ij. yards.

A Turquoy carpett of Norwiche work, in length ij. yards, in breadth j. yard quarter.

Fyve Turquoy carpetts, the grounde red and blewe, with a green liste at each end, 4 yards by 2 yards.

Two Turquoy carpetts of different colours, each 5 yards in length and ij. yards in breadth.

An other Tuorquoy carpett of the same dimensions.

An other Turquoy carpett, redd and blewe, with a liste of blewe at each end; length iij. yards iij. quarters, breadth ij. yards.

Three Turquoye carpetts, the grounde white and garnished with other colours; two yards in breadth, and of different lengths, from iij. yards 3 quarters to iiij. yards 3 quarters: one of them sent to the Queen by order of my Lord, 20th October, 1588.

Twenty-six Turquoy carpetts, small, all of one making, betweene two ells and 3 ells a peece in length, in breadth betweene one ell and 1 ell 3 quarters.

Fower other Turquoy carpetts.

A Persian carpett, like Turquoie worke, the grounde redd; length iiij. yards 3 quarters, breadth ij. yards quarter.

Carpetts of Clothe.

Three carpetts of stamell clothe, fringed with gould and crimson silck, all of the breadth of the clothe, and in length iij. yards quarter, ij. yards quarter, and ij. yards quarter.

A long carpet of blew clothe, lyned with Bridges sattin, fringed with blew silck and gould; in length vj. yards lack a quarter, the whole breath of the clothe.

Six square carpetts, whereof iij. stamell, the other of greene clothe; in length, one with the other, 11 yards.

Fyve wyndowe carpetts of blew clothe, fringed with blewe silck on the one side, and both ends embr. with black vellet; in length one yard iij. quarters the peece, in breadth one yard lack a naile.

Two others of the same bredth and length, in like manner fringed, the one embr. with black vellet and white silck, the other with black vellet and yello silck.

A square carpett of blew clothe, with like imbrotherie, fringed with blew silck.

A carpett of greene clothe, fringed with greene silck and silver, in length ij. yards and quarter.

A carpett of greene clothe, fringed with green silck rounde, in length xj. yards quarter, the full bredth of the clothe.

Six carpetts of greene clothe, fringed with silck, for cupboards.

Three of very darke green clothe, for cupboards, containing, one with another, vj. yards of broade clothe.

Two carpetts of blew clothe and one of greene, fringed with silck of their own collour.

Curtens.

Eight windowe peeces of course vardures, of different lengths and bredths; six windowe peeces of tapistrie; two curtaines of crimson taff., lyned with Bridges sattin; two curtaines of green taff., lyned with Bridges sattin; one of greene taff. sarsenett; fower curtaines of striped Bridges sattin, of different length and bredths; eight curtaines of blew Bridges sattin, of different l. and b.; two of greene Bridges sattin; two window curtaines of redd, and fower of redd and greene Bridges sattin.

Pictures.

Two great tables of the Queenes Majesties pictures, with one curtaine changeable silck; two great pictures of my Lord, in whole proporcion, the one in armor, the other in a sute of russett sattin; with one curtaine to them.

An other picture of my Lo., in halfe proporcion, done in black garments.

The picture of St. Jerom naked, with a curtaine of silcke.

The picture of the Lord of Arundell,[1] with a curtaine.

The picture of the Lord Maltrevers,[2] with a curtaine.

Two pictures of the Lord of Pembroke,[3] with curtaines.

Two pictures of the Count Egmondt, with curtaines.

The picture of the Queene of Scotts, with a curtaine.

The picture of King Phillip, with a curtaine.

The picture of the Baker's Daughter.[4]

[1] See note page 266. [2] Ibid. [3] See note page 267. [4] Ibid.

Picture of the Duke of Feria,[1] in clothe, whole proportion.
The picture of Alexander Magnus, with a curtaine.
The pictures of two Yonge Ladyes, with curtaines.
Two pictures of Pompoea Sabina.
The picture of Frederick Duke of Saxony,[2] without frame and curtaine.
The picture of the Emperor Charles, with a curtaine.
The picture of King Phillips Wife, with a curtaine.
The picture of the Prince of Orange, with a curtaine.
The picture of the Wife[3] of the Prince of Orange.
The picture of the Marques of Berges,[4] with a curtaine.
The picture of the Wife of the Marques, with a curtaine.
The picture of the Count de Horne,[5] with a curtaine.
The picture of Count Holstrate, with a curtaine.
The picture of Monsieur Brederode, with a curtaine.
The picture of the Duke Alva, with a curtaine.
The picture of the Cardinall Granville, with a curtaine.
The picture of the Duches of Parma, with a curtaine.
The picture of Henrie Earl of Pembroke.
The picture of the young Countess [Mary Sydney, niece of the E. of Leycester.]
The picture of the Countis Essex, in a wainscot case.
The picture of Occacion and Repentance.
The picture of the Lord Mowntacute, with a curtaine.
The picture of Sir James Crofts,[6] with a curtaine.
The picture of Sir Walter Mildmay.[7]
The picture of Sir William Pickering,[8] in clothe, whole proportion.
The picture of Edwin [Sandys], 2d Archbishop of York, with a curtaine.
A tabell of an historie of men, women, and children, molden in wax.
A little foulding table of ebanie, garnished with white bone, wherein are written verses with letters of goulde.
A table of my Lords Armes.
Fyve of the Plannetts, painted in frames.
Twentie-three cards or maps of Countries.

[1] See note, page 267.   [2] Ibid.   [3] Ibid.
[4] Ibid.   [5] Ibid.   [6] Ibid.
[7] See note page 268.   [8] Ibid.

Instruments.

An instrument of organns, ryalls, and virginalls, covered with crimson velvet, and garnished with goulde lace.
A faier pair of double virginalls.
A ffaier pair of double virginalls, covered with black velvet.
A cheast of vialls; a case of fluits flewed with silver, containing xij. peeces.
Three bandoracs, in a case of leather.
Three lutes, in leather cases.

Cabonetts.

A cabonett of crimson sattin, richlie embr. with a device of hunting the stagg, in gould, silver, and silck, with iiij. glasses in the topp thereof, and xvj. cupps of flowers, made of golde, silver, and silck, in a case of leather, lyned with greene sattin of Bridges.
A cabonett of purple vellett, richlie embr. with gold and silver, with three brainches of flowers of gold, silver, and silck, and a case for the same.
A deske of redd leather, printed and gilded with a standyshe in it lyned with greene sattin of Bridges.
A chess boarde of ebanie, with checkars of christall and other stones layed with silver, garnished with beares and ragged staves, and cinquefoiles of silver; the xxxij. men likewise of christall and other stones sett, the one sorte in silver white, the other gilte; in a case of leather, gilded and lyned with greene cotton.
A chess-borde of bone and ebanie, with thirtie and fower men to it, in a leather case.
A pair of tabells of bone inlaid, with divers colors and men to them, in a case of leather.

Chestes.

A jewel coffer, with sundrie boxes and partitions of redd leather, covered with fustian of Naples, nailed all over with yello nailes, barred with iron; and iiij. locks and keies.
Fower faier flatt Venecian chests of wallnuttree, carved and gilte, with locks and keys.
A greate redd standard, bound with iron, with lock and key.

Nine other chests of different sizes, covered with leather and Naples fustian.

A Byble covered withe redd leather gilte, with the beares and ragged staves printed upon it.

Seaven Psalters Bookes, covered with redd leather.

Candlesticks.

A dozen pewter candlesticks of a serviceable sorte.
One dozen and six of a second sorte.
A dozen of a thirde sorte.
One dozen and ij. of a fourth sorte.
One dozen and a halfe of a fifte sorte.
A great cestern of pewter to sett at a cupborde.
A great brason candlestick to hang in the roofe of the house, verie fayer and curiuslye wrought with xxiiij. branches, xij. greate, and xij. of lesser size, 6 rowlers and ij. wings for the spreade eagle; xxiiij. socketts for caudells, xij. greater and xij. of a lesser sorte; xxiiij. sawcers or candle cupps, of like proportion, to putt under the socketts.

iiij. images of men and iij. of weomen, of brass, verie finelie and artificiallie done.

Six candlesticks, with chaines, to hang in the roofe of the house, whereof 5 with 5 socketts a peece and one with 4.

Twentie other candlesticks of sundrie sortes; xvij. greate and small plates for candles, six of a lesser sorte.

Three greate cesters to sett at cupbordes:

A greate copper pann, to boile.

NOTES.

P. 263. *Notes on the Pictures.* Lord of Arundell was probably Henry Fitzalan, last Earl of Arundel. The picture is perhaps the same with that now at Longleat.

P. 263. *Lord Maltrevers.* Only son of the above-mentioned Earl of Arundel, by whose death, during the lifetime of his father, the honors of the family devolved to the Howards, by the marriage of Thomas Duke of Norfolk with Mary, one of the daughters, and at length the heiress of her father, Henry Earl of Arundel, and of her brother, Henry Lord Maltravers.

P. 263. *The Lord of Pembroke.* Probably Henry Earl of Pembroke, who married a niece of the Earl of Leicester, Mary Sydney, daughter of Sir Henry Sydney by the Lady Mary Dudley. He died in 1601.

P. 263. *The Picture of the Baker's Daughter.* This entry is of extreme interest in connexion with its most probable allusion to the same subject which is mentioned in the tragedy of Hamlet—" The owl was a baker's daughter." Is it impossible that this very picture had been seen by Shakespeare, and had furnished him with the idea of introducing the subject of the legend, which is thus related by Douce from oral tradition :—" Our Saviour went into a baker's shop where they were baking, and asked for some bread to eat. The mistress of the shop immediately put a piece of dough into the oven to bake for him, but was reprimanded by her daughter, who, insisting that the piece of dough was too large, reduced it to a very small size. The dough, however, immediately afterwards began to swell, and presently became of a most enormous size. Whereupon the baker's daughter cried out—Heugh, heugh, heugh, which owl-like noise probably induced our Saviour for her wickedness to transform her into that bird."[1]

P. 264. *The Duke of Feria.* Don Gomez Saures de Figueroa y Cordova came into England with Phillip II, and was afterwards created Duke of Feria in Spain. He married Jane daughter of Sir William Dormer, Knight of the Bath, maid of honour to Queen Mary, and sister of the first Lord Dormer of Wenge. The Duke of Feria was also employed in several embassies from Philip to Elizabeth, in the beginning of her reign. There is a small etching of him noticed by Granger, half length, 12mo.

P. 264. *Frederick Duke of Saxony.* This was probably the portrait of John Frederick the Magnanimous, Elector of Saxony, the protector of Luther and of the Reformation, who was deprived of his dignity and liberty by the Emperor Charles V. He died 1554.

P. 264. *The Wife of the Prince of Orange.* William, first founder of the Belgic liberties, had four wives (ob. assassinated 1584) :—1. Anne of Egmont, ob. 1558. 2. Anne, daughter of Maurice Elector of Saxony, ob. 1579. 3. Charlotte de Bourbon Montpensier, ob. 1582. 4. Louisa, daughter of Gaspard de Coligny, Admiral of France, ob. 1620. This was probably the one whose portrait is noticed.

P. 264. *The Marques of Berges and the Wife of the same.* I conceive these to have been the portraits of William, third Count of Bergen in Tutphen, and his countess, Mary of Nassau, sister of William Prince of Orange. He died 1586; she survived till 1599.

P. 264. *The Count de Horne.* This was most probably the portrait of the unfortunate Count de Hornes, who, with the Comte d'Egmondt, before mentioned, was beheaded in 1568, by the D'Alva, in the Low Countree.

P. 264. *Sir James Crofts.* "This personage was well known in the reign of Elizabeth, to whom he was Comptroller of the Household, and whom

[1] See also note by Wm. J. Thoms, page 269.

he also served in repeated embassies and in other employments. He was of a Herefordshire family, and a portrait of him, the only one I have ever seen, is at Rudhall, in that county. Margaret, the daughter and coheiress of Sir James Crofts, having married William Rudhall, Esq., accounts for the portrait being at that house." Malone notices a copy of the Rudhall portrait as being in the possession of Mr. Tighe.

P. 264. *Sir Walter Mildmay.* Sir Walter Mildmay was Surveyor of the Court of Augmentations in the reign of Henry VIII, and Privy Councillor, Chancellor, and Under-Treasurer of the Exchequer to Elizabeth, and founder of Emmanuel College, Cambridge. His portrait has been engraved by Faber, among the Founders.

P. 264. *Sir William Pickering.* Sir William Pickering had served four Sovereigns with distinction in military and civil capacities. Bishop Kennett says that he aspired to become the husband of Elizabeth. He died in 1574, aged 58, and was buried in the Church of Great St. Helen's, where a splendid monument was erected to his memory by his four executors, Sir Thomas Heneage, John Astley, Sir Drue Drury, and Thomas Wotton.

The above notes on the pictures are almost exclusively taken from some MS. notes signed R. S. T., attached to a transcript of the original manuscript, but I am unacquainted with the name of their author.

Mr. J. G. Nichols, in his interesting preface to the Unton Inventories, 4to, 1841, p. 10, has given a list of inventories then printed. A few important ones have lately been published by the Camden and Surtees Society, amongst which may be specially noticed the valuable volume of early Bury wills and inventories, edited by Mr. Tymms; but any large collection is still a desideratum. It is almost impossible to overrate the importance of this class of documents, in investigating the habits of our ancestors, and the character of their domestic life.[1]

---

[1] See "*Halliwell's Ancient Inventories,*" 4to, printed "*for private circulation only,*" by J. E. Adlard, 1854. Of this elegantly printed volume *only* 25 *copies* were printed, as certified by the printer.

PICTURES

OF THE

GREAT EARL OF LEICESTER.

Mr. WILLIAM J. THOMS communicates to the 'Notes and Queries¹ in 1862 a list of the PICTURES at KENILWORTH, prefacing the list by the following observations :

"I am enabled, by the kindness of the noble lord to whom the MS. belongs, to lay before the readers of 'Notes and Queries' a very interesting catalogue of the pictures which were in the possession of the Earl of Leicester at the time of his death, Sept. 4, 1588. It is extracted from an inventory taken in October following; and I think those who are interested in the history of art in England, will join me in thanking the owner of the manuscript for thus putting them in possession of information which would have gladdened the heart of Horace Walpole."

By comparing the list of pictures given by Mr. THOMS in 'Notes and Queries (in 1862) with the inventory in Mr. HALLIWELL'S 'Ancient Inventories' (printed in 1854), it will appear that they were both from the same source. Mr. Thoms was evidently not aware that his list had before been printed; the circumstance that Mr. Halliwell's book was for private circulation only, and that not more than 25 copies had been printed, may probably account for this.

At the end of the list Mr. Thoms says : "There is one picture in this list respecting which I would make a special query—What is the picture of the Baker's Daughter? Could we suppose it to represent the legend to which Shakspeare refers in 'Hamlet,'

¹ 'Notes and Queries,' 3rd series, No. 37, Sept. 13, 1862.

'The owl was a baker's daughter:' we might see in this allusion a recollection of one of the many visits which Shakspere doubtless paid to the glories of Kenilworth." In the following number of 'Notes and Queries,' Mr. Thoms again alludes to the same subject,—" Since my first communication appeared, my friend Mr. HENRY FOSS has suggested to me that the picture of the Baker's Daughter—of which, it will be seen, there was another copy at Wanstead—is the well-known Fornarina of Raffaele; while Mr. J. G. NICHOLS, judging from the pictures of Philip and the Baker's Daughter being together, inclines to the opinion that they were companions, and that the latter was a portrait of a female respecting whom there was scandal current during Mary's lifetime: it being said in an old ballad that Philip loved—

"The baker's daughter, in her russet gown,
Better than Queen Mary without her crown."

Mr. Thoms has also given, in the latter number of 'Notes and Queries,' a list of the pictures at LEICESTER HOUSE and at WANSTEAD.

Among the Burghley papers in the Lansdowne collection of MSS.,[1] we find the following inventory and valuation of the hangings and carpets, which form part of the inventory of "household stuff" given by Mr. Halliwell in his 'Ancient Inventories.' The paper has neither place, nor signature stated, and is merely indorsed—

"Novemb. '88.—A note of hangings and carpets of the Earl of Leycester."

"*Hangings and Carpets belonging to Robert, Earl of Leycester.*"

Hangings.

	£	s.	d.
Imprimis. Six pieces of the story of Hercules of 5 ells, 3 quarters deep, containing in all 333¼ ells at 20 pence the ell	22	17	0
8 pieces of Judith and Holofernes, 5 ells deep, containing in all 215¼ ells at 2s. 6d. the ell	26	17	6
Item—6 pieces of Flowers and Beasts, of 5 ells deep, containing 181 ells at 4s. the ell	36	5	0

[1] Lansdowne MSS., British Museum, Vol. 57.

KENILWORTH CASTLE. 271

	£	s.	d.

Item—6 pieces of Naaman the Syrian, 5 ells deep, containing 157¼ ells at 4s. the ell . . 31 10 0

Item—8 pieces of Flowers and Beasts, 5 ells deep containing 215 ells at 3s. 4d. the ell . . 35 16 8

Item—8 pieces of Histories, 5 ells deep, containing 213 ells, 3qrs., at 2s. the ell . . . 21 7 6

Item—9 pieces of Hawking and Hunting, of 5 ells deep, containing 230 ells, at 3s. 8d. the ell . 42 3 4

Item—4 pieces of Flowers and Beasts, being 4½ ells deep, containing 106 ells, at 3s. the ell . . 15 18 0

Item—9 pieces of the Story of Hercules, antiques, 7 ells deep, containing 533 ells, at 7s. the ell . 186 16 0

Item—8 pieces of Alexander Magnus, of 5 ells deep, containing in the whole 215 ells, 4s. 6d. the ell 48 7 6

Item—6 pieces of the Story of Hyppolitus, 5 ells deep, containing in all 115 ells and 3 qrs., at 6s. 8d. the ell 51 18 4

Item—7 pieces of Histories, of 5 ells deep, containing 321¼ ells, at 2s. 6d. the ell . . . 40 3 1

Item—8 pieces of the Story of Jacob, of 5 ells 3 qrs. deep, containing 243 ells and 3 qrs., at 4s. the ell 49 15 0

Item—6 pieces of Abraham, of 5 ells deep, containing 153 ells 3 qrs., at 2s. 4d. the ell . . 17 10 0

Item—5 pieces of David, of 5 ells deep, containing 137 ells, at 2s. 8d. the ell . . 18 10 4

Item—[ ] pieces of Flowers and Beasts, of 5 ells deep, containing 241 ells, at 4s. the ell . . 48 4 0

Item—8 pieces of Flowers and Beasts, 5 ells deep, at 3s. the ell, containing 216 ells and qr. . 36 10 0

Item—7 pieces of Jezebel, of 5 ells deep, containing 28 ells, at 2s. 8d. the ell . . . 27 16 8

Item—8 pieces of Forest work, 6 ells deep, containing 250½ ells, at 2s. the ell . . . 25 0 12

Item—8 pieces of old hangings, containing 331 ells, at 16d. the ell 22 0 16

Item—4 pieces of the Story of King Saul, containing 120 ells at 2s. 6d. the ell . . . 15 0 0

Bedsteads and Beds.

	£	s.	d.
One field bedstead of crimson satin, laid on with rich bone lace of gold, with curtains and a counterpoint embroidered, with two chairs, two stools, and two long cushions for the window, with a curtain, a cupboard-cloth, all suitable, with a quilt of crimson satin embroidered all over	70	0	0
A field-bedstead, varnished and gilt, with the cover, the double vallance, the counterpoint, the bases, one carpet for the table, with four chairs and five cushions, all of green velvet, embroidered with guards of satin gold twist, with the chair-frames gilt	40	0	0
Item—One rich square bed, embroidered with the Queen's Arms, which was sometime King Henry the Seventh's, with counterpoint and curtains to the same	30	0	0
Item—One field bed of scarlet, with the tops and vallance embroidered all over with crimson silk and gold. The curtains with guards suitable to the same, with one quilt, &c., with one chair, two stools, and one long cushion striped	25	0	0
Item—12 Quarters featherbeds, at £4 the bed,			
Item—11 Quarters featherbeds, at £3 10s. the piece.			
Item—10 Quarters featherbeds, 50s. the piece.			
Item—9 Quarters featherbeds, at 26s. 8d. the piece.			
Great window-curtains of satin of bridges [Bruges], 6 at 20s. a piece	6	0	0
Long needlework cushions, at 30s. a piece	4	10	0
Twenty pair of down pillows, at 10s. a pair	10	0	0
Andirons 4 pair, with fire-shovel and tongs, suitable to them	4	0	0
Two pair of bellows of walnut-tree carved, at 2s. a pair	0	4	0
Close stools, 10 at 10s. a piece	5	0	0
Corsletts[1]	60		

---

[1] Query, 60 in number, not £60.

Carpets.

	£	s.	d.
A Turkey carpet, 10 yards long, and 4 yards broad	20	0	0
A Turkey carpet, 7 yards long, 4 yards broad	15	0	0
A Turkey carpet, 5 yards long, 2½ yards broad	5	0	0
A Turkey carpet, 4½ yards long, 2½ yards broad	4	10	0
A Turkey carpet of 3½ yards long, 2½ yards broad	3	10	0
A Turkey carpet of 4½ yards long, 2½ yards broad	4	10	0
A Turkey carpet of 3½ yards long, 2½ yards long, [broad]	3	10	0
20 Turkey carpets for Court cupboards, at 13s. 4d. 1¼ yard broad	13	6	8
A fair needlework carpet, 7 yards long, lined with green satin	13	6	8

END OF HISTORY OF KENILWORTH CASTLE.

SIR ROBERT DUDLEY.

MEMOIRS AND CORRESPONDENCE

OF

SIR ROBERT DUDLEY,

(SON OF THE EARL OF LEICESTER)

WITH HIS

PROPOSITION TO BRIDLE THE IMPERTINENCE OF PARLIAMENTS

SUBMITTED TO JAMES I.

TOGETHER WITH A SHORT ACCOUNT OF

ALICE, DUCHESS DUDLEY,

SECOND WIFE OF SIR ROBERT.

SIR ROBERT DUDLEY,

SON OF THE EARL OF LEICESTER.

DOUGLAS, LADY SHEFFIELD, mother of Sir Robert Dudley, born about 1545, was the daughter of William Howard, first Lord Howard of Effingham, and Lord Admiral, who was the youngest son of Thomas, 2d Duke of Norfolk. She married Lord Sheffield about 1561 or 62, by whom she had a son, created by Charles I. Earl of Mulgrave. Lord Sheffield died Decr. 1568. Douglas was married to the Earl of Leicester in May, 1573. Dugdale says they were privately married in a house in Cannon Row, and two years afterwards, the ceremony was again more solemnly performed "in her chamber at Asher (or Esher) in Surrey, by a lawful minister, according to the form of matrimony by law established in the Church of England, in the presence of Sir Edward Horsey, Knight, that gave her in marriage, as also of Robert Sheffield, Esq., and his wife, Dr. Julio, Henry Frodsham, gentleman, and five other persons whose names are not specified." Two days after the first or secret marriage she was brought to bed of a boy, who was born at Sheen, now Richmond, and "there christened by a minister sent from Sir Henry Lee, having to his godfathers the Earl of Warwick and Sir Henry Lee, and to his god-mother the Lady Dacres, of the South, by their deputies." It is said that she received a letter from Leicester in which "he thanked God for the birth of his said son, who might be their comfort and staff of their old age,"—and that he subscribed himself her " Loving Husband."

It has been stated that there was besides a daughter born at Dudley Castle; but of this we have no authentic account. Lady Sheffield, in 1578, married Sir Edward Stafford, of Grafton. In the same year Leicester married Lady Lettice, the widow of Walter, Earl of Essex, and daughter of Sir Francis Knolles, who after his death married Sir Christopher Blount.[1]

Mary, sister of Douglas, Lady Sheffield, was the third wife of Edward, Lord Dudley, after whose death she married Richard Mompesson.

From another account we have the following:

SIR ROBERT DUDLEY, son to the Earl of Leicester, by the Lady Douglas Sheffield, was born at Sheen,[2] in Surrey, in the year 1573. His birth was carefully concealed, in order to prevent the Queen's knowledge of the Earl's engagement with his mother. He was, however, considered and treated as his lawful son till the Earl's marriage with the Countess Dowager of Essex, when he was about five years of age; and then he was declared to be only his natural issue by Lady Douglas. Out of her hands the Earl was very desirous to get him, in order to put him under the care of Sir Edward Horsey, Governor of the Isle of Wight; which some have imagined to have been done, not with any view to the child's disadvantage, whom he is said to have always loved tenderly, but with a view of bringing him upon the stage at some proper time, as his natural son by another lady. He was not, however, able to get him for some time; but at last effecting it, he sent him to school at Offington, near Worthing, in Sussex, in 1583. His uncle, the Earl of Warwick, had a seat near Worthing, still standing, and bearing the name of 'Warwick House.' At this school he was under the care of one Owen Jones, to whom, upon a certain occasion, the Earl is said to have expressed himself to this purpose. "Owen, thou knowest that Robin, my boy, is my lawful son; and as I do, and have charged thee, to keep it secret, so I charge

[1] See Dugdale's 'Warwickshire,' i, 250; 'Baronage,' ii, 262; 'Romance of the Peerage,' vol. iii, 1849.
[2] Sheen, now Richmond, near London.

thee not to forget it; and, therefore, see thou be careful of him." After remaining four years in this private school he was removed, in 1587, to the University of Oxford, and there entered of Christ Church by the style of " *Comitis Filius,*" *i. e.* an Earl's son.[1] In about a year after he came to the University, and when he was about the age of fifteen, his father died, leaving him, after the decease of his uncle Ambrose, Earl of Warwick, his noble castle of Kenilworth, and the Lordships of Denbigh and Chirk, and the bulk of his estate, which, before he was of age, he in a good measure enjoyed, notwithstanding the enmity borne him by the Countess Dowager of Leicester.

" He was not slow, however, in assuming the man. Nature had given him great activity of mind and quickness of faculty; he was to an unusual extent his own master, and free from all the ordinary restraints and entanglements. All the peculiar circumstances of his birth and position impelled an ardent, projecting, and ambitious spirit like his to seek distinction, and to seek it out of the common path. Perhaps it may have been his uncle Warwick who first turned his young imagination to the field of maritime adventure and discovery; that nobleman had been among the earliest patrons of the famous Frobisher, and no doubt had often told his listening nephew the story of the black stones which the great navigator brought home from his first expedition in search of the north-west passage, and which had afterwards thrown the nation into such a ferment, when one of them, having been accidentally cast on the fire, had blazed forth, not with the flame of a common coal, but with the glitter of gold.[2]

" He was at this time looked upon as one of the finest gentlemen in England; in his person tall and well shaped, having a fresh and fine complexion, but red-haired; learned beyond his age, more especially in the mathematics; and of parts equal, if not superior, to any of his family. Add to all this, that he was very expert in his exercises, and particularly in

---

[1] In 'Nichols's Leicestershire' it is stated that he was educated under Sir Thomas Chaloner, the accomplished governor of Prince Henry.

[2] Craik's 'Romance of the Peerage,' vol. iii.

riding the great horse, in which he was allowed to excel any man of his time.

"His genius prompting him to great exploits, and having a particular turn to navigation and discoveries, he projected a voyage into the South Seas, in hopes of acquiring the same fame thereby as his friend the famous Thomas Cavendish, whose sister, it is said, he had married.

The following, in a measure, corroborates the inference of the marriage having taken place:

[1592-3.] "*At St. James's*, 18 *March*, 1592.

"A letter to the Mayor and Officers of the Port of Portsmouth. Whereas Mr. Robert Dudley Esq. hath taken a letter of Administration of the goods of Thomas Cavendish Esq. lately deceased at the seas. These shall be, notwithstanding any former letters written from the Galleon Leicester and the Roebuck, two ships that did appertain to the said Mr. Cavendish, to require you to cause the said ships, with their lading, to be delivered to Mr. Dudley, or such as he shall appoint to receive the same. Wherein we require you to give the gentleman your best help and assistance, &c., &c."[1]

"But, after he had taken much pains and spent a great deal of money in preparation for this design, the Government would not suffer him to proceed, looking upon it as a dangerous voyage, in which they thought it not fit to hazard the lives of the Queen's subjects. However, notwithstanding this disappointment, he fitted out a small squadron for the river Oronoko and the coasts adjacent, of which he took the command in person. An account of this voyage, written by himself, is published in Hakluyt's collection,[2] entitled, 'A Voyage of the Honourable Gentleman, Mr. Robert Dudley, now Knight, to the Isle of Trinidad and the Coast of Paria.' 'Having ever,' he commences his narrative, 'since I could conceive of anything, been delighted with the discoveries of navigation, I fostered in myself that disposition till I was of

[1] Privy Council Registers, Elizabeth, vol. ii.
[2] 'Hakluyt,' vol. iii, pp. 574–7. 1600.

more years and better ability to undertake such a matter. To this purpose I called to me the advice of sufficient seamen, and principally undertook a voyage for the South Seas; but, by reason that many before had miscarried in the like enterprise, I could not be suffered to hazard more of her Majesty's subjects upon so uncertain a ground as my desire, which made me by constraint (great charges already by me defrayed) to prepare another course for the West Indies.' But upon that, he says, he had set out 'without hope there to do anything worth note.' Such a voyage was become so common, indeed, as not to be worth the registering. It was only Hakluyt's importunity that had prevailed with him to send his journal to fill any vacant space that might be left by more important discourses. In making provision for the enterprise, he had had in view rather 'some practice and experience than any wonders or profit.'

"The adventure was noteworthy for one thing, at least—the youth of the conductor. Dudley, when he set out upon this enterprise, would be scarcely one and twenty, if he was so old. They weighed anchor from Southampton Road on the 6th of November, 1594; himself in the 'Bear,' of two hundred tons, as Admiral, and Captain Monk in the 'Bear's whelp' as Vice-Admiral; two small pinnaces, the 'Frisking' and the 'Earwig,' accompanying them. Dudley had 140 men under his own command in the "Bear." He was soon left to pursue his way alone, his Vice-Admiral, before they had been many days out at sea, having made two prizes (Spaniards), with which it was thought best that he should return to England. Under Teneriffe Dudley also captured two caravels, having previously, however, lost one of his two pinnaces. On reaching the coast of South America they waited some time for Sir Walter Raleigh. It seems to have been arranged that they should meet there; but Raleigh did not sail from Plymouth till after the beginning of February, 1595, and did not reach the South American coast till six or eight weeks after the time when Dudley expected him. Upon his not making his appearance Dudley determined to return home. By this time he was, he says, worse manned by half than he went forth. In fact he had only fifty men left. With this small crew, however, he maintained a fight of two days with a great Spanish armada of 600 tons; and though he did not succeed in compelling her to strike, yet left her, at 300 leagues from land, in such a state as that it was apparently impossible for her to escape sinking. He afterwards heard that the ship, which was said to have been very rich, had actually gone down. Our adventurers, or the few of them that survived, regained their native country in the latter end of May, 1595, landing at St. lves, in Cornwall. 'In this voyage,' says Dudley, ' I and my fleet took, sunk, and burnt nine Spanish ships, which was loss to them, though I got nothing.'

"It was the special command of the Queen which put a stop to Dudley's South Sea project; and it was not without some difficulty that her Majesty was brought to consent even to the West Indian voyage. She would have had 'this noble gentleman' to remain in quiet at home till he was of riper years, not doubting but that time and experience would work a most excellent perfection in one whom nature had so singularly endowed.[1]

" In the following year he fitted out two ships and two pinnaces for the South Seas, under command of Capt. Benjamin Wood, at his own expense; and attending the Earl of Essex and the Lord High Admiral in their expedition against the Spaniards, he received the honour of Knighthood for his gallant behaviour at the taking of Cadiz. In the latter end of Queen Elizabeth's reign, having buried his first wife, he married Alice, the daughter of Sir Thomas Leigh. He then began to entertain hopes of reviving the honours of his family; and in the beginning of the reign of King James I. he commenced a suit in the Archbishop of Canterbury's Court of Audience, with a view of proving the legitimacy of his birth; and the plague being then at London, he obtained a commission directed to Dr. Zachary Babington, Chancellor of the Diocese of Litchfield, to examine witnesses on that head, which was accordingly done.

[1] Craik's ' Romance of the Peerage,' vol. iii.

SIR ROBERT DUDLEY. 285

The following letter to his Father's Secretary, Arthur Atye, has reference to these proceedings :

[1605.] *"Sir Robert Dudley to Arthur Atye. 2d Nov., 1605.*[1]
"Mr. Atye,
"I remember my best love unto you as to one of the truest lovers of my father, and me for his sake.
"I am sure you hear of my proceeding to prove my legitimation and the Council's authority for me to proceed in the Court of Arches; for as much as I understood by Mr. Barker's deed that you were acquainted with an instrument my father made, of this last reputed marriage, under the hands and seals and oathes of them that were at it, and it is thought that he might procure sentence of the same secretly from Doctor Aubrey to colour aught better which afterwards he seriously repented that matter. Now because this point being known, is of little effect; a marriage proved good before it, yet not known, might do harm in proceeding, wherefore I pray you most earnestly that you will acquaint this bearer, Mr. Ward, my proctor, with your directions therein, of the substance of the deed; and if there were sentence, in what kind, and what parties made, and about what years to be sought for. This courtesy I desire most earnestly from you, as one I desire to love as nearly as my father did. I know you refused my father to be any actor in this matter, but in his nearness to you, he acquainted you with it, which was not to be avoided. So resting most assured of your love to me, I commit you to your happiest desires.

"*From Stoneleigh, this 2d of November, 1605.*

" Your very faithful friend,
" Ro. DUDDELEY.
(Superscribed)
" To my most especial friend
Mr. Arthur Atye, give these, at his house at Kilborne,
or elsewhere."[2]

---

[1] Arthur Atye was secretary to Dudley's father, the Earl of Leicester. In the *burial* register of St. Dunstan's in the West, London, we find the following—
"1604. Sir Arthur Atye, Knight, out of Shire Lane, Secretary to the Great Earl of Leicester, attendant on the unfortunate Earl of Essex." Also—
" Neare the Globe in Sheer Lane " lived Elias Ashmole, the Antiquary.
[2] Lansdowne MSS., 89.

"But no sooner had Lettice, Countess of Leicester, notice of these proceedings, than she procured an information to be filed by Sir Edward Coke, the King's Attorney-General, in the Star Chamber, against Sir Robert Dudley, Sir Thomas Leigh, Dr. Babington, and others, for a conspiracy; and upon the petition of Lord Sydney, an order, issued out of that Court, for bringing in all the depositions that had been taken by virtue of the Archbishop's commission, sealing them up, and depositing them in the Council chest. In order, however, to keep up some appearance of impartiality, Sir Robert Dudley was allowed to examine witnesses as to the proofs of his legitimacy, in that Court; which, when he had done, in as full a manner as in such a case could be expected, a sudden order was issued for stopping all proceedings, and locking up the examinations, of which no copies were to be taken but by the King's license.

"This unfair proceeding was such a blow to the hopes of Sir Robert Dudley, and gave him such disgust, that, obtaining a license to travel for three years,[1] which was easily granted him, he quitted the kingdom, leaving behind him Alice Dudley his wife, and four daughters.[2] He did not, however, go abroad without a female, for, as he inherited some of the vices, as well as most of the great qualities of his ancestors, he prevailed upon a young lady, at that time esteemed one of the finest women in England, to bear him company in the habit of a page. The name of this lady was Elizabeth Southwell; and she was daughter to Sir Robert Southwell, of Woodrising, in Norfolk. He was afterwards married to her by virtue of a dispensation from the Pope.[3]

"Though Sir Robert Dudley had a license to travel for

25th June, 1605.
[1] 1605. "A license for Sir Robert Dudley, Knight, to travel beyond the seas for three years next after his departure, with three servants, four geldings or nags, and £80 in money, with usual provision. Dated at Greenwich the 25th of June, 1605. Procured by Sir Thomas Lake."—*Privy Council Register.*
[2] Sir Robert had by his wife Alice, seven daughters. In 1616, five were living, and four grown to woman's estate.—[*Letter of Sir Thomas Leigh, in State Paper Office, London.*]
[3] A sister of hers married Sir Grevil Verney, of Warwickshire.

three years, yet, under a pretence of his assuming, in foreign countries, the title of Earl of Warwick, he was in a short time commanded to return home.

"2nd February, 1606-7.

[1607.] "*A form of revocation of a pass, Sir Robert Dudley from foreign parts.*[1]

"James, by the grace of God, King of England, Scotland, France, and Ireland, Defender of the Faith, &c. To our subject Robert Dudley, Knight, greeting. Whereas, we, out of our special favour, did grant you license to travel out of our realm of England into foreign parts, in hope that you might thereby prove the better enable to the service of us and our State, as you pretended, we do now certainly understand that contrarywise in those parts you do bear and behave yourself inordinately, and have intended and attempted many things prejudicial to us and our crown, which we cannot suffer or endure. We do, therefore, by these presents, will and straightly charge and command you, upon your faith and allegiance, and upon the pain of all that you may forfeit unto us, that forthwith upon the receipt and understanding thereof, you do, all excuses and pretences set apart, make your personal repair and return into this our realm of England with all speed, and that presently upon your arrival here, you do yield and render your body to some of our Privy Council, to the intent we may be truly advertised of the day and time of your return, and hereof fail you not, as you will answer the contrary at your uttermost peril. Given under our Privy Seal at our palace of Westminster, the second day of February, in the fourth year of our reign of England, France, and Ireland, and of Scotland the fortieth.

"(Signed)   THOMAS CLERKE."[2]
"To our subject Robt. Dudley, Kt."

"On his refusing to obey, his whole estate was seized during his life by the Crown. A few years after, his right to the magnificent castle of Kenilworth, with the manors adjoining, were purchased, in consequence of an agreement with him, by Henry, Prince of Wales, for £14,500, of which,

[1] Apparently the original draft.   [2] State Paper Office.

though much less than the value, but £3000 was ever paid, and that to a merchant, who soon after failed.

"The place which Sir Robert Dudley chose for his retreat abroad was Florence, where he was very kindly received by Cosmo II., Grand Duke of Tuscany; and in process of time he was made Grand Chamberlain to his Serene Highness's consort, the Archduchess Magdalen of Austria, sister to the Emperor, Ferdinand II., with whom he was a great favorite. He discovered in that Court those great abilities for which he had been admired in England. He contrived several methods of improving shipping, introduced new manufactures, excited the merchants to extend their foreign commerce, and, by other services of still greater importance, obtained so high a reputation, that, at the desire of his mistress, the Archduchess, the Emperor, by letters patent dated at Vienna, March 9th, 1620, created him a Duke of the Holy Roman Empire. Upon this he assumed his grandfather's title of Northumberland; and ten years after got himself enrolled by Pope Urban VIII. among the Roman nobility. Under the reign of the Grand Duke, Ferdinand II, he became still more famous, on account of that great project which he formed of draining a vast tract of morass between Pisa and the sea; for by this he raised Livorno or Leghorn from a mean and pitiful place into a large and beautiful town; and, having engaged his Serene Highness to declare it a free port, he, by his influence, drew many English merchants to settle and set up houses there. In consideration of his services, and for the support of his dignity, the Grand Duke bestowed upon him a handsome pension, which, however, went but a little way in his expenses, for he affected magnificence in all things; built a noble palace for himself and his family at Florence, and much adorned the Castle of Carbello, three miles from that capital, which the Grand Duke gave him for a country retreat, and where he died in September, 1649.

"Sir Robert Dudley was not only admired by princes, but also by the learned; among whom he held a very high rank, as well on account of his skill in philosophy, chemistry, and physic, as his perfect acquaintance with all the branches of the mathematics, and the means of applying them for the service and benefit of mankind. He wrote several things. His principal work is 'Del Arcano, del Mare,' &c., Fiorenze, 1630, 1646, in 3 vols. folio. This work, which is very scarce,[1] is full of schemes, charts, plans, and other marks of its author's mathematical learning; but it is chiefly valuable for the projects contained therein for the improvement of navigation and the extension of commerce. Anthony Wood tells us that he wrote also a medical treatise, entitled 'Catholicon,' which was well esteemed by the faculty. There is also another piece written by him, the title of which, as it stands in Rushworth, runs thus :—'A proposition for his Majesty's service, to bridle the impertinence of Parliaments. Afterwards questioned in the Star Chamber.'

This proposition or treatise was written by Sir Robert Dudley in 1612, and was sent by him to Sir David Foulis, to be presented to Prince Henry, with the view of ingratiating himself with King James, and procuring a pardon, so that he might return to England. A copy of this Proposition or Treatise, with the letter to Sir David, which accompanied it, is here given,[2] from the originals in the State Paper Office, dated from Florence, 14 Nov. 1612. Prince Henry, however, had previously died, viz. on the 6th of the same month.

It does not appear whether the paper was presented to the King; but in the year 1629 considerable commotion was excited by copies being found in circulation, one of which, in the possession of Sir Robert Cotton, had been borrowed by Mr. St. John, of Lincoln's Inn; and being afterwards shown to several persons, it was reported to the Privy Council, who thereupon instituted an inquiry, and Mr. St. John was charged with being the author. This led to the apprehension of Sir Robert Cotton, the Earls of Clare, Somerset, and Bedford, Mr. John Selden, and Mr. Oliver St. John, to answer for the same in the Court of Star Chamber. An interesting account of this is given in Sir Simond Dewes's Journal, copy of which is here given,[3] together with the proceedings in the Star Chamber, from the MSS. in the State Paper Office.

[1] Two copies are in the British Museum.
[2] See pages 295 et seq.   [3] See pages 291 et seq.

The proceedings were, however, suddenly stopped, and the defendants discharged by the King, on the joyful occasion of the birth of his son Charles, afterwards Charles II., and not, as has been stated by several writers, on the discovery of the true author.

The imprisonment of Sir Robert Cotton, with the deprivation of the use of his library, is said to have killed him. He died 6 May, 1631.

This treatise of Dudley's was afterwards printed and published in 1641, immediately after the execution of the Earl of Strafford, attributing it to the pen of that nobleman, under the title of "Strafford's Plot Discovered and the Parliament vindicated in their justice executed upon him, by the late discovery of certain propositions delivered to his Majesty by the Earl of Strafford a little before his trial, with this inscription —'Propositions for the Bridling of Parliaments, and for the increasing of His Majesty's Revenue.'"

Sir Robert Dudley was also the author of a famous powder, called "Pulvis comitis Warwicensis, or the Earl of Warwick's powder," he being known in Italy by the title of Earl of Warwick, before the Emperor created him a Duke.

Sir Robert Dudley, as he was styled in England, or the Duke of Northumberland, as he was styled abroad, had by the daughter of Sir Robert Southwell (who went into Italy with him in the habit of a page, and to whom he was afterwards married, as we before observed) a son, named Charles, who assumed the title of Earl of Warwick, and four daughters, who were all honorably married in Italy, viz. the eldest to the Prince of Piombino, the second to the Marquis of Clivola, the third to the Duke of Castilion del Lago, and the fourth to the Count of Carpegna, brother to the Cardinal of that name. The son Charles inherited the title as Duke of Northumberland, and is stated to have married, in France, Mary Magdalen Gouffier, of the family of the Duke of Rohanet, and by her to have had many children. His eldest son, Robert, went by the name of the Earl of Warwick, as he himself had done during his father's life-time. One of his daughters married the Marquis of Palliotti, of Bologna, and was by him the mother of a son and daughter, who both found their way back to the native country of their great grandfather, in the beginning of the next century, and figure diversely in the romance of our English family history of that period; the lady dying Duchess of Shrewsbury, her brother on the gallows at Tyburn.

Charles, 12th Earl (and only) Duke of Shrewsbury, married Adelhida, daughter of the Marquis of Paliotti, of Bologna, in Italy, descended by her mother from Sir Robert Dudley, son of Robert, "Earl of Leicester."[1]

As to this lady of Sir Robert Dudley (Elizabeth Southwell), though her following him into Italy, when he had another wife, justly exposed her to much censure, yet her conduct was in other respects without exception; and as she lived in honour and esteem, and had all the respect paid her that her title of Duchess could command, so it is said that Sir Robert loved her with great tenderness to the last, and caused a noble monument to be erected to her memory in the Church of St. Pancratius, in Florence, where her body lies buried, and he by her. She died some years before her husband. He had caused a sumptuous marble monument to be erected over her grave, in the intention that, when his own funeral came to be celebrated, his remains should be deposited beside hers.[2]

SIR ROBERT DUDLEY AND HIS TRACT IN MS., "PROPOSITIONS FOR THE BRIDLING OF PARLIAMENTS," &c.

Sir Simon D'Ewes's journal contains the following in reference to Sir Robert Cotton being accused of having written a book of a dangerous tendency, and imprisoned:

[1631, May.] "Amongst other Books, he (Richard James, Fellow of Corpus Christi College, Oxford, and custodian of Sir Robert Cotton's library,) lent out,—one Mr. St. John, of Lincoln's Inn, a young studious gentleman, borrowed of him, for money, a dan-

[1] Collins's 'Peerage.'
[2] From the "British Biography," published in Dodsley's 'Annual Register for 1768'; 'Romance of the Peerage,' by George Lillie Craik, vol. iii, 1849, and Collins's 'Peerage.'

gerous pamphlet that was in a written hand, by which a course was laid down how the Kings of England might oppress the liberties of their subjects, and forever enslave them and their posterities. Mr. St. John showed the book to the Earl of Bedford, or a copy of it: and so it passed from hand to hand, in the year 1629, till at last it was lent to Sir Robert Cotton himself, who set a young fellow [1] he then kept in his house to transcribe it; which plainly proves that Sir Robert knew not himself, that the written tract had originally come out of his own library. This untrusty fellow imitating, it seems, the said James, took one copy secretly for himself, when he wrote another for Sir Robert; and out of his own transcript, sold away several copies, till at last one of them came into Wentworth's hands of the North,[2] now Lord Deputy of Ireland. He acquainted the Lords and others of the Privy-Council, with it. They sent for the said young fellow, and examining him where he had the written tract, he confessed Sir Robert Cotton delivered it to him. Whereupon in the beginning of November in the same year, 1629, Sir Robert was examined; and so divers others, one after the other, as it had been delivered from hand to hand, till at last, Mr. St. John himself was appeached, and being conceived to have been the author of the book, was committed close prisoner to the Tower, being in danger to have been questioned for his life about it. Upon his examination upon oath, he made a clear, full and punctual declaration, that he had received the same MS. pamphlet [3] of that wretched mercenary fellow, James, who by this means proved the wretched instrument of shortening the life of Sir Robert Cotton; for he was presently thereupon sued in the Star-chamber, his library locked up from his use, and two or more of the guard set to watch

---

[1] Sir Simond D'Ewes says it was affirmed, "that this young fellow, whom Sir Robert kept in his house, and had employed to transcribe the said written tract, was his illegitimate son."

[2] At the period here spoken of, the great champion of the House of Commons for the liberties of the people. It is singular enough that shortly after he was beheaded, this very tract, having lain in his study from the year 1629, was turned against himself, he being charged as the author of it, in a treatise, entitled, "Strafford's Plot discovered, and the Parliament vindicated in their justice executed upon him, by the late discovery of certain Propositions delivered to his Majesty by the Earl of Strafford, a little before his trial, with the inscription, "Proposition for the bridling of Parliaments."

[3] This very curious pamphlet may be found in 'Rushworth,' vol. i, App., p. 12. Howell's 'State Trials,' and on pp. 295-7 of the present work.

his house continually. When I went several times to visit and comfort him, in the year 1630, he would tell me, "they had broken his heart, and had locked up his library from him." I easily guessed the reason, because his honor and esteem were much impaired by this fatal accident; and his house, that was formerly frequented by great and honorable personages, as well as by learned men of all sorts, remained now upon the matter, desolate and empty. I understood from himself and others, that Dr. Neale and Dr. Laud, two prelates that had been stigmatised in the first session of Parliament in 1628, were his sore enemies. He was so outworn, within a few months, with anguish and grief, as his face, which had been formerly ruddy and well colored, (such as the picture I have of him shows) was wholly changed into a grim blackish paleness, near to the resemblance and hue of a dead visage."

"It may be necessary, in order to elucidate this matter still further, to take notice, that one of the articles in the Attorney General's information against Sir Robert Cotton, was, that the discourse or project was framed and contrived within five or six months past here in England; but Sir David Foulis testified, upon oath, being thereunto required, that it was contrived at Florence, seventeen years before, by Sir Robert Dudley, son of the famous Robert Dudley, Earl of Leycester, by the Lady Douglas Sheffield, widow of John, Lord Sheffield, who at the time of his birth, in 1573, and for some years after, was considered as the Earl's lawful son, though he was carefully concealed, as well to prevent the Queen's knowledge of the Earl's engagement with his mother, as to hide it from the Countess Dowager of Essex, to whom Leycester was then contracted, if not married. But when this son was about five years of age, his father married the Countess openly, and thereupon Robert was no longer treated as his lawful child. The Earl died while his son was at Oxford in 1588; and at his leaving the University he was deservedly looked upon as one of the most accomplished men in England, his parts, being not only equal, but superior to those of any of his family. In 1594, he fitted out a small squadron at his own expense, and went on an expedition to the West Indies, where he sunk and took nine Spanish ships, and performed much more than could have been expected. An account of this voyage is published by Hakluyt, (Voy. Vol. 3, p. 574) to whom Mr. Dudley gave it. In 1595 he was knighted by the Earl of Essex, for his gallant behaviour at the siege of Cadiz. In the beginning of King James's reign, having some years before married Alice, daughter of Sir Thomas Leigh, and gained by this marriage some powerful friends, he endeavoured to prove the legitimacy of his birth; which no doubt would have been authenticated, had not all proceedings been stopped and the examinations locked up, by the influence of the Countess Dowager of Leycester. Upon this, Sir Robert, in disgust left the Kingdom; and as he inherited some of the vices, as well as most of the great qualities of his ancestors, he took with him, disguised as a Page, (his wife being living,) a young lady of distinguished beauty, the daughter of Sir Robert Southwell, of Norfolk. This lady, by the Pope's dispensation, he afterwards married, and in every other respect her conduct was irreproachable. She lived in honour and esteem, and died truly lamented by her husband, by whom she left a numerous issue, and who erected a noble tomb to her memory in the Church of St. Pancrace[1] in Florence. His other wife, Alice, and four daughters, remained in England. Though he had a license to travel for three years, yet under a pretence of his assuming in foreign countries, the title of Earl of Warwick, he was in a short time, commanded to return home; and on his refusing to obey, his whole estate was seized, during his life, by the Crown. A few years after, his magnificent castle of Kenilworth with the manors adjoining, was purchased by Henry, Prince of Wales for £14,500, of which, though much less than its value, but £3,000 was ever paid, and that to a merchant, who soon after failed. Sir Robert was so well received at Florence that he resided there for the remainder of his life, though, to ingratiate himself with King James, and to facilitate his return, he drew up the scheme above mentioned. But though he failed in this, foreign Princes saw, and rewarded his merits. The Arch-Duchess Magdalen of Austria, then Regent of Tuscany, made him her Grand Chamberlain. In 1620, her brother, the Emperor, Ferdinand II., at her desire, gave him that rank to which he was entitled, by creating him a Duke of the Holy Roman Empire, upon which he assumed his grandfather's title of Northumberland; and in 1630, he was enrolled by Pope Urban VIII. amongst the Roman nobility. Under the reign of the Grand Duke, Ferdinand II., he became still more famous for his useful projects for improving shipping, manufactures and commerce, and particularly

[1] So his son informed Anthony Wood.

by his schemes for draining the great morass between Pisa and the sea; for building a mole at Leghorn, making it a free port, and settling an English factory there; for which great services, the Grand Duke gave him a pension of 2000 sequins per annum. In short, by his practical skill in Philosophy, Chemistry, Physic, Navigation, Architecture and the Mathematics, his exile was a public benefit to Italy, a public loss to England. But with a Prince who could sacrifice a Raleigh, how could a Dudley find esteem! At length, after building a noble palace at Florence, this Duke died, at his Castle of Carbello, which the Grand Duke had given him for a country seat, in 1649, aged 66. His wife Alice, was afterwards created by King Charles I., Duchess Dudley, Sir Robert's legitimacy being acknowledged in her patent. She lived till 1668, and was as distinguished for her charities, as her husband was for his learning and abilities.

"Sir Robert Dudley's principal work, which is now very scarce, is intituled, "Dell Arcano del Mare, di Roberto Dudleo, Duca di Nortumbria e Conte di Warvick, con mult. fig.," Fiorenze, 1646-47, 3 vols. folio. It abounds with schemes, plans, useful projects, &c. A copy of it was sold among Dr. Campbell's books a few years ago,[1] and another remains in the Bodleian Library. The little tractate that occasioned this detail, though Wood[2] supposes it to have remained a MS., was published by Rushworth, and though neither King James I. nor Charles I., nor their ministers, made use of it, yet it was turned to their prejudice, as has been already mentioned.

"The following is an abstract of the contents of this Tract.

"The first part which is styled, 'A PROPOSITION TO SECURE THE STATE AND TO BRIDLE THE IMPERTINENCY OF PARLIAMENTS.'

"1. To have a fortress in every considerable town.

"2. To suffer none to wear arms, but such as are enrolled.

"3. To cause highways to be made through the fortified towns.

"4. Not to let the soldiers of such fortresses be inhabitants of the place.

"5. To let no persons pass through such places without a ticket.

"6. To have the names of all lodgers taken by all innkeepers.

---

[1] Now in the British Museum, as well as another copy, '*Impressione Seconda, Fiorenza,*' 1661, 3 vols.

[2] Wood's 'Athenæ Oxoniensis,' vol. ii, 128.

"7. To impose an oath of allegiance upon all the subjects. "To each fort he allots 3000 men, and £40,000 per annum.

"The second part entitled ' MEANS TO INCREASE HIS MAJESTY'S REVENUES.'

£

" 1. To demand a tenth of all estates, real and personal, in lieu of all other subsidies. This, by his calculation, will increase the revenue,—at least 500,000
" 2. To buy out all leases upon the Crown lands,—at least 140,000
" 3. To take the salt into his Majesty's own hands,—at least 150,000
" 4. To demand a rate for sealing the weights and measures every year, at 6d. each weight,—near 60,000
" 5. To demand an impost for wools, as in Spain, at 5 per cent. of the true value at the shearing . 140,000
" 6. To lay a tax of five per cent. upon every lawyer's fee 50,000
" 7. To lay a tax of £10, £5, or £1 per annum, upon all inns, taverns, alehouses, &c., for a licence . 100,000
" 8. To lay a tax of three or four per cent. upon all Cattle, flesh and horses sold in the market as in Tuscany. (N.B.—All flesh, fish and victuals to be sold by weight.) 200,000
" 9. To lay a tax upon all things alienated, and marriage portions, at seven per cent., as in Tuscany . 100,000
"The subjects (in return for this) to be eased of hardships, to be of age at 18, and not to forfeit their lands by condemnation, except for high treason.
" 10. To demand a rate upon all offices in his Majesty's grant. Notaries, attornies, &c., to pay towards it 100,000
" 11. By some other taxes, not specified . . 200,000
" 12. To reduce his Majesty's household to board wages 60,000
" 13. By an assured course in the Navy, not specified,— at least 40,000
" 14. To demand a rate for license to eat eggs, cheese, and white meats at 10s. the rich, and 1s. 6d. the poor 100,000

"15. To take an imposition upon the Catholics' lands. Particulars not named,— at least 200,000

"Total Increase . . £2,140,000
"Besides some sums of money in present, by the following courses:

£

"1. At the Prince's marriage, all the Earls to be made Grandees of Spain and Principi,—at £20,000 each . . . . . .
"2. All the Barons to be made Earls, at £19,000 each   500,000
"3. To ennoble 200 of the richest commoners, as is usual in Naples,
"A Duke to pay . . £30,000 ⎫
"A Marquiss . . . 15,000 ⎬
"An Earl . . . 10,000 ⎭ at least 1,000,000
"A Viscount, or Baron . 5,000
N.B.—The ancient nobility to precede all these.
"4. To make gentlemen of low degree, and rich farmers *Esquires*, the price not named.
"By another course not specified,— at least 300,000
"He concludes by recommending also a sumptuary law.[1]

[1612.] "*Sir Robert Dudley (son of Earl of Leycester) to Sir David Fowlis.*

"*Florence*, 14 *Nov.* 1612.
"Sir,

"Although I have had heretofore a sufficient taste of your readiness in doing many good offices for me, whereby I hold myself obliged unto you very much, yet I have been since advertised by some letters from Mr. Yates, of the increase of your extraordinary good respect unto me, which now, at his coming to Florence, he hath so fully confirmed, (affirming you to be a principal agent in the speedy effecting of my business with the Prince, my Master,) that I cannot devise how to give fit correspondency to this your exceeding loving kindness towards me; seeing therefore that I need not doubt of your constant perse-

[1] Nichols's 'Bibliotheca Topog. Brit.,' vol. vi, and 'Gent.'s Mag.,' 1767, pp. 403-4.

verance therein, I will not be dainty to make you a party to my designs. I have sent unto his highness a little treatise, much importing his own security and profit, the copy whereof I have herewith sent unto you,[1] that you may the better instruct yourself to encourage his highness to undertake a matter of that consequence for his own safety and perpetual good. It cannot be unknown to you that I have given his highness my estate of Kenilworth for a small matter, considering the worth thereof: I have only reserved the Constableship of the Castle, that I may have some command there under his highness, whensoever I shall happen to come into England, and also that he will protect me (and that but justly) in the sale of Ichington and Balsall, that I might settle my estate, to be the better able to do his highness service, for without the sale thereof, I shall be in far worse case than I was before. I have given warrant to Mr. Yates to undergo all my businesses whatsoever in my behalf, in my absence; and he hath so confirmed me in the assurance of your forward and ready assistance upon all occasions, that I need not any more solicit you therein; but he can likewise assure you, that upon the sale of those lands I have proportioned a thankful gratuity for you, as a testimony of my exceeding love and thankfulness unto you, protesting withal ever to remain,

"Your most affectionate and assured true friend,
"WARWICK.

"*Florence;* 14*th November*, 1612.
(Superscribed)
" To my honorable and much esteemed
good friend Sir David Fowlis, Knight,
Gent. of the Prince's Bed-Chamber and
Cofferer to his Highness."[2]

[1] The treatise alluded to, consists of sixteen pages of MS. in a plain neat hand (not Dudley's), and is indorsed "Coppie of Sr. Rob. Dudley his service offered to the Prince, 1612, November," and in another hand " Sr Davie Fowles' papers, presented to the King, the first of Januarie, 1629."

It commences with the heading, " A proposition for his Highness, my master, the Prince of Wales." It points out the necessity of a thorough attention to the navy, as the best means of keeping up the greatness of the country. In the second part, he speaks of his invention of a new ship to be called the " Gallizabra," to carry fifty great pieces, drawing only ten feet of water, to sail faster than any other vessel. That the same can be maintained at much less charge, and may be managed by fewer men, and with greater readiness. Dated Florence, 22nd Nov., 1612. Prince Henry, to whom it is addressed, died on the 6th of the same month.

[2] State Paper Office, London.

[1612.] Indorsed, "Copy of Sir Robert Dudley, his service offered to the Prince, 1612, November;" also, in another hand, under the above, "Sir David Fowlis's Papers, presented to the King, the first of January, 1629."

"A PROPOSITION FOR HIS HIGHNESS, MY MASTER, THE PRINCE OF WALES.

"It is held for the surest reason of state amongst some of good understanding, that what king soever is most powerful by sea hath the best means to secure his own greatness; and if his ambition pass further, hath the like occasion to hazard others.

"The consequence of this proposition is to be confirmed by many examples, observed in the revolution of such like affairs, especially by the success of the late Queen of England, that so infinitely affronted the King of Spain; as also those States of the Low Country, defending very easily their long war, to his great expense and loss; so as well looked into what was done and what might have been done, maketh demonstrable the former proposition; and to explain it more particularly, we will briefly show, how much it importeth, and may be applied to your Highness's more greatness and security.

1. "First for England, as their good and safety hath always been upheld by their sea-force, so on the contrary, if the King of Spain had been more potent by sea, and able to invade England, in the time of these wars, it might have much hazarded that kingdom; the private reasons whereof I omit, as not fit for this discourse.

2. "Touching France, as the sundry affronts England in times past, by invasions hath done them, by being their master at sea, lost them their crown; so in their last war, the same force of England preserved them from the Spaniard, who possessed their best ports, and was besides strongly planted on their firm land.

3. "The Hollanders, being more strong by sea than the King of Spain, have not only much consumed that great King in a lingering and long war, but also at last made their peace upon good advantage; and this chiefly in being able to give succour by sea, as their long siege of Ostend doth verify; and is allowed by great Captains, that the sea relief importeth more than the best fortresses or fortifications; so as by the contrary reason, had the King of Spain known to accomplish the means presented your Highness, (in the second part of this discourse,) by such fleet and forcible vessels to enter his ports of Dunkirk, &c., the Low Coun-

tries could not stand in the terms of safety they do, nor England flourish in that state it doth and may.

4. "Touching Spain and Portugal; their losses to England by sea; we know by the battles they have lost, by their prizes taken, and by their cities burned, as well in the Indies, as in Spain and Portugal; the losses whereof may import many millions, and by the impoverishment of the King himself, all which considered and applied to my end, I know and dare boldly say, England may have the means to dispose of both their Indies, and that by such demonstrable means, as if I should discover them, not be gainsayed.

5. "The like application may be employed to hurt Italy, who want not many occasions, I know, to have taken upon them, the like advantage, and may no less hurt the King of Spain; in Italy, and Italians themselves, and many other territories of his, than before hath been pronounced against the Indies.

6. "Touching the state of Venice, which I place by itself, from Italy, being the most forcible part thereof by sea and thereby maintaineth their greatness and wealth and esteem, to the heighth it is of, so on the contrary any Prince having Ports in their Adriatic Seas, (being but narrow); and withal we are of more force than they; it is most assured, they might be barred from all manner of traffic and relief, which importeth altogether their good and safety.

7. "Upon the great Turk are the like or easier occasions by sea; his force less, and his riches of more value, so as he hath some straits giveth them this occasion, as whosoever can maintain that passage, (as is easy,) may not only hinder him from receiving that wealth, (which importeth above thirty millions yearly,) but also avoid the prejudice of his galleys; either to hurt the Christianity or relief of the Grecian Islands, he possesseth in the Archipelago, the state whereof standeth so, as by such a course he may both easily and assuredly lose them, to the great benefit of Christianity, wherein I could speak very particularly, having invented the same design for the Grand Duke Ferdinand, and embraced by him as the best course for his war and greatness against the Turk.

"Now having shown your Highness the great advantage by sea to dispose of the potentest territories of the world, the inferiors are easily bridled, by the same rule, as cannot be denied. I may withal conclude this part, that whosoever is patron of the sea, commandeth the land. Now in respect of the manner of sea force yet known in ordinary practice to the world, either these of England or elsewhere, is of little moment to these ends: for many reasons, especially their great draught, whereby they can offend or defend but in some few places and less occasions, I have therefore ordered this second part following for your Highness better understanding my intention and desire, when time may serve to do you service, in such a degree as I dare boldly say unto you, (without ostentation,) that no man living is able to offer you a matter of so much consequence for the state and security thereof, as now it standeth; nay, hardly wish you a greater, much less accomplish it.

The Second Part.

"By the former part is shown the great importance for so great a Prince as your Highness to be master of the seas, as well to secure your own estate as to endanger others thereby; the means to dispose of great matters, which being so, my intention is how to augment the same with more advantage than hitherto hath been penetrated, and (as I conceive) may consist in these three points following:

1. "First, to invent such a sort of vessel, as by the condition and quality thereof, may be fitter for all uses required, than those already made.

2. "That the same invention may be maintained at much less charge, &c.

3. "That their employment may be by fewer men, and easier expense and readiness.

"Touching the first, I may pretend a vessel of my invention, I name *Gallizabra*, which carry 50 great pieces, and those I make lighter, by one third at least, than others; and no less in force, every way; whereof each of these vessels to carry 30 of those demi-cannons, and 20 demi-culverines; and though the draught of this vessel passeth not ten feet, yet are they good, both in long and short voyages; in swiftness to sail, no ship nor pinnace can arrive near them, especially (*a la bolnino*) or upon a tack; and besides, they have all other good conditions, both in foul or fair weather, for a ship to have; being indeed altogether contrary to the vulgar opinions. Further they are contrived to be hardly sunk by the enemy's ordnance, and less easy to be boarded; they may carry oars, if need be, to unite themselves in calms, to the great hurt of enemies' ships, that in such case cannot stir; these under sail are so stiff-sided, to indure forcible winds as no vessel whatsoever is able to do the like; now whereas the sea force consisteth merely in these qualities and secrets how to manage them in fight, and not in the number or hugeness of ships, as the demonstration hereof doth manifest: I may assuredly pretend 30 of these gallizabras, double in force to the King's Majesty's navy, and sufficient to affront in battle the armadas of any other potent state by sea; with these advantages, more that they can leave or take, and gain the wind of any other fleet; that they can by their exceeding floatness [? buoyancy] enter into every ordinary ports, and such places where ships of burthen may not hazard to go, thereby fitter for more employment, and not to be prevented. upon any landing or invasion. That the charge to build one of them, (the body I mean,) besides timber, may import £1300, or thereabouts, other provision of the King's Navy will serve to furnish these with little help, therefore, in the building doth consist most part of the charge, and shall not in all pass £60,000 or £70,000, with no doubt for so good purpose will be defrayed by the counties and chief cities thereof, rateably *scompartited*,[1] the King allowing for the work, wood and iron only.

"That these vessels succeeding in practice, as here propounded, the rest of the ancient navy may be ordered as best shall please his Highness's wisdom, and therein also worth consideration, to make the merchants-venturers of London and other port-towns, to employ a good part of them that are strong and serviceable; though they sell the worst of their own, and have these for little, (their hulls I mean,) for so their force may be kept for the use of the State; and not lost, and albeit the setting forth of these may be more chargeable in merchandise (ton for ton) than their own, yet in respect of their daily losses by pirates, and great disgraces received to the whole nation, to be so beaten and spoiled every day as they have been, the difference of charges or other trifling objections, ought not so much to be regarded as the sure transporting their goods, besides the reputation and strength to the Kingdom, but howsoever in this I remit me to their liking.

2. "Touching the second point of maintaining these gallizabras at less charge, I pretend their fashion and proportion such as they may be kept in a kind of arsenal, and order, according to my

[1] Scompartire, to share or divide. (Italian.)

direction, where they shall need both few men to look to them, as also not to decay their furniture, by weather, nor themselves so often to be repaired, and yet be kept with far more safety than now they are, either for wind, weather, or fire, and three parts less charge, and less means of abuse by ill officers; which benefits cannot be applied to his Majesty's present navy, their forms not comporting such ends.

3. "Touching the third point of setting forth these vessels, &c., I conceive, may be much more commodious and easier in them, than in other ships of war, and ordered according to my directions need require fewer men, that is, for each, 130 mariners and 110 soldiers; but counting the mariners to furnish 30 gallizabras (which importeth most) will not pass 4000, the ease whereof is such, as their employment need not hinder the foreign trade of merchants.

"If it shall be thought necessary to keep some galleys, as his Majesty doth, then I will, with another sort of vessel of that kind, of mine own invention, also called by me *Gallea Reale*, which row as swift, and sail faster, than the English galleys, and in draught nearly equal; but for force to fight, so far surpassing, as one of these, carrying 60 pieces of good ordnance, is able to beat 20 galleys, besides they are framed of purpose to endure much more foul weather; that they may use their navigation with shipps, which galleys cannot do, four of these *galley reales* may be sufficient, and are fit to attend a fleet for these reasons:

1. "That in calms they can do great hurt to any enemies' ships scattered.

2. "That they are more swift of sail to fetch up any prize, than any other vessel of square sails can be.

3. "They are excellent to land men upon any occasion, and hinder others to do the like.

4. "That they are ready to relieve any vessel distressed, or come aground.

5. "That they can both put out of ports, and enter into them, when ships cannot, and therefore better for sudden actions.

6. "That they are good to enter into rivers, and to defend straight or shoal passages, or any other service a galley can do.

7. "Lastly, these can tow away any vessel distressed in fight, either by loss of her masts, or burning her sails, or chief ropes, or such like accidents, and so save her from being taken; or lead in

ships to fight, in calms, in little winds, upon more advantage than otherwise can be taken.

" These vessels may be armed for rowing with condemned men, or watermen, four vessels whereof may be sufficient in any armada, being of more force than 80 galleys, and in charge, little more than seven or eight galleys.

" The same *galliæ realei* are of such consequence in an armada, as they would require a particular command, with other officers for their government, being greatly different in all orders to these of gallizabras, or ships, and albeit their force is so great as mentioned, yet are they not of the kind of Galliares, but in use and swiftness far beyond them.

" In these propositions your highness need but search the benefit and necessaries of the offer, for the rest I can secure you to be able to do what herein is contained, and perchance much more to purpose, than is fit in this discourse to be manifest.

" Further, I must profess, that whereas I have found no friendship nor favor in England, but from your Highness, my gracious Master, so do I renounce all other obligation (his Majesty only excepted) but yourself, and therefore do resolve confidently not to do any of these services spoken of, upon any contentment whatsoever, unless your Highness be pleased to take the Admiralty wholly into your hands, for in these courses belonging to it, or any other of mine, I will depend upon none but his Majesty, your gracious father, and yourself. And when it shall please God, I may with my honor, return to serve you (which point I am above all things to respect, or else were unworthy to be your servant,) I can then promise divers other services, not inferior to this, as well for your profit, as force, being the two chief ends I study and endeavour for you. So praying God for your Highness's long happiness, I humbly take my leave. From Florence, the 22d of November, 1612." (O. S. 12th Nov.)

[1613-14.] *Indorsed*, " *Copy of a part of a letter sent from Livorno* [*Leghorn*] *to London, by Sir Robert Dudley, to a friend of his, in January*, 1613.

"HIS INVENTION OF A SHIP OF STRANGE FORCE, &c."

" The words of Sir Robert Dudley, his letter touching his new invented ship.

" You have heard, I am sure, of the great Turkish Prince come to the Grand Duke with offer of his country and self and all; he hath been Prince of the Holy Land, a matter of such consequence as his Highness meaneth to do honorably in it, and is begun to arm his galleons. Now his highness, of his favour, much depending of my counsel in this business, and matter of great consequence, I, in studying upon it, of vessels fit for this business, if some Christian Prince will give help in it, as is hoped, now by occasion of this diligent study in a matter of so much consequence, I have found out a certain manner of vessel, that I can do, of so wonderful consequence in force and swiftness, as I dare boldly say, the like was never known to the world, and wonderfully far beyond those I mentioned in my discourse to the Prince, my master, of famous memory, so as I do hold them nothing in comparison of this, being as float as they, not passing 10 foot water, but tidyer, as swift in sailing as all ships are they, besides these, can road [ride] as well as any galliass,[1] but endure the seas and storms as well as the King's ships, which is the importance of the secret and advantage in fight, besides their huge force, which is the greatest that ever the world saw; for some skilful [persons] that I have showed my design, (though they are not the nearer for doing of it,) yet can judge and conclude absolutely that no three of the King's greatest ships royal, though you make the Princes one, is able to endure the force of one of these; in fine, it is not credible her force and qualities. I call this a countergalliass, being invented upon the occasion mentioned to overthrow them, because where these come the galliasses must depart, though they be five or six for one. I write to you this much, because this sort of vessel is so great a secret for England, as if the King had of them, he would not leave it for millions, I know; and though I invented this against the Turk only, for which I know he would be glad, but if by this occasion this secret should come to the hands of others, to have but ten of these, were in some such a Prince, were absolute patron of these seas, in despite of ships, and by reason of their orders and force, land men where they list, being besides so floaty as I said. Now out of my affection to my country, and duty to his Majesty, I would not do it, nor propound it, without offering it first to him, though privately to none but to himself, as a secret I can do, and esteem at a great value, as the sure card of my advancement wheresoever I be, therefore had rather have my desire and advancement in my

[1] Galliass, a large kind of galley (Halliwell).

own country than elsewhere, especially to do it so great service as I can in this, and avoid it so great an ill as may happen in discovering it elsewhere, though my intent be not to do anything but against the Turk. The Venetians have heard an inkling of this vessel and seek wonderfully after it under hand; and others greater than they. I have stayed answer or offering it any, till I know what the King will say to it, or that he esteem to have it, or me in it, as I esteem myself and the value of it, that know the benefit, for this is a matter of such consequence as I will treat it so. If his Majesty will not apprehend this offer, which I do out of duty and love, I know he will, out of his bounty, give me leave, without his displeasure, (as I deserve, making him the first offer,) to make my best use of it for my advancement that I can abroad; wherefore I write this much unto you, that you may confer it with Sir David Foulis, for none else will I have know of it, yet to acquaint the King with what I write, and the respect I owe him in this offer, if he like, it being in his power to command me and it; if not, that he dare not trust my skill so far as I write, to give me leave, without dislike, to make my best use of it, having now as I live, no country, nor means to raise myself, but my knowledge. In this, I pray you, work very secretly and carefully, that I may have a speedy answer, and that you and Sir David be witnesses of my loyalty in my offer, and that by this occasion you work yourself in person with Sir David, to deliver the effect of this I write; that from you two I may credit what his Majesty sayeth, because few else I shall credit to be the King's answer to me, only out of love and duty to his Majesty and my Country do I write thus much, because else it is indifferent if it be not accepted, because I know where to make the use of it, the times here offering great occasion, &c."

[1614.] In May following Sir Robert made further application in respect to his invention, as appears by another paper, indorsed,

"THE COMMODITY OF SIR R. D., HIS VESSEL, 1614."

The paper is headed,

"What I promise touching the vessel offered his Majesty, if he please to accept it."

In this paper, he reiterates the contents of the Tract or

Proposition of Nov. 1612, divided into ten sections, and he closes, with these words,

"Therefore do subscribe it and write it with my own hand as an obligo, by my word to be able to perform what here written. Dated the 11th of May, 1614.

"Ro. Dudl. &c."[1]

[1614.] *Sir Robert Dudley (Earl of Warwick, &c.) to Sir David Foulis*, 15 *July*, 1614. [*Holograph.*]

"My very honorable and worthy friend,

"It is near two months since I wrote you full answer to satisfy his Majesty of my ability to make those forcible and swift vessels offered him, which as touching his sea force and strength, I know to be an offer of greatest consequence; and only duty made me do it, and love to my country, else that proffer had not sailed so far Northwards. Touching the same, I wrote something to my Lord of Somerset,[2] of all which I expect now shortly to hear some resolution.

"Having had a mind, in this my absence, to enable myself to do his Majesty some faithful services, that he might one day thank me for, as well in his matters of profit at home, and safely within land, as money matters, I thought of some application for his service, of much I have seen and had extraordinary means to learn, from the school of the Great Duke Ferdinand, of famous memory; and I remember well I was then most thinking of some ends for his service; even then, when his agent, Sir Stephen Leasure[3] (I thank him) proclaimed me in his cups for a rebel and I know not what; but leaving him where he deserved, I thought it not amiss at this present to write you a word of some importunate matter for his Majesty's good, upon the occasion of the thwartness I understand of late the Parliament useth towards him; neither consenting to such subsidies accustomed and necessary, but rather with much presumption, standing upon worse terms; and I, conceiving to understand something, their natures I doubt in time may grow to a bad obstinacy, especially understanding their malice much pretendeth against the Scottish nation, to whom I have been particularly beholden, maketh me, out of gratitude,

[1] State Paper Office, London.
[2] The favorite minion of the King.
[3] Sir Stephen Leasure was knighted in 1609.

write this, which for a time I had thought to have prolonged; neither would I do it to any other but yourself, knowing your fidelity to the King, and worth. Having long suspected some mischiefs I see creeping on, I kept in store a certain design of mine, which, followed in England, by his Majesty, I know may make him secure against all these rubs for his profit, and make him safe to do what he please with his own (as an absolute monarch as he is), without dangerous resistance, and as free from the possibility of foreign invasions, if any such should ever be attempted, and keep the bridle in his own hand, so strong, and never King had a greater in those parts; nay, I doubt not by the same means I know, he may to increase his revenues to a much greater value—I hope double; and I make no question, without discontent of his people, and not to be vexed with the variety of so many men's minds as the Parliaments afford. In fine, to make him so absolute patron of his own as he may do what himself thinketh fit, without contradiction of moment by any that can hazard prejudice, &c. First, I protest to you I wrote this out of love and duty, merely to his Majesty, and gratitude for some favours his Majesty hath done me, and not least for being father to a Prince, my master, I so dearly loved (as it maketh my heart bleed to remember), and not out of any design or desire to leave home, being farthest from my desire, having received so many discourtesies from my friends and kindred in those parts, which are the most and greatest of the kingdom, as it maketh me least think of home; and therefore to avoid that suspicion I profess I can better do him the service, and more willingly, where I am, than at home. True it is I will trust no English with my design therein, for his Majesty's greater happiness, if [it] please him to follow it; but if he give commission to some wise and faithful servant and Scottish gentleman, to treat with me therein privately, I will open to him a course for his Majesty's service, under writing, that I know he will say I am the faithfullest servant of his kingdom, and I may say, without interest, because I offer it without particular conditions, yet that his commission may be large to answer for some generality on his Majesty's part, were not amiss for some reason necessary, I presume, when his gracious Majesty shall be partaker of my intent for his service to prevent the former mischiefs that methinks creep on too fast. I doubt not, upon the view thereof, his vexations, or what else I may term it, fit for his greatness, will be much satisfied and eased in this course, or rather counsel (if I may without presumption so call it); he must be his own Counsellor, or some one most trusted, to digest it, with his Majesty's great wisdom, and most trusted by him, which I conceive of, or rather wish it may be my Lord of Somerset;[1] for many reasons the faithful person employed in it, I wish either yourself or some one as trusty to the King and affectionate to you, as yourself, for I doubt not the service, as I said, will be extremely grateful, and be a sure way as I pretend (if my brains fail me not, and daily examples I see), to make his Majesty powerful and rich at home, to his own pleasure, secure from rebellions or foreign invasions. I do not use to write so confidently and liberally in a matter so weighty, if I knew not what I say, sure I am I shall not fail in my duty and loyalty to his Majesty, which may answer for any other want in me; so not to tire you with longer discourse, only that you will be pleased to make privately known to his Majesty what I write. I bid you most affectionately farewell, from Florence, this 15 of July, 1614.

"Your most faithful friend to command,
"WARWICK, &c."

"Because my leisure is not at this time to keep a copy of what I write, I pray you keep it safely, that if the business proceed to a tractation, you may send me this letter, or copy thereof, that I may maintain my word in every point here written. If you trust any with this business of the nation, I think you may best Mr. Yeats, who I have proved a very faithful, honest man, wise and secret, and I know a most faithful mind to the King to be employed."

(Superscribed)
"To my very honorable and worthy
friend, Sir David Foulis.
At the Court."[2]

(Superscribed)
[1614.] "*To my honorable friend Sir Robert Dudley, Knight, &c. &c.*

"Sir,

"I have received your letters, wherein you testify so honorable a conceit of me, that I cannot but take it very thankfully,

[1] Robert Carr, Viscount Rochester, created Earl of Somerset, 3rd Nov., 1613.
[2] State Paper Office, London.

and will ever answer the trust you repose in me with such care as becometh me, whether it shall concern his Majesty's benefit, or the country's, or your own particular, in whatsoever shall be reasonable and just. And if the offer made in your letters prove answerable, that you promise I shall be ready to employ myself to procure you such favor and reward as shall be suitable to the service, as upon the return of this messenger, and his Majesty's satisfaction, by his report of the business, you shall more particularly understand. So wishing the good event of so great a project and much contentment to yourself, I rest,

"Your loving friend,

"R. S."[1]

"*Wansted*, 12*th Sept.*, 1614.

(Indorsed)

"M. to R. Dudley, 12th Sept., 1614."

[1616.] *At Greenwich*, 21*st May*, 1616. [From Privy Council Regrs.]

"Sir Thomas Leigh, Knight and Baronet, having exhibited a Petition unto his Majesty, humbly praying; that whereas Sir Robert Dudley, Knight, after he had taken to wife the daughter of the said Sir Thomas Leigh, and cohabiting with her the space of ten years, had by the said Lady seven daughters, five living, and four of them now grown to woman's estate, did afterwards not only depart and absent himself out of the Kingdom, into parts beyond the seas, where he yet remaineth, in contempt of his Majesty's laws and express commandment, signified under his Highness's Privy Seal, and hath disloyally forsaken his said wife and children, but also now endeavoureth utterly to defeat them of all means of livelihood from him, by selling all such lands of his as are left unsold within this realm. It would therefore please his Majesty that some course might be taken for the restraining of him in the execution of his intended purpose. The said Petition being thereupon referred by his Majesty unto the Right Honorable the Lord Chancellor of England, the Lord Zouch, and Mr. Secretary Lake; upon perusal thereof, and of the particulars annexed, setting forth the state of the cause concerning the said Lady Dudley; They have this day ordered, that Sir David Fowlis and Mr. Gates, who do pretend, (as it is therein informed,) to have the inheritance

[1] Robert Carr, Earl of Somerset, then Lord Chamberlain.—The corrupt favorite of James I. He was implicated in the murder of Sir Thomas Overbury.

of certain manors conveyed unto them by Sir Robert Dudley, since his departure, shall attend their Lordships at their next meeting, for this business, to show what estate they have, and upon what consideration the same is passed unto them; whereupon their Lordships will further advise what is fit to be done. And in the meantime they are of opinion, that it is requisite Order be given by the Lord Chancellor that no Dedimus potestatem be granted to take any fine, or other assurance, from Sir Robert Dudley for the aliening of any of his lands. And they are also of opinion that it is in no sort fit, or to be allowed, that either the eight hundred pounds yearly rent, or the eight thousand pounds ready money, or any part thereof, (mentioned in the said particular or abstract, remaining now in the hands of the Clerk of the Council,) should be conveyed out of this kingdom, either in specie or by exchange, to the said Sir Robert Dudley, or to any other to his use, whereby to encourage him to persist in the continuance of his wilful contempt and disobedience to his Majesty's commandment. But that the said money be stayed here in this Kingdom, to the end the Lady, his wife, who brought him a fair portion, may be relieved and provided for, towards the maintenance of herself and family, and some competent portions also raised for their said children, out of the same."[1]

[1621.] *Sir Thomas Chaloner to Sir Robert Dudley, at Livorno.*

"Sir,

30 *July*, 1621. (*Holograph.*)

"Albeit I have not written unto you, notwithstanding I remained as desirous of your good as any friend you have; in testimony whereof you shall understand that since you took a course to repair your offence by submitting yourself to his Majesty's grace, and resolved therein to use the mediation of his Highness, I have not failed to do you all the good offices that lay in my poor ability; and as it beseemeth a friend to deal plainly with him, to whom I profess friendship, let me persuade you to apply yourself to such actions as may rejoice those that wish you well, and have sorrowed much for your late misfortune. The means in my opinion to effect this, consist chiefly in giving evident tokens of your loyalty, and to make good by your service what by your

[1] Pr. Coun. Regr., Jas. I, vol ii.

neglect you have forfeited. Which point being happily won, and his Majesty's favorable conceit gained, it followeth next, that to your Lady's friends and allies here in England you endeavour to give present satisfaction, to the end that both herself and your children may have portions allotted them, or some such assurance thereof as you, in your fatherly care, are bound to provide for them. Neither am I unmindful to put you in mind of that which I presume you will not omit, that before your return to England you will take order that some that with you have suffered loss of friends and other prejudices, for your sake, be honorably settled with a convenient estate.[1] Believe me, Sir, by these endeavours, you shall return a welcome guest to all your country; and the Prince, whom you vow, next unto the King, only to honour and serve, shall not be ashamed to have such a servant; for I can assure you that his purpose is never to aim at anything whereunto the advancement of his reputation shall not be his director. To which purpose it hath seemed good to his Majesty and his Highness that I should enclose the articles or writing herein,[2] to the end that, upon notice given by you of your humble readiness to give way unto your own happiness, by subscribing dutifully thereunto, you may forthwith receive that gracious pardon which you so much thirst for. And as you have received my Lord of Northampton's especial care (as I may justly term it) the life of your estate, which through your debts and other intricacies was ready to perish, so let me advise you to acknowledge it, with the best terms and fashion you may. Not detaining you longer, I will end, though not end to be a friend to him that shall apply himself to all loyal duties.

"Yours,
"THOMAS CHALONER."

"*Richmond, July* 30.

(Superscribed)
"To Sir Robert Dudley, Knight,
Livorno."

---

[1] Evidently alluding to Elizabeth Southwell,—his third wife.
[2] Not found with the letter.
[3] State Paper Office, London.

[1621.] Indorsed, "Kenilworth let to Prince by Sir Robert Dudley."

"A relation of the passages in the conveyance of Kenilworth to the Prince by Sir Ro. Dudley."

"Sir Ro. Dudley did ever seek all means before his going over, to let his Majesty understand his loyal and true heart, and to that purpose tendered his service to his late Highness, who vouchsafed to call him servant; and Sir Robert, to give him a further taste of his true affection, by Sir Thomas Chaloner, offered Kenilworth at a low price to his Highness, but the Lord Treasurer Dorset said the King was not furnished with money.

"Sir Robert, after his departure out of England, finding that his adversaries laid many imputations on him, ceased not to write many letters to his friends, especially assuring his Highness that he would live and die the King's faithful subject and his servant; and whereas his Majesty was to pay £26,000 or £25,000 for Kenilworth, and as it was informed him, to grant withall a pardon for his contempt (which he protested he was driven unto with grief of mind), he was contented upon some conditions to let his Highness have it at a lower rate, forasmuch as the bruit was in England that his Majesty meant to bestow it upon him, and to that purpose required that he might be assured whether his Highness would accept of it or no. It pleased the Prince to signify that his purpose was to have it, which, being by his servant Wyatt, related to Sir Ro. Dudley, he offered to give it freely to the Prince, and so would have done, but that the Prince partly refused it; and then Sir Robert required only such a sum of money as might serve his turn to pay some present debts, which Sir Robert did not because nobody else would buy it, for divers offered money for it, and it was in his power to sell it to whom he would; besides that, he hath three manors worth £20,000 yet to sell, if he were disposed so to do; whereby Sir Robert desired his Highness to inform his Majesty that no other motive induced him to pass such a rich castle at so low a price, but only to give his Majesty satisfaction for the contempt; and as for treasons unjustly imputed against him, he would stand to the uttermost trial of law. And for service in shipping he propounded an overture of great consequence for his Majesty, letting his Highness also know that, in point of religion, he was different many years before his going out of England, and did not change his opinion, as is imputed to him since his departure.

"It pleased his highness, therefore, before he would conclude, to ask leave of his Majesty (which he said he had obtained), and to confer also with the late Lord Treasurer, who encouraged him to accept the bargain at £15,000, for so much was demanded, and his Highness had such a confidence that the King would pardon the contempt, considering that Sir Robert, to regain his Majesty's gracious favour, thought he had parted with more in the bargain than by any profit of the seizure could ever arise, that he sent to Mr. Attorney to make ready a pardon, against such time as it should please the King resolutely to grant it; but finding a cross at Windsor, a messenger went to Sir Robert to let him know it was not the Prince his fault, that the condition of the pardon was not performed.

"Now, albeit that Sir Robert had always refused to part with Kenilworth, in case his pardon was not procured, notwithstanding his answer was, that, to the end the King and the Prince might know the openness of his heart, he would put himself into their hands freely, hoping that by how much he humbled himself, so much the more his Majesty would take commiseration of his case; he therefore resolved to proceed in the bargain upon condition his Highness would undertake, in convenient time, to procure his pardon; and whereas he reserved to himself and his heirs, the Constableship and command of the game of Kenilworth, he agreed to have it put into Sir Thomas Chaloner's hands during their two lives; and to that purpose humbly presented his Highness with such conditions as he thought safe and honorable to accept, and by letter assured him of the performance thereof.

"Since which time with much travel and pain of messengers sent into Italy to accomplish the business, all hath been brought to pass on Sir Robert's part, and there resteth behind part of the money to be paid, which was promised to be performed above a year past, and for default whereof Sir Robert hath sustained great exclamation of his creditors, whereas out of his other lands he could have provided himself, if this expectation had not delayed him.

"And now that his Majesty and the Prince have in their hands one of the goodliest and stateliest castles of this land, Sir Robert's desire is, that his Majesty will extend his grace, without the hope whereof no money could have drawn his estate therein out of his possession.

"And albeit that Sir Robert offered his service in matter of shipping, and the delivery of Kenilworth, notwithstanding his Highness was advised by Sir Thomas Chaloner not to meddle therewith until all had obtained first his Majesty's license, and had means to pay what should be promised, which by conference with my Lord Treasurer he was assured of, and that also thoroughly informed whether the claim made to Kenilworth were of value or not, which course his Highness followed, and under his Counsel's hands was certified, that their opinion was, that they held not the ground of the claim to be good or sufficient in law, besides that there was a strong decree in Chancery on Sir Robert Dudley's behalf."[1]

[1629, 14 Nov.] A copy of the information exhibited into the Star Chamber by Sir Robert Heath, Knight, his Majesty's Attorney General, against Francis, Earl of Bedford; Robert, Earl of Somerset; John, Earl of Clare; Sir Robert Cotton, Knight and Baronet; John Selden, Esq.; and Gilbert Barrett, Gent. Tero. Michaelis, Anno 5 Carolus Regis."

As to "The Proposition," written by Sir Robert Dudley in 1612, requesting his Majesty to issue his orders for the above persons to appear before his Majesty and the Council at the Star Chamber.

[―― 15 *Nov.*]   "*At Whitehall the* 15*th of November*, 1629.

" This day his Majesty, sitting in Council, was pleased to impart to the whole Board the cause for which the Earls of Clare, Somerset, and Bedford, Sir Robert Cotton, Knight, and sundry other persons of inferior quality, had been lately restrained and examined by a special commission appointed by him for that purpose. Which cause was this; his Majesty declared that there came to his hands, by mere accident, the copy of a certain discourse or Proposition (which was then by his commandment read at the Board), pretended to be written for his Majesty's service, and bearing this title—' The Proposition for your Majesty's service, containing two parts; the one to secure your estate, and to bridle the impertinency of Parliaments; the other to increase your Majesty's revenue much more than it is.'

" Now, the means propounded in this discourse for the effecting thereof are such as are fitter to be practised in a Turkish state

[1] State Paper Office, London.

than amongst Christians, being contrary to the justice and mildness of his Majesty's government, and the sincerity of his intentions; proceeding from a pernicious design, both against his Majesty and the State. Which, notwithstanding the aforesaid persons had not only read and concealed the same from his Majesty and his Council, but also communicated and divulged it to others. Whereupon his Majesty did further declare, that it is his pleasure that the aforesaid Earls and Sir Robert Cotton shall answer this their offense in the Court of Star Chamber, to which end they had already been summoned, and that now they should be discharged and freed from their restraint, and permitted to return to their several houses, to the end that they might have the better means to prepare themselves. And lastly, he commanded that his pleasure should be signified by the Board unto them, who were then attending without, having for that purpose been sent for. His Majesty, having given this order and direction, rose from the Board; and when he was gone the three Earls were called in severally, and the Lord Keeper signified to each of them his Majesty's pleasure in that behalf, shewing them withall how graciously he had been pleased to deal with them, both in the manner of their restraint, which was only during the time of the examination of the cause (a thing usual and requisite, especially in cases of that consequence), and in that they had been committed to the custody of eminent and honorable persons, by whom they were treated according to their qualities; and likewise in the discharging of them now from that restraint, that they might have the better convenience and means to prepare themselves for the defense of their cause in that legal course, by which his Majesty had thought fit to call them to an account and trial. The like was also signified by his Lordship to Sir Robert Cotton, who was further told, that although it were his Majesty's pleasure that his studies should as yet remain shut up, yet he might enter into them, and take such writings, whereof he should have use, provided, that he did it in the presence of a Clerk of the Council, and that whereas the clerk attending hath the keys of two of the studies, he might put a second lock on either of them, so that neither doors might be opened but by him and the said Clerk, both together."[1]

[1] State Paper Office, London.

[1629.] Indorsed "From the Lords of the Council to Sir David Fowlis, the 25th of November 1629."

"After our hearty commendations, we have received and communicated, to his Majesty your letter of the 16th of this present [month], in answer of ours of the 9th, together with the two writings thereunto annexed; and having thereupon new charge from his Majesty to send again unto you, we will first let you know the contentment his Majesty hath, in the freedom and ingenuity of your answer; but because the business, bred by those writings, proves a matter of much moment, importing his Majesty greatly in honor, and some persons of rank and quality are in question about them, it is thought necessary by his Majesty for the further clearing of some weighty circumstances, you come hither with all convenient speed; and that you bring with you a certain letter[1] specified in the Proposition at the summing up the account of the value of the projects contained in the said proposition, as much more than was promised by the said letter, whereby the said letter appears to be written and sent before this proposition; and it is very requisite it should be had; wherefore his Majesty will expect you should look it out, and produce it with the same fidelity you have done the rest; which we let you know once more for your comfort and encouragement, his Majesty doth graciously interpret as an acceptable service. So we bid you heartily farewell; from the Court at Whitehall the 25th of November 1629."[2]

[1629.] *Sir David Foulis to the Earl of Dorchester (Lord Carleton).*

"*Inglebye, Yorkshire; 9th Dec.*, 1629.

"May it please your Lordship,—

"I did yesterday receive a letter from yourself and others of his Majesty's Honorable Privy Council, intimating his Majesty's pleasure, that with convenient speed, I should address myself to Court, which upon the very instant I had performed, but that there were in my hands, a number of divers sorts of felonies to be examined, whereof some were to be tried at the next general Quarter-sessions, and other some at the next Assizes and general jail delivery, to be holden within the County of York; the per-

[1] The letter referred to by the Council may be found under date, 15 July,1614. See page 307.
State Paper Office, London.

fecting of which, with the recognizances and evidences belonging thereunto, will hold me at least ten days; neither durst I omit so great a duty to the Crown, to the Country, and to my own conscience, as to leave them at random without bringing them to be heard according to law. All which I am forced to do myself alone, being here without the assistance of any to help me, in this Hundred of Langbargh, where I dwell, consisting of 70 constabularies. So as I hope that this necessary excuse will be allowed, that I do not come so soon as I willingly would; but (by God's grace) I will set forward as soon as possibly I can, though I know (as I do always find here) that the disorders of the country will swell much about Christmas, especially when wicked people shall see none here to look to the government; yet notwithstanding all impediments (if God grant me continuance of health,) I hope to attend your Lordship about twelfthtide;[1] for I will endeavour it with all my power, and will not fail to bring with me such papers as are in my possession, touching the matters your Lordships write of, which, in truth, was neglected and forgotten in a manner by me. Thus humbly beseeching your best construction and allowance of my proceedings herein, according to my true relation and upright meaning, I take my leave and rest,

"Your Lordship's humble servant to command,
"DA. FOULIS."

"*Inglebye; the 9th of December* 1629."

(Superscription)
" To the right honorable my very
good Lord, the Earl of Dorchester,
principal Secretary to the King his
Majesty, and one of his Majesty's most
honorable Privy Counsel. At Court."[2]

[1630.] Proceedings were commenced in the Star Chamber against (Francis Russell) Earl of Bedford; (John Hollis) Earl of Clare; (Robert Carr) Earl of Somerset; Sir Robert Cotton, John Selden, Esq., Oliver St. John, Esq., and others, for publishing a seditious and scandalous writing. 26th May, 1630; VI Charles 1.

This was the "Proposition," written by Sir Robert Dudley,

[1] Twelfth-day (Halliwell).
[2] State Paper Office, London.

which was sent over in time of James I (1612) by Mr. Yates to Sir David Fowlis, who delivered it to the Earl of Somerset (Carr), and the Earl communicated it to the King (Jas.). The Proposition is printed in 'Rushworth.'[1] And also in 'Howell's State Papers.'[2]

The Earl of Somerset pleaded that, conceiving it to be no scandal to the present Government, he had casually imparted it to the Earls of Bedford and Clare. After the proceedings had commenced, viz. on the 29th May, in the presence of the nobility and gentry, the King sent word to the Lord Keeper, "that in respect of the great joy upon the birth of his son,[3] he should immediately order the proceedings to be stopped, and the defendants to be discharged." Upon which the said writing was ordered to be burned, as seditious and scandalous, and the proceedings were taken off the file.[4]

[1633.] Sir David Fowlis was one of his Majesty's sworn counsel in the northern parts, one of the Deputy Lieutenants, and Justice of the Peace of the North Riding, Yorkshire. He was, with Sir Thomas Layton and Henry Fowlis, Esq., prosecuted in the Star Chamber in 1633, (9 Chas. I,) on a charge of opposing the King's service, in respect to dissuading persons from compounding for fines for Knighthood, and in traducing the character of Lord Wentworth, one of the Commissioners for compounding for fines, for which Sir David was ordered to be committed to the Fleet, to be fined £5000 to the King, and to lose the places of office he then held. And also to pay a fine of £3000 to Lord Wentworth.

On the prosecution of Lord Wentworth, Earl of Strafford, in 1640 and 41, Sir David Fowlis and Sir Thomas Layton were material witnesses against his Lordship.[5]

[1] 'Rushworth,' vol. i, Appendix, p. 12.
[2] 'Howell,' vol. iii, pp. 389, *et seq.* See also pp. 299—304 of the present work.
[3] Charles, Prince of Wales; afterwards Chas. II.
[4] State Paper Office, London.
[5] 'Howell's State Trials,' 8vo, 1816, vol. iii.

DUCHESS DUDLEY.

DUCHESS DUDLEY.

SIR ROBERT DUDLEY's other wife, who was left by him in England, LADY ALICE DUDLEY, third daughter of Sir Thomas Leigh, of Stoneley, is said to have been a woman of great parts, and of distinguished piety. King Charles I. granted to her, by letters patent under the Great Seal, the rank, style, and title of a Duchess, during the term of her natural life; and also the same privileges and precedencies to her daughters, as if they had been a Duke's daughters; and in the preamble to the letters patent for this purpose, the legitimacy of Sir Robert Dudley is asserted, and the injustice that had been done him is acknowledged. Duchess Dudley also, by the assistance of her friends, secured to herself and her daughters the remains of that great fortune which devolved to Sir Robert Dudley, in consequence of the Earl of Leicester's will, and other conveyances. She lived many years after the title of Duchess was conferred on her, and distinguished herself by her uncommon charity and benevolence. She had five daughters: Aliza and Douglas, died unmarried; Katherine, married Sir Richard Leveson, K.B.; Frances, married Sir Gilbert Kniveton, Knight; and Anne, married Sir Robert Holborne, Solicitor-General to Charles I.

"The Duchess outlived all her five daughters,[1] except the youngest. She resided for many years in the parish of St. Giles-in-the-fields, London; and she died there 22nd Jan., 1668-9, in her ninetieth year. Her brother, Sir John Leigh, was the father of the first Lord Leigh, of Stoneley, which

[1] She had seven daughters, see note ² at foot of page 286.

title subsisted till the latter part of the last century, and has, since it became extinct or dormant, been the subject of one of the most remarkable of modern Peerage cases."[1]

St. Giles-in-the-fields, London, was, soon after the dissolution of the monasteries by Hen. VIII., granted by that monarch to JOHN DUDLEY (then LORD LISLE and GREAT ADMIRAL of England), grandfather to Duchess Dudley's husband.

The Hospital of St. Giles was founded in 1117 by Matilda (or Maud), daughter of Malcolm King of Scotland, and Queen of Hen. I. Edward III. attached this hospital to that of Burton St. Lazar, in Leicestershire, 4 April, 1354.

"On the dissolution of the monasteries, Hen. VIII. kept the Hospital and its precincts six years in his possession, and in 1545 bestowed it on LORD LISLE, together with Burton St. Lazar, by the following grant. (Rent to the Crown £4 . 6 . 3.)

"'The King, to all to whom it may concern, sends greeting. Be it known that we, in consideration of the good, true, faithful, and acceptable councel and services to us, by our beloved counsellor *John Dudley*, Knight of the most noble order of the Garter, *Viscount Lisle*, and our *Great Admiral* of England, before time done and performed, of our special grace, and of our certain knowledge and mere motion, have given and granted, and by these presents do give and grant, to the said John Dudley, Viscount Lisle, all the late dissolved *Hospital of Burton St. Lazar*, otherwise called the Hospital of St. Lazarus of Burton, with all its rights, members, and appurtenances, in our County of Leicester, lately dissolved, and in our hands now being, and all the late *Hospital of St. Giles in the Fields*, without the bars of London, with all its rights, members, and appurtenances, in our said County of Middlesex, in like manner dissolved of late, and in our hands now being. And also all that our *Rectory and Church of Feltham*, with all its rights, members, and appurtenances, in our said County of Middlesex, to the late hospital of Burton aforesaid, belonging and appertaining, or being part or possession thereof, and the advowson, donation, free-disposition, and right of patronage of the vicarage of the parish of *Feltham*, in our said County of Middlesex,

---

[1] 'Romance of the Peerage,' by George Lillie Craik, vol. iii, 1849.

of the possessions of the late hospital of Burton aforesaid, being, belonging, and appertaining.

" 'And also all and singular the manors, messuages, rectories, churches, &c. (amongst others) and the parish of *St. Giles in the Fields*, without the bars of London, and in Holbourne, Feltham, and Edmonton (Edlemeton) in our said County of Middlesex, and in the City of London, and elsewhere, and wheresoever, within our Kingdom of England, to the said late hospital of Burton St. Lazarus otherwise the hospital of Burton St. Lazar, and of the said late hospital of St. Giles in the Fields, without the bars of London, or either of the same late hospitals of Burton aforesaid, in anywise belonging, or appertaining, or as parcel or possession of the said late hospital of Burton aforesaid, and the said late hospital of St. Giles in the Fields, or either of the said late hospitals, heretofore possessed, known, accepted, used, are reputed to belong.'

" By this Grant, all the possessions of the Hospital of St. Giles (not expressly mentioned in the exchange with the King) were vested in Lord Lisle. They consisted of the Hospital, its site and gardens, the Church and Manor of St. Giles, the Pittaunce Croft, Newland, Le Lane and other lands in the Parish of St. Giles. Also of the Church of Feltham, and Lands at Edmonton, and of the several rent charges, and hereditaments in the City of London and in the suburbs thereof, and in the fields of Westminster, and at Charing, as described in the hospital possession.

" After this Grant Lord Lisle fitted up the principal part of the hospital for his own residence, leasing out other subordinate parts of the structure, and portions of the adjoining grounds, garden, &c., and at the end of two years he conveyed the whole of the premises to John Wymonde Carewe, Esq., by license from the King, in the last year of his reign, to wit—

" ' The King, to all whom it may concern, sends greeting. Know ye, that we, of our special grace, and in consideration of the sum of Seven pounds and sixteen shillings, paid to us in our hanaper, do grant and give license, and by these presents, have granted and given license, for us and our heirs, as much as in us lies, unto our beloved *John Dudley*, Knight of our order of the Garter, *Viscount Lisle*, and our *Great Admiral* of England, to Grant and Sell, dispose of, alienate or acknowledge by fine in our Court, before our Justices of our Common bench, or in any manner whatsoever at his pleasure, unto John Wymonde Carewe, Esq., all that his mansion, place or capital house, late the house of the dissolved Hospital of St. Giles in the Fields, in the County of Middlesex,' &c.

"This Charity, founded by royal munificence, had subsisted under varied circumstances from 1117 to 1547, forming a period of 430 years, when it finally fell a prey to the rapacity of a monarch, whose 'catalogue of vices,' as Hume remarks, 'would comprehend many of the worst qualities incident to human nature.'

"The capital mansion or residence which Lord Lisle fitted up for his own accommodation, was situate where the soap manufactory of Messrs. Dix and Co. now is [1829], in a parallel direction with the Church, but more westward. It was afterwards occupied by the much celebrated *Alice, Duchess Dudley*, who was buried therefrom in the reign of Charles II. anno 1669, aged 90. This house was afterwards the town residence of Lord Wharton.

"A building situate on the site where Dudley Court now stands, was with a garden attached, purchased by Duchess Dudley in 1646, and was given for a perpetual mansion for the Incumbent. Some time previous to 1722 it was probably taken down, Dudley Court having been erected on the ground it had before occupied. It was, there is little doubt, as well as Dudley House which adjoined it, once part of the ancient hospital. The Rector of St. Giles, for the time being, is still entitled to receive the rents, &c., of Dudley Court, where this residence stood."[1]

Stow, in his 'Survey of London' (Strype, 1720), says—

"But of all the benefactors of St. Giles's Church and Parish, the Lady Alice, Duchess Dudley, must stand in the fore front. She lived in her house near the Church, and there she died, at the age of ninety years, and hath a monument in the said Church, though her corpse was conveyed to the Church of Stoneleigh in Warwickshire, and there entombed; in which parish she was born. But now to give a catalogue of this Lady's charities, as Dr. Boreman, sometime Incumbent, took them out of the Church's Register, and published them with her funeral sermon, anno 1669.

Sir Robert Dudley died at Florence in 1649. Lady Alice,

[1] Dobie's 'Hist. of the United Parishes of St. Giles and St. George, Bloomsbury,' 8vo, Lond., 1829.

Duchess Dudley, died possessed of a portion of the vast fortune of her husband's father, (the Earl of Leicester,) at her house near the Church, 22d Jany., 1668-9, aged 90.

"Doctor Boreman, in his funeral sermon, says, 'She was a magazine of experience; her vast memory, which was strong and vigorous to admiration, was the storehouse and treasury of observation and knowledge of occurrences for many years.'

"When the former Church of St. Giles, which was decayed by age, lay, as it were, in rubbish, there being a void space at the upper end of the chancel, wherein were old coffin boards and the bones of dead men thrown, she, being offended at the unhandsome prospect, erected a decent screen to divide the said chancel from that place, to hide it from the eyes of those that passed by.

"When the foresaid old church was fallen, with the fall thereof, that screen was demolished, the parishioners erected a new church in the room and place where the former stood. It began to be built anno 1623, and was finished with the wall about it, anno 1631; many hundreds of good Christians in other parishes contributing to so good a work. And then did this Lady give to the said work, and the wall encompassing the Church, many hundred pounds. Of which her magnificent bounty, the then grateful parishioners erected a monument, which is placed over the great gate on the north side of the Church. The words engraven on a large square stone, are these:

"'Quod fœlix bonumque fit Posteris, Hoc Templum loco Veteris ex annosa Vetustate collapse, mole et splendore auctum multo, Parœcorum charitas Instauravit. Inquibus pientissimæ Heroinæ D. Aliciæ Duddeley, munificentia gratum marmoris hujus meretur Eloquium. Huic etiam accessit aliorum quorundam pietas. Quibus provisæ in cælo sunt Grates.'

"*Translation.*—'This Temple, (may it be a blessing to posterity,) was built in the place of a former one, which had fallen from the effects of time. But augmented in size, and with great splendour, by the Christian beneficence of the parishioners, among whom the munificence of the pious Lady Alice Dudley deserves the grateful tribute of this marble. The pious contributions of some others, whose reward is in heaven, aided the work.'"[1]

"The Church being finished, that the inside of it might correspond with that which is without, the said Lady gave hangings

[1] Dobie's 'Hist. of St. Giles and St. George, Bloomsbury,' 8vo, 1829.

of Watchet taffata to cover the upper end of the chancel, and those bordered with a silk and silver fringe.

"Item. For the back of the altar, a rich green velvet cloth, with these three letters in gold, I.H.S., embroidered on it.

"Two service books, in folio, embossed with gold.

"A green velvet cloth, with a deep gold fringe, to cover the altar on Sundays.

"A cambric altar cloth, with a deep bone lace round about.

"Another fine damask altar cloth.

"Two cushions for the altar, richly embroidered with gold.

"A large Turkey carpet, to be spread on the week days over it.

"A beautiful screen of carved work, which was placed where the former in the old Church stood.

"Moreover, she gave a neat pair of organs, with a case richly gilded.

"Item. Very costly handsome rails, to guard the altar, or the Lord's table, from profane abuses.

"Item. The communion plate of all sorts, in silver and gilt, for that sacred use, which is as large and rich as any in the city and suburbs.

"Besides all this, she was at the charge of paving the upper end of the Church with marble. And gave the great bell in the steeple; which as oft as it ringeth sounds her praise. And was at the charge of casting and hanging the other five bells.

"Only this bell and the foresaid plate excepted, all the forenamed ornaments of the Church, (being counted superstitious and Popish,) were demolished and sold, (under pretence of relieving the poor out of the money received for them,) by the Reformers, (as they were called,) in the civil war time.

"Besides these largesses and Christian liberalities to St. Giles', she gave long since to the Churches of Stoneleigh, Manchester, Leke Wotton, Ashow, Kenilworth, and Monks Kirby, all in Warwickshire, twenty pounds and upwards per annum, apiece, for a perpetual augmentation to the poor Vicarages of those respective Churches for ever.

"Moreover, she bestowed on the same Churches, and likewise upon the Churches of Bidford, in the foresaid County of Warwick, Acton in Middlesex, St. Albans in Hertfordshire, Patshil in Northampton, divers pieces of fair and costly plate, to be used at the celebration of the holy communion in each of them.

"Besides all this, she purchased a fair house and garden near the Church of St. Giles, aforesaid; and gave it for a perpetual mansion to the incumbents after three lives, whereof two were expired, anno 1669.

"She also allowed a yearly stipend to the Sexton of this Church, to toll the great bell, when the prisoners condemned to die, shall be passing by, and to ring out after they shall be executed.

"She likewise gave great sums of money for the repairing of the Cathedral Church at Litchfield, and for the re-edifying of St. Sepulchres in London.

"All these, with many more, were the products and fruits of her noble charity while she lived. And at her death she made the following bequests.

I. "For the redemption of Christian captives from the hands of infidels, £100 per annum for ever.

II. "To the Hospital situate near the Church here in St. Giles, £400 for £20 a year for ever.

III. "For the placing out for ever of poor parish children of St. Giles', apprentices, £200, to purchase a piece of land at £10 per annum; and two to be put out every year.

IV. "To the poor of the foresaid parishes of Stoneleigh, Kenilworth, Leke Wotton, Ashow, Bidford, in the foresaid County of Warwick; and Patshill, Litchborough and Blakesley, in the County of Northampton, £100 per annum to be disposed and distributed among them, in such sort and manner as her Will directs her Executrix. And

V. "Upon the day of her funeral, £50 to be distributed among the poor of the said parish of St. Giles', and other adjoining parishes.

VI. "To Fourscore and ten widows, according to the number of years she lived, she bequeathed to each a gown, and a fair white kerchief, to attend the hearse wherein her body was carried, and one shilling apiece for their dinner after that solemnity was performed; which was on the 10th day of March 1668-9.

VII. "She appointed by her will £5, to be given to every place or town where her corpse should rest in its passage from London unto Stoneleigh, where she had a noble monument, long since prepared by herself.

VIII. "She ordered that sixpence should be given to every poor body that should meet her corpse on the road.

IX. "She gave to Blakesley, Litchborough and Patshill £10

apiece, to be distributed among the poor, the same day her corpse was interred.

X. "To the parish of Stoneleigh £50, which was distributed the same day.

"There is a monument set up for her in St. Giles' Church, thus inscribed,

"'ALICE, DUTCHESS DUDDELEY.

"'A Lady of a vast charitable mind, and who did many good deeds to that parish. She died anno 1669, third daughter of Sir Thomas Leigh of Stoneleigh in Warwickshire, Knt. and Bart. Her mother was Katharine, daughter to Sir John Spencer of Wormleighton, Knt., and great grandfather to Earl Sunderland. The foresaid Sir Thomas Leigh had by the said Katharine, John Leigh, Knt., who was the father of the Lord Leigh, Baron of Stoneleigh.

"'There is her funeral sermon preached by Dr. Boreman, Minister of St. Giles, and a narrative of her life and death, which was published after the sermon.

"'She was the relict of Sir Robert Dudley, Knt., son to Robert, late Earl of Leicester; and for his excellent merits created a Duke by Ferdinand 2d, late Emperor of Germany. She was by letters patent, bearing date, at Oxford the 20 of May, 20 Chas. I., advanced by him to the title of a Duchess; being by the foresaid Robert, the mother of five[1] daughters, Alice; Douglas; Frances, wife of Sir Gilbert Kniveton, Knt.; Anne, wife of Sir Robert Holborn, late of Lincoln's Inn. All these deceased; and Katharine, the only surviving picture, in piety and goodness of her Lady mother, and widow of Sir Richard Levison, Knt. of the Bath. She was born in the town of Stoneley.'

"There is a catalogue of her charities to the reparation and rebuilding of the Church and the ornaments of the altar; besides her charity to Stoneley, where her body lies entombed, and many other Churches and augmentations of poor Vicarages. She purchased a fair house and garden near the Church of St. Giles for the incumbent there, and other charities; which we all set down in an account of her good deeds in her life and at her death.[2]

A monument was erected towards the lower end of the Church of St. Giles in the Fields to "The Right Honorable the Lady Frances Kniveton, wife of Sir Gilbert Kniveton of Bradley in the

[1] She had seven daughters, see note [2] at foot of page 286.
[2] Stow's 'Survey,' by Strype, Book iv, 82-4.

County of Derby, Bart. She was one of the five daughters and co-heirs of Sir Robert Dudley, Knt., Duke of the Empire, by the Lady Alice his wife and Dutchess. The honor and title of Dutchess Dudley was by letters patent of King Charles I. allowed, and confirmed by King Charles 2d.

"The Right Honorable the Lady Anne Holborne, sister of the said Lady Frances. Another daughter of the said Duke and Duchess, died 1663."[1]

In this year (1669) was published—

"A mirror of Christianity and a miracle of charity," or a true and exact narrative of the life and death of the most virtuous Lady Alice Duchess Dudley. Sm. 4to, 1669.

Dedicated to Catharine Levison, relict of Sir Richard, and only surviving daughter of the Duchess. The Duchess died in her house near St. Giles's Church, 22d Jany. 1669, in her 90th year.

Her patent stated to be 20 May, 20 Chas. I.[2]

[1669.] In Heraldic Collections, Addl. MSS., 12,514, fo. 277, is the following, in the handwriting of Sir Wm. Dugdale:

"Order of the proceeding to the funeral of the Right Honorable Lady Alice, Duchess Dudley, 16th March, 1668-9.

"The hearse covered with velvet, &c., drawn by six horses, harnessed with velvet, &c., on each side, whereof the banner rolls, in number eight, borne by gentlemen, and eight footmen attending thereon.

"The Lady Katherine Leveson, chief mourner, in her coach, covered with black.

"The Lady's assistants in other coaches.

"The coaches of the nobility, and others, in due order."

Heralds and pursuivants, Dr. Boreman, Parson of St. Giles, among the attendants on the funeral.[3]

[1] Stow's 'Survey,' by Strype.
[2] B.M., 'Grenville Cat.,' 1376.
[3] 'Additional MSS.'—British Museum.

[1669.] Sir William Dugdale, in his 'Diary,' says, under date 1668-9—

"Mar. 16. I came out of London with the corpse of the Duchess Dudley (who died at her house near St. Giles Church in Holborn, 22d Jany.) to St. Albans.

"17. To Layton in Bedfordshire.—18. To Northampton.—19. To Dunchurch.—20. To Stoneleigh—where the said corpse was interred."

[1670.] "Concerning Duchess Dudley's Gift for Redemption of Captives."

"*At Whitehall, the 9th of September*, 1670.

"Upon reading this day at the Board, the humble petition of John Cooke, Solicitor for poor captives, praying, that the Trustees in the will of the late Duchess Dudley may be commanded to make a legal settlement of the sum of One hundred pounds per annum for ever, for the redemption of poor English captives taken by the Turks, given to that use by the last Will and Testament of the said Duchess. It was ordered by his Majesty in Council, that the said petition be, and it is hereby, referred to the Right Honorable the Lord Keeper of the Great Seal of England, who is desired speedily to take it into consideration, and by the most effectual ways and means he can to settle the said gift, that the same, together with the arrears thereof, may be employed to the use for which it was intended by the donor.'"[1]

[1673.] Lady Katherine Leveson, the only surviving daughter of the Duchess, died at Trentham, in Staffordshire, in 1673. A mural tablet to the memory of this lady, one of the daughters of Sir Robert Dudley, is in the Collegiate Church of St. Mary, WARWICK, over the door leading from the Chapel to the Oratory, with the following inscription:

"To the memory of the Lady Katherine (late wife of Sir Richard Leveson, of Trentham, in the County of Staff., Knt. of the Bath), one of the daughters and coheirs of Sir Robert Dudley, Knt., son to Robert late Earl of Leicester, by Alicia his wife,[2] daughter to Sir Tho. Leigh of Stoneley, Knt. and Bart. (created

[1] 'Privy Council Register,' Chas. 2d, Vol. 9.

[2] A noble monument to the memory of this lady is erected in the chancel of Stoneleigh church.

Duchess Dudley by K. Charles I. in regard that her said husband, leaving this Realm, had the title of a Duke confer'd upon him by Ferdinand II. Emp'r of Germany,) which honorable Lady taking notice of these Tombs of her noble Ancestors[1] being much blemished by consuming time, but more by the rude hands of impious people, were in danger of utter ruin by the decay of this Chapel, if not timely prevented; did in her life time give Fifty pounds for its speedy repair: and by her last Will and Testament, bearing date xviii° Dec. 1673 bequeath forty pounds *per annum*, issuing out of her manor of FOXLEY, in the County of Northampton, for the perpetual support and preservation of these monuments in their proper state; the surplusage to be for the poor Brethren of her Grandfather's Hospital in this Borough [Warwick]. Appointing WILLIAM DUGDALE, of BLYTHE HALL, in this County, Esq. (who represented to her the necessity of this good work,) and his heirs,[2] together with the Mayor of WARWICK for the time being, to be her Trustees therein.[3]

[1] The tombs referred to are those of Robert Dudley, Earl of Leicester, Ambrose Dudley, Earl of Warwick, and the young Lord Denbigh, infant son of the Earl of Leicester.
[2] William Stratford Dugdale, Esq., the representative of this family and trustee in 1849.
[3] 'Description of the Collegiate Church of St. Mary, Warwick,' by Hands, 12mo.

APPENDIX.

1.

APPENDIX.

JOHN APPLEYARD (*See Note*, p. 10).

THE following entries in reference to John Appleyard appear in the Privy Council Register Books:

[1553] 26th July. "It is ordered that John Appleyard, Esq., of Brakenashe, in Norfolk, shall not be dismissed, but is commanded to attend from time to time within four miles of the Court, wheresoever it shall be, until other order be taken for him, and to give knowledge to her [the Queen's] Counsell, where he bestoweth himself.

"The said John Appleyard is charged with v^{li} remaining in his hands of the goods of the Lord Robert [Dudley], and to make payment thereof when he shall be thereto required by the order of the Counsell."

1556. *At St. James's the 20th May*, 1556.[1]

A letter of appearance to John Appleyard, Esq.

At St. James's the 28th May, 1556.

"Johannis Appleyarde de Brakenasshe, in Com. Norff. armiger, recognovit se debere sereniss. Dnus Regi et Regine, quingentas marcas bone et legalis monete Angliæ." &c.

"The condicion of this recognizance is such that if the above-named John Appleyard, Esq., do give from henceforth his continual attendance upon the Queen's highness's Commissioners, who lately sent for him, and do not depart hence without express license of them obtained thereunto, that then this present recognizance to be void and of none effect, or else to stand, &c. &c.

(Signed) "JOHN APPLEYARDE."

[1] Pr. Council Reg., Mary, vol. i.

1565. *At Westminster, 22nd Dec.*, 1565.[1]

"A letter to the Earl of Bedford that whereas the Queen's Majesty hath appointed John Appleyard, Esq., to be Gentleman Porter of that town of Berwick, he is required to give order that the said Appleyard may receive all such fees and profits as are incident to that office, and are reserved since the death of Selby, late porter there, &c. According to the minute in the Council chest."

1574. *At Greenwich, 6th April,* 1574.[2]

"A letter to the Sheriff of Norfolk, that whereas the Queen's Majesty's pleasure was that John Appleyard, prisoner in the Castle of Norwich, should, for his better health's sake, have liberty to remain in the said [sheriff's house, he is therefore to receive him accordingly, there to remain till he had other order to the contrary."

1574. *At Greenwich,* 31*st May,* 1574.[3]

"A letter to the sheriff of Norwich signifying that her Majesty's pleasure is, that John Appleyard should be committed to the custody of the Dean of Norwich.

"A letter to the said Dean to receive him and suffer him to enjoy such liberty as he may always be forthcoming when occasion shall require."

In 1553, when Lord Robert was confined to the Tower, Amye Dudley was permitted occasionally to visit him there. The following is one of the orders issued by the Privy Council for that purpose:

At Richmond the 5*th September,* 1553.

"Another letter to the Lieutenant of the Tower, whereby he is willed to permit these ladies following, to have access unto their husbands, and there to tarry with them so long and at such times, as by him shall be thought meet. That is to say, the Lord Ambrose's wife, the Lord Robert's wife, Sir Francis Jobson's wife, Sir H. Gates' wife, and Sir Richard Corbett's wife."[4]

[1] Pr. Council Reg., Eliz., vol. i.   [2] *Ibid.* vol. ii.
[3] *Ibid.* vol. ii.   [4] *Ibid.* Mary, vol. ii.

WILL OF SIR JOHN ROBSART.

(See Note to p. 12.)

In the Norwich Register—WALPOLE, p. 77.

"In the name of God, Amen. I, John Robsart, Esq., bequeath my soule to Almightie God, and my bodie to be buried where it shall please God. *Item*, I give and bequeath to Elizabeth my wiffe all that my Manor of Sydesterne and Newton in the Countie of Norf., with all appurtenances to them belonginge, both free and bonde, wheresover they lie. And also I give and bequeath to the same Elizabeth all that my mannor of Bostentim [?] in the Countie of Suff., with all the singular appurtenances to that belonginge, both free and bond, wheresoever they lie within the said countie, for tearme of her liffe, the remainder to Amye my dawter and her heirs for ever. And as for all my other goodes, both moveables and unmoveables, I give them holie to Elizabeth my wiffe whom I ordeign and make my sole Executrix.

"In witness, &c., dated 6th October, 28 Henry 8th (1537), King of Englande and ffrance, lorde of Ireland, and within the said realme supreme hede of the Church. Immediatlie under God.

"Proved at Norwich 5th July, 1554 [1st Mary] and Administration granted to the widow in the person of [J]ames Biggott."[1]

"Per me, Thomam Alchracke,
"Ricardum Cattyn."

SEDISTERN (page 5). Bloomfield states that Sedistern was granted 3 and 4 Philip and Mary [1557] to Lord Robert for life. Presuming that Sir John Robsert died in 1554, by the terms of the above Will Lord Robert must have come into possession in that year. Amye's mother died in 1549.

[1] James Biggot, or Bigot, was m. to Anna, daughter of Elizabeth Scott, (by her first husband,) and half sister to Amye Robsart. (*See Pedigree on page* 11.)

STANFIELD HALL (p. 12).

"Sir JAMES ALTHAM, an eminent lawyer in his time, was third son of James Altham, of Marks Hall, Essex, Esq., by his first wife, who was sister and heir of Sir Thomas Blancke. He was Reader at Grays Inn, 1602, Sergeant-at-law, 1603, Baron of the Exchequer, 9 Feb., 1606, Knighted by James I. at Whitehall, 15th February following. He raised a plentiful fortune by his profession, and died 21st February, 1616-17 at his seat at Oxley, in Hertfordshire, and buried in the chapel there with his lady" [Daughter of Auditor Sutton.][1]

RAINTHORP HALL (page 15). Now in the possession of the Honorable FREDERICK WALPOLE, M.P. for Norfolk, brother of the Earl of Orford.

COUSIN BLOUNT (note to page 32). Mr. *Craik*, in his "Romance of the Peerage,"[2] thinks that "Cousin [Thomas] Blount" was the second son of Thomas Blount, Esq., of Kidderminster.

Clutterbuck, in his History of Hertfordshire,[3] says, "In 1555, the Princess Elizabeth was taken from the monastery of Ashridge, in the County of Bucks, upon the false pretence of being engaged in Sir Thomas Wyat's rebellion, and was placed at Hatfield under the charge of Sir Thomas Pope, whose wife, Margaret, was the daughter of Walter Blount, of Osbaston, County of Leicester (younger branch of the family of Lord Mountjoy). She was succeeded by her nephew *Thomas Blount*, who is usually called Sir Thomas Pope Blunt."

The latter may have been the "Cousin Blount" to whom Leycester's letters were addressed at the time of the Coroner's Inquest.

[1] Nichols's Biblioth. Topog. Brit., vol. ii, p. 18.
[2] Craik, vol. i, p. 130   [3] Clutterbuck, vol. i, p. 208.

AUTHORS CITED, addition to (p. 62).

EDMUND LODGE, in his Biography of eminent persons, attached to "Portraits of Illustrious Personages," falls into the errors of his predecessors in attaching importance to Ashmole's narrative, without stopping to inquire whence Ashmole derived his information; the circumstance that Ashmole omitted all reference to authority for the statements he made ought to have awakened suspicion, or at all events to have induced some inquiry.

MRS. HYDE, a connection of the family (p. 63).

The Grandfather of Sir Edward Unton, who married Anne, Countess of Warwick (widow of John Earl of Warwick) was Thomas Unton, and he married Elizabeth, daughter and co-heir of John Hyde, of Denchworth.

VERNEY (p. 88). Sir Greville Verney married Catherine daughter of Sir Robert Southwell. Richard Verney, 2nd son, married 1st Mary, daughter of Sir John Prettyman; 2nd Frances Dove, of Upton, co. Northamp.

VERNEY (p. 89). [2] Frances, daughter of George Raleigh, or Rawley, of Farnborough, co. Warwick.

[3] Jane was the sister of Sir Thomas Lucy.

"The DICTUM de KENILWORTH" (referred to on page 102,) was made by twelve persons, bishops and peers of the King's selection; the object of which was to soften the severity of the parliament holden at Winchester, which had entirely confiscated the estates of the rebels and their adherents; instead of which, this decree—that they might not be rendered desperate—sentenced them only to a pecuniary fine of not more than five years' income of their estates nor less than two."

(Beattie's Castles of England, p. 217.)

KENILWORTH (Note to page 106).

On the occasion of the Queen's visit it is stated that she was attended by thirty-one barons, the ladies of her Court, and four hundred inferior servants.—*Beattie.*

"It was in his castle of KENILWORTH that Leicester first married Lady Essex privately; but her father, Sir Francis Knolles, being well acquainted with Leicester's inconstancy, refused to give any credit to it unless the marriage was solemnized in his own presence. In consequence of this resolution, the ceremony was again performed at Wanstead, in presence of the said Sir Francis, Ambrose Earl of Warwick, the Lord North, a public notary, and several other witnesses."

(Beattie's Castles of England, p. 247.)

GROUND PLAN OF KENILWORTH CASTLE, at the time of the Queen's visit in 1575 (facing page 106).

"Consulting the *ground plan* of KENILWORTH, we find that the dungeons lay at the western extremity of the castle, the part which is now most ruinous. They were situated under Mervyn's Tower—a sallyport of the castle, and which we apprehend formed, with Cæsar's Tower, the substance of the original fortress— probably Saxon. This portion of the ruins we examined, but found it a mere shapeless heap, with some indications of strong vaultings, sufficient to justify the belief of their having been places of confinement in the ruder and more warlike days of the Barony. Kenilworth, in the absence of additions absolutely modern, affords specimens of the architecture of more various periods than most English castles. The KEEP or CÆSAR'S TOWER (No. 1) corresponds in some important points with the recognised specimens of Saxon building extant at Bamborough, showing the same narrow buttresses traversing the entire elevation; and a window remaining on the eastern face of the keep, narrow, with a circular arch, and diminishing inward to a mere slit, is of corresponding time. Supposing the body of the Keep to date before the Norman Conquest, we take the wings to be of Norman addition, from their being similar to the castle at Newcastle-on-Tyne, built immediately after the Conquest. Some portions on the western side indicate additions made about the time of Edward the Third, by John of Gaunt, and called Lancaster's Building (No. 2); some of the windows of the Great Hall (15) are beautiful examples of this period. Near this quarter, on the southwestern angle of the group, are some turrets constructed so as to be defended by three arches back to back, the loopholes extending outwards, and giving them the means of annoying an invading party under a sufficient cover. In Leicester Buildings (No. 3) are some elegant remains, particularly a superb Oriel; and in this part are the details of a very delicate and elaborate style."

(*Beattie's Castles of England*, p. 258.)

ROOMS OF STATE (see pages 111, 112).

"THE HALL, in which were held so many splendid reunions and banquets, is still magnificent in decay. Its proportions are ninety feet in length, forty-five in breadth, and the same in height—proportions which were generally observed by the ancient builders in all edifices where harmony of parts and grandeur of effect were to be combined. In the windows the richness of the mouldings and tracery still remains as a proof of what they must have been when, on the decoration of this castle, all that art could accomplish or wealth command was lavishly bestowed . . . On each side of the hall is a fireplace; near to the inner court is an oriel, in plan comprehending five sides of an octagon, and a fireplace. On the side opposite is a recess with a single window and a small closet, said to have been Queen Elizabeth's dressing-room."

LEYCESTER CHIMNEY PIECE (facing page 112).

"This justly-admired specimen of art is of alabaster, finely sculptured with bears and rugged staves, and the monogram of the Earl of Leycester. When freshly gilded, and placed in a becoming situation, it justly deserved, says a writer of taste, to be eulogised as a work of decided skill and merit. Having happily escaped the Cromwellian devastation, the mantel-piece, together with the oaken pillars which surmount it, were removed from one of the principal apartments or presence chamber of Leicester-Buildings, to the room which they now occupy—an oak-pannelled chamber in the old Gate House."

(*Beattie's Castles of England*, p. 260.)

(Page 286.)

WOOD, in his *Athenæ Oxoniensis*,[1] in speaking of Sir Robert Dudley, says:

" It was plainly proved in open Court, before those that were then judges, that he was legitimate.

" He missed his design (that of proving his legitimacy) by the endeavours of Lettice his father's widow, who well knew that if he could obtain it, it would have much redounded to her dishonour, she being his father's reputed wife when this our Robert Dudley was born."

[1] By Bliss, vol. iii, p. 359.

FINIS.

PRINTED BY J. E. ADLARD, BARTHOLOMEW CLOSE, LONDON.

A Catalogue of Books on

HISTORY,
BIOGRAPHY,
TOPOGRAPHY,
HERALDRY,
OLD POETRY,

THE DRAMA,
PHILOLOGY,
BIBLIOGRAPHY,
FINE ARTS,
DIVINITY,

FOLK-LORE,
ARCHÆOLOGY,
AND
MISCELLANEOUS
LITERATURE.

THE PROPERTY OF JOHN RUSSELL SMITH,

On Sale, by Retail, at the annexed Prices, by

ALFRED RUSSELL SMITH,
36, SOHO SQUARE, LONDON, (W.)

HAND-BOOK to the POPULAR, Poetical, and Dramatic Literature of England, from Caxton the first English Printer, to the year 1660. By W. CAREW HAZLITT, one thick vol, 8vo, pp. 716, *in double columns*, half morocco, Roxburghe style. £1. 11s 6d
—— LARGE PAPER, royal 8vo, HALF MOROCCO, ROXBURGHE STYLE. £3. 3s

It will be found indispensable to Book-Collectors and Booksellers. It is far in advance of anything hitherto published on Old English Literature.—Forming a supplement to Lowndes, giving the prices the rare articles have sold for at sales since his time, also of thousands not mentioned by him.

MARTYR TO BIBLIOGRAPHY: A Notice of the Life and Works of JOSEPH-MARIE QUERARD, the French Bibliographer. By OLPHAR HAMST. 8vo (*only 200 printed*). 3s

HANDBOOK for FICTITIOUS NAMES, being a Guide to Authors, chiefly of the Lighter Literature of the XIXth Century, who have written under assumed names; and to Literary Forgers, Impostors, Plagiarists, and Imitators. By OLPHAR HAMST, Esq., *Author of a Notice of the Life and Works of J. M. Querard.* 8vo, *cloth.* 7s 6d
—— THICK PAPER (only 25 copies printed). 15s

An exceedingly curious and interesting book on the bye ways of Literature.

BIBLIOGRAPHY of the Writings of Lord Brougham. By OLPHAR HAMST. Fcap. 8vo. 1s 6d

BLARD (George).—The Sutton-Dudleys of England, and the Dudleys of Massachusetts, in New England. 8vo, *pedigrees, &c., cloth.* 15s

An interesting volume to the English genealogist, it contains a good deal of new matter relating to this old English Family and their collateral branches.

ÆSCHYLUS.—The Orestes of Æschylus, translated into English Verse. By C. N. DALTON, B.A., of Trin. Coll., Camb. Fcp. 8vo, *cloth*, 2s 6d (original price 5s)

AGINCOURT.—A Contribution towards an Authentic List of the Commanders of the English Host in King Henry the Fifth's Expedition. By the Rev. JOSEPH HUNTER, post 8vo. 2s 6d

AKERMAN'S (John Yonge, *Fellow and late Secretary of the Society of Antiquaries*) Archæological Index to Remains of Antiquity of the Celtic, Romano-British, and Anglo-Saxon Periods. 8vo, *illustrated with numerous engravings, comprising upwards of five hundred objects, cloth.* 15s

This work, though intended as an introduction and guide to the study of our early antiquities, will, it is hoped, also prove of service as a book of reference to the practised Archæologist.

AKERMAN'S (J. Y.) Coins of the Romans relating to Britain. Described and Illustrated. *Second edition*, greatly enlarged, 8vo, *with plates and woodcuts, cloth,* 10s 6d

"Mr. Akerman's volume contains a notice of every known variety, with copious illustrations, and is published at a very moderate price; it should be consulted, not merely for these particular coins, but also for facts most valuable to all who are interested in Romano-British History."—*Archæol. Journal.*

AKERMAN'S (J. Y.) Tradesman's Tokens struck in London and its Vicinity, from 1648 to 1671, described from the originals in the British Museum, &c. 8vo, *with 8 plates of numerous examples, cloth.* 7s 6d (original price 15s.)—LARGE PAPER in 4to, *cloth.* 15s

This work comprises a list of nearly 3000 Tokens, and contains occasional illustrative, topographical, and antiquarian notes on persons, places, streets, old tavern and coffee-house signs, &c., &c., with an introductory account of the causes which led to the adoption of such a currency.

AKERMAN'S (J. Y.) Ancient Coins of Cities and Princes, Geographically Arranged and Described—Hispania, Gallia, Britannia. 8vo, *with engravings of many hundred Coins from actual examples*. Cloth 7s 6d (original price 18s)

AKERMAN'S (J. Y.) Introduction to the Study of Ancient and Modern Coins. Foolscap 8vo, *with numerous engravings from the original Coins (an excellent introductory book)*, cloth. 6s 6d

CONTENTS:—SECT. 1—Origin of Coinage—Greek Regal Coins—2. Greek Civic Coins—3. Greek Imperial Coins—4. Origin of Roman Coinage—Consular Coins—5. Roman Imperial Coins—6. Roman British Coins—7. Ancient British Coinage—8. Anglo-Saxon Coinage—9. English Coinage from the Conquest—10. Scotch Coinage—11. Coinage of Ireland—12. Anglo-Gallic Coins—13. Continental Money in the Middle Ages—14. Various Representatives of Coinage—15. Forgeries in Ancient and Modern Times—16. Table of Prices of English Coins realized at Public Sales.

AKERMAN'S (J. Y.) Spring Tide; or, the Angler and his Friends. 12mo, *plates*, cloth. 2s 6d (original price 6s)

These Dialogues incidentally illustrate the Dialect of the West of England.
"Never in our recollection has the contemplative man's recreation been rendered more attractive, nor the delights of a country life set forth with a truer or more discriminating zest than in these pleasant pages."—*Gent.'s Mag.*

AKERMAN'S (J. Y.) Wiltshire Tales, illustrative of the Manners, Customs, and Dialect of that and adjoining Counties. 12mo, *cloth*. 2s 6d

ALFRED (KING)—Memorials of King Alfred, being Essays on the History and Antiquities of England during the Ninth Century—the Age of King Alfred. By various Authors. Edited and in part written by the Rev. Dr. GILES. Royal 8vo, pp. 400, *coloured plate of K. Alfred's Jewel, seven plates of Anglo-Saxon Coins, and views of Grimbald's Crypt*, cloth, 7s 6d

ALLIES (JABEZ, F.S.A.) The Ancient British, Roman, and Saxon Antiquities and Folk-Lore of Worcestershire. 8vo, pp. 500, *with 6 plates and 40 woodcuts*, Second Edition, cloth. 7s 6d (original price 14s)

"The good people of Worcestershire are indebted to Mr. Jabez Allies for a very handsome volume illustrative of the history of their native county. His book, which treats *On the Ancient British, Roman, and Saxon Antiquities and Folk-lore of Worcestershire*, has now reached a second edition; and as Mr. Allies has embodied in this, not only the additions made by him to the original work, but also several separate publications on points of folk-lore and legendary interest, few counties can boast of a more industriously or carefully compiled history of what may be called its popular antiquities. The work is very handsomely illustrated."—*Notes and Queries*.

AMADIS of GAUL. — The Renowned Romance of Amadis of Gaul, by VASCO LOBEIRA, translated from the Spanish version of GARCIORDONEZ DE MONTALVO by ROBT. SOUTHEY. A new edition in 3 vols, fcap. 8vo, *cloth*. 15s.
—— Large Paper. 3 vols, post 8vo, £1. 2s 6d

Amadis of Gaul is among prose, what Orlando Furioso is among metrical romances; not the oldest of its kind, but the best.

AMYE ROBSART and the EARL of Leicester: a Critical Inquiry into the Authenticity of the various Statements in relation to the Death of Amye Robsart, and of the Libels on the Earl of Leicester, with a Vindication of the Earl by his Nephew Sir Philip Sydney: with a History of Kenilworth Castle, including an Account of the splendid entertainment given to Queen Elizabeth, by the Earl of Leicester, in 1575, from the Works of Robert Laneham and George Gascoigne; together with Memoirs and Correspondence of Sir Robert Dudley, Son of the Earl of Leicester. By GEORGE ADLARD, author of "The Sutton-Dudleys of England." A handsome vol, 8vo, pp. 368, *with fine plates*, cloth. 12s

ANCIENT ROLLS of ARMS, No 1. Glover's Roll of the Reign of Henry III, Edited by GEORGE J. ARMYTAGE, F.S.A. 4to, *with frontispiece of Shields*, sewed. 4s
—— No. 2.—Roll of the Reigns of Henry III. and Edward I. By N. CHARLES, *Lancaster Herald*. Edited by GEORGE J. ARMYTAGE, F.S.A. Small 4to, *frontispiece of Arms*. 10s

ANDERSON (WM.) Genealogy and Surnames, with some Heraldic and Biographical Notices. 8vo, *woodcuts of Arms and Seals*, cloth. 3s 6d (original price 6s)

ANECDOTA LITERARIA, a Collection of Short Poems in English, Latin, and French, illustrative of the Literature and History of England in the XIIIth Century, and more especially of the Condition and Manners of the Different Classes of Society, Edited by THOMAS WRIGHT, M.A. 8vo, *cloth, only 250 copies printed*. 5s

ANGLING.—BLAKEY (ROBERT) Historical Sketches of the Angling Literature of all Nations, to which is added a Bibliography of English Writers on Angling by J. R. Smith. Fcap. 8vo, *cloth*. 5s

ANGLING.—SMITH (J. R.) A Bibliographical Catalogue of English Writers on Angling and Ichthyology, (reprinted from the foregoing). Post 8vo. 1s 6d

ANGLO-SAXON.—A Compendious Anglo-Saxon and English Dictionary, by the Rev. J. BOSWORTH, D.D., F.R.S., &c., *Anglo-Saxon Professor in the University of Oxford.* 8vo, *closely printed in treble columns.* 12s

This is not a mere abridgment of the large dictionary, but almost entirely a new work. In this compendious one will be found, at a very moderate price, all that is most practical and valuable in the former expensive edition of 1838, with a great accession of new words and matter."—AUTHOR'S PREFACE.

ANGLO-SAXON.—VERNON'S (E. J., B.A., *Oxon*) Guide to the Anglo-Saxon Tongue, on the Basis of Professor Rask's Grammar; to which are added Reading Lessons in Verse and Prose, with Notes, for the Use of Learners. 12mo, *cloth.* 5s

"Mr. Vernon has, we think, acted wisely in taking Rask for his model; but let no one suppose from the title that the book is merely a compilation from the work of that philologist. The accidence is abridged from Rask, with constant revision, correction, and modification; but the syntax, a most important portion of the book, is original, and is compiled with great care and skill; and the latter half of the volume consists of a well-chosen selection of extracts from Anglo-Saxon writers, in prose and in verse, for the practice of the student, who will find great assistance in reading them from the grammatical notes with which they are accompanied, and from the glossary which follows them. This volume, well studied, will enable anyone to read with ease the generality of Anglo-Saxon writers.—*Literary Gazette.*

ANGLO-SAXON. — Analecta Anglo-Saxonica: a Selection in Prose and Verse, from Anglo-Saxon Authors of various Ages; with a Glossary. Designed chiefly as a first book for students. By BENJAMIN THORPE, F.S.A. A new Edition with corrections and improvements. Post 8vo, *cloth.* 7s 6d

ANGLO-SAXON.—A Delectus; Serving as a First Class-Book to the Language, by the Rev. W. BARNES, B.D., of St. John's College, Cambridge. 12mo, *cloth.* 2s 6d

"To those who wish to possess a critical knowledge of their own Native English, some acquaintance with Anglo-Saxon is indispensable; and we have never seen an introduction better calculated than the present to supply the wants of a beginner in a short space of time. The declensions and conjugations are well stated, and illustrated by reference to Greek, the Latin, French, and other languages. A philosophical spirit pervades every part. The Delectus consists of short pieces on various subjects, with extracts from Anglo-Saxon History and the Saxon Chronicle. There is a good Glossary at the end."—ATHENÆUM.

ANGLO-SAXON.—Introduction to Anglo-Saxon Reading, comprising Ælfric's Homily on the Birthday of St. Gregory, with a Copious Glossary, &c., by L. Langley, F.L.S. 12mo, *cloth.* 2s 6d

Ælfric's Homily is remarkable for beauty of composition, and interesting, as setting forth Augustine's mission to the "Land of the Angles.'

ANGLO-SAXON VERSION of the Life of St. Guthlac, Hermit of Croyland. Printed, for the first time, from a MS. in the Cottonian Library, with a Translation and Notes by CHARLES WYCLIFFE GOODWIN, M.A., Fellow of Catherine Hall, Cambridge. 12mo, *cloth.* 5s

ANGLO-SAXON VERSION of the Hexameron of St. Basil, and the Anglo-Saxon Remains of St. Basil's Admonitio ad Filium Spiritualem. Now first printed from MSS. in the Bodleian Library, with a Translation and Notes by the Rev. H. W. NORMAN. 8vo, *second edition, enlarged, sewed.* 4s

ANGLO - SAXON.—Narratiunculæ Anglice Conscriptæ. De pergamenis exscribebat notis illustrabat eruditis copiam, faciebat T. OSWALD CÓCKAYNE, M.A. 8vo. 5s

Containing Alexander the Great's Letter to Aristotle on the situation of India—Of wonderful things in the East—The Passion of St. Margaret the Virgin—Of the Generation of Man, &c.

ANGLO-SAXON.—A FRAGMENT of Ælfric's Anglo-Saxon Grammar, Ælfric's Glossary, and a Poem on the Soul and Body, of the XIIth Century, discovered among the Archives of Worcester Cathedral, by Sir THOMAS PHILLIPPS, Bart. Folio, PRIVATELY PRINTED, *sewed.* 1s 6d

ANGLO-SAXON and GOTHIC. — Four Versions of the Holy Gospels, viz., in Gothic, A.D. 360; Anglo-Saxon, 995; Wycliffe, 1389; and Tyndale, 1526, in parallel columns, with Preface and Notes by the Rev. Dr. BOSWORTH, Professor of Anglo-Saxon in the University of Oxford, assisted by GEORGE WARING, M.A., of Cambridge and Oxford. One vol, 8vo, *above 600 pages, cloth.* 12s

A very low price has been fixed to ensure an extended sale among students and higher schools.

"The texts are printed in four parallel columns, and very great care appears to have been taken in their collation and correction."—ATHENÆUM.

"We heartily welcome this volume, brought out with so much care and ability . . . It does credit to the printers of the University. . . . . The work is scholarlike, and is a valuable contribution to the materials for Biblical Criticism . . . We heartily commend it to the study of all who are interested either in the philology of the English language, or in the history and formation of our Authorised Version."—THE CHRISTIAN REMEMBRANCER, *a Quarterly Review.*

"It may almost be a question, whether the present volume possesses greater interest for the divine or for the philologist. To the latter it must certainly be interesting from the opportunity which it affords him of marking the gradual development of our language. The four versions of the Gospel, . . . with a learned and instructive preface, and a few necessary notes, form a volume, the value and importance of which need scarcely be insisted upon."—NOTES AND QUERIES.

ARCHÆOLOGIA CAMBRENSIS.—A Record of the Antiquities, Historical, Genealogical, Topographical, and Architectural, of Wales and its Marches. First Series, complete, 4 vols, 8vo, *many plates and woodcuts, cloth.* £2. 2s

Odd Parts may be had to complete Sets.

ARCHÆOLOGICAL INSTITUTE.— Report of the Transactions of the Annual Meeting of the Archæological Institute held at Chichester, July, 1853. 8vo, *many plates and woodcuts, cloth.* 7s 6d

Printed uniformly with the other Annual Congresses of the Institute.

ARCHER FAMILIES.—Memorials of Families of the Surname of Archer in various Counties of England, and in Scotland, Ireland, Barbadoes, America, &c. By Capt J. H. LAWRENCE ARCHER. 4to, *but few copies printed, cloth.* 12s 6d

ARCHERY.—Toxophilus; the School of Shooting (the first English Treatise on *Archery.*) By ROGER ASCHAM, reprinted from the Rev. Dr. Giles's Edition of Ascham's Whole Works. Fcap. 8vo, *cloth.* 2s

ARTHUR (KING). La Mort d'Arthur. The History of King Arthur and the Knights of the Round Table. Compiled by Sir THOMAS MALORY, Knight. Edited from the Edition of 1634, with Introduction and Notes, by THOMAS WRIGHT, M.A., F.S.A. 3 vols. Fcp. 8vo, SECOND AND REVISED EDITION. *cloth.* 15s.

——LARGE PAPER, 3 vols, post 8vo, *cloth.* £1. 2s 6d

The only uncastrated edition. Several others have appeared since this was published, but they all have been abridged or adapted to the capacity of young ladies and gentlemen. It is the storehouse of the legends which Tennyson, Morris, Westwood, Lytton, and others have turned into Poetry.

ASCHAM (ROGER)—The Whole Works OF ROGER ASCHAM, now first collected and revised, with Life of the Author. By the Rev. Dr. GILES, formerly Fellow of C. C. C., Oxford. 4 vols. fcp. 8vo, *cloth.* £1.

——LARGE PAPER, 4 vols, post 8vo, *cloth.* £1. 10s

Ascham is a great name in our national literature. He was one of the first founders of a true English style in prose composition, and of the most respectable and useful of our scholars.—*Retrospective Review.*

AUBREY'S (JOHN, *the Wiltshire Antiquary*) MISCELLANIES. FOURTH EDITION. With some Additions and an Index. Fcp. 8vo, *portrait and cuts, cloth.* 4s

CONTENTS:—Day Fatality, Fatalities of Families and Places, Portents, Omens, Dreams, Apparitions, Voices, Impulses, Knockings, Invisible Blows, Prophecies, Miracles, Magic, Transportation by an Invisible Power, Visions in a Crystal, Converse with Angels, Corpse Candles, Oracles, Ecstasy, Second Sight, &c.; with an Appendix, containing his Introduction to the Survey of North Wiltshire.

AUTOBIOGRAPHY of JOSEPH LISTER (a Nonconformist), of Bradford, Yorkshire, with a contemporary account of the Defence of Bradford and Capture of Leeds, by Parliamentarians, in 1642. Edited by THOS. WRIGHT, F.S.A. 8vo, *cloth.* 2s

AUTOBIOGRAPHY of Thomas Wright, of Birkenshaw, in the County of York, 1736-1797. Edited by his Grandson, THOMAS WRIGHT, M.A., F.S.A. Fcp. 8vo, pp. 376, *cloth.* 5s

Particularly interesting about Bradford, Leeds, Halifax, and their neighbourhoods, and a curious picture of manners and persons in the middle of the last century.

AUTOGRAPHICAL MISCELLANY; A Collection of Autograph Letters, Interesting Documents, &c., executed in facsimile by FREDK. NETHERCLIFT, each facsimile accompanied with a page of letter-press by R. SIMS, of the British Museum. Roy. 4to, A HANDSOME VOL, *extra cloth.* £1. 1s (*original price* £1. 16s)

Containing sixty examples of hitherto unpublished Letters and Documents of Blake, Boileau, Buonaparte, Burns, Calvin, Camden, Carrier, Catherine de Medicis, Charles I., Chatterton, Congreve, Crammer, Cromwell, Danton, D'Aubigne, Dryden, Edward VI., Elizabeth, Elizabeth (sister of Louis XVI.), Franklin, Galilei, Glover, Goethe, Goldsmith, Henry VIII., Hyde (Anne), James II., Jonson, Kepler, Kotzebue, Latimer, Loyola, Louis XIV., Louis XVI., Luther, Maintenon, Maria Antoinette, Marlborough, Marmontel, Mary Queen of Scots, Melancthon, Newton, Penn, Pompadour, Pole (Cardinal), Raleigh, Ridley, Robespierre, Rousseau, Rubens, Sand, Schiller, Spenser, Sterne, Tasso, Voltaire, Walpole (Horace), Washington, Wolfe, Wolsey, Wren, and Young.

For the interesting nature of the documents, this collection far excels all the previous ones. With two exceptions (formerly badly executed), they have never been published before.

AUTOGRAPHS.—A Hand-book to Autographs, being a Ready Guide to the Handwriting of Distinguished Men and Women of every Nation, designed for the Use of Literary Men, Autograph Collectors, and others. Executed by FREDERICK GEO. NETHERCLIFT. 8vo, *above* 700 *specimens, cloth.* 10s 6d

— Printed *upon* one side only. 8vo, *cloth.* 15s

The specimens contain two or three lines each besides the signature, so that to the historian such a work will recommend itself as enabling him to test the genuineness of the document he consults, whilst the judgment of the autograph collector may be similarly assisted, and his pecuniary resources economized by a judicious use of the "Manual." To the bookworm, whose name is "legion," it may be observed that daily experience teaches us the great value and interest attached to books containing "marginal notes" and "memoranda," when traced to be from the pens of eminent persons.

Books on Sale at Smith's, 36, Soho Square, London.   5

AUTOGRAPH SOUVENIR; a Collection of Autograph Letters, Interesting Documents, &c., Selected from the British Museum, and from other sources, Public and Private, *executed in facsimile* by FREDERICK GEO. NETHERCLIFT, with Letterpress Transcriptions and occasional Translations, &c., by RICHARD SIMS, *of the British Museum.* 4to, *cloth, a handsome volume, gilt leaves.* £2. 2s

The examples are different from any other collection.

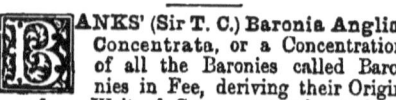ANKS' (Sir T. C.) **Baronia Anglia, Concentrata,** or a Concentration of all the Baronies called Baronies in Fee, deriving their Origin from Writ of Summons, and not from any Specific Limited Creation, showing the Descent and Line of Heirship, as well of those Families mentioned by Sir William Dugdale, as of those whom that celebrated Author has omitted to notice: interspersed with Interesting Notices and Explanatory Remarks. Whereto is added, the proofs of Parliamentary Sitting, from the Reign of Edward I. to Queen Anne; also, *a Glossary of Dormant English, Scotch, and Irish Peerage Titles, with reference to presumed existing Heirs.* 2 vols, 4to, *cloth.* 15s (original price £3. 3s)

—— LARGE PAPER COPY (*very few printed*). 2 vols. £1. 1s

A book of great research, by the well-known author of the "Dormant and Extinct Peerage," and other heraldic and historical works. Those fond of genealogical pursuits ought to secure a copy while it so cheap. It may be considered a supplement to his former works. Vol. ii., pp. 210-300, contains an Historical Account of the first Settlement in Nova Scotia, and the foundation of Nova Scotia Baronets, distinguishing those who had seizin of lands there.

BARBER (G. D., *commonly called Barber-Beaumont*) Suggestions on the Ancient Britons, in 3 parts. Thick 8vo, *cloth.* 7s 6d (*original price* 14s)

BARKER.—Literary Anecdotes and Contemporary Reminiscences of Professor Porson and others, from the Manuscript Papers of the late E. H. Barker, Esq., of Thetford, Norfolk, with an Original Memoir of the Author. 2 vols, 8vo, *cloth.* 12s

A singular book, full of strange stories and jests. Only 120 copies were printed.

BARNES' (Rev. **William,** *of Came Rectory, Dorchester*) A Philological Grammar, grounded upon English, and formed from a comparison of more than Sixty Languages. Being an Introduction to the Science of Grammars of all Languages, especially English, Latin, and Greek. 8vo, (pp. 322), *cloth.* 9s

BARNES' (Rev. **W.**) **Tiw; or a View of the Roots and Stems of the English as a Teutonic Tongue.** Fcap. 8vo, *cloth.* 5s

"I hold that my primary roots are the roots of all the Teutonic languages; and, if my view is the true one, it must ultimately be taken up by the German and other Teutonic grammarians, and applied to their languages."—*The Author.*

BARNES' (Rev. **W.**) **Early England and the Saxon English**; with some Notes on the Father Stock of the Saxon English, the Frisians. Fcap. 8vo, *cloth.* 3s

BARNES' (Rev. **W.**) **Notes on Ancient Briton and the Britons.** Fcap. 8vo, *cloth.* 3s

"Mr. Barnes has given us the result of his collection for a course of Lectures on the subject, and has produced a series of Sketches of the Ancient Britons, their language, laws, modes of life, and of their social state as compared with that of the Saxons, which will be read with considerable interest."—*Notes and Queries.*

BARNES' (Rev. **W.**) **Views of Labour and Gold.** Fcp. 8vo, *cloth.* 3s

"The title, 'Views of Labour and Gold,' cannot be said to indicate the scope of the Essays, which open with pictures of primitive life, and pass on, through an agreeably diversified range of topics, to considerations of the rights, duties, and interests of Capital and Labour, and to the enquiry, What constitutes the utility, wealth, and positive well-being of a nation? Subjects of this class are rarely handled with so firm a grasp and such light and artistic manipulation."—*Athenæum.*

BERKSHIRE.—History and Antiquities of the Hundred of Bray, in Berkshire. By the Rev. CHAS. KELLY. 8vo, *cloth.* 7s 6d

—— The same, *with* 10 *folding pedigrees, cloth.* 10s 6d

BERKSHIRE.— WINDSOR.—ANNALS of Windsor, being a History of the Castle and Town, with some Account of Eton and Places Adjacent. By R. R. TIGHE and J. E. DAVIS, Esqs. In 2 thick vols, royal 8vo, *illustrated with many engravings, coloured and plain, extra cloth,* £1. 5s (*original price* £4. 4s)

"We have read, not indeed every word, but not much less than the whole of this book, with a satisfaction which we think every one will share who has given any serious study or attention to English history, and with a strong impression of the good taste, industry, and literary skill of the authors. . . . . We have chosen only one or two illustrations of the contents of the 'Annals of Windsor,' in order to show their historical value; but they furnish a vast quantity of information, possessing much general and literary interest, at which our space will not allow us even to glance."—*The Saturday Review.*

"Windsor is a grand subject! The historian, the poet, the artist, the statesman, the soldier, the courtier, the player,—from mantled king to gaping citizen,—there does not exist a man who is not interested in this old pile, its vicinity, and its traditions. . . . . These volumes may be consulted with good result by any one anxious to discover any circumstance, important or trivial, concerning Windsor, which has ever been recorded."—*The Athenæum.*

BEDFORD'S (Rev. W. K. Riland) The Blazon of Episcopacy, being a complete List of the Archbishops and Bishops of England and Wales, and their Family Arms, drawn and described, from the first introduction of Heraldry to the present time. 8vo, 144 *pages, and* 62 *pages of drawings of Arms, cloth.* 15s
This work depicts the arms of a great number of English Families not to be found in other works.
" There has been an amount of industry bestowed upon this curious work which is very creditable to the author, and will be found beneficial to all who care for the subject on which it has been employed."—ATHENÆUM.

BERRY'S (W.) Pedigrees and Arms of the Nobility and Gentry of Hertfordshire. Folio (only 125 printed), *bds.* £1. 10s (*original price* £3. 10s)

BIBLIOTHEQUE ASIATIQUE et Africane, ou Catalogue des Ouvrages relatifs a l'Asie et a l'Afrique qui ont paru jusqu'en 1700, par H. TERNAUX-COMPANS. 8vo, *avec supplement et index, sewed.* 10s 6d

"BIBLIA PAUPERUM." One of the earliest and most curious BLOCK BOOKS, reproduced in facsimile from a copy in the British Museum, by J. Ph. BERJEAU. Royal 4to, *half bound.* £2. 2s.
As a specimen of the earliest woodcuts and of printed block-books, destined to supersede the manuscripts anterior to the valuable invention of Guttenberg, the BIBLIA PAUPERUM is well worthy the attention of the amateur of Fine Arts as well as of the Bibliographer. It consists of 40 engravings, printed on one side only of the leaves, and disposed so as to have the figures opposite to each other.
The engravings were printed by friction, with a substance of a brownish colour instead of printing ink, which was unknown at this early period. To imitate as nearly as possible the original, the plates in this facsimile are disposed opposite each other, and printed in a brownish colour. Various editions of this BlockBook have been discovered, without any writer being able to say which is the first one. A review of them is given in the printed Introduction of the book.
Besides the rhymed Latin Poetry—of which part was given by Heinecken, and after him by Ottley—the Introduction gives, for the first time, the whole of the Text printed on both sides in the upper compartment, as well as an English Explanation of the subject.
ONLY 250 COPIES HAVE BEEN PRINTED, UNIFORMLY WITH MR. S. LEIGH SOTHEBY'S *Principia Typographica.*

BLOOMFIELD.—Selection from the Correspondence of Robert Bloomfield, the Suffolk Poet. Edited by W H. HART, F.S.A. 8vo, pp. 28, *sewed.* 1s 6d

BROOKE (R.) A Descriptive Account of Liverpool, as it was during the last Quarter of the XVIIIth Century, 1775—1800. A handsome vol, royal 8vo, *with illustrations, cloth.* 12s 6d (*original price* £1. 5s)

BROOKE (RICHARD, F.S.A.) Visits to Fields of Battle in England, of the XVth Century, with some Miscellaneous Tracts and Papers, principally upon Archæological Subjects. Royal 8vo, *plates, cloth.* 15s
The work contains a descriptive account of the scenes of most of the memorable conflicts in the Wars of York and Lancaster, comprising the celebrated battles of Shrewsbury, Blore Heath, Northampton, Wakefield, Mortimer's Cross, Towton, Barnet, Tewkesbury, Bosworth, and Stoke, and genealogical and other particulars of the powerful, warlike, and distinguished personages who were the principal actors in those stirring and eventful times, with plans of some of the fields of Battle, and an Appendix containing the principal Acts of Attainder relative to the Wars of the Roses, and Lists of the Noblemen, Knights, and other personages attainted by them.

BUCKHURST (LORD) The Dramatic and Poetical Works of THOMAS SACKVILLE Lord Buckhurst, and Earl of Dorset. With Introduction and Life by the present LORD BUCKHURST. Fcap. 8vo, *cloth, fine portrait from a picture at Buckhurst, now first engraved.* 4s.

BURKE'S (JOHN) GENEALOGICAL and Heraldic History of the Extinct and Dormant Baronetcies of England, Ireland, and Scotland. Medium 8vo, SECOND EDITION, 638 *closely printed pages,* in *double columns, with about* 1000 *Arms engraved on wood, fine port. of* JAMES I., *cloth.* 10s (*original price* £1. 8s)
This work engaged the attention of the author for several years, comprises nearly a thousand families, many of them amongst the most ancient and eminent in the kingdom, each carried down to its representatives still existing, with elaborate and minute details of the alliances, achievements, and fortunes, generation after generation, from the earliest to the latest period.

BURN'S (J. S.) History of Parish Registers in England, and Registers of Scotland, Ireland, the Colonies, Episcopal Chapels in and about London, the Geneva Register of the Protestant Refugees, with Biographical Notes, etc. *Second edition, greatly enlarged,* 8vo, *cloth.* 10s 6d

BURN'S (J. S.) The High Commission, Notices of the Court and its Proceedings. 8vo, *cloth, only* 100 *printed.* 3s.

BURN'S (J. S.) The Star Chamber.— Notices of the Court and its Proceedings, with a few Additional Notes on the High Commission. 8vo, *cloth.* 5s

ALTON'S (R. BELL) Annals and Legends of Calais, with Sketches of Emigré Notabilities, and Memoirs of Lady Hamilton. Post 8vo, *with frontispiece and vignette, cloth.* 5s
A very interesting book on England's first Colony, the only English book written on this singular place.

Books on Sale at Smith's, 36, Soho Square, London. 7

CAMDEN'S (WILLIAM) REMAINS Concerning Britain. Fcp. 8vo, *fine portrait, cloth.* 6s

—— LARGE PAPER, Post 8vo, *cloth.* 7s 6d

The eighth edition of this interesting volume by Camden, the famous Antiquary, consisting of little essays and scraps, which did not come within the scope of his "Britannia."

CARDWELL (REV. DR., *Professor of Ancient History, Oxford*) Lectures on the Coinage of the Greeks and Romans, delivered in the University of Oxford. 8vo, *cloth.* 4s (*original price* 8s 6d)

"A very interesting historical volume, and written in a pleasing and popular manner.

CARTWRIGHT.—Memoirs of the Life, Writings, and Mechanical Inventions of Edmund Cartwright, D.D., F.R.S., *Inventor of the Power Loom, &c.* Edited by E. H. STRICKLAND. Post 8vo, *engravings, boards.* 2s 6d (*original price* 10s 6d)

It contains some interesting literary history, Dr. Cartwright numbering among his correspondents, Sir W. Jones, Crabbe, Sir H. Davy, Fulton, Sir S. Raffles, Langhorne, and others. He was no mean Poet, as his legendary tale of "Armine and Elvira" (given in the Appendix) testifies. Sir W. Scott says it contains some excellent poetry,expressed with unusual felicity.

CHATTO (W. A., *Author of "Jackson's History of Wood Engravings"*) Facts and Speculations on the History of PLAYING CARDS in Europe. 8vo, *profusely illustrated with engravings, both plain and coloured, cloth.* £1. 1s

"The inquiry into the origin and signification of the suits and their marks, and the heraldic, theological, and political emblems pictured from time to time, in their changes, opens a new field of antiquarian interest : and the perseverance with which Mr. Chatto has explored it, leaves little to be gained by his successors. The plates with which the volume is enriched add considerably to its value in this point of view. It is not to be denied that, take it altogether, it contains more matter than has ever before been collected in one view upon the same subject. In spite of its faults it is exceedingly amusing ; and the most critical reader cannot fail to be entertained by the variety of curious outlying learning Mr. Chatto has somehow contrived to draw into the investigation."

"THE GAME OF THE CHESSE," the First Book printed in England by William Caxton, reproduced in facsimile from a copy in the British Museum, with a few Remarks on Caxton's Typographical Productions by Vincent FIGGINS. 4to, pp. 184, *with* 23 *curious woodcuts, half morocco, uncut.* £1. 1s—or, *in antique calf, with bevelled boards and carmine edges.* £1. 8s

Frequently as we read of the works of Caxton and the early English Printers, and of their Black Letter Books, very few persons ever had the opportunity of seeing any of these productions, and forming a proper estimate of the ingenuity and skill of those who first practised the "Noble Art of Printing."
THE TYPE HAS BEEN CAREFULLY IMITATED, AND THE WOODCUTS FACSIMILED BY MISS BYFIELD. The Paper and Watermarks have also been made expressly, as near as possible, like the original : and the book is accompanied by a few remarks of a practical nature, which have been suggested during the progress of the count, and the necessary study and comparison of

Caxton's Works with those of his contemporaries in Germany, by Mr. V. FIGGINS, who spent two years' "labour of love" in cutting the matrixes for the type.

COLLECTION OF LETTERS, on Scientific Subjects, illustrative of the Progress of Science in England. Temp. Elizabeth to Charles II. Edited by J. O. HALLIWELL. 8vo, *cloth.* 3s

Comprising letters of Digges, Dee, Tycho Brahe, Lower, Hariott, Lydyatt, Sir W. Petty, Sir C. Cavendish, Brancker, Pell, etc. ; also the Autobiography of Sir Samuel Morland, from a MS. in Lambeth Palace, Nat. Tarpoley's Corrector Analyticus, etc.

COMBERBACH FAMILY.—Collection for a Genealogical Account of the Family of Comberbach (of Cheshire, etc.) By G. W. MARSHALL. 8vo, *plate of Arms, &c., cloth.* 5s

CORNWALL. — Footprints of Former Men in Far Cornwall (Sketches of Places, Men, and Manners). By the Rev. R. S. HAWKER, Vicar of Morwenstow, Author of "Cornish Ballads," etc. Crown 8vo, *cloth.* 5s

CORNWALL. — HALLIWELL's (J. O.) Rambles in Western Cornwall, by the Footsteps of the Giants ; with Notes on the Celtic Remains of the Land's End District and the Isles of Scilly. Fcp. 4to, *elegantly printed by Whittingham, cloth.* 7s 6d

CORNWALL. — EDMOND'S (R., *late of Penzance*) The Land's End District. its Antiquities, Natural History, Natural Phenomena, and Scenery ; also a Brief Memoir of Richard Trevithick, C. E. 8vo, *maps, plates, and woodcuts, cloth.* 7s 6d

CORNWALL.—KYNANCE COVE ; or, The Cornish Smugglers, A Tale of the Last Century. By W. B. FORFAR, *Author of* "Pentowan," "Pengersick Castle," *etc.*, Fcp. 8vo, *boards.* 2s

CORNWALL.—PEDLER (E. H., *of Liskeard*) The Anglo-Saxon Episcopate of Cornwall, with some Account of the Bishops of Crediton. 8vo, *cloth.* 3s 6d (*original price* 7s 6d)

COSIN'S (MR., *Secretary to the Commissioners of Forfeited Estates*) Names of the Roman Catholics, Non Jurors, and others, who Refused to take the Oaths to King George I., together with their Titles, Additions, Places of Abode, the Parishes and Townships where their Lands lay,the Names of the then Tenants, and the Annual Value of them as returned by themselves. *Reprinted from the Edition of* 1745. 8vo, *cloth.* 5s

A curious book for the Topographer and Genealogist.

CRASHAW. — The Poetical Works of RICHARD CRASHAW, Author of "Steps to the Temple," "Sacred Poems, with other Delights of the Muses," and " Poemata," now first collected. Edited by W. B. TURNBULL. Fcp. 8vo, *cloth*. 5s.

"*He seems to have resembled Herbert in the turn of mind, but possessed more fancy and genius.*"—ELLIS.

EFOE.—The Life and Times of Daniel De Foe, with Remarks, Digressive and Discursive. By WILL. CHADWICK. 8vo, pp. 472, *portrait, cloth*. 5s. (original price 10s 6d)

DERBYSHIRE.—BATEMAN'S (Thos., *of Youlgrave, Derbyshire*) Vestiges of the Antiquities of Derbyshire, and the Sepulchral Usages of its Inhabitants, from the most Remote Ages to the Reformation. 8vo, *with numerous woodcuts of Tumuli and their contents, Crosses, Tombs, &c., cloth*. 15s

DERBYSHIRE.—BIGSBY's (ROBERT, M.A., LL.D.) Historical and Topographical Description of Repton, in the County of Derby, with Incidental View of objects of note in its Vicinity. 4to, a handsome volume, *with* SEVENTY *illustrations on copper, stone, and wood, cloth*. 18s (*original price* £3. 3s)

DEVON.—KING'S (R. J.) The Forest of Dartmoor and its Borders in Devonshire, an Historical Sketch. Foolscap 8vo, *cloth*. 3s

DORSET.—WARNE'S (CHARLES, F.S.A.) The Celtic Tumuli of Dorset ; and Account of Personal and other Researches in the Sepulchral Mounds of the Durotriges. Folio, *plates and woodcuts, cloth*. £1. 10s

DRUMMOND's (WILLIAM, *Of Hawthornden*) Poetical Works. Now first published entire. Edited by W. B. TURNBULL. Fcp. 8vo, *fine portrait, cloth*, 5s

"*The sonnets of Drummond,*" says Mr. Hallam, "*are polished and elegant, free from conceit and bad taste, and in pure unblemished English.*"

DURHAM.—RAINE (REV. JAMES) History and Antiquities of North Durham, as subdivided into the Shires of Norham, Island, and Bedlington, which from the Saxon period until 1844 constituted part of the County of Durham, but are now united to Northumberland. BOTH PARTS complete, folio, *fine plates* (wanting 3 plates in the first part) bds. £1. 5s

——— Part II. (*wanting by many Subscribers*) quite complete. 18s. LARGE PAPER. £1. 1s

DURHAM.—RAINE (REV. JAMES) Historical Account of the Episcopal Castle or Palace of Auckland. Royal 4to, *fine views, portraits, and seals, cloth*. 10s 6d (*original price* £1. 1s)

DURHAM.—Illustrations of the Architectural Antiquities of the County of Durham, Ecclesiastical, Castellated, and Domestic. By R. W. BILLINGS. 4to, 61 *fine plates, bds*. £1. 1s (*original price* £2. 2s)

ARLY POPULAR POETRY.— Remains of the EARLY POPULAR POETRY OF ENGLAND, collected and edited by W. CAREW HAZLITT. 4 vols, fcp. 8vo, *with many curious woodcut facsimiles, cloth*. £1

——— LARGE PAPER, 4 vols, post 8vo, *cloth*. £1. 10s

ELLIS'S (W. SMITH) Antiquities of Heraldry, collected from Literature, Coins, Gems, Vases, and other Monuments of Pre-Christian and Mediæval Times ; with a Catalogue of EARLY ARMORIAL SEALS ; tending to show that Modern Heraldry embodies or is derived from the Religious Symbols, the Military Devices, and the Emblems of the Heathen Deities of Antiquity. A handsome volume, 8vo, pp. 300, *with* 20 *plates, cloth*. 7s 6d (*original price* 15s)

ELLIS FAMILIES. — Notices of the Ellises of England, Scotland, and Ireland, including the Families of Alis, Fitz-Elys, Helles, &c. By W. SMITH ELLIS, of the Middle Temple. 8vo, *arms and plates*, (very few printed) *cloth*. £1. 1s

ENGLAND as seen by Foreigners in the Days of Elizabeth and James and the First, comprising Translations of the Journals of the two Dukes of Wirtemberg in 1592 and 1610, both illustrative of Shakespeare. With Extracts from the Travels of Foreign Princes and others. With Copious Notes, an Introduction, and Etchings. By WILLIAM BRENCHLEY RYE, *Assistant Keeper of the Department of Printed Books, British Museum*. Thick foolscap 4to, *elegantly printed by Whittingham, extra cloth*. 15s

"*This curious volume has been the labour of a scholar's love, and will be read with ease by all. The idea of assembling the testimonies of foreign visitors, and showing us how we appeared to others in the days of Bess, by way of contrast and comparison to the aspect we present in the days of Victoria, was one which involved much arduous research. Mr. Rye had had no predecessor. . . . . He has not only added an introduction to the works he assembles and translates, but has enriched them with some hundred pages of notes on all kinds of subjects, exhibiting a wide and minute research.*"—*Fortnightly Review*. (G. H. LEWES.)

"*A book replete both with information and amusement, furnishing a series of very curious pictures of England in the Olden Times.*"—*Notes and Queries*.

Books on Sale at Smith's, 36, Soho Square, London. 9

ENGLISH COINS.—A Guide to the Study and Arrangement of English Coins. By H. W. HENFREY, Member of the Numismatic Society of London. *With plates and woodcuts*, post 8vo, *cloth*. 7s 6d
A very useful and compendious History of English Coins, and what will interest collectors, it gives the price the rarest coins have sold for in auctions of late years.

ENGLISH RETRACED, or Remarks on the "Breeches" Bible (the Genevan Version) and the English of the present day. Post 8vo, *cloth*. 2s (pub at 5s)
An ingenious and instructive volume, the result of a good deal of reading.

EPITAPHS—NORFOLK'S (H. E.) Gleanings in Graveyards: a Collection of Curious Epitaphs. *Third Edition, revised and enlarged*, fcap. 8vo, *cloth*. 3s

EPITAPHS.—A Collection of Curious and Interesting Epitaphs copied from the Monuments of Distinguished and Noted Characters in the Ancient Church and Burial Grounds of Saint Pancras, Middlesex. By F. T. CANSICK. Post 8vo, *plates, cloth*. 7s 6d
———LARGE PAPER, 4to, *cloth*. 15s
———VOL II (Completing the Parish of St Pancras, including Highgate Cemetery). Post 8vo, *cloth*. 7s 6d
———LARGE PAPER 4to, *cloth*. 15s

ESSAYS on the DRAMA. BY W. BONHAM DONNE (*the present Licenser of Plays*). Post 8vo, *cloth*. 2s (original price 6s)
CONTENTS: — Athenian Comedy; Beaumont and Fletcher; Plays and their Providers; Songs from the Dramatists; The Drama; Charles Kemble; The Drama Past and Present; Popular Amusements.

ESSEX.—HADFIELD (JAMES, *Architect*) Ecclesiastical Architecture of the County of Essex, from the Norman Era to the Sixteenth Century, with Plans, Elevations, Sections, Details, &c., from a Series of Measured Drawings, and Architectural and Chronological Descriptions. Royal 4to, 80 *plates, leather back, cloth sides*. £1. 11s 6d

ESSEX.—The Parish of Waltham Abbey, its History and Antiquities. By JAMES MAYNARD. Post 8vo, *engravings, sewed*, 1s—*cloth*. 2s

EVANS (JOHN, F.S.A., *Secretary to the Numismatic Society*) Coins of the Ancient Britons, Arranged and Described. Thick 8vo, *many plates, engraved by F. W. Fairholt, F.S.A., and cuts, cloth, a handsome volume*. £1. 1s
The "Prix de Numismatique" has been awarded by the French Academie des Inscriptions et Belles Lettres, to the author, for this book.

**INLAYSON (JAMES) Surnames and Sirenames, the Origin and History of certain Family and Historical Names, and Remarks on the Ancient Right of the Crown to Sanction and Veto the Assumption of Names, and an Historical Account of the Names of Buggey and Bugg. 8vo. 1s 6d (*original price 3s 6d*)

FRENEAU (PHILIP) Poems on Various Subjects, but chiefly illustrative of the Events and Actors in the American War of Independence, *reprinted from the rare edition printed at Philadelphia in 1786, with a Preface*. Thick fcap. 8vo, *elegantly printed, cloth*. 6s
Freneau enjoyed the friendship of Adams, Franklin, Jefferson, Madison, and Munroe, and the last three were his constant correspondents while they lived. His Patriotic Songs and Ballads, which were superior to any metrical compositions then written in America, were everywhere sung with enthusiasm. See Griswold's "Poets and Poetry of America," and Duyckinck's "Cyclop. of American Literature."

ILES (REV. DR.) The Writings of the Christians of the Second Century, namely, Athenagoras, Tatian, Theophilus, Hermias, Papias, Aristides, Quadratus, etc., collected and first translated, complete. 8vo, *cloth*. 7s 6d
Designed as a continuation of Abp. Wake's *Apostolical Epistles*, which are those of the first century.

GILES (REV. DR.) Heathen Records to the Jewish Scripture History, containing all the Extracts from the Greek and Latin Writers in which the Jews and Christians are named, collected together and translated into English, with the original Text in juxtaposition. 8vo, *cloth*. 7s 6d

GILES (REV. DR.) Codex Apocryphus Novi Testamenti the Uncanonical Gospels and other Writings referring to the First Ages of Christianity, in the original Languages of Arabic, Greek, and Latin, collected together from the editions of Fabricius, Thilo and others. 2 vols, 8vo, *cloth*. 14s

GRENVILLE (HENRY) A Chronological Synopsis of the Four Gospels, on a new plan, with Notes. 8vo, *cloth*. 1s 6d
The most useful and comprehensive Synopsis ever published, it will be found of great utility to Preachers and Students in Divinity.

GUDE AND GODLIE BALLATES, a Compendious Book of Psalms and Spiritual Songs commonly known as "The Gude and Godlie Ballates," Reprinted from Edinburgh edition of 1578, with Introduction, Glossary, etc., by David Laing. Fcp. 8vo, *cloth*. 7s 6d

GWYNN AND OTWAY. — A Memorial of Nell Gwynne the Actress, and Thomas Otway the Dramatist. By W. H. HART. 4to. 6d

HAIGH'S (DANIEL HENRY, *M.A.*) The Conquest of Britain by the Saxons. A Harmony of the History of the Britons, the Works of Gildas, the "Brut," and the Saxon Chronicle, with reference to the Events of the Fifth and Sixth Centuries. 8vo, *plates of Runic Inscriptions, cloth.* 15s

HAIGH'S (DANIEL HENRY, *M.A.*) The Anglo-Saxon Sagas, an Examination of their value as aids to History, serving as a Sequel to "The Conquest of Britain by the Saxons." 8vo, *cloth.* 8s 6d
It analyses and throws new historical evidence on the origin of the Poems of Beowulf, the Lament of Deor, the Saga of Waldhere, Scyld Scefing, the fight at Finnesham, the Story of Horn, the Lay of Hildebrand, etc.

HALLIWELL'S (J. O., *F.R.S., &c.*) Dictionary of Archaic and Provincial Words, Obsolete Phrases, Proverbs, and Ancient Customs, from the Reign of Edward I. 2 vols, 8vo, containing upwards of 1,000 pages, *closely printed in double columns, cloth, a new and cheaper edition.* 15s
It contains above 50,000 words (embodying all the known scattered glossaries of the English language), forming a complete key for the reader of our old Poets, Dramatists, Theologians, and other authors, whose works abound with allusions, of which explanations are not to be found in ordinary Dictionaries and books of reference. Most of the principal Archaisms are illustrated by examples selected from early inedited MSS. and rare books, and by far the greater portion will be found to be original authorities.

HALLIWELL'S (J. O.) The Manuscript Rarities of the University of Cambridge. 8vo, *bds.* 3s (*original price* 10s 6d)
A companion to Hartshorne's "Book Rarities" of the same university.

HALLIWELL'S (J. O.) A Dictionary of Old English Plays, existing either in print or in manuscript, from the earliest times to the close of the 17th Century, including also notices of Latin Plays written by English Authors during the same period, with particulars of their Authors, Plots, Characters, &c. 8vo, *cloth.* 12s
Twenty-five copies have been printed on THICK PAPER, price £1. 1s.

HALLIWELL'S (J. O.) Introduction to the Evidences of Christianity. Fcp. 8vo, 2nd EDITION, *cloth.* 1s 6d (*original price* 3s 6d)
The only book which contains in a popular form the Ancient Heathen unconscious testimonies to the truth of Christianity.

HANTS.—AN Extension of the Latin text and an English translation of the Domesday Book for HAMPSHIRE, with notes by H. MOODY. 4to, *cloth.* 7s 6d

HANTS.—BAIGENT (F. J., *of Winchester*) History and Antiquities of the Parish Church of Wyke, near Winchester. 8vo, *engravings.* 2s 6d

HANTS.—WILLIAM RUFUS, his Tomb in Winchester Cathedral, Account of the Opening, &c. By T. W. Richards. 8vo, 36 pp., 3 *plates, sewed.* 1s 6d

HART'S (W. H.) Index Expurgatorius Anglicanus, or a Descriptive Catalogue of the Principal Books printed or published in England, which have been Suppressed, or Burnt by the Common Hangman, or Censured, or for which the Author, Printer, or Publisher have been Prosecuted. 8vo, Part I. 2s

HARTLIB.—A Biographical Memoir of Samuel Hartlib, Milton's familiar friend, with Bibliographical Notices of Works published by him, and a reprint of his Pamphlet entitled "An Invention of Engines of Motion." By HENRY DIRCKS, C.E., author of the Life of the Marquis of Worcester, &c. Post 8vo, *cloth.* 3s 6d
To have been the familiar friend of Milton, the correspondent of Boyle and Evelyn, Pepys and Wren, and to have had the honour of suggesting to Milton his tract on Education, and of receiving his high praise in his own lofty and sonorous language, is honour enough to make Hartlib's name and life worthy of a special work.

HEARNE. — Reliquæ Hearnianæ. The Remains of THOMAS HEARNE, (the Antiquary) M.A., of Edmund Hall, Oxon, being Extracts from his Diaries. Edited by Dr. P. BLISS, late Principal of St. Mary Hall. SECOND EDITION, *with additions and a new index.* 3 vols, fcp. 8vo, *port., cloth.* 15s
——— LARGE PAPER, 3 vols, post 8vo, *cloth,* £1. 2s 6d
One of the most gossipping diaries that has ever been published more so to those fond of bibliography, biography, and antiquities. Poor Tom's inveterate Jacobinical tendencies often led him into amusing scrapes.

HERALDRY OF SMITH, being a Collection of the Arms borne by, or attributed to most Families of that Surname in Great Britain, Ireland, and Germany, compiled from the Harleian MSS., and other Authentic Sources. By H. SYDNEY GRAZEBROOK. Small 4to, *elegantly printed in antique type by Whittingham, cloth.* 15s
The above work contains a correct heraldic description of the Armorial Insignia of nearly every known armigerous Family of the surname of Smith, Smyth, etc., (about 250 in number) and is illustrated with 32 plates.

Books on Sale at Smith's, 36, Soho Square, London.

comprising 125 Shields of Arms copied in facsimile from a curious manuscript in the Harleian Collection in the British Museum.
A few copies are issued with the Arms coloured, for which early application is necessary. Price £2. 2s

HERALDRY of SMITH of Scotland with Genealogical Annotations. By F. M. SMITH, Capt., R. A. 4to, 3s 6d
Forming a supplement to H. S. Grazebrook's Heraldry of Smith (the previous article.)

HERBERT'S (Hon. Algernon) *Cyclops Christianus*, or an Argument to disprove the supposed Antiquity of Stonehenge and other Megalithic Erections in England and Brittany. 8vo, *cloth*. 4s (*original price* 6s)

HEREFORD.—Helps to Hereford History, Civil and Legendary, in an Ancient Account of the Ancient-Cordwainers' Company of the City, the Mordiford Dragon, and other Subjects. By J. D. DEVLIN. 12mo, *cloth* (*a curious volume*). 3s 6d

HERRICK.—Hesperides, The Poems and other Remains of Robert Herrick, now first collected and edited by W. Carew Hazlitt. 2 vols, fcap. 8vo, *frontispiece after Marshall, cloth*. 8s.
—— LARGE PAPER, 2 vols, post 8vo, *cloth*. 15s

HOMER.—THE ILIADS OF HOMER, Prince of Poets, never before in any language truly translated, with a Comment on some of his chief Places. Done according to the Greek by GEORGE CHAPMAN, with Introduction and Notes by the Rev. RICHARD HOOPER. 2 vols, sq. fcp. 8vo. SECOND and REVISED EDITION, *with portrait of Chapman, and frontispiece*. 12s

"The translation of Homer, published by George Chapman, is one of the greatest treasures the English language can boast."—*Godwin.*
"With Chapman, Pope had frequent consultations, and perhaps never translated any passage till he read his version."—*Dr. Johnson.*
"He covers his defects with a daring, fiery spirit, that animates his translation, which is something like what one might imagine Homer himself to have writ before he arrived at years of discretion."—*Pope.*
"Chapman's translation, with all its defects, is often exceedingly Homeric, which Pope himself seldom obtained."—*Hallam.*
"Chapman writes and feels as a Poet—as Homer might have written had he lived in England in the reign of Queen Elizabeth."—*Coleridge.*
"I have just finished Chapman's Homer. Did you ever read it?—it has the most continuous power of interesting you all along. . . . The earnestness and passion which he has put into every part of these poems would be incredible to a reader of a mere modern translation."—*Charles Lamb.*

HOMER'S ODYSSEY, Translated according to the Greek by GEORGE CHAPMAN. With Introduction and Notes by Rev. RICHARD HOOPER. 2 vols, sq. fcp. 8vo, Second and Revised Edition, *with facsimile of the rare original frontispiece*. 12s

HOMER'S Battle of the F HESIOD'S Works and I Hero and Leander; JU tire. Translated by GI Edited by Rev. RICH. H fcp. 8vo, *frontispiece afte*

"The Editor of these five rare w calculable service to English George Chapman's folios out o noured libraries, by collating the patience, and through the ager publisher, bringing Chapman within the reach of those who c least afford to purchase th *Athenaeum.*

HORNE'S (R. H.) Ball 12mo, pp. 248, *cloth*. 3s

"Containing the Noble Heart, the Monk of Swineshead Abbe of the Death of King John ; Camelott, a Fairy Tale : The E Passion of Andrea Como ; Bed gend : Ben Capstan, a Ballad the Elfe of the Woodlands, a C
"Pure fancy of the most abunda scription. Mr. Horne should tales : we know none to equal l Drayton and Herrick."—EXAM
"The opening poem in this volu entitled the 'Noble Heart' an in treatment well imitates the Fletcher."—ATHENÆUM.

**RISH FAMILIE** (John, *Barrister-at* Illustrations, Hist alogical, of the mo LIES of IRELAND (500) N held Commissions in K vice in the War of the Re in their respective Origi Forfeitures, and ultima set forth. 2 thick vols, 8v TION, pp. 1400, *cloth*. £

ISLE OF MAN.—HALLI Roundabout Notes, chie cient Circles of Stones in Fcp. 4to, *only 100 printe*

JOHNES (ARTHUR J. Proofs of the original U Origin of the Human R a Comparison of the Lang Asia, Africa, and Ame 6s (*original price* 12s 6d)
Printed at the suggestion of Dr. works it will be found a useful s

JONES (REV. H. LO Essays and Papers on L torical Subjects. 8vo, 4s. 6d (*original price* 12s)

"CONTENTS :—How to build a H Something like a Country Ho France (Biron and the Bastile. Versailles)—Modern Schools Belgium, and Switzerland—The 16th, 17th, and 18th Centuries. the Benedictines.

KELLY (WM., *of Leicester*) **Notices** illustrative of the Drama, and other Popular Amusements, chiefly in the Sixteenth and Seventeenth Centuries, incidentally illustrating Shakespeare and his Contemporaries, Extracted from the Chamberlain's Accounts and other Manuscripts of the Borough of Leicester, with an Introduction and Notes. Post 8vo, *plates, cloth.* 9s

KENRICK (REV. JOHN, *Curator of Antiquities in the Museum at York, author of* " *Ancient Egypt under the Pharaohs,*" "*History of Phœnicia,*" &c.) Papers on Subjects of Archæology and History communicated to the Yorkshire Philosophical Society. 8vo, *cloth.* 3s 6d. (Original price 9s.)

CONTENTS.
The Rise, Extension, and Suppression of the Order of Knights Templars in Yorkshire.
Historical Traditions of Pontefract Castle, including an Enquiry into the Place and Manner of Richard the Second's Death.
Relation of Coins to History, illustrated from Roman Coins found at Methal, in Yorkshire.
The Causes of the Destruction of Classical Literature.
The History of the Recovery of Classical Literature.
The Reign of Trajan, illustrated by a monument of his reign found at York.
Roman Wax Tablets found in Transylvania.
New Year's Day in Ancient Rome.

KENT.—LAMBARDE'S (WILLIAM, *Lawyer and Antiquary*) A Perambulation of Kent, containing the Description, Hystorie, and Customs of that Shire. Written in 1576. Thick 8vo, *cloth.* 5s (*original price* 12s)
The first county history published, and one of the most amusing and *naive* old books that can be imagined.

KENT.—SMITH (J. R.) Bibliotheca Cantiana.—A Bibliographical Account of what has been published on the History, Topography, Antiquities, Customs, and Family Genealogy of the County of Kent, with Biographical Notes. 8vo, (pp. 370) *with two plates of facsimiles of autographs of 33 eminent Kentish writers.* 5s (original price 14s)

KENT.—Liber Estriæ, or Memorials of the Royal Ville and Parish of Eastry, in the County of Kent. By W. F. SHAW, M.A., Vicar of Eastry. A handsome volume, *elegantly printed,* 4to,*plates, cloth.* £1. 8s

KENT.—SANDYS' (C.) Critical Dissertation on Professor Willis's "Architectural History of Canterbury Cathedral." 8vo. 2s 6d
"Written in no quarrelsome or captious spirit ; the highest compliment is paid to Professor Willis where it is due. But the author has made out a clear case, in some very important instances, of inaccuracies that have led the learned Professor into the construction of serious errors thoughout. It may be considered as an indispensable companion to his volume, containing a great deal of extra information of a very curious kind."—*Art-Union.*

KENT.—CONSUETUDINES KANCIÆ. A History of Gavelkind, and other remarkable Customs, in the County of Kent. By CHARLES SANDYS, *of Canterbury.* 8vo, *illustrated with facsimiles, a very handsome volume, cloth.* 15s.

KENT.—A Register of the Lands held by Catholics and Nonjurors in the County of Kent in the Reign of George the I., edited by W. H. Hart, F.S.A. 8vo, pp. 43, *sewed.* 1s

KENT.—KNOCKER'S (EDW., *Town Clerk of Dover*) Account of the Grand Court of Shepway, holden on Bredonstone Hill, at Dover, for the Installation of Viscount Palmerston as Constable of Dover and Warden of the Cinque Ports, in 1861. With Notes on the Origin and Antiquity of the Cinque Ports, Two Ancient Towns, and their Members. Foolscap 4to, *engravings, elegantly printed by Whittingham, cloth.* 15s

KENT.—Cæsar's British Expeditions from Boulogne to the Bay of Apuldore, and the subsequent formation Geologically of Romney Marsh. By F. H. APPACH, M.A. Post 8vo, *map, cloth.* 4s 6d

KENT.—A History of the Weald of Kent, with an Outline of the Early History of the Country. By ROBERT FURLEY, F.S.A., also a Sketch of the Physical Features of the District, by Henry B. Mackeson, F.G.S., thick 8vo, *with maps,* vol 1 (to be completed in 2 vols), *cloth.* 12s

KENT. — Passages from the Autobiography of a "MAN OF KENT," (ROBERT COWTAN *of the British Museum*) together with a few rough Pen and Ink Sketches by the same hand of some of the people he has met, the changes he has seen, and the places he has visited, 1817-1865. Thick post 8vo. *Cloth.* 5s. (original price 10s 6d)

KENT.—Some Account of Stone Church, near Dartford. By G. E. STREET, Architect. Imp 8vo, *fine engravings.* 5s

KENT. — History of the Fraternity of the Assumption of the Blessed Virgin Mary at Hythe. By H. B. MACKESON, F.G.S. 8vo, *facsimile of the MS.* 1s 6d
The curious documents here analyzed are of a class of which only two are known to exist in the Record Office, where they are regarded as of great interest and value.

KENT.—An Essay on the Tragedy of " Arden of Faversham." By C. E. DONNE. 8vo. 1s

KENT, SUSSEX, & SURREY.—HUSSEY (Rev. Arthur) Notes on the Churches in the Counties of Kent, Sussex, and Surrey mentioned in Domesday Book, and those of more recent date; with some Account of the Sepulchral Memorials and other Antiquities. Thick 8vo, *fine plates*, cloth. 12s (*original price* 18s)

LANCASHIRE.—HUTTON (W., *of Derby*) Description of Blackpool, in Lancashire. 8vo, *3rd edition.* 1s 6d

LATHBURY'S (REV. THOMAS) HIS-tory of the Nonjurors : their Controversies and Writings, with Remarks on some of the Rubrics in the Book of Common Prayer. Thick 8vo, *cloth.* 6s (*original price* 14s)

LATHBURY'S (REV. T.) History of the Convocation of the Church of England from the Earliest Period to the Year 1742. *Second edition, with considerable additions.* Thick 8vo, *cloth.* 5s (*original price* 12s)

LAWRENCE (SIR JAMES, *Knight of Malta*) On the Nobility of the British Gentry, or the Political Ranks and Dignities of the British Empire compared with those on the Continent. Post 8vo. 2s

Useful for foreigners in Great Britain, and to Britons abroad, particularly those who desire to be presented at Foreign Courts, to accept Foreign Military Service, to be invested with Foreign Titles, to be admitted into foreign orders, to purchase Foreign Property, or to Intermarry with Foreigners.

LETTERS of the KINGS of ENGLAND— Now first collected from the Originals in Royal Archives, and from other Authentic Sources, Private as well as Public. Edited, with Historical Introduction and Notes, by J. O. HALLIWELL. *Two handsome volumes,* post 8vo, *with portraits of Henry VIII. and Charles I.*, cloth. 8s (*original price* £1. 1s)

These volumes form a good companion to Ellis's Original Letters.

The collection comprises, for the first time, the love-letters of Henry VIII. to Anne Boleyn, in a complete form, which may be regarded, perhaps, as the most singular documents of the kind that have descended to our times ; the series of letters of Edward VI. will be found very interesting specimens of composition ; some of the letters of James I., hitherto unpublished, throw light on the Murder of Overbury, and prove beyond a doubt the King was implicated in it in some extraordinary and unpleasant way ; but his Letters to the Duke of Buckingham are of the most singular nature ; only imagine a letter from a Sovereign to his Prime Minister commencing thus ; " My own sweet and dear child, blessing, blessing, blessing on thy heart-roots and all thine." Prince Charles and the Duke of Buckingham's Journey into Spain has never been before so fully illustrated as it is by the documents given in this work, which also includes the very curious letters from the Duke and Duchess of Buckingham to James I.

LIBRARY of OLD AUTHORS.
JOHN MARSTON'S Dramatic Works, 3 vols. 15s.
PIERS PLOUGHMAN, his Vision and Creed. 2 vols. 10s.
MATHER'S Remarkable Providences of Early American Colonization. 5s.
JOHN SELDEN'S Table Talk. 5s—LARGE PAPER. 7s 6d
WILLIAM DRUMMOND'S Poetical Works 5s.
FRANCIS QUARLES' Enchiridion. 3s.
SIR THOMAS OVERBURY'S Works. 5s.
GEORGE WITHER'S Hymns and Songs of the Church. 5s.
GEORGE WITHER'S Hallelujah. 6s.
ROBERT SOUTHWELL'S Poetical Works. 4s
JOSEPH SPENCE'S Anecdotes of Books and Men. 6s.—LARGE PAPER. 7s 6d.
COTTON MATHER'S Wonders of the Invisible World. 5s.
REMAINS of the Early Popular Poetry of England. 4 vols. £1—LARGE PAPER. £1. 10s.
JOHN AUBREY'S Miscellanies. 4s.
GEORGE CHAPMAN'S Translation of Homer's Iliad. 2 vols. 12s
——— Odyssey. 2 vols. 12s.
——— Battle of the Frogs, and other Pieces. 6s.
JOHN WEBSTER'S Dramatic Works (more complete than any other). 4 vols. £1.—LARGE PAPER. £1. 10s.
JOHN LILLY'S Dramatic Works. 2 vols. 10s.—LARGE PAPER. 15s.
RICHARD CRASHAW'S Poetical Works. 5s.
LA MORTE D'ARTHUR.—History of King Arthur and the Knights of the Round Table (the only uncastrated Edition). 3 vols. 15s.—LARGE PAPER. £1. 2s 6d
SACKVILLE'S (Lord Buckhurst) Works. 4s.
RICHARD LOVELACE'S (The Cavalier) Poetical Works. Now first collected. 5s.—LARGE PAPER. 7s 6d
CAMDEN'S Remains concerning Britain. 8th edition, *new portrait.* 6s.—LARGE PAPER. 7s 6d.
ROBERT HERRICK'S Poetical Works. 2 vols. 8s. — LARGE PAPER. 15s
THE DIARIES OF THOMAS HEARNE the Antiquary. 3 vols. 15s. — LARGE PAPER. £1. 2s 6d.
ROGER ASCHAM'S Whole Works. Now first collected. 4 vols. £1.—LARGE PAPER. £1. 10s.
DUCHESS OF NEWCASTLE'S Autobiography and Life of her Husband. 5s.—LARGE PAPER. 7s 6d.

GEORGE SANDYS' Poetical Works. 2 vols. 10s.—LARGE PAPER. 15s.

THE Renowned Romance of Amadis of Gaul. 3 vols. 15s.—LARGE PAPER. £1. 2s 6d.

MICHAEL DRAYTON'S Poetical Works. Now first collected, *in the press.*
All elegantly printed and carefully edited with portraits, woodcuts and facsimiles. The title of each work is given more fully in this Catalogue.

LILLY'S (JOHN *the Euphist*) Dramatic Works. Now first collected, with Life and Notes by F. W. FAIRHOLT. 2 vols, fcp. 8vo, *cloth.* 10s.
——LARGE PAPER, 2 vols, post 8vo, *cloth.* 15s

LOVELACE (RICHARD) Lucasta.— The Poems of RICHARD LOVELACE, now first edited and the Text carefully revised, with Life and Notes by W. CAREW HAZLITT. Fcp. 8vo, *cloth, with 4 plates.* 5s.
—— LARGE PAPER. Post 8vo, *cloth.* 7s 6d

LOWER'S (MARK ANTONY, *M.A., F.S.A.*) Patronymica Britannica, a Dictionary of Family Names. Royal 8vo, 500 *pages, with illustrations, cloth.* £1. 5s
This work is the result of a study of British Family Names, extending over more than twenty years.

LOWER'S (M. A.) Curiosities of Heraldry, with Illustrations from Old English Writers. *With illuminated Titlepage, and numerous engravings from designs by the Author.* 8vo, *cloth.* 14s
"Mr. Lower's work is both curious and instructive, while the manner of its treatment is so inviting and popular, that the subject to which it refers, which many have hitherto had too good reason to consider meagre and unprofitable, assumes, under the hands of the writer, the novelty of fiction with the importance of historical truth."—*Athenæum.*

LOWER'S (M. A.) Contributions to Literature, Historical, Antiquarian, and Metrical. Post 8vo, *woodcuts, cloth.* 7s 6d
Contents: 1. Local Nomenclature—2. The Battle of Hastings, an Historical Essay—3. The Lord Dacre, his mournful end, a Ballad—4. Historical and Archæological Memoir on the Iron Works of the South of England, *with numerous illustrations*—5. Winchelsea's Deliverance, or the Stout Abbot of Battayle, in Three Fyttes—6. The South Downs, a Sketch, Historical, Anecdotical, and Descriptive—7. On the Yew Trees in Churchyards—8. A Lytte Geste of a Greate Eele, a pleasaunt Ballad—9. A Discourse of Genealogy—10. An Antiquarian Pilgrimage in Normandy, *with woodcuts*—11. Miscellanea, &c., &c.

LOWER'S (M. A.) Chronicle of Battel Abbey, in Sussex, originally compiled in Latin by a Monk of the Establishment, and now first translated, with Notes and an Abstract of the subsequent History of the Abbey. 8vo, *with illustrations, cloth.* 9s
This volume, among other matters of local and general interest, embraces—New Facts relative to the Norman invasion—The Foundation of the Monastery—The Names and Rentals of the Original Townsmen of Battel—Memoirs of several Abbots and Notices of their Disputes with the Bishops of Chichester, respecting Jurisdiction—The Abbey's Possessions—A Speech of Thomas a Becket, then Chancellor of England, in favour of Abbot Walter de Luci—Several Miracles—Anecdotes of the Norman Kings—and an Historical Sketch of the Abbey, from 1176 to the present time by the Translator.

LONDON.—Liber Albus; the White Book of the City of London. Compiled A.D. 1419, by JOHN CARPENTER, *Common Clerk*; RICHARD WHITTINGTON, *Mayor.* Translated from the Original Latin and Anglo-Norman, by H. T. Riley, M.A. 4to, pp. 672 (*original price* 18s) *the few remaining copies offered, in cloth, at* 9s—*Half morocco (Roxburghe style)* 10s 6d—*Whole bound in vellum, carmine edges,*12s—*Whole morocco, carmine edges,* 13s 6d
Extensively devoted to details which must of necessity interest those who care to know something more about their forefathers than the mere fact that they have existed. Many of them—until recently consigned to oblivion ever since the passing away of the remote generations to which they belonged—intimately connected with the social condition, usages, and manners of the people who—uncouth, unlearned, ill-housed, ill-fed, and comfortless though they were, still formed England's most important, most wealthy, and most influential community throughout the chequered and troublous times of the 13th and 14th centuries. During this period, in fact, there is hardly a phase or feature of English national life, upon which, in a greater or less degree, from these pages of the "Liber Albus," some light is not reflected.

LONDON.—Chronicle of London, from 1089 to 1483, written in the 15th Century, and for the first time printed from MSS. in the British Museum, with numerous Contemporary Illustrations of Royal Letters, Poems, descriptive of Public Events and Manners and Customs of the Metropolis. (Edited by SIR HARRIS NICOLAS.) 4to, *facsimile, bds.* 15s
Only 250 copies printed. It forms a Supplement to the Chronicles of Harding, Crafton, Hall, and others.

LONDON.—History of the Church of St. Mildred, in the Poultry, London, with some particulars of the Church of St. Mary, Colechurch, destroyed in the great Fire, A.D. 1666. By THOMAS MILBOURN, late Hon. Sec. to the London and Middlesex Archæological Society. 8vo, *engravings, cloth.* 9s
The large extracts from the Parish Registers will interest the Genealogist, as it was an important parish in the olden time.

LUKIS (REV. W. C.) Account of Church Bells, with some Notices of Wiltshire Bells and Bell-Founders, containing a copious list of Founders, a comparative Scale of Tenor Bells, and Inscriptions from nearly 500 Parishes in various parts of the Kingdom. 8vo, 13 *plates, cloth.* 3s 6d (*original price* 6s)

Books on Sale at Smith's, 36, Soho Square, London. 15

LYNDSAY'S (SIR DAVID) Poetical Works, a new edition, carefully revised, etc., by DAVID LAING. 2 vols, post 8vo, cloth. 12s

ADDEN (FRED. W., *of the Medal Room, British Museum*) Handbook to Roman Coins. Fcap. 8vo, *plates of rare examples, cloth.* 5s
A very useful and trustworthy guide to Roman Coins.

MARSTON'S (JOHN) Dramatic and Poetical Works. Now first collected and edited by J. O. HALLIWELL, F.R.S., &c. 3 vols, fcp. 8vo, *cloth.* 15s
"The edition deserves well of the public; it is carefully printed, and the annotations, although neither numerous nor extensive, supply ample explanations upon a varitey of interesting points. If Mr. Halliwell had done no more than collect these plays, he would have conferred a boon upon all lovers of our old dramatic poetry."—*Literary Gazette.*

MATHER'S (Dr. INCREASE) Remarkable Providences of the Earlier Days of American Colonization. With Introductory Preface by GEORGE OFFOR. Fcp. 8vo, *Portrait, cloth.* 5s
A very singular collection of remarkable sea deliverances, accidents, remarkable phenomena, witchcraft, apparitions, &c., &c., connected with inhabitants of New England, &c., &c. A very amusing volume, conveying a faithful portrait of the state of society, when the doctrine of a peculiar providence and personal intercourse between this world and that which is unseen was fully believed.

MATHER'S (DR. COTTON) Wonders of the Invisible World, being an account of the Trials of several Witches lately executed in New England, and of the several remarkable curiosities therein occurring. To which are added Dr. INCREASE MATHER's Further Account of the Tryals, and Cases of Conscience concerning Witchcrafts, and Evil Spirits Personating Men. *Reprinted from the rare original editions of* 1693, with an Introductory Preface. Fcp. 8vo, *Portrait, cloth.* 5s

MENZIES (LOUISA J.) Legendary Tales of the Ancient Britons, rehearsed from the Early Chronicles. Fcp. 8vo, *cloth.* 3s
Contents: 1. Esyllt and Sabrina. 2. Lear and his three daughters. 3. Cynedda and Morgan. 4. The Brothers Beli and Bran. 5. Ellidure the Compassionate. 6. Alban of Verulam. 7. Vortigern. 8. Cadwallon and the Final Struggle of the Britons.

MICHAEL ANGELO Considered as a Philosophic Poet, with translations by JOHN EDWARD TAYLOR. Post 8vo. SECOND EDITION. *Cloth.* 2s 6d (*original price* 5s)

MILTON; A Sheaf of Gleanings after his Biographers and Annotators. By the Rev. JOSEPH HUNTER. Post 8vo. 2s 6d

MOORE (THOMAS) — Notes from the Letters of Thomas Moore to his Music Publisher, James Power (*the publication of which was suppressed in London*), with an Introduction by Thomas Crofton Croker, F.S.A. Post 8vo, *cloth.* 3s 6d
The impression on the mind of a reader of these Letters of Moore in Lord Russell's edition will be not only incomplete, but erroneous, without the information to be derived from this very interesting volume.

ARES' (ARCHDEACON) Glossary, or Collection of Words, Phrases, Customs, Proverbs, &c., illustrating the Works of English Authors, particularly Shakespeare and his Contemporaries. A New Edition, with considerable Additions, both of Words and Examples. By JAMES O. HALLIWELL, F.R.S., and THOMAS WRIGHT, M.A., F.S.A. 2 thick vols, 8vo, *cloth.* £1. 1s
The Glossary of Archdeacon Nares is by far the best and most useful work we possess for explaining and illustrating the obsolete language and the customs and manners of the 16th and 17th Centuries, and it is quite indispensable for the readers of the literature of the Elizabethan period. The additional words and examples are distinguished from those in the original text by a † prefixed to each. The work contains between FIVE and SIX THOUSAND additional examples, the result of original research, not merely supplementary to Nares, but to all other compilations of the kind.

NASH'S (D. W.) Taliesin, or the Bards and Druids of Britain. A Translation of the Remains of the earliest Welsh Bards, and an examination of the Bardic Mysteries. 8vo, *cloth.* 14s

NASH'S (D. W.) The Pharoah of the Exodus. An Examination of the Modern Systems of Egyptian Chronology. 8vo, *with frontispiece of the Egyptian Calendar, from the ceiling of the Ramasseum, at Thebes, cloth.* 12s

NEWCASTLE'S.—The Lives of William Cavendish, Duke of Newcastle, and of his wife Margaret Duchess of Newcastle, written by the thrice noble and illustrious, Princess MARGARET, DUCHESS OF NEWCASTLE. Edited with a Preface and Occasional Notes by M. A. LOWER, A.M., etc. Fcap. 8vo, *fine portrait of the Duchess, cloth.* 5s.
—— LARGE PAPER, post 8vo, *cloth.* 7s 6d

NORFOLK. — On the True Derivation of the Names of Towns, Villages, Rivers, and other Great Natural Features of the County of Norfolk. By the Rev. GEO. MUNFORD, *Vicar of East Winch.* 8vo, *cloth.* 4s (published at 7s)

NORFOLK.--Analysis of Domesday Book for the County of Norfolk. By the Rev. George Munford, *Vicar of East Winch.* In 1 vol., 8vo, *with pedigrees and arms, cloth.* 10s 6d

" Many extracts have been made, at various times, for the illustration of local descriptions, from the great national (but almost unintelligible) record known as *Domesday Book*; but Mr. Munford has done more in the case of his own county, for he supplies a complete epitome of the part of the survey relating to Norfolk, giving not only the topographical and statistical facts, but also a great deal that is instructive as to the manners and condition of the people, the state of the churches and other public edifices, the mode of cultivation and land tenure, together with a variety of points of interest to the ecclesiologist and antiquary."—*Bury Post.*

NORFOLK. — SURTEES' (Rev. Scott F.) Julius Cæsar, Did he Cross the Channel? Post 8vo, *cloth.* 1s 6d

" In giving an answer in the negative to the above question, we ask for a fair and dispassionate hearing, and in order to avoid circumlocution pass at once our Rubicon, and propound as capable of all proof the following historical heresy, viz., that Cæsar never set foot at Boulogne or Calais, never crossed the Channel, or set eyes on Deal or Dover, but that he sailed from the mouths of the Rhine or Scheldt, and landed in Norfolk on both his expeditions."—AUTHOR.

—— **JULIUS CAESAR how he sailed from Zealand and landed in Norfolk** (a sequel to the foregoing). Post 8vo. 1s

—— **JULIUS CAESAR did he CROSS the Channel?** Reviewed (a Reply to Mr. Surtees' books). By JOHN WAINWRIGHT. post 8vo. 2s 6d.

NOTTS.—CRESWELL'S (REV. S. F.) Collections towards the History of Printing in Nottinghamshire. Small 4to, *sewed.* 2s

NOTTS and YORKSHIRE.—The History and Antiquities of the Parish of Blyth, in the Counties of Nottingham and York, comprising Accounts of the Monastery, Hospitals, Chapels, and Ancient Tournament Field, of the Parish of the Castle and Manor of Tickill, and of the Family Possessions of De Buili, the First and Norman Lord thereof, together with Biographical Notices of Roger Mowbray, Philip of Olcotes, Bishop Sanderson, John Cromwell, and others, with Appendix of Documents. By the Rev. JOHN RAINE, *Vicar of Blyth.* 4to, *plates and pedigrees, cloth.* 15s (original price, £1. 6s)

—— LARGE PAPER, royal 4to. £1. 5s

These copies have an additional view of the Remains of Scrooby Palace, not issued with the early copies.

NUMISMATIC CHRONICLE and Journal of the Numismatic Society. NEW SERIES, Edited by W. S. W. VAUX, JOHN EVANS, and F. W. MADDEN. Nos. 1 to 48 Published Quarterly. 5s *per Number*
This is the only repertory of Numismatic intelligence ever published in England. It contains papers on coins and medals, of all ages and countries, by the first Numismatist of the day, both English and Foreign Odd parts may be had to complete a few of this and the former series in 20 vols.

LD BALLADS.—CATALOGUE of a unique Collection of 400 Ancient English Broadside Ballads, printed entirely in the **Black letter,** lately on sale by J. RUSSELL SMITH. With Notes of their Tunes, and Imprints. Post 8vo, *a handsome volume, printed by Whittingham, in the old style, half bound.* 5s

—— A Copy on thick paper, *without the prices to each, and a different title-page, only 10 copies so printed.* 10s 6d

OVERBURY'S (SIR THOMAS) Works in Prose and Verse, now first collected. Edited, with Life and Notes, by E. F, RIMBAULT. Fcp. 8vo, *portrait after Pass cloth.* 5s

OXON. — GILES (REV. DR.) History of the Parish and Town of Bampton, in Oxfordshire, with the District and Hamlets belonging to it. 8vo, *plates, second edition, cloth.* 7s 6d

OXON.—GILES (REV. DR.) History of Witney and its Neighbouring Parishes, Oxon. 8vo, *plates, cloth.* 6s

OXON.—TURNER's (Sir Gregory Page) Topographical Memorandums for the County of Oxford. 8vo, *bds.* 2s

OXON. — Memorials of the Parish of Westcott Barton. By the Rev. JENNER MARSHALL, *Lord of the Manor.* 8vo, *plate of the Church, cloth.* 2s 6d

EDIGREES. — BRIDGER'S (CHARLES) Index to the Printed Pedigrees of English Families contained in County and Local Histories, the "Herald's Visitations," and in the more important Genealogical Collections. Thick 8vo, *cloth.* 10s 6d

A similar work to Sims' "Index of Pedigrees in the MSS. in the British Museum." What that is for Manuscripts this is for Printed Books. It is the most complete Index of its kind, and contains double the matter of another hasty production.

PEDIGREES.—A Catalogue of Pedigrees hitherto unindexed. By G. W. MARSHALL. 8vo. 3s 6d

A useful supplement to Bridger's Index of Printed Pedigrees as it touches books not comprehended in the scope of that work—as the "Gentleman's Magazine" "Notes and Queries," " Gough's Sepulchral Monuments," " Family Histories," "Peerage Cases," also those Pedigrees not in tabular form in " Morant's Essex" " Hasted's Kent," &c.

PETTIGREW (THOS. JOS.) On Super- stitions connected with the History and Practice of Medicine and Surgery. 8vo, *frontispiece, cloth.* 4s (original price 8s)

Books on Sale at Smith's, 36, Soho Square, London. 17

PETTIGREW'S Biographical Memoirs of the most celebrated Physicians, Surgeons, &c., who have contributed to the advancement of Medical Science. Imp. 8vo, 25 *fine portraits, cloth.* 7s 6d

PETTIGREW (THOS. JOS.) Inquiries into the particulars connected with the Death of Amy Robsart (Lady Dudley) at Cumnor Place, Berks., Sept. 8, 1560; being a refutation of the Calumnies charged against Sir Robert Dudley, Anthony Forster, and others. 8vo. 2s

PIERS PLOUGHMAN. — The Vision and Creed of PIERS PLOUGHMAN. Edited by THOMAS WRIGHT; a new edition, revised, with additions to the Notes and Glossary. 2 vols, fcp. 8vo, *cloth.* 10s

"The Vision of Piers Ploughman" is one of the most precious and interesting monuments of the English Language and Literature, and also of the social and political condition of the country during the fourteenth century. . . . . But its time of composition can, by internal evidence be fixed at about the year 1362. On this and on all matters bearing upon the origin and object of the poem, Mr. Wright's historical introduction gives ample information."—*Literary Gazette.*

PILGRIM FATHERS.—HUNTER (Rev. Joseph, F.S.A.) The Pilgrim Fathers— Collections concerning the Church or Congregation of Protestant Separatists formed at Scrooby, in North Nottinghamshire, in the time of James I., the Founders of New Plymouth, the Parent Colony of England. 8vo, *with view of the Archiepiscopal Palace at Scrooby inserted, cloth.* 8s

This work contains some very important particulars of these personages, and their connections previously to their leaving England and Holland, which were entirely unknown to former writers, and have only recently been discovered through the indefatigable exertions of the author. Prefixed to the volume are some beautiful Prefatory Stanzas by Richard Monckton Milnes, Esq., M.P. (now Lord Houghton).

PIOZZI.—Love Letters of Mrs. Piozzi (formerly Mrs. Thrale, the friend of Dr. Johnson), written when she was eighty to the handsome actor, William Augustus Conway, aged Twenty-seven. Edited by W. A. CHATTO. 8vo, *sewed.* 2s

"————written at three, four, and five o'clock (in the morning) by an octogenary pen! a heart (as Mrs. Lee says) twenty-six years old, and as H. L. P. feels it to be, *all your own*."—*Letter V., 3rd. Feb. 1820.*
"This is one of the most extraordinary collections of love epistles we have chanced to meet with, and the well known literary reputation of the lady—the Mrs. Thrale of Doctor Johnson and Miss Burney celebrity —considerably enhances their interest. The letters themselves it is not easy to characterise: nor shall we venture to decide whether they more bespeak the drivelling of dotage, or the folly of love; in either case they present human nature to us under a new aspect, and furnish one of those riddles which nothing yet dreamt of in our philosophy can satisfactorily solve."—*Polytechnic Review.*

POPE.—Facts and Conjectures on the Descent and Family Connections of Pope, the Poet. By the Rev. JOSEPH HUNTER. Post 8vo. 2s

POPE.—Additional Facts concerning the Maternal Ancestry of Pope, in a Letter to Mr. Hunter. By ROBERT DAVIES, F.S.A. Post 8vo. 2s

POPULAR TREATISES ON SCIENCE, written during the Middle Ages, in Anglo-Saxon, Anglo-Norman, and English. Edited by Thomas Wright, M.A. 8vo, *cloth.* 3s

CONTENTS.—An Anglo-Saxon Treatise on Astronomy of the Tenth Century, now first published from a MS. in the British Museum, with a translation. Livre des Creatures, by Phillippe de Thaun, now first printed, with a translation (extremely valuable to Philologists, as being the earliest specimens of Anglo-Norman remaining, and explanatory of all the symbolical signs in early sculpture and painting); the Bestiary of Phillippe de Thaun, with a translation; Fragments on Popular Science from the Early English Metrical Lives of the Saints (the earliest piece of the kind in the English Language.)

PORTRAITS OF ILLUSTRIOUS PER- sons in English History, drawn by G. P. Harding, F.S.A., from original Pictures, with Biographical and Historical Notices, by Thomas Moule, F.S.A. In a handsome roy. 4to volume, *bound in cloth extra, bevelled edges, and gilt leaves.* £1. 1s

Contents : King Henry VIII. and the Emperor Charles the Fifth. Sir Robert Dudley, son of the Earl of Leicester, Queen Catherine of Aragon. Sir William Russell, Lord Russell of Thornhaugh, Sir Anthony Browne. Anthony Browne, Viscount Montagu. Margaret Cavendish, Duchess of Newcastle. Sir Anthony Shirley. Sir Charles Scarborough, M.D. Henry Carey, Viscount Falkland. Flora Macdonald, the preserver of Prince Charles Stuart. William Lenthall, Speaker of the House of Commons, 1649. Edward Vere, Earl of Oxford. William Camden, Antiquary. Sir Thomas Browne, of Norwich, M.D. Separate prints may be had on folio, India paper proofs 3s 6d each.

POSTE'S (REV. BEALE, M. A.) Britannic Researches ; or new Facts and Rectifications of Ancient British History. 8vo (pp. 448). *with engravings, cloth.* 15s

"The author of this volume may justly claim credit for considerable learning, great industry, and above all, great faith in the interest and importance of his subject. . . . . On various points he has given us additional information, and afforded us new views, for which we are bound to thank him. The body of his book is followed by a very complete index, so as to render reference to any part of it easy ; this was the more necessary, on account of the multifariousness of the topics treated, the variety of persons mentioned and the many works quoted."—*Athenaeum.*

POSTE'S (REV. B.) Brittannia Antiqua or Ancient Britain brought within the Limits of Authentic History. 8vo (pp. 386), *map, cloth.* 14s

A Sequel to the foregoing work.

POSTE'S Vindication of the "Celtic In- scriptions on Gaulish and British Coins." 8vo, *plates and cuts, cloth.* 1s

18 *Books on Sale at Smith's, 36, Soho Square, London.*

POSTE'S (REV. B.) Celtic Inscriptions on Gaulish and British Coins, intended to supply materials for the Early History of Great Britain, with a Glossary of Archaic Celtic Words, and an Atlas of Coins. 8vo, *many engravings, cloth.* 10s 6d

PROVENÇAL.—A Hand-book to the Modern Provençal Language, spoken in the South of France, Piedmont, &c., comprising a Grammar, Dialogues, Legends, Vocabularies, &c., useful for English Tourists and others. By Rev. J. D. CRAIG. Roy. 12mo, *cloth.* 3s 6d

This little book is a welcome addition to our literature of comparative philology in this country, as we have hitherto had no grammar of the sweet lyrical tongue of Southern France.

PROVINCIAL DIALECTS OF ENGLAND.

A DICTIONARY of Archaic and Provincial Words, Obsolete Phrases, etc. By J. O HALLIWELL, F.R.S., &c. 2 vols, 8vo, 1000 pp. in double columns. SEVENTH EDITION *cloth.* 15s

GLOSSARY of Provincial and Local Words Used in England. By F. GROSE, F.S.A., with which is now incorporated the Supplement. By SAMUEL PEGGE, F.S.A. Post 8vo, *cloth.* 4s 6d

SPECIMENS of Cornish Provincial Dialect, collected and arranged by Uncle Jan Treenodle, with some Introductory Remarks and a Glossary by an Antiquarian Friend ; also a Selection of Songs and other Pieces connected with Cornwall. Post 8vo, *with a curious portrait of Dolly Pentreath, cloth.* 4s

CUMBERLAND BALLADS. By Robert ANDERSON, with Autobiography, Notes, and Glossary. Edited by SIDNEY GILPIN. Fcp. 8vo, *cloth.* 2s

THE Folk Speech of Cumberland, and some Districts adjacent, being short Stories and Rhymes in the Dialects of the West Border Counties. By ALEX. CRAIG GIBSON, F.S.A. Post 8vo, SECOND EDITION, *cloth.* 3s 6d

"CUMBERLAND TALK," being Short Tales and Rhymes in the Dialect of that County, by JOHN RICHARDSON, of St. John's. Fcp. 8vo, *cloth.* 3s 6d

NATHAN HOGG'S Letters and Poems in the Devonshire Dialect. *The Fifth Edition, with additions.* Post 8vo. *Coloured wrapper.* 1s

*These letters, which have achieved considerable popularity, evince an extensive acquaintance with the vernacular of the county and its idioms and phrases, while the continuous flow of wit and humour throughout cannot fail to operate forcibly upon the risible faculties of the reader. In the Witch story Nathan has excelled himself, and it is to be hoped we have not seen his last effort in this branch of local English literature. The superstitions of Jan Vaggis and Jan Plant are most graphically an and the various incidents wher " Evil Eye" is sought to be co ludicrous and irresistible."—*i*

NATHAN HOGG'S New Ser Devonshire Dialect, in(Story of Mucksy Lane, Ghost. *Dedicated by Highness Prince Louis.* Post 8vo, *4th edition wrapper.* 1s

A GLOSSARY of Words us the County of Durham DALE. Post 8vo, *cloth.* 2s

POEMS of Rural Life in tl By the Rev. WILLIAM Rectory, Dorchester. Fcp. 8vo, SECOND EDITI(

JOHN NOAKES and MAR] exhibiting some of the gual localisms peculiar Glossary. By CHARLE Great Totham Hall, *cloth.* 2s

A GLOSSARY of the Cots shire) Dialect, illustra from ancient Authors. RICHARD WEBSTER H Boxwell Court, Glouces *cloth.* 2s

DIALECT of South Lan Bobbin's Tummas and M Corrected, with his Rh larged Glossary of W(chiefly used by the Ru the Manufacturing D Lancashire. By SA) 12mo, *sewed edition, clot*

A GLOSSARY of the Wor Furness (North Lancasl tive Quotations, princip Northern Writers. B. 12mo, *cloth.* 3s 6d

A GLOSSARY of Northam and Phrases, with Ex Colloquial Use, with various Authors, to whi Customs of the County BAKER. 2 vols, post (*original price £1. 4s*)

"The provincial dialects of Eng serve the elements and rudin tongue. In Miss Baker's adr shire Glossary,' we have r archaisms than vulgarisms. than a vocabulary ; it preserv peculiarities, but odd and disa] there is hardly a page in it wh on some obscurity in our write and practices."—*ChristianRe Review.*

RUSTIC SKETCHES, bei " Skits" on Angling and one of the South-wester copious Glossary and ge Country Talk. By G. Post 8vo. THIRD EDITI

Books on Sale at Smith's, 36, Soho Square, London. 19

)RNESS Folk, their Sayin's an' Dewin's, or Sketches of Life and Characters in Lonsdale, North of the Sands. By ROGER PIKETAH. 12mo, sewed. 1s

THE Dialect of Somersetshire, with a Glossary, Poems, &c., exemplifying the Dialect. By J. JENNINGS. Second Edition, edited by the Rev. J. K. JENNINGS. Fcp. 8vo, cloth. 4s 6d

GLOSSARY of the Provincialisms of the County of Sussex. By W. DURRANT COOPER, F.S.A. Post 8vo, second edition, enlarged, cloth. 3s 6d.

ESTMORELAND and Cumberland.—Dialogues, Poems, Songs, and Ballads, by various Writers, in the Westmoreland and Cumberland Dialects, now first collected, to which is added a Copious Glossary of Words peculiar to those Counties. Post 8vo, (pp. 408), cloth. 9s.

IE WESTMORELAND DIALECT, in four familiar dialogues. By Mrs. ANN WHEELER, a new edition, to which is added a Copious Glossary of Westmoreland and Cumberland Words. Post 8vo, cloth. 3s 6d
Printed separately from the foregoing work.

GLOSSARY of Provincial Words in use in Wiltshire, showing their Derivation in numerous instances, from the Language of the Anglo-Saxon. By JOHN YONGE AKERMAN, Esq., F.S.A. 12mo, cloth. 3s

IE DIALECT of Leeds and its Neighbourhood, illustrated by Conversations and Tales of Common Life, etc., to which are added a Copious Glossary, Notices of the various Antiquities, Manners, and Customs, and General Folk-lore of the District. (By C. C. ROBINSON.) Thick 12mo, pp. 458, cloth. 6s
This is undoubtedly the best work hitherto published on the dialects of Yorkshire in general, and of Leeds in particular. The author, we believe one of our fellow townsmen—for his introductory remarks are dated 'Leeds, March, 1861'—has used not only great industry, but much keen observation, and has produced a book which will everywhere be received as a valuable addition to the archæological literature of England.—Leeds Intelligencer.

GLOSSARY of Yorkshire Words and Phrases, collected in Whitby and its Neighbourhood, with examples of their colloquial use and allusions to local Customs and Traditions. By an INHABITANT. (F. K. Robinson). 12mo, cloth. 3s 6d

GLOSSARY of the Dialect of the district of Cleveland in the North Riding of Yorkshire. By the Rev. J. C. ATKINSON, Incumbent of Danby. Thick small 4to, 662 pages, cloth. £1. 4s

GLOSSARY, with some Pieces of Verse of the Old Dialect of the English Colony in the Baronies of Forth and Bargy, Co. Wexford, Ireland. Formerly collected by JACOB POOLE, of Growton, now edited with Notes and Introduction by the REV. W. BARNES, Author of the Dorset Poems and Glossary. Fcap. 8vo, cloth. 4s 6d

SMITH (J. R) A Bibliographical List of all the Works which have been published towards illustrating the Provincial Dialects of England. Post 8vo. 1s 1839

UARLES' (FRANCIS) Enchiridion containing Institutions — Divine, Contemplative, Practical, Moral, Ethical, Economical, and Political. Fcp. 8vo, Portrait, cloth. 3s
"Had this little book been written at Athens or Rome, its author would have been classed with the wise of his country."—Headley.

QUEEN DAGMAR'S CROSS, facsimile in gold and colours of the Enamelled Jewel in the Old Northern Museum, Copenhagen, with Introductory Remarks by Prof. GEORGE STEPHENS, F.S.A. 8vo, sewed. 3s

QUINTUS SMYRNÆUS.—Select Translations from the Greek of Quintus Smyrnæus. By the Rev. Alexander Dyce. 12mo, bds. 2s (original price 5s 6d)

ELIQUIÆ ANTIQUÆ. Scraps from Ancient Manuscripts, illustrating chiefly Early English Literature and the English Language, Edited by Wright and Halliwell. 8vo, Vol II., Nos. in 12s
Many subscribers want the second volume. A number of odd parts of both vols. to complete copies.

RETROSPECTIVE REVIEW (New Series) consisting of Criticisms upon, Analysis of, and Extracts from, curious, useful, valuable, and scarce Old Books. 8vo, Vols I., and II., all printed, cloth. 10s 6d (original price £1. 1s) 1853—54
These two volumes form a good companion to the old series of the Retrospective, in 16 vols; the articles are of the same length and character.

REYNOLDS (SIR JOSHUA) Notes and Observations on Pictures chiefly of the Venetian School, being Extracts from his Italian Sketch Books; also the Rev. W. Mason's Observations on Sir Joshua's Method of Colouring, with some unpublished Letters, of Dr. Johnson, Malone, and others; With an Appendix, containing a Transcript of Sir Joshua's Account-Book, showing the Paintings he executed, and the Prices he was paid for them. Edited by William Cotton, Esq, 8vo, cloth. 5s.
"The scraps of the Critical Journal kept by Reynolds of Rome, Florence. and Venice, will be esteemed by high-class virtuosi."—Leader.

RIMBAULT (E. F., LL.D., F.S.A., &c.)—A Little Book of Songs and Ballads, gathered from Ancient Music Books, MS. and Printed. Elegantly printed in post 8vo, pp. 243, half morocco. 6s

RIMBAULT (DR. E. F.) Bibliotheca Madrigaliana.—A Bibliographical Account of the Musical and Poetical Works published in England during the Sixteenth and Seventeenth Centuries, under the Titles of Madrigals, Ballets, Ayres, Canzonets, &c., &c. 8vo, *cloth*. 5s

It records a class of books left undescribed by Ames, Herbert, and Dibdin, and furnishes a most valuable Catalogue of Lyrical Poetry of the age to which it refers.

ROBERT'S (GEORGE, *of Lyme-Regis*)—Life, Progresses, and Rebellion of James, Duke of Monmouth, &c., to his Capture and Execution, with a full account of the "Bloody Assize," under Judge Jeffries, and Copious Biographical Notices. 2 vols, post 8vo, *plates and cuts, cloth*. 7s 6d (*original price* £1. 4s)

Two very interesting volumes, particularly so to those connected with the West of England. Quoted for facts by Lord Macaulay.

ROBERTS' (GEORGE) The Social History of the People of the Southern Counties of England in Past Centuries, illustrated in regard to their Habits, Municipal Bye-laws, Civil Progress, &c. Thick 8vo, *cloth*. 7s 6d (*original price* 16s)

An interesting volume on old English manners and customs, mode of travelling, punishments, witchcraft, gipsies, pirates, stage-players, pilgrimages, prices of labour and provisions, the clothing trade of the West of England, &c., compiled chiefly from original materials, as the archives of Lyme-Regis, and Weymouth, family papers, church registers, &c. Dedicated to Lord Macaulay.

ROBIN HOOD.—THE GREAT HERO of the Ancient Minstrelsy of England, "Robin Hood," his Period, Real Character, &c., investigated and ascertained. By the Rev. JOSEPH HUNTER. Post 8vo. 2s 6d

RUNIC MONUMENTS.—The Old Northern Runic Monuments of Scandanavia and England, now first collected and deciphered by GEORGE STEPHENS, F.S.A., Professor of English in the University of Copenhagen. Folio, *many hundred engravings, some in gold, silver, bronze, and colours*, pp. 1112, *in two parts (the complete work)*. £5.

SACRED MUSIC.—BY THE REV. W.Sloane Evans, M.A. Royal 8vo, third edition, *sewed*. 1s 6d (*original price* 6s)

Consisting of Psalm Tunes, Sanctusses, Kyrie-Eleisons, &c., and fifty-four Single and Double Chants (Major, Changeable, and Minor).

ST. CUTHBERT.—RAINE'S (Rev. Jas.) Saint Cuthbert, with an Account of the State in which his Remains were found upon the Opening of his Tomb in Durham Cathedral, 1827. 4to, *plates and woodcuts, bds. (a very interesting* vo 10s 6d. (*original price* £1. 11s 6d)

SALOP.—The Roman City of Uriconium at Wroxeter, Salop; illustrative of t History and Social Life of our mano-British Forefathers. By J. Cor Anderson. *A handsome volume, post 8 with numerous cuts drawn on wood from actual objects by the author, extra cloth.*

SALVERTE'S (EUSEBIUS) Histo of the Names of Men, Nations, and F ces, in their Connection with the P gress of Civilization. Translated by Rev. L. H. Mordaque, M.A., Oxon. 2 v 8vo, *cloth*. £1. 4s

"Notre nom propre c'est nous-memes."
"Nomina si nescis periit cognitio rerum."
"Full of learning, well written, and well translated *Daily News.*
"These two volumes are filled with a minute and ph sophical enquiry into the origin of names of all so among all nations, and show profound scholarship patient skill in wide and elaborate research. Muc the work is necessarily too profound for general ders—particularly the appendices to the second ume—but the larger part of the enquiry is so curi and interesting that any ordinary reader will appr ate and profit by the researches."—*Birmingh Journal.*

SANDYS' (W., F.S.A.) — Christmasti its History, Festivities, and Car (*with their music*). In a handsome 8vo, *illustrated with 20 engravings af the desings of F. Stephanoff, extra cloth,* edges. 5s (*original price* 14s)

"Its title vouches that *Christmastide* is germane to time. Mr. Sandys has brought together, in an oct of some 300 pages, a great deal of often interest information beyond the stale gossip about 'Christ in the olden time," and the threadbare make-believe jollity and geniality which furnish forth most book the subject. His carols, too, which include some in French and Provencal, are selected from numer sources, and comprise many of the less known more worth knowing. His materials are presen with good feeling and mastery of his theme. On whole the volume deserves, and should anticipat welcome."—*Spectator.*

SANDYS' (W.) and S. A. FORSTER History of the Violin and other Inst ments played on with a Bow, from Earliest Times to the Present, also Account of the Principal Makers, glish and Foreign. Thick 8vo, pp. 4 *with many engravings, cloth.* 14s

SANDYS' (GEORGE) Poetical Wor now first collected, with Introduct and Notes by the Rev. RICHARD HOO M.A., Editor of Chapman's Homer, the Music to the Psalms, by HE LAWES, revised by Dr. E. F. RIMBA 2 vols, fcap. 8vo, *portrait, cloth*. 10s

—— LARGE PAPER, 2 vols, post 8vo, cl 15s

BULL (W. D.) On the Connection between Astronomical and Geological Pheonomena, addressed to the Geologists of Europe and America. 8vo, *diagrams, sewed.* 2s

OTT (HENRY, *Minister of Anstruther Wester).* **Fasti-Ecclesiæ Scoticanæ;** the Succession of Ministers to the Parish Churches of Scotland, from the Reformation, A.D. 1560, to the Present Time. 4to, Parts I to VI (*each containing about* 400 *pages*) £1. 10s each.

THE design of the present work is to present a comprehensive account of the SUCCESSION OF MINISTERS of the Church of Scotland, since the period of the Reformation. An attempt is made to give some additional interest by furnishing incidental notices of their lives, writings, and families, which may prove useful to the Biographer, the Genealogist, and the Historian. A similar work to "Wood's Athenæ Oxoniensis."

RASE FAMILY.—Genealogical Memoir of the Family of Scrase, of Sussex. By M. A. LOWER. 8vo. 1s 6d

LDEN'S (JOHN) Table Talk, with a Biographical Preface and Notes by S. W. SINGER. *Third edition,* fcp. 8vo, *portrait, cloth.* 5s

—— LARGE PAPER. Post 8vo, *cloth.* 7s 6d

Nothing can be more interesting than this little book, containing a lively picture of the opinions and conversations of one of the most eminent scholars and most distinguished patriots England has produced. There are few volumes of its size so pregnant with sense, combined with the most profound learning; it is impossible to open it without finding some important fact or discussion, something practically useful and applicable to the business of life. Coleridge says, 'There is more weighty bullion sense in this book than I ever found in the same number of pages in any uninspired writer.' . . . . Its merits had not escaped the notice of Dr. Johnson, though in politics opposed to much it inculcates, for in reply to an observation of Boswell, in praise of the French Ana, he said, 'A few of them are good, but we have one book of the kind better than any of them—Selden's Table Talk.'—*Mr. Singer's Preface.*

SHAKESPERIANA.

LIFE of Shakespeare, including many particulars respecting the Poet and his Family, never before published. By J. O. HALLIWELL, F.R.S., etc. 8vo, *illustrated with 75 engravings on wood, most of which are of new objects, from drawings by Fairholt, cloth.* 15s. 1848

This work contains upwards of forty documents respecting Shakespeare and his family, *never before published,* besides numerous others, indirectly illustrating the Poet's biography. All the anecdotes and traditions concerning Shakespeare are here, for the first time, collected, and much new light is thrown on his personal history, by papers exhibiting him as selling Malt, Stone, &c. Of the seventy-six engravings which illustrate the volume, *more than fifty have never before been engraved.*

It is the only life of Shakespeare to be bought separately from his works.

W Illustrations of the Life, Studies, and Writings of Shakespeare. By the Rev. JOSEPH HUNTER. 2 vols, 8vo, *cloth.* 7s 6d (*original price,* £1. 1s). 1845

Supplementary to all editions of the works of the Poet.

SHAKESPEARE'S Versification, and its Apparent Irregularities Explained by Examples from Early and Late English Writers. By W. SIDNEY WALKER. Edited by WM. NANSOM LETTSOM. Fcp. 8vo, *cloth.* 6s 1854

"The reader of Shakespeare would do well to make himself acquainted with this excellent little book previous to entering upon the study of the poet."—*Mr. Singer, in the Preface to his New Edition of Shakespeare.*

A CRITICAL Examination of the Text of Shakespeare; together with Notes on his Plays and Poems, by the late W. SIDNEY WALKER. Edited by W. NANSOM LETTSOM. 3 vols, foolscap 8vo, *cloth.* 18s. 1860

"Very often we find ourselves differing from Mr. Walker on readings and interpretations, but we seldom differ from him without respect for his scholarship and care. His are not the wild guesses at truth which neither gods nor men have stomach to endure; but the suggestions of a trained intelligence and a chastened taste. Future editors and commentators will be bound to consult these volumes, and consider their suggestions."—*Athenæum.*

"A valuable addition to our Philological Literature, the most valuable part being the remarks on contemporary literature, the mass of learning by which the exact meaning and condition of a word is sought to be established."—*Literary Gazette.*

"Mr. Walker's Works undoubtedly form altogether the most valuable body of verbal criticism that has yet appeared from an individual."—*Mr. Dyce's Preface to Vol. I. of his Shakespeare,* 1864.

NARES (Archd.) Glossary, or Collection of Words, Phrases, Customs, Proverbs, etc., illustrating the Works of English Authors, particularly Shakespeare and his Contemporaries. A new edition, with Considerable Additions both of Words and Examples. By James O. Halliwell, F.R.S., and Thomas WRIGHT, M.A., F.S.A. 2 thick vols, *cloth.* £1. 1s. 1867

Other "*Shakesperiana*" will be found at *p.* 27.

WORKS BY SAMUEL SHARPE.
Author of the "History of Ancient Egypt," etc.

THE EGYPTIAN ANTIQUITIES in the British Museum described. Post 8vo, *with many woodcuts, cloth.* 5s

"Mr. Sharpe here presents the student of Egyptian antiquity and art with a very useful book. . . . . To the accomplished student this book will be useful as a reminder of many things already known to him; to the tyro it may serve as a guide and *aide-memoire*; to the mere visitor to the Galleries in the British Museum, this will be a handy guide book, in which an immediate answer may be sought and found for the oft-repeated questions before these wondrous remains—of what are their natures? what their meanings? what their purposes?"—*Athenæum.*

EGYPTIAN MYTHOLOGY and Egyptian Christianity, with their Influence on the Opinions of Modern Christendom. Post 8vo, *with* 100 *engravings, cloth.* 3s

EGYPTIAN Hieroglyphics, being an attempt to explain their Nature, Origin, and Meaning, with a Vocabulary. 8vo, *cloth.* 10s 6d

HISTORY of the Hebrew Nation and its Literature. Post 8vo, *cloth.* SECOND AND ENLARGED EDITION. 5s

The first edition has been translated into German, but it is not a proper reflex of the work: the translator has made omissions and alterations to suit his views. Germans will please note this.

TESTAMENT (Old).—The Hebrew Scriptures, translated by Samuel Sharpe, being a revision of the authorised English Old Testament. 3 vols, fcap. 8vo, *cloth, red edges.* 7s 6d (A Second and Revised Edition now ready).

TESTAMENT (The New) Translated from Griesbach's Text. By Samuel Sharpe. 12TH THOUSAND. 12mo, pp. 412, *cloth.* 1s 6d

CRITICAL NOTES on the Authorised English Version of the New Testament, being a Companion to the Author's "New Testament translated from Griesbach's Text." Fcap. 8vo, *second edition, cloth.* 2s 6d

ON THE CHRONOLOGY OF THE BIBLE. Fcap. 8vo, *cloth.* 1s 6d

TEXTS FROM THE HOLY BIBLE, explained by the help of Ancient Monuments. By SAMUEL SHARPE. *With 166 drawings on wood, chiefly by* JOSEPH BONOMI, *Curator of Soane's Museum.* Post 8vo, SECOND EDITION ENLARGED, *cloth.* 3s 6d

THE DECREE OF CANOPUS in Hieroglyphics, and Greek, with Translations and an Explanation of the Hieroglyphical Characters. 8vo, 16 *plates, cloth.* 7s 6d
This inscription or tablet was discovered in Egypt in 1865, and is preserved in the Khedive's museum at Cairo.

THE ROSETTA STONE (*in the British Museum*) in Hieroglyphics and Greek, with Translations and an Explanation of the Hieroglyphical Characters. 8vo, 8 *plates, cloth.* 4s

SHEPHERD'S (Charles) Historical Account of the Island of Saint Vincent, in the West Indies, with large Appendix on Population, Meteorology, Produce of Estates, Revenue, Carib Grants, etc. 8vo, *plates, cloth.* 3s (*original price* 12s)

SIMS' (RICHARD, *of the Dept. of MSS. in the British Museum*) A Manual for the Genealogist, Topographer, Antiquary, and Legal Professor, consisting of Descriptions of Public Records, Parochial and other Registers, Wills, County and Family Histories, Heraldic Collections in Public Libraries, &c. 8vo, SECOND EDITION, pp. 540, *cloth.* 15s
This work will be found indispensable by those engaged in the study of Family History and Heraldry, and by the compiler of County and Local History, the Antiquary and the Lawyer.

SINDING'S (PROFESSOR, *of Copenhagen,*) History of Scandinavia, from the early times of the Northmen, the Seakings, and Vikings, to the present day. First English Edition, thoroughly revised and augmented. 8vo, pp. 490, *large map and portrait of Q. Margaret, cloth.* 6s

SLOANE.—EVA British Heral and Marshalli the Rise and Ensigns. 8v *plates, cloth.*

SOMERSET.—T of the Count of Bath and V nals of their I the earliest ti Mary. By Re *A handsome half morocco,*

SOMERSET.—H By the Rev. *ptales, cloth.*

SOUTHWELL'S *Loretto*) Poeti pletely edited 8vo, *cloth.* 4 "His piety is simpl gentleness and ki is equally disting sweetness of expr

SPENCE (JOSE racters of Bc from the Con other eminer With Notes, I The second e *cloth.* 6s
———— LARGE PAP
"The 'Anecdotes' friend of Pope, is English language.

SPROTT'S (THO *circa* 1280) Ch cred History. ginal MS., on possession of verpool. By morocco, accom *mile of the ent round case*, PR *rious.* £2. 2s

STAFFORDSHI Historical anc Dudley Castle *folding pedigre*

STIRRY'S (Tho Bishops, or a of Canterbury blems, to ple (*A Satire on A woodcut emblen*
A facsimile of the ve at Bindley's sale f

Books on Sale at Smith's, 36, Soho Square, London. 23

TUART FAMILY.—TOWNEND'S (W.) The Descendants of the Stuarts. An unchronicled Page in England's History. 8vo, *portraits and folding pedigrees*, SECOND EDITION, WITH ADDITIONS, *half morocco*. 5s (*original price* 10s 6d)
This volume contains a most minute, precise, and valuable history of the Stuart Family. Neither of our Historians from Hume to Macaulay give even the more prominent facts in connection with many branches of the House of Stuart.

FFOLK.—Notes or Jottings about Aldborough, in Suffolk, relating to Matters Historical, Antiquarian, Ornithological, and Entomological. By NICHOLAS FENWICK HELE, *Surgeon there*. Post 8vo, *plates, cloth*. 7s 6d

SSEX.—A Compendious History of County of Sussex; Topographical, Archæological, and Anecdotal. By M. A. LOWER, author of "Patronymica Britannica," "Curiosities of Heraldry," &c. 2 vols, 8vo, *cloth*. 12s 6d (*original price* £1. 5s)

SSEX.—The Churches of Sussex. Etched by R. H. NIBBS, with Historical and Archæological descriptions by M. A. LOWER. 4to, 86 *plates, half bd., top edge gilt*. £1. 11s 6d

SSEX.—LOWER's (M. A.) Memorials of the Town of Seaford, Sussex. 8vo, *plates*. 3s 6d

SSEX.—LOWER'S (M. A) Bodiam (in Sussex), and its Lords. 8vo, *engravings*. 1s

SSEX.—MANTELL (Dr. GIDEON) A Day's Ramble in and About the Ancient Town of Lewes, Sussex. 12mo, *engravings, cloth*. 2s

SSEX.—History and Antiquities of the Town and Port of Rye. By W. HOLLOWAY. Thick 8vo, pp. 624, *cloth* (*only* 150 *printed*). £1. 1s

SSEX.—TIERNEY'S (REV. CANON) History and Antiquities of the Castle and Town of Arundel, including the Biography of its Earls. 2 vols, royal 8vo, *fine plates, cloth*. 14s (*original price* £2. 10s)

SSEX.—Descriptive Catalogue of the Original Charters, Grants, Donations, &c., constituting the Muniments of Battle Abbey; also the Papers of the Montagus, Sidneys, and Websters, embodying many highly interesting and valuable Records of Lands in Sussex, Kent, and Essex, with Preliminary Memoranda of the Abbey of Battel, and Historical Particulars of the Abbots. 8vo, 264 *pages, cloth*. 1s 6d

SWISS ECCLESIOLOGY.—Histoire de l'Architecture Sacree du quatrieme au dixieme siecle dans les anciens eveches de Geneve, Lausanne et Sion. Par J. D. Blavignac, Architecte. One vol, 8vo, pp. 450, *and* 37 *plates; and a* 4to *atlas of* 82 *plates of Architecture, Sculpture, Frescoes, Reliquaries, &c., &c.* £2. 10s
A very remarkable book, and worthy the notice of the Architect, the Archæologist, and the Artist.

TESTAMENT (OLD).—The Hebrew Scriptures, translated by SAMUEL SHARPE, being a revision of the authorised English Old Testament. 3 vols, fcp. 8vo, *cloth, red edges*. 7s 6d
"In the following Revision of the Authorised Version of the Old Testament, the aim of the Translator has been to shew in the Text, by greater exactness, those peculiarities which others have been content to point out in Notes and Commentaries. He has translated from Van der Hooght's edition of the Hebrew Bible, printed in Amsterdam in 1705; except when, in a few cases, he has followed some of the various readings so industriously collected by Dr. Kennicott."—*Preface*.

TESTAMENT (THE NEW) Translated from Griesbach's Text. By SAMUEL SHARPE, Author of the History of Egypt, &c. 5th edition. 12mo, pp. 412, *cloth*. 1s 6d
The aim of the translator has been to give the meaning and idiom of the Greek as far as possible in English words. The book is printed in paragraphs (the verses of the authorised version are numbered in the margins) the speeches by inverted commas, and the quotations from the "Old Testament" in italics, those passages which seem to be poetry in a smaller type. *It is entirely free from any motive to enforce doctrinal points*, Six large Impressions of the volume sufficiently test its value.
We cordially recommend this edition of the New Testament to our readers and contributors.—*British Controversialist*.
Upon the whole, we must admit that this is the most correct English Version in existence, either of the whole or of any portion of the New Testament.—*The Ecclesiastic*, and repeated by the *English Churchman*.

THOMPSON'S (EBENEZER) A Vindi-cation of the Hymn "Te Deum Laudamus," from the Corruptions of a Thousand Years, with Ancient Versions in Anglo-Saxon, High German, Norman-French, &c., and an English Paraphrase of the XVth Century, now first printed. Fcap. 8vo, *cloth*. 3s
A book well worth the notice of the Ecclesiastical Antiquary and the Philologist.

THOMPSON (EBENEZER) On the Ar-chaic Mode of expressing Numbers in English, Anglo-Saxon, Friesic, etc. 8vo, (*and ingenious and learned pamphlet, interesting to the Philologist*). 1s

TITIAN.—Notices of the Life and Works of Titian the Painter. By SIR ABRAHAM HUME. Royal 8vo, *portrait, cloth*. 6s

26 Books on Sale at Smith's, 36, Soho Square, London.

WRIGHT's (THOMAS) Saint Patrick's rick's Purgatory, an Essay on the Legends of Hell, Purgatory, and Paradise, current during the Middle Ages. Post 8vo, *cloth*. 6s

"A complete history of the legends and superstitions relating to the subject, from the earliest times, rescued from old MSS. as well as from old printed books. It embraces a singular chapter of literary history omitted by Warton, and all former writers with whom we are acquainted: and we think we may add, that it forms the best introduction to Dante that has yet been published."—*Literary Gazette*.
"This appears to be a curious and even amusing book on the singular subject of Purgatory, in which the idle and fearful dreams of superstition are shown to be first narrated as tales, and then applied as means of deducing the moral character of the age in which they prevailed."—*Spectator*.

YORKSHIRE.—THE HISTORY of the Township of Meltham, near Huddersfield. By the late Rev. JOSEPH HUGHES. Edited with addition by C. H. Post 8vo, *cloth*. 7s 6d

YORKSHIRE.—RAINE'S (REV. JAS.), Catterick Church, Yorkshire, a correct copy of the contract for its building in 1412. Illustrated with Remarks and Notes. With 13 *plates of views, elevations and details*, by A. SALVIN, Architect. 4to, *cloth*. 6s.—LARGE PAPER, *cloth*. 9s

YORKSHIRE.—DAVIES (ROBT., F.S.A Town Clerk of York) Extracts from the Municipal Records of the City of York during the Reign of Edward IV., Edward V., and Richard III., with Notes illustrative and explanatory, and an Appendix, containing some account of the Celebration of the Corpus Christi Festival at York, in the Fifteenth and Sixteenth Centuries. 8vo, *cloth*. 4s (*original price* 10s 6d)

YORKSHIRE.—DAVIES (ROBT.) THE Fawkes's of York in the 16th Century, including Notices of Guy Fawkes, the Gunpowder Plot Conspirator. Post 8vo. 1s 6d

YORKSHIRE.—THE HISTORY AND Topography of Harrogate and the Forest of Knaresborough. By W. Grainge. 8vo, 521 pp., *map and illustrations, cloth*. 10s 6d

YORKSHIRE.—SURTEES(REV. SCOTT F., of *Sprotburgh, Yorkshire*) Waifs and Strays of North Humber History. Post 8vo, 3 *plates, cloth*. 3s 6d

YORKSHIRE.—HISTORY AND ANTI- quities of the Parish of Blyth in the Counties of Notts and Yorkshire. By the Rev. JOHN RAINE, Vicar. 4to, *plates and pedigrees, cloth*. 15s (*original price* £1. 6s)

PUBLICATIONS OF THE CAXTO SOCIETY.
OF CHRONICLES AND OTHER WRITINGS ILLUSTRATIVE OF THE HISTORY AND MISCELLANEOUS LITERATURE OF THE MIDDLE AGES.
Uniformly printed in 8vo, with English Preface and Notes. Of several of the Volumes only 100 copies have been printed.

CHRONICON Henrici de Silgrave. No first printed from the Cotton MS. By HOOK. 5s 6d
GAIMAR (Geoffrey) Anglo-Norman Metric Chronicle of the Anglo-Saxon King Printed for the first time entire, with A pendix, containing the Lay of Havel the Dane, the Legend of Ernulph, a Life of Hereward the Saxon. Edited T. WRIGHT, Esq., F.S.A. Pp. 284 (or to be had in a set)
The only complete edition; that in the Monumenta F torica Britannica, printed by the Record Commissi is incomplete.
LA REVOLTE du COMTE de WARWICK cont le Roi Edouard IV., now first printed fro a MS. at Ghent, to which is added French letter, concerning Lady Ja Grey and Queen Mary, from a MS. Bruges. Edited by Dr. GILES. 3s 6d
WALTERI Abbatis Dervensis Epistolæ, no first printed from a MS. in St. John's Co lege, Cambridge. By C. MESSITER.4s
BENEDICTI Abbatis Petriburgensis de Vi et Miraculis St. Thomae Cantaur, no first printed from MSS. at Paris and Lar beth. By Dr. GILES. 10s
GALFRIDI le Baker de Swinbroke, Chron con Angliæ temp. Edward II. et II now first printed. By Dr. GILES. 10s
EPISTOLA Herberti de Losinga, primi Ep copi Norwicensis, et Oberti de Clara, Elmeri Prioris Cantuariensis, now fir printed. By Col. ANSTRUTHER. 8s
ANECDOTA Bedæ Lanfranci, et alioru (inedited Tracts, Letters, Poems, & by Bede, Lanfranc Tatwin, etc.) By L GILES. 10s
RADULPHI Nigri Chronica Duo, now fir printed from MSS. in the British Museum By Lieut. Col. ANSTRUTHUR. 8s
MEMORIAL of Bishop Waynflete, Found of St. Mary Magdalene College, Oxfor By Dr. Peter HEYLYN. Now first edite from the original MS. By J. R. BLOXA D.D., Fellow of the same College. 5s 6
ROBERT GROSSETETE (Bishop of Linco "Chasteau d'Amour," to which is add "La Vie de Sainte Marie Egyptien and an English Version (of the 13th C tury) of the "Chasteau d'Amour," n first edited. By M. COOKE. 6s 6d
GALFREDI Monumentis Historia Briton nunc primum in Anglis novem codd. MS collatis. Editit J. A. GILES. 10s

Books on Sale at Smith's, 36, Soho Square, London. 27

]antuariensis postea Abbatis nsis, Scripta quæ extant.]ILES. 6s 6d
nglið Petriburgense, iterum im cum cod. MSS. contulit. 6s 6d
m Anglo-Saxonum, Original glo-Saxons and others who the Conquest (*in Latin*). r. GILES. 10s
Rerum Gestarum Wilhelmi . In Unum collecti. Ab J. 0s

3revis relatio de Willelmo nobilissimo norum. 2. Protestatio Willelmi pri-
]antuariensis Ecclesiæ. 3. Widonis larmen de Hastingensi. 4. Charta Ji. 5. Epistola Will. conquestoris ad am. 6. Excerpta de vita Willelmi r. De Morte Will Conq. 8. Hymnus]onq. 9. De Morte Lanfranci. 10. is Normannorum. 11. Excerptum ex uberti. 12. Annalis Historia brevis Monasterii S. Stephani Cadomensis. Morte Lanfranci. 14. Charta a rege Anglo Saxonice scripta. 15. Du Roi rleterre par Chretien de Troyes. 16. ime d'Angleterre.

ESPEARIANA.
Genius of Shakespeare, with 1arks on the Characters of let, Juliet, and Ophelia, by ES. Post 8vo, *cloth*. 2s 6d e 5s 6d) 1826
an Historical Play, repre- rury Lane, April 2, 1796, as newly discovered Drama of by WILLIAM HENRY IRE-
) *Edition, with an original*), *facsimile*. 1s 6d (*original* 1832
)tb interesting and curious, from the nation it gives respecting the Shake-s, containing also the substance of the ssions."
:Y Anecdotes of Shakespeare, Warwickshire in 1693. 8vo, 1838
[S on an Autograph of Shake-he Orthography of his Name, 1. MADDEN. 8vo, *sewed*. 1s 1831
E'S Autobiographical Poems, nnets clearly developed, with er, drawn chiefly from his :. A. BROWN. Post 8vo, *cloth*. 1838
iNA, a Catalogue of the ons of Shakespeare's Plays, ommentaries and other Pub-strative of his works. By J. LL. 8vo, *cloth*. 3s 1841
) everybody who wishes to carry on onnected with Shakespeare, or his cy for Shakespeare Bibliography."—

New Edition of Shakespeare's . PAYNE COLLIER. 8vo. 1s
1842

ACCOUNT of the only known Manuscript of Shakespeare's Plays, comprising some inportant variations and corrections in the "Merry Wives of Windsor," ob- tained from a Playhouse Copy of that Play recently discovered. By J. O. HALLIWELL. 8vo. 1s 1843
'WHO was Jack Wilson,' the Singer of Shake- speare's Stage?" An Attempt to prove the identity of this person with John Wilson, Doctor of Music in the University of Oxford, A.D. 1644. By E. F. RIMBAULT, LL.D. 8vo. 1s 1846
HAMLET.—An Attempt to ascertain whether the Queen were an Accessory before the Fact, in the Murder of her First Hus- band. 8vo, *sewed*. 2s 1856
"This pamphlet well deserves the perusal of every student of Hamlet."—*Notes and Queries*.
PERICLES, Prince of Tyre, a Novel, by Geo. Wilkins, printed in 1608, and founded upon Shakespeare's Play, edited by PRO- FESSOR MOMMSEN, with Preface and Ac- count of some original Shakespeare edi- tions extant in Germany and Switzerland, and an Introduction by J. P. COLLIER. 8vo, *sewed*. 5s 1857
LLOYD (W. Watkiss) Essays on Life and Plays of Shakespeare contributed to the Edition by S. W. SINGER, 1856. Thick post 8vo, *half calf gilt, marbled edges*. 9s 1858
Only 50 copies privately printed.
THE Sonnets of Shakespeare, *rearranged* and divided into Four Parts, with an Intro- duction and Explanatory Notes. By Dr. Robt. Cartwright. Post 8vo, 2s 6d 1859
THE Shakespeare Fabrications, or the MS. Notes of the Perkins folio, shown to be of recent origin ; with Appendix on the Authorship of the Ireland Forgeries, by C. MANSFIELD INGLEBY, LL.D. Fcp. 8vo, *with a facsimile shewing the pseudo old writing and the pencilled words, cloth*. 3s. 1859
STRICTURES on Mr. Collier's New Edi- tion of Shakespeare, published in 1858, by the Rev ALEXANDER DYCE. 8vo, *cloth*. 5s (*original price* 7s 6d) 1859
STRICTURES on Mr. Hamilton's Inquiry into the Genuineness of the MS. Correc- tions in J. Payne Collier's Annotated Shakespeare. Folio, 1632. By SCRU- TATOR. 8vo, *sewed*. 1s. 1860
SHAKESPEARE and the Bible, showing how much the great Dramatist was indebted to Holy Writ for his profound knowledge of Human Nature. By the Rev. T. R. EATON. Fcp. 8vo, *cloth*. 2s 6d 1860
CRITICISM applied to Shakespeare. By C. BADHAM. Post 8vo. 1s 1846
CROKER (Crofton).—Remarks on an Article inserted in the Papers of the Shakespeare Society. Small 8vo, *sewed*. 1s 1849

Lancashire and Cheshire. Transactions of the Historic Society of Lancashire and Cheshire. FIRST SERIES, *complete*, 10 vols, 8vo, *many engravings*. £3. 3s

Baines's History of the County of Lancaster, a new, revised, and improved edition. Edited by J. HARLAND, F.S.A. 2 handsome vols, 4to, *cloth*. £1. 11s 6d (*original price* £3. 3s)
——— LARGE PAPER, 2 vols, royal 4to, *cloth*, £3. 3s (*original price* £6. 6s)

History of the Bishoprick of Lincoln, from its Origin to and Endowment at Sidnacester, until the removal of the Seat of the See to Lincoln. Thick 8vo, (*very few printed*) *cloth*, 12s (*original price* £1. 1s)

Derbyshire Gatherings; a Fund of Delight for the Antiquary, the Historian, the Topographer, and Biographer, and General Reader. By J. B. ROBINSON, of Derby. A *handsome* 4to, *with engravings, extra cloth, gilt edges*. £1. 5s

Smith's (Toulmin) Memorials of Old Birmingham, Men and Names, Founders, Freeholders, and Indwellers, from the 13th to the 16th Century, with particulars as to the earliest Church of the Reformation built and endowed in England, from original and unpublished documents. Royal 8vo, *plates, cloth*. 4s 6d

History of the Weald of Kent, with an Outline of the History of the County from the Earliest Period. By ROBERT FURLEY, F.S.A. 2 vols, 8vo, *plates and maps, cloth*. £1. 4s
The second volume may be had separately for 12s.

Pilgrimages to St. Mary of Walsingham and St. Thomas of Canterbury. By DESIDERIUS ERASMUS. Newly Translated. With the Colloquy of Rash Vows, by the same Author, and his characters of Archbishop Warham and Dean Colet, with Notes by J. GOUGH NICHOLS. Post 8vo, *engravings, cloth*. 4s 6d (*original price* 6s)

Lays and Legends of the English Lake Country, with copious Notes. By JOHN PAGEN WHITE. Fcp. 8vo, *cloth*. 6s.

Brockett's (J. T.) Glossary of North Country Words, with their Etymology and affinity to other Languages, and occasional notices of Local Customs and Popular Superstitions. THIRD EDITION, *corrected and enlarged*. By W. E. BROCKETT. 2 vols in one, post 8vo, *cloth*, 10s 6d (*original price* £1. 1s)

The Hamilton Manuscripts, containing some Account of the settlement of the Territories of the Upper Clandeboye,

Great Ardes, and Dufferi of Down. By SIR JAM Kut. (afterwards Viscou in the reigns of James I. with Memoirs of him a and grandson, James a first and second Earls of and of their Families, C Descendants. Edited by LL.D. 4to, *very few* £1. 1s

History of Drogheda, with in the county of Louth JOHN D'ALTON, Author Irish Army Lists, &c. *plates, cloth:* 14s (*origin*

Account of the Territory o Farney, in the Province land. By EVELYN PH Esq. 4to, *woodcuts, a ha cloth, only 250 printed*.

England and Scotland. R pêches, Rapports, Instru moires des Ambassadeur Angleterre. Corresponc tique de BERTRAND DE LA MOTHE FENELON, A France en Angleterre d publie pour la premièr PORTON COOPER. 7 vo 1840, *sewed*. £1. 10s £3. 10s)

France and Spain with S lations Politiques de la l'Espagne avec l'Ecosse a Papiers d'Etat, Pièces inédites ou peu connus, thèques et des Archive Publie par ALEX. TEU: *aux Archives de l'Empi Paris*, 1862, *sewed*. £1 *price* £3)

Della Valle (Pietro) Viagg medesimo civé la Turch India. cello Vita dell A vols, 8vo, *Italy*, 1843, *seu* An amusing old traveller of the earl teenth century.

Walckenaer (Le Baron). Gé cienne, historique et Gaules Cisalpine et Tra d'Analyse Géographique Anciennes. 3 vols, 8vo, *a Paris*, 1839, *sewed*. £1 *price* £1. 16s)

Virgil. Quæ Vices quæqu et Virgilium ipsum et eju Mediam ætatem excepe: tentavit Franciscus Mich 1846, 1s 6d
It will also be found interesting Medieval literature.

Books on Sale at Smith's, 36, Soho Square, London. 31

elepierre (Octave). Macaroneana, : Mélanges de Littérature Macaronique des différent Peuples de l'Europe, avec Notes, Extraits, &c. 8vo, *vellum paper, Paris*, 1852, *sewed.* 7s
'Dans cet ouvrage plein de finesse et d'erudition, M. Octave Delepierre, dont les connaissances littéraires et Bibliographiques sont bien connues à réuni tout ce que l'on pouvait désirer sur les Macaronées et les ouvrages en style Macaronique. On sait combien Ch. Nodier affectionnoit ce genre de Littérature, il ne laissait passer aucune occasion de parler dans ses opuscules Bibliographiques. Bien avant lui encore, Naudé disait: "La Macaronée est à mon avis, la plus divertissante raillerie que l'on puisse jamais faire, et je me flatte d'avoir en cela aussi bon gout que le Cardinal Mazarin, qui en recitait quelquefois trois et quatre cent vers de suite."

alderon. Las Comedias de Don Pedro Calderon de la Barca, cotejadas con las mejores Ediciones hasta aliora publicadas corregidas y dadas a luz por J. J. Kiel. 4 thick vols, royal 8vo, *sewed*, 1827. £1. 4s (*original price £2.* 10s)

necdotes of the English Language, chiefly regarding the Local Dialect of London and its Environs. By SAMUEL PEGGE, F.S.A. *Third Edition enlarged and corrected by the* REV. H. CHRISTMAS. 8vo, *boards.* 6s 6d (*original price* 12s)

aintings. A Catalogue of Pictures Composed and painted chiefly by the most admired Masters of the Roman, Florentine, Parman, Bolognese, Venetian, Flemish, and French Schools, with critical remarks by ROBERT FOULIS. 3 vols, 12mo, 1776, *boards.* 7s 6d

aintings. Memoirs of Painting, with a Chronological History of the Importation of Pictures by the Great Masters into England since the French Revolution. By W. BUCHANAN. 2 vols, 8vo, *boards.* 7s 6d (*original price £1. 6s*)
This and the foregoing are useful Works to trace the original Paintings of the Great Masters.

andor (Savagius). Poemata et Inscriptiones. 12mo, pp. 356, *cloth.* 3s (*published at 7s*) 1847

bliographical Miscellany. Edited by JOHN PETHERAM. 8vo, Nos. 1 to 5 (all published), *with general title.* 1s
CONTENTS.—Particulars of the Voyage of Sir Thomas Button for the Discovery of a North-West Passage, A.D. 1612—Sir Dudley Digges' Of the Circumference of the Earth, or a Treatise of the North-East Passage, 1611-13—Letter of Sir Thomas Button on the North-West Passage, in the State-Paper Office—Bibliographical Notices of Old Music Books, by Dr. Rimbault—Notices of Suppressed Books—Martin Mar-Prelate's Rhymes—The Hardwicke Collection of Manuscripts.

oman Coins. Records of Roman History from Cnæus Pompeius to Tiberius Constantius, as exhibited on the Roman Coins, Collected by FRANCIS HOBLER, formerly Secretary to the Numismatic Society of London. 2 vols, royal 4to, *frontispiece and numerous engravings. in cloth.* £1. 1s (*original price £2. 2s, only 250 printed*)
"A work calculated not only to interest the professed numismatist, but also to instruct the classical student and the historian. The unpublished Coins are rather numerous, especially when we consider how many works have been printed on the Roman series, and how much it has been studied. . . . The value of the work is much enhanced by the illustrations, executed by Mr Fairholt, with the peculiar spirit and fidelity which indicate his experienced hand."—*C. Roach Smith's Collectanea Antiqua.*

Numismata Cromwelliana: or the Medallic History of Oliver Cromwell, illustrated by his Coins, Medals, and Seals. By HENRY W. HENFREY, F.R. Hist. Soc., &c., Author of a "Guide to English Coins." 4to, *plates*, Part I. (to be completed in 6 parts) 3s 6d
In this work, a complete historical description of all the Coins, Medals and Pattern Pieces of Oliver Cromwell is attempted for the first time. Vertue, Snelling, Folkes, and Ruding, have all left but very imperfect notes and sketches of Cromwellian numismatics, and Mr. Hawkins never published anything on the subject; thus many vexed questions have not yet been properly discussed.
The collector and student of English Coins will find amongst the numismatic information numerous facts, details, and elucidations which are absolutely unpublished; and the numerous Autotype plates will furnish the first correct, and in some instances, the only illustrations yet published of many places.

Greenhow (Robt., Librarian to the Dept. of State, U.S.A.). History of Oregon and California, and the other Territories on the North-West Coast of America, accompanied by a Geographical View and Map, and a number of Proofs and Illustrations of the History. 8vo, *large map, cloth.* 7s 6d (*original price* 16s)

Fitzgerald's (J. E.) Examination of the Charter and Proceedings of the Hudson's Bay Company with reference to the Grant of Vancouver's Island. 12mo, *map, cloth.* 2s 6d (*original price* 6s)

Fancourt's (Charles) History of Yucatan from its Discovery to the close of the 17th Century. 8vo, *map, cloth.* 4s (*original price* 10s 6d)

Hooper's (Lieut.) Ten Months among the Tents of the Tuski, with incidents of an Arctic Boat Expedition in search of Sir John Franklin. Thick 8vo, *map, and coloured plates, cloth.* 5s 6d (*original price* 16s)

Turnbull's (D.) Travels in Cuba, with Notices of Porto Rico. Thick 8vo, *map, cloth.* 5s (*original price* 15s)

Hawkins (J. S., F.S.A.). History of the Origin and Establishment of Gothic Architecture, and an Inquiry into the mode of Painting upon and Staining Glass, as practised in the Ecclesiastical Structures of the Middle Ages. Royal 8vo, 1813, 11 *plates, boards.* 4s (*original price* 12s)

Books on Sale at Smith's, 36, Soho Square, London.

Porson. The Life of Richard Porson, Professor of Greek in the University of Cambridge from 1792 to 1808. By the Rev. J. S. WATSON. 8vo, *portrait, cloth.* 5s (*original price* 14s)

Bowles' (Rev. W. Lisle) Hermes Britannicus, a Dissertation on the Celtic Deity Teutates, the Murcurius of Cæsar, in further proof and corroboration of the origin and designation of the Great Temple at Abury, in Wiltshire. 8vo, *bds.* 4s (*original price* 8s 6d)

Reliquiæ Isurianæ; the Remains of the Roman Isurium, now Aldborough near Boroughbridge, Yorkshire. By H. ECROYD SMITH. Royal 4to, 37 *plates, cloth.* £1. 5s

Ridpath's (George) Border History of England and Scotland, with accounts of remarkable antiquities and anecdotes of the most considerable Families and Characters. A NEW EDITION, 1848. 4to, *boards.* 8s 6d. (*original price* £1. 1s)

Narratives from Criminal Trials in Scotland. By JOHN HILL BURTON. 2 vols, post 8vo, *cloth* (*a very interesting book*). 5s 6d. (*original price* £1. 1s)

Heemskerck. Catalogue of the Prints which have been engraved after Martin Heemskerck. By T. KERRICH, Librarian to the University of Cambridge. 8vo, *portrait, bds.* 3s 6d

Whistler's Etchings. A Catalogue Raisonné of Etchings and Drypoints of JAMES ABBOTT MACNEIL WHISTLER. 8vo, 100 pp. £1. 1s
Only 50 copies printed for private circulation.

CATALOGUES IN PRINT.

BIBLIOTHECA AMERICANA.—A CATALOGUE OF FOUR THOUSAND BOOKS and Pamphlets relating to North and South America and the West Indies. An 8vo. vol., *in cloth, sent free for 2s worth of postage labels, and for 3s worth of postage labels for America.* Published this day.

A CATALOGUE OF ENGRAVED PORTRAITS (MOSTLY OF ENGLISH Persons), Parts I. to VI., 6600 Articles [A to PHI]. Priced from 3d upwards. *Sent for six penny postage labels.*

A CATALOGUE OF FOUR THOUSAND FOUR HUNDRED TOPOGRAPHICAL Prints on Beds, Berks, Bucks, Cambridge, Channel Islands, Cheshire, Cornwall, Cumberland, Derby, Devon, Dorset, Durham, Essex, Gloucester, Hants, Hereford, Herts, Hunts, and Isle of Man. *Sent for three penny postage labels.*

A CATALOGUE OF FOUR THOUSAND PAMPHLETS ON DIVINITY AND Ecclesiastical History, from 1840 to 1860, classified under Baptisms, Catechisms, Catholic Controversy, Church of England, Commentaries on the Scriptures, Canons, Convocations, Jesuits, Jews, the Eucharist, Luther, Methodism, Miracles, Prophecies, Puseyism, Quakers, Unitarians, Warburton, Waterland, Whiston, and many others. *Post free for six penny postage labels.*
The most curious Catalogue of the kind ever offered to the literary public.

CATALOGUES OF CHOICE, USEFUL, AND CURIOUS SECOND HAND BOOKS are published every few weeks. *A specimen sent for a penny postage label.*

www.ingramcontent.com/pod-product-compliance
Lightning Source LLC
Chambersburg PA
CBHW051243300426
44114CB00011B/867